Women's Ritual Competence in the Greco-Roman Mediterranean

Contributions in this volume demonstrate how, across the ancient Mediterranean and over hundreds of years, women's rituals intersected with the political, economic, cultural, or religious spheres of their communities in a way that has only recently started to gain sustained academic attention. The volume aims to tease out a number of different approaches and contexts and to expand existing studies of women in the ancient world as well as scholarship on religious and social history.

The contributors face a famously difficult task: ancient authors rarely recorded aspects of women's lives, including their songs, prophecies, and prayers. Many of the objects women made and used in ritual were perishable and have not survived; certain kinds of ritual objects (lowly undecorated pots, for example) tend not even to be recorded in archaeological reports. However, the broad range of contributions in this volume demonstrates the multiplicity of materials that can be used as evidence – including inscriptions, textiles, ceramics, figurative art, and written sources – and the range of methodologies that can be used, from analysis of texts, images, and material evidence to cognitive and comparative approaches.

Matthew Dillon is an Associate Professor of Classics and Ancient History in the School of Humanities, University of New England, Armidale, Australia. He has written several articles and a book on women's religion in ancient Greece, *Girls and Women in Classical Greek Religion* (2002). He is interested in all ancient religions and in Greek society.

Esther Eidinow is Associate Professor of Ancient Greek History at the University of Nottingham, UK. She has particular interest in ancient Greek religion and magic, and her publications include *Oracles, Curses, and Risk among the Ancient Greeks* (2007), *Luck, Fate and Fortune: Antiquity and its Legacy* (2010), and *Envy, Poison and Death: Women on Trial in Classical Athens* (2015).

Lisa Maurizio is an Associate Professor of Classical and Medieval Studies at Bates College, Maine, USA. She is interested in interplay between gender, oral poetry, and Greek religion and has published articles on Delphic divination as well as *Classical Mythology in Context* (2015).

Women's Ritual Competence in the Greco-Roman Mediterranean

Edited by Matthew Dillon,
Esther Eidinow, and Lisa Maurizio

LONDON AND NEW YORK

First published 2017
by Routledge
2 Park Square, Milton Park, Abingdon, Oxon OX14 4RN

and by Routledge
711 Third Avenue, New York, NY 10017

Routledge is an imprint of the Taylor & Francis Group, an informa business

© 2017 selection and editorial matter, Matthew Dillon, Esther Eidinow, and
Lisa Maurizio; individual chapters, the contributors

The right of the editors to be identified as the authors of the editorial
material, and of the authors for their individual chapters, has been asserted
in accordance with sections 77 and 78 of the Copyright, Designs and
Patents Act 1988.

All rights reserved. No part of this book may be reprinted or reproduced or
utilised in any form or by any electronic, mechanical, or other means, now
known or hereafter invented, including photocopying and recording, or in
any information storage or retrieval system, without permission in writing
from the publishers.

Trademark notice: Product or corporate names may be trademarks or
registered trademarks, and are used only for identification and explanation
without intent to infringe.

British Library Cataloguing in Publication Data
A catalogue record for this book is available from the British Library

Library of Congress Cataloging-in-Publication Data
Names: Dillon, Matthew, 1963– editor. | Eidinow, Esther, 1970– editor. |
    Maurizio, Lisa, editor.
Title: Women's ritual competence in the Greco-Roman Mediterranean /
    edited by Matthew Dillon, Esther Eidinow, and Lisa Maurizio.
Description: Abingdon, Oxon ; New York, NY : Routledge, 2016. |
    Series: Routledge monographs in classical studies | Includes
    bibliographical references and index.
Identifiers: LCCN 2016018591 | ISBN 9781472478900 (hardback : alk. paper) |
    ISBN 9781315546506 (ebook)
Subjects: LCSH: Women—History—To 500. | Civilization, Greco-Roman. |
    Women—Greece—Social life and customs. | Women—Rome—Social
    life and customs. | Rites and ceremonies—Greece—History. | Rites and
    ceremonies—Rome—History. | Rome—History. | Greece—History.
Classification: LCC HQ1134 .W66 2016 | DDC 305.40938—dc23
LC record available at https://lccn.loc.gov/2016018591

ISBN: 978-1-4724-7890-0 (hbk)
ISBN: 978-1-315-54650-6 (ebk)

Typeset in Times New Roman
by Apex CoVantage, LLC

Contents

List of figures	vii
Acknowledgements	viii
Abbreviations and spelling	ix
Notes on contributors	x

Introduction — 1

ESTHER EIDINOW, LISA MAURIZIO, AND MATTHEW DILLON

PART I
Objects and offerings — 9

1 **The forgotten things: Women, rituals, and community in Western Sicily (eighth–sixth centuries BCE)** — 11

MERITXELL FERRER

2 **Materiality and ritual competence: Insights from women's prayer typology in Homer** — 32

ANDROMACHE KARANIKA

3 **Power through textiles: Women as ritual performers in ancient Greece** — 46

CECILIE BRØNS

4 **Silent attendants: Terracotta statues and death rituals in Canosa** — 65

TIZIANA D'ANGELO AND MAYA MURATOV

PART II
Authority and transmission — 95

5 **Shared meters and meanings: Delphic oracles and women's lament** — 97

LISA MAURIZIO

vi *Contents*

6 Priestess and polis in Euripides' *Iphigeneia in Tauris*   115
LAURA McCLURE

**7 Owners of their own bodies: Women's magical knowledge
and reproduction in Greek inscriptions**   131
IRENE SALVO

**PART III
Control and resistance**   149

8 Bitter constraint? Penelope's web and "season due"   151
LAURIE O'HIGGINS

**9 Women's ritual competence and domestic dough:
Celebrating the Thesmophoria, Haloa, and Dionysian
rites in ancient Attica**   165
MATTHEW DILLON

**10 Inhabiting/subverting the norms: Women's ritual agency
in the Greek West**   182
BONNIE MACLACHLAN

**PART IV
Denial and contestation**   197

**11 Women's ritual competence and a self-inscribing
prophet at Rome**   199
J. BERT LOTT

**12 "A devotee and a champion": Reinterpreting the female
"victims" of magic in early Christian texts**   213
ESTHER EIDINOW

**13 "What the women know": Plutarch and Pausanias
on female ritual competence**   229
DEBORAH LYONS

Index   241

Figures

1.1	Map of Sicily.	14
1.2	Planimetry of Monte Polizzo.	19
1.3	*Pignatte* from the acropolis of Monte Polizzo and *pignatte* from domestic contexts of Monte Maranfusa.	21
1.4	Planimetry of Montagnola di Marineo's city wall.	25
3.1	Boiotian relief *pithos.*	49
3.2	Woman placing a folded textile in a chest.	50
3.3	*Peplophoria. Pinax* from Lokris.	51
4.1	Map of Daunia, south-eastern Italy.	66
4.2	Terracotta statue of a maiden, from Canosa.	69
4.3	Terracotta statue of a maiden, from Canosa.	70
4.4	Terracotta statue of a maiden, from Canosa.	71
4.5	Terracotta statue of a maiden, from Canosa.	72
4.6	Wall painting depicting a journey to the Underworld, from the façade of the Sant'Aloia Hypogaeum, Canosa.	77
4.7	Terracotta group depicting an *ekphora*, from a burial in Vari.	83
4.8	Reconstruction drawing of a set of Canosan terracotta statues on a wheeled platform.	83
8.1	*Penelope Unraveling Her Work at Night.*	153
9.1	Woman tending to dough phalloi.	173

Acknowledgements

We would like to thank the Program in Classical and Medieval Studies at Bates College and the Costas and Mary Maliotis Charitable Foundation Fund for their generous support of the conference that led to this volume; and Matt and Esther want to say a special thank you to Lisa and Bates College for the wonderful hospitality they provided. We are very grateful to Michael Greenwood at Routledge for his unfailing support and encouragement. Finally, many thanks to all our contributors for their patience and wisdom.

Abbreviations and spelling

For ancient authors, works, and journal abbreviations we have used those given in the *Oxford Classical Dictionary* 4th ed. (Oxford: Oxford University Press, 2012). Abbreviations not listed there are provided here:

IGLS   *Inscriptions Grecques et Latines de la Syrie.*

P. Par.   *Notices et textes des papyrus du Musée du Louvre et de la Bibliothèque Impériale*, edited by Antoine Jean Letronne, Wladimir Brunet de Presle, and Émile Egger (Paris: Imprimerie Impériale, 1865).

Notes on contributors

Cecilie Brøns received her PhD in Classical Archaeology in 2015 from the National Museum of Denmark, Department of Ancient Cultures of Denmark and the Mediterranean, and the Danish National Research Foundation's Centre for Textile Research (CTR) at the University of Copenhagen. Her dissertation, entitled *Gods and Garments: Textiles in Greek Sanctuaries in the 7th to the 1st Century BC*, will be published by Oxbow Books in 2017. She is currently a postdoctoral research fellow at the Ny Carlsberg Glyptotek, Copenhagen, and director of the research project *Transmission and Transformation: Ancient Polychromy in an Architectural Context*, funded by the Carlsberg Foundation. Her research currently focuses on ancient textiles and polychromy.

Tiziana D'Angelo is Temporary Lecturer in Classical Art and Archaeology at the University of Cambridge and Fellow of St. Edmund's College. She received her PhD in Classical Archaeology from Harvard University in 2013. Her research interests include ancient wall painting and its reception during the nineteenth and twentieth centuries, funerary art, ancient ethnic and cultural identity, and history of collecting. Her current book project focuses on pre-Roman funerary painting from southern Italy.

Matthew Dillon is Associate Professor of Classics and Ancient History at the University of New England – Australia. He publishes primarily on Greek religion but also on Greek history in general. In Greek religion, the role of women is also a particular interest but also how the Greeks "communicated" with the gods and how they actually worshipped them. He is currently writing a monograph, *Omens and Oracles. Divination in the Archaic and Classical Greece*, and is the author of *Girls and Women in Classical Greek Religion* (2002).

Esther Eidinow is Associate Professor in Ancient Greek History at the University of Nottingham. Her research focuses on ancient Greek magic and religion, and she has published *Oracles, Curses, and Risk Among the Ancient Greeks* (Oxford University Press, 2007, ppbk 2013); and *Luck, Fate, and Fortune: Antiquity and its Legacy* (I. B. Tauris, 2011), as well as a number of articles. Her latest book is *Envy, Poison, and Death: Women on Trial in Classical Athens* (Oxford University Press, 2015).

Notes on contributors xi

Meritxell Ferrer is a Beatriu de Pinós postdoctoral research fellow at the Universitat Pompeu Fabra (Barcelona, Spain). Previously, she was postdoctoral research fellow in the Classics Department of Stanford University. She earned her PhD from IUHJVV-UPF (Barcelona, Spain) in 2012 with a dissertation entitled "Acrópolis sicilianas: comunidades, rituales y poderes (ss. X-V a.C.)." Her research specializes in the archaeology of the Mediterranean during the Iron Age, mainly Phoenician and Greek colonization in the western Mediterranean, with a particular interest in Sicily and the Iberian Peninsula. Meritxell has done fieldwork in Spain, Portugal, Sicily, and Sardinia. Among her recent publications are "Feasting the Community: Ritual and Powers on the Sicilian Acropolis (10th–6th centuries BC)" in *Journal of Mediterranean Archaeology* (2013); "Life and Death in Ancient Colonies: Domesticity, Material Culture and Sexual Politics in the Western Phoenician World, 8th–6th B.C." in *The Archaeology of Colonialism: Intimate Encounters and Sexual Effects*, edited by B. Voss and E. Cassella (2012); "Representing Communities in Heterogeneous Worlds: Staples Foods and Ritual Practices in Phoenician Diaspora" in *Guess Who's Coming to Dinner: Feasting Rituals in the Prehistoric Societies of Europe and the Near East* edited by G. Aranda *et al.* (2012).

Andromache Karanika is Associate Professor of Classics at the University of California, Irvine. She received her PhD at Princeton University and has published articles on Homer, women's oral genres, lament, pastoral poetry, and, recently, on Homeric reception in Byzantine literature. Her book *Voices at Work: Women, Performance and Labor* is published by Johns Hopkins University Press (2014); she has also co-authored a textbook on Modern Greek. She is currently working on a book on wedding songs and poetics and the interactions of lyric and epic.

J. Bert Lott is Professor of Greek and Roman Studies at Vassar College in Poughkeepsie, New York. He is the author of *The Neighborhoods of Augustan Rome* and *Death and Dynasty in Early Imperial Rome*, published by Cambridge University Press and *Roman Historical Documents*, forthcoming from Wiley-Blackwell.

Deborah Lyons is the author of *Dangerous Gifts: Ideologies of Gender and Exchange in Ancient Greece* (Texas, 2012) and *Gender and Immortality: Heroines in Ancient Greek Myth and Cult* (Princeton, 1997) and co-editor (with Raymond Westbrook) of *Women and Property in Ancient Near Eastern and Mediterranean Societies* (Washington, DC, 2005). She is currently working on ancient Greek views of immortality. She is Associate Professor of Classics at Miami University.

Bonnie MacLachlan is Professor Emerita/Adjunct Research Professor, Department of Classical Studies, University of Western Ontario. She has recently led seminars on Greek thought at the University of Siena, October 2014. Her most recent book publications include (ed.) *Thalia Delighting in Song. Essays on Ancient Greek Poetry by Emmet Robbins*, 2013; *Women in Ancient Greece. A* xii *Notes on contributors*

Sourcebook, 2012; and *Women in Ancient Rome. A Sourcebook*, 2013. She has recently published "The Grave's a Fine and Funny Place: Chthonic Rituals and Comic Theater in the Greek West," in *Theatre Outside Athens. Drama in Greek Sicily and South Italy*, 2012, "Ritual Katábasis and the Comic," in *Cahiers des études anciennes XIII*, 83–111, and four articles on comic theatre in the Greek West for *The Encyclopedia of Greek Comedy* (Wiley-Blackwell).

Lisa Maurizio is currently Associate Professor of Classical Medieval Studies at Bates College. Her research interests are in the area of oral poetry, gender, and religion. She has published articles on Delphi, oral poetry, religious festivals, and, most recently, Heraklitos, in addition to having two of her plays that borrow conventions from Japanese Noh theater, Bunraku puppets, and ancient Greek tragedy produced by Animus Ensemble at the Boston Center for the Arts. She has recently published a textbook on Greek mythology (Oxford, 2015) and is working on an electronic edition of Delphic oracles.

Laura McClure is Professor of Classics at the University of Wisconsin–Madison. Her research focuses on Athenian drama, the study of women in the ancient world and Classical reception. Her publications include books on the representation of women in Athenian drama and the courtesan in the Greek literary tradition: *Spoken Like a Woman: Speech and Gender in Athenian Drama* (Princeton, 1999) and *Courtesans at Table: Gender and Greek Literary Culture in Athenaeus* (Routledge 2003). She has edited three volumes on the subject of women in antiquity as well as numerous articles, most recently an analysis of the role of women in tragic recognition scenes. She is currently completing a textbook about women in ancient Greece and Rome (under contract with Blackwell). Her current work explores the reception of the Greek chorus.

Maya Muratov, currently Associate Professor of Art History at Adelphi University, received her PhD in Ancient Art and Archaeology from the Institute of Fine Arts, New York University. Her research interests, which include cultural, religious, and social history of the Greek colonies in the Northern Black Sea area and interactions between the colonists and the indigenous populations, are reflected in her fieldwork: for the past 25 years, Maya has been participating in the excavation of Pantikapaion, the ancient capital of the Bosporan Kingdom. She is also involved in research projects dealing with multicultural and multilingual societies and the complex roles the interpreters played within them; as well as a project on theater culture and popular entertainment in the ancient Mediterranean and marionette theater in antiquity.

Laurie O'Higgins was educated at Trinity College Dublin, and received her PhD from Cornell. She works on women's voices in Classical literature and wrote *Women and Humor in Classical Greece*, Cambridge 2003. Her most recent major project is a book on the reception of Classical literature among sub-elites in eighteenth-century Ireland.

Irene Salvo is Post-doctoral Gerda Henkel Scholar in Ancient History at the Royal Holloway, University of London. Her new research project is on gender and

Notes on contributors   xiii

religion in Greek inscriptions. She analyses women's agency in ancient Greek society through documents of religious interest, such as curse tablets, oracle enquiries, "confession inscriptions," and healing miracle stories. She received her PhD from the Scuola Normale Superiore (Pisa) in 2011 with a dissertation titled *Unclean Hands. Blood Pollution and Civic Rites of Purification in the Ancient Greek World*. She has published various articles on Greek social and cultural history, focusing on Greek epigraphy, pollution and purification, and emotions. Two forthcoming book chapters are on gender and emotions in Greek curse tablets.

Introduction

*Esther Eidinow, Lisa Maurizio,
and Matthew Dillon*

Over the last 50 years, women as ritual agents in the ancient world have increasingly become the subject of scholarly scrutiny. While the reasons for this are manifold, two crucial dimensions can be highlighted: first and foremost, religion is the major sphere where women in antiquity left evidence of their activities; second, ritual itself continues to be an object of intense scholarly attention both within and outside of the field of Classics, not only, but perhaps especially, since Frazer published his *Golden Bough* (1925) on ritual. These two dimensions, combined with broader historical dynamics, have developed both separately and together – the one informing the other and vice versa.

In part this is accounted for by the dynamic nature of the scholarship in each area, which continues to evolve. Only relatively recently, for example, have long-standing assumptions that formed the basis of scholarly inquiry into studies of women been challenged. Scholars have recognized the inter-relational nature of society: scholarship on women has borne studies in gender, which consider how notions of femininity *and* masculinity, as well as female *and* male identities, are shaped – and shape each other – through social and ritual practices. Not only does this mean that studies of men and masculinity in the ancient world have increased (Arnold and Brady 2011; Foxhall and Salmon 2013 [1998]; Masterson 2013; Williams 2010 [1999]) but also that new paths in the analysis of ancient women are being forged, prompting more encompassing investigations of gender and society that allow significant interactions and ambiguities in the social construction of ancient gender ideologies to emerge. The focus of resulting scholarship spreads across a spectrum of relevant themes, from explorations rooted, as it were, in the mind (e.g. on myth and its social influence, such as the papers in Bodiou and Mehl 2009) to work that carefully investigates the interaction of body and behavior (e.g. Holmes 2012; Masterson, Rabinowitz and Robson 2015); there is also the welcome development of thoughtful guides to methodology for researchers at all levels (Foxhall 2013).

Similar pathways can be traced in the directions taken by recent research into ritual, which can be broadly categorized as those that focus on either the role of the body or more closely on the internal experience of the ritual practitioner. Examples of the former range widely, including, for example, explorations of the performativity of ritual (e.g. Lonsdale 2000; Bierl 2001; Kowalzig 2007) or the use of archaeological remains to reconstitute ritual practice (Mylonopoulos and Röder

2 *Esther Eidinow et al.*

2006), while the latter include studies of ritual as an emotional experience (e.g. Alexiou 2002 [1974]). In turn, these categories are themselves blurred in scholarship that examines ritual as a mode of communication (e.g. Chaniotis 2006; Stavrianopoulou 2006) or probes perceptions and representations of ritual as public and/ or private events (Connelly 2007; Blok 2010). As this suggests, the recognition of the interrelational nature of society is also a factor here, as ritual studies embrace an increasingly holistic approach to the topic. Moreover, in this field, as well, scholarly conventions are being challenged, as a number of recent studies have disputed enduring paradigms of particular (categories of) rituals such as, for example, that of offerings (e.g. Patera 2012), sacrifice (e.g. Naiden 2013), and so-called "initiation" rituals (Dodd and Faraone 2003).

In both areas, gender and ritual, these developments demonstrate how completely an explanatory paradigm can take root as a tenet of scholarship and how "the more eyes use the same glasses, the fuzzier their focus has to become" (Graf 2003, 20). Studies that take gender as a category of analysis, thereby conceptually separating the term "men" from "human," a conflation that is often implicit in ancient sources and scholarship, have illuminated and reshaped both the conceptual and actual role of men and women. In turn, reconsiderations of ritual, particularly those that eschew functional paradigms that treat ritual as reinforcing social structures rather than shaping them, have similarly revised the conceptual and actual role of ritual in its social settings and historical period. And when scholars bring these two strands of scholarship together, we find these developments sharpen our vision of the role that ritual may have played with regard to women in ancient society – and vice versa (Tzanetou 2007 offers a critical and comprehensive review of scholarship in this area; see also Burrus 2007; Foxhall 2013, 4–15).

We highlight here two areas in particular. First, there is the visibility of the evidence and the methodologies that can be brought to bear in analyzing that material. It is hard to deny (as Cole has eloquently argued 2004, 92–145) that men's and women's rites were divided by their social roles: in contrast to the lives of women, men operated in the public sphere, so that many of their activities, ritual or otherwise, left visible traces. At one level, this means that, although "the vital ritual tasks that women discharged on behalf of their families and the community were less widely noticed and commemorated than those of men" (as Tzanetou 2007, 16), nevertheless, there are opportunities to broaden and deepen our investigations into the lived experience of ancient women. For example, Susan Cole (2004) has shown the essential role of women – even if only as regulated bodies – in the formation of public, civic ritual and therefore of the polis itself; Lisa Nevett (2011), has challenged the common understanding of a women's "space" in the ancient Greek city and offered evidence for the idea that (588) "women were present in the urban landscape in a range of contexts" and how "gender associations of certain spaces within the city may . . . have changed on a cyclical basis over a relatively short time-frame." Certainly, it is the case that "like any other social practice, ritual is an ideologically charged activity, and as such one of its goals in ancient Greece was to produce women who performed successfully within a male-dominated and often explicitly

Introduction 3

misogynist community" (Goff 2004, 4). Yet, at the same time, the nature of (women's) ritual potentially offered a range of opportunities for self-articulation. In other words, accomplishing "an ideologically charged activity" does not remove women (or men, and here we might consider the hoplite) from the historical stage or as subjects of modern scholarship. Indeed, the private nature of some of women's activities and the conformity to social norms that ritual seemingly compels need not determine how they are studied. Instead, it suggests, as many scholars have recognized, that women's rituals within the ancient city bear further examination from a range of perspectives.

The contributions in this volume seek to put this examination into practice. They developed from a conference "Women's Ritual Competence in the Ancient Mediterranean." The conference's call for papers gave only the most sparing accounts of the terms "ritual" and "competence" and asked rather for examples of "expertise" in situations that involved communication with supernatural powers. The aim of this more open invitation was to prompt a broader view of ritual and religion so as to encourage reflection on the ways certain actions, manners and situations can differentiate the secular from the sacred; and to enable the exploration of how women's rituals in this broader sense might be said to intersect with the political, economic, and cultural spheres of their communities. In this way, we hoped to identify how the rituals that women created and in which they participated were enacted and served various purposes. These rituals would therefore not necessarily lie directly in the realm of "religious" activity, but might integrate sacred and secular (as Cole 2004), shaping the rhythms of daily life in myriad ways.

In response, the chapters in this collection examine the multiplicity of ritual as a lived experience, reflecting the range of women's activities in which ritual was involved and the range of rituals in which women participated. This includes, for example, not only directly religious rituals such as prayer, prophecy, and sacrifice, but also baking, weaving and the creation of textiles, preparing for birth and lamenting death. To do this, they focus on a wide range of evidence for the ritual activities of women in the ancient world, employing and integrating epigraphic, material, iconographic, and literary sources, and embracing a wide-ranging geographical and temporal perspective on women's ritual in Greco-Roman cultures of the ancient Mediterranean, extending from Magna Graecia to Lydia and Phrygia; from Iron Age Greece to Imperial Rome.

The chapters also take a variety of theoretical approaches to analyzing evidence. Most contributors take as their premise a definition of ritual that entails competence (or its absence), that is, as the explicit or implicit internalization of a number of cultural scripts that practitioners are able to maintain, manipulate, innovate, or even distort in their ritual performances. The ways in which they approach this idea varies – but can perhaps be grouped under three broad headings. In their approach to ritual competence, a number of chapters show particular affinities with Catherine Bell's definition of ritual practice and, in particular, ritualization as a "strategic way of acting in specific social situations" (67). This is a touchstone in Bonnie MacLachlan's chapter in the volume; the

4   *Esther Eidinow et al.*

approach also plays a key, albeit implicit, conceptual role in Dolores O'Higgins' chapter on the ways in which Penelope's ritual agency disrupts time. This aspect of Bell's theory reinforces and elaborates her notion of "acceptable ritual," which draws attention to the ways in which ritual competence may be understood as assessed by the community in which a particular activity is performed; a negative assessment will result in unacceptable ritual or no ritual at all. A number of contributors work with this idea, using very different kinds of evidence. Using epigraphic sources, Irene Salvo's chapter demonstrates how the skills or competence to perform acceptable rituals relating to reproduction may have been attributed to women – by other women. Tiziana D'Angelo and Maya Muratov illustrate how the community's commemoration of the competence of women can be recovered from material evidence, specifically the Canosan terracotta statuettes (and its dissipation from their disappearance from the material record). Literary evidence is also important: Laura McClure interprets the presentation of Iphigenia in Euripides' *Iphigeneia in Tauris* as demonstrating the polis' approval of female priesthoods, while Deborah Lyons' chapter also considers the judgment of literary writers and uses it to examine the implications for our understanding of rituals by women that we scarcely hear about.

Unacceptable ritual can be recognized, if not theorized, by audiences of ritual acts in the way that speakers of a language can hear grammatical errors without necessarily having the capacity to explain them. In this volume, the idea of a grammar of ritual is explored in at least three chapters in very different ways: Bert Lott uses the action-representation system of ritual identified by Robert N. McCauley and E. Thomas Lawson (Lawson and McCauley 1990; McCauley and Lawson 2002). They argue that religious rituals across cultures demonstrate a structural regularity, and thus religious ritual actions must depend on an underlying universal conceptual scheme, a common ritual form that was independent of cultural context. Lott uses this approach to examine the representation of a female prophet in Republican Rome. Andromache Karanika's chapter takes a different approach to the "grammar of ritual." She pursues the linguistic analogy for ritual through the work of Richard L. Grimes, who explicitly considers the question of ritual competence: "Ritual Competence is like grammar, most of us learn to speak before we can articulate rules of grammar" (Grimes 2013, quoted by Karanika). Finally, Lisa Maurizio's chapter about the ritual competence of the Pythia turns on the ways in which women will have acquired the competence to create ritual speech – and the ways in which the power of such speech was contained, negotiated, or simply curtailed in different social and political settings. These conceptualizations of ritual as strategy or grammar have several points in common: each allows for the question of competence or incompetence to be assessed through an examination of a ritual's performance and its reception among its onlookers and participants. Each entertains the question of an actor's intentionality or lack thereof, without making assumptions that ritual demands intentionality or curtails it. Each sets ritual and ritual actor within their social world but does not assume that the social world dictates, explains, or wholly shapes ritual and actor.

Introduction 5

This focus on the interaction between individual and culture has particular affinities with practice theory (also deployed in Barbara Goff's recent book on women and Greek religion, 2004) and with the approach to agency developed by Sherry Ortner (2006). Practice theory, developed with varying emphases in the works of Pierre Bourdieu, Anthony Giddens, Marshall Sahlins, Michel de Certeau and James Scott, rejects what Sherry Ortner defines as "constraint theories" (Ortner 2006, 14 and chapter 6), such as functionalism (which presumes that ritual supports or works within social structures) and symbolist approaches (which asks what ritual objects and actions symbolize within a given social structure). Rather, it recognizes "human behavior as shaped, molded, ordered, and defined by external social and cultural forces and formations" (Ortner 2006, 1). Unlike functionalism and symbolism, it asks how such constraints exist in a dialectical rather than an oppositional relationship with the practices of individuals.

When defining agency within practice theory, Ortner (2006, 147) makes a distinction between what she calls "an agency of power and an agency of projects," which is also useful for analyzing the intersection of women and ritual in antiquity. An agency of power refers to a person's power to act for their own or others' benefit, and their ability (whether in terms of social, economic, political, or cultural resources) to act on others; it also refers to a person's power to refuse or side-step social imperatives. An agency of power then concerns domination and resistance. Often, acts of resistance in or through ritual are taken to be indicators of agency because the person's intentionality is most apparent in oppositional acts or critical words (e.g. Winkler 1989). An agency of projects, on the other hand, considers the capacity of people to pursue projects and agendas in a way that does not directly engage power, either the exercise or resistance of it. The two categories of agency, although usefully distinguished for heuristic purposes, are usually found acting together in real-life events. Both Meritxell Ferrer's and Cecilia Brøn's chapters illustrate this overlap: Ferrer's chapter shows how women's use of daily objects in the development of ritual practices supported their broader role in the mortal community, while Brøns's chapter shows how women used textiles to interact with cult images and hence the gods themselves; she also introduces the work of Alfred Gell to highlight the sensory side of religion in this context. The views of ritual and agency adopted by a number of other contributors also align with Ortner's approach. Esther Eidinow uses Ortner's work explicitly to discuss the representation of women as "victims" of magical attacks in early Christian texts, questioning traditional analyses of these descriptions as undermining women. In addition, both Bonnie MacLachlan and Matthew Dillon, in their chapters on women's ritual laughter, show how dominated groups, such as women, are accorded agency when they can be seen to resist or oppose those around them.

The arrangement of the chapters in this volume draws on these observations about their theoretical underpinnings. Chapters in the first section concern the ways in which ritual agency and/or competence were expressed – and can be traced – through mundane objects and activities. The next three sections are organized around themes of claims to ritual agency and reactions to those claims: section II

6 *Esther Eidinow et al.*

is concerned with women who claimed or acquired ritual authority and the ways in which that authority appears to have been transmitted. Different kinds of evidence offer a variety of representations of processes of transmission, from the language of the Pythia (Maurizio), to Euripides' portrayal of Iphigenia at Tauris (McClure), to inscriptions that suggest the transmission of knowledge of rituals to influence female fertility (Salvo). The question of how women may assert control of a ritual space as a form of resistance to dominant forms of power is examined by the chapters in the third section, using a variety of evidence from literary (O'Higgins) to material (Dillon and McLachlan). The final section investigates some examples of women whose claims to ritual agency have been denied or contested by those interpreting the evidence. The examples range from Republican Rome (Lott), to early Christian texts (Eidinow), to the descriptions of ritual in Pausanias and Plutarch (Lyons).

While the chapters in this volume may vary in their employment of the terms "ritual," "competence," and "agency," they share a common concern to identify the ways in which these phenomena can be traced in ancient lived experience. The range of approaches and case studies that result suggests that these are best observed in particular instances, but some generalizations still emerge. Ritual is identified by the majority of our contributors as not simply repeated or routine actions, but as dynamic and creative activities. The implications of these activities may vary – they may replicate or reorder the context in which they occur. But, as these chapters show, this variety itself is significant, helping to enrich our understanding of the possible relationships between women and ritual. It moves the discourse away from a simple division between, say, autonomous or regulated activity to more nuanced depictions of ancient women's engagement with their communities – a potential spectrum of "agency" – and it helps us to identify and map the many different spheres that comprised ancient women's social worlds.

Works consulted

Alexiou, Margaret. 2002 [1974]. *The Ritual Lament in Greek Tradition*. Revised by Dimitrios Yatromanolakis and Panagiotis Roilos. Cambridge: Cambridge University Press.

Arnold, John H. and Sean Brady, eds. 2011. *What is Masculinity? Historical Dynamics from Antiquity to the Contemporary World*. Basingstoke: Palgrave Macmillan.

Bierl, Anton. 2001. *Der Chor in der Alten Komödie: Ritual und Performativität (unter besonderer Berücksichtigung von Aristophanes' Thesmophoriazusen und der Phallosliede fr. 851 PMG)*. Munich and Leipzig: Saur.

Blok, Josine H. 2010. "Citizenship in Action: 'Reading' Sacrifice in Classical Athens." In *Rollenbilder in der athenischen Demokratie: Medien, Gruppen, Räume im politischen und sozialen System: Beiträge zu einem interdisziplinären Kolloquium in Freiburg i. Br., 24.–25. November 2006*, edited by Christian Mann, Matthias Haake and Ralf von den Hoff, 89–111. Wiesbaden: Reichert.

Bodiou, Lydie and Véronique Mehl. 2009. *La religion des femmes en Grèce ancienne: mythes, cultes et société*. Rennes: Presses universitaires de Rennes.

Burrus, Virginia. 2007. "Mapping as Metamorphosis: Initial Reflections on Gender and Ancient Religious Discourses." In *Mapping Gender in Ancient Religious Discourses*, edited by Todd C. Penner and Caroline Vander Stichele, 1–10. Leiden: Brill.

Introduction 7

Chaniotis, Angelos. 2006. "Rituals between Norms and Emotions: Rituals as Shared Experience and Memory." In *Ritual and Communication in the Graeco-Roman World.* Kernos Suppl. 16, edited by Eftychia Stavrianopoulou, 211–38. Liège: CIERGA.

Cole, Susan G. 2004. *Landscapes, Gender, and Ritual Space: the Ancient Greek Experience.* Berkeley: University of California Press.

Connelly, Joan Breton. 2007. *Portrait of a Priestess: Women and Ritual in Ancient Greece.* Princeton: Princeton University Press.

Dodd, David B. and Christopher Faraone, eds. 2003. *Initiation in Ancient Greek Rituals and Narratives: New Critical Perspectives.* London and New York: Routledge.

Foxhall, Lin. 2013 [1998]. *Studying Gender in Classical Antiquity.* Cambridge: Cambridge University Press.

Foxhall, Lin and John Salmon. 2013 [1998]. *When Men Were Men: Masculinity, Power and Identity in Classical Antiquity.* New York and London: Routledge.

Goff, Barbara. 2004. *Citizen Bacchae: Women's Ritual Practice in Ancient Greece.* Berkeley: University of California Press.

Graf, Fritz. 2003. "Initiation: A Concept with a Troubled History." In Dodd and Faraone 2003, 3–24.

Grimes, Ronald L. 2013. *The Craft of Ritual Studies.* Oxford: Oxford University Press.

Holmes, Brooke. 2012. *Gender: Antiquity and Its Legacy.* Oxford: Oxford University Press.

Kowalzig, Barbara. 2007. *Singing for the Gods: Performances of Myth and Ritual in Archaic and Classical Greece.* Oxford: Oxford University Press.

Lawson, E. Thomas and Robert N. McCauley. 1990. *Rethinking Religion: Connecting Cognition and Culture.* Cambridge and New York: Cambridge.

Lonsdale, Stephen H. 2000. *Dance and Ritual Play in Greek Religion.* Baltimore, MD: The Johns Hopkins University Press.

Masterson, Mark. 2013. "Studies in Ancient Masculinity." In *A Companion to Greek and Roman Sexualities*, edited by Thomas Hubbard, 17–30. Malden, MA: Wiley-Blackwell.

Masterson, Mark, Nancy Rabinowitz and James Robson. 2015. *Sex in Antiquity: Exploring Gender and Sexuality in the Ancient World.* New York and London: Routledge.

McCauley, Robert N. and E. Thomas Lawson. 2002. *Bringing Ritual to Mind: Psychological Foundations of Cultural Forms.* Cambridge and New York: Cambridge University Press.

Mylonopoulos, Joannis and Hubert Röder, eds. 2006. *Archäologie und Ritual. Auf der Suche nach der rituellen Handlung in den antiken Kulturen Ägyptens und Griechenlands.* Wien: Phoibos Verlag.

Naiden, Fred S. 2013. *Smoke Signals for the Gods: Ancient Greek Sacrifice from the Archaic through Roman Periods.* Oxford: Oxford University Press.

Nevett, Lisa C. 2011. "Towards a Female Topography of the Ancient Greek City: Case Studies from Late Archaic and Early Classical Athens (*c.* 520–400 BCE)." *Gender and History* 23: 576–96.

Ortner, Sherry B. 2006. *Anthropology and Social Theory: Culture, Power, and the Acting Subject.* Durham and London: Duke University Press.

Patera, Ioanna. 2012. *Offrir en Grèce ancienne: gestes et contextes.* Potsdamer Altertumswissenschaftliche Beiträge, 41. Stuttgart: Franz Steiner Verlag.

Stavrianopoulou, Eftychia. 2006. "Introduction." In *Ritual and Communication in the Graeco-Roman World.* Kernos Suppl. 16, edited by Eftychia Stavrianopoulou, 7–22. Liège: CIERGA.

8 *Esther Eidinow et al.*

Tzanetou, Angeliki. 2007. "Ritual and Gender: Critical Perspectives." In *Finding Persephone: Women's Rituals in the Ancient Mediterranean*, edited by Maryline Parca and Angeliki Tzanetou, 3–28. Bloomington, IN: Indiana University Press.

Williams, Craig. 2010 [1999]. *Roman Homosexuality: Ideologies of Masculinity in Classical Antiquity*. Oxford: Oxford University Press.

Winkler, John J. 1989. *The Constraints of Desire: The Anthropology of Sex and Gender in Ancient Greece*. New York and London: Routledge.

Part I
Objects and offerings

1 The forgotten things

Women, rituals, and community in Western Sicily (eighth–sixth centuries BCE)

Meritxell Ferrer

Introduction[1]

Despite the importance that gender studies and feminist perspectives have achieved in archaeology in the last decades, their impact has been quite limited in Italian archaeology. This is especially true for Italian archaeology of the Iron Age, where only in the last decade have a few works begun to consider questions of gender and women's lives (Robb 1997; Whitehouse 2001, 2013; Cuozzo 2003; Gleba 2008; Perego 2011). In the field of the archaeology of Sicily during the first millennium BCE, studies of the colonies increasingly focus on gender, especially on intermarriages (Hodos 1999; Shepherd 1999; Delgado and Ferrer 2007, 2011a, 2011b; Péré-Noguès 2008), but almost none considers the active participation of women in the everyday life and development of the colonies (Delgado and Ferrer 2007, 2011a, 2011b). Moreover, such studies almost completely ignore native Sicilian populations. In fact, most studies related to the Italian peninsula and Sicily reproduce traditional views of gender in which agency, that is the ability to act with consequence, is granted only to men, particularly those understood to have a higher rank or status, in contexts traditionally interpreted as masculine, such as trade, production, politics, and the public sphere. Conversely, women are denied any capacity to act and hence any role in the success and growth of colonies.

Ruth Whitehouse (2013) has recently pointed out that the lack of interest in gender issues in Italian and, by extension, Sicilian archaeology responds to the maintenance of historical-cultural paradigms in its almost exclusive interest in describing different patterns to place material objects in a frame of space and time. Women, as well as children, elders, commoners – that is, everyone who is not a member of the male elite – simply do not fit in or contribute to the historical cultural paradigms that archaeologists implicitly assume in their analyses. Consequently, most studies ignore these "others" and thereby reinforce a view of society in which only elite males act and have agency. In the case of Sicily during the first half of first millennium BCE, we could add two more causes for the general neglect of women beyond the one highlighted by Whitehouse. First, archaeological practice from its beginnings at the end of the nineteenth century until relatively recently has been dominated by the archaeology of monumentality and objects. In Sicily, this long-held predilection has resulted in the exclusive examination of contexts

12 *Meritxell Ferrer*

traditionally associated with power – such as city walls and ritual spaces – as well as other contexts that potentially provide complete artifacts suitable for museum display, like cemeteries. This bias in the Sicilian archaeological record has taken place at the expense of other areas where gender studies could be more preeminent, such as the domestic context, which is usually considered to be both unrelated to power and, by extension, to the masculine sphere and less likely to produce complete objects. Indeed, only two domestic areas from western Sicily – four houses from Monte Polizzo (Mühlenbock 2008) and one from Monte Maranfusa (Spatafora 2003) – have been published.

The second reason for the lack of attention to gender issues lies in the hegemony of colonial archaeology and colonist discourses. The persistence of the gaze from the colonies – mainly the Greek ones, but also Phoenician ones – has led to a continued interpretation of colonist groups as the leading actors in any kind of action or change in the island. The local populations, on the other hand, have been traditionally imagined as being passive and static actors; they are mere recipients of the technological, social, and cultural advances of their "outstanding" colonial neighbors. As a result most studies of the native Sicilian world of the first half of the first millennium BCE place a very large emphasis on imported objects, especially those of Greek origin. In fact, these objects have been traditionally considered to be "exceptional" and have been granted a higher aesthetic, symbolic, or economic value based on a modern and subjective "ceramics hierarchy" made by archaeologists. On the other hand, artifacts that are not considered to be "extraordinary" have largely been undervalued. This is the case, for example, for the many objects of local production that have usually been categorized as artifacts of poor aesthetic, symbolic, or economic interest and placed in the lower levels of this imagined "ceramics hierarchy." This is the category where all material objects related to the domestic sphere and, in particular, to activities traditionally associated with the world of women, such as cooking ware, can be found. Scant attention is paid to material culture related to the domestic sphere, especially to culinary practices, in most of the monographs and articles related to Sicilian acropoleis, the main ritual space of most native Sicilian settlements (see, for example: Castellana 1990, 1992; Vassallo 1999; Guzzone 2009; Panvini *et al.* 2009). This usual meager presence – or even absence – contrasts with the materials documented in these ritual spaces. On the acropolis of Monte Polizzo, for example, cooking ware accounts for 22.92 percent, while native plain ware accounts for 51.29 percent of all ceramic sherds recorded in this ritual space (percentages extracted from Morris and Tusa 2004, table 1).

Despite the challenges that the published archaeological records pose for any study of native populations, especially women, the main goal of this chapter is to recover the agency of some women in communal celebrations carried out periodically on the acropoleis of native Sicilian settlements, through the analysis of one of the largely forgotten objects strongly connected with domestic practices and, by extension, women: cooking ware, especially *pignatte* or cooking pots. To do this, first I analyze the acropoleis, as well as the meaning that these settings had for the local population of the island. Second, I review ritual practices carried on during

The forgotten things   13

these communal ceremonies, in particular feasting. Finally, I highlight how women constructed a sense of community and the hierarchical relationships within it, as well as created strong bonds between these ritual events and the daily world, through their ritual activities. The visibility of these women's agency and ritual competence is possible when we consider ritual as an action, in particular as a specialized form of behavior that stresses some aspects of the daily life through some kind of performance (Bell 1992; Barrett 1994; Humphrey and Laidlaw 1994; Brück 1999; Bradley 2005). In this case, I explicitly consider the "ritualization" of the act of cooking that some women carried out in the periodic celebrations hosted on the acropoleis.

Sicilian acropoleis: Communal ritual spaces in Sicily during the first millennium BCE

Since the end of the second millennium BCE and during all the first millennium BCE, native Sicilian populations mostly settled the upper part of certain hills. The settlements were placed at strategic points along routes of travel and transport and with easy access to the Sicilian river network, which favored convenient communication not only between them but also with the colonies scattered along the coast (Fig. 1.1). The elevated topography of these centers determined their internal organization, using the slope to distinguish, visually and spatially, the three areas that usually form these settlements. At lower levels were the cemeteries. At a second level were located the areas of habitation. Finally, at the highest point or in the most visually conspicuous area was located the acropolis, the place devoted to the periodic celebration of communal ritual ceremonies. This topographic placement endowed the acropolis with a visual and geographic dominance over the whole settlement, its surrounding areas, and the links established between them and the rest of the island (Ferrer 2010, 2012).

The prominence of the acropoleis was reinforced through architecture that stressed their monumentalization, distinguishing them from contemporary domestic contexts and maximizing their difference from the rest of the settlement (Ferrer 2010, 2012). This distinction was achieved through the use of Archaic architectural styles, such as circular buildings – as, for example, at Polizzello (Panvini *et al.* 2009), Montagnoli (Castellana 1990, 1992), or Monte Polizzo (Morris *et al.* 2002) – that were dominant in domestic architecture in western Sicily (second millennium BCE) until being gradually replaced with rectangular buildings (eighth to seventh centuries BCE) (Ferrer 2010, 2012). This distinction was also achieved by integrating elements belonging to foreign architectural traditions, such as the erection of a Phoenician stele-baetyl at Monte Polizzo (Morris *et al.* 2002; Ferrer 2012), the use of Greek silenic antefixes (Guzzone 2009), and the almost complete adoption of a Doric temple in Segesta used for native ritual practices (Burford 1961).

Another aspect of these communal ritual places is their high level of complexity and temporal dynamism. The acropoleis are quite large spaces, allowing the celebration of ritual events in which a considerable number of people assisted and participated. In most of these settings, there are several buildings, some devoted

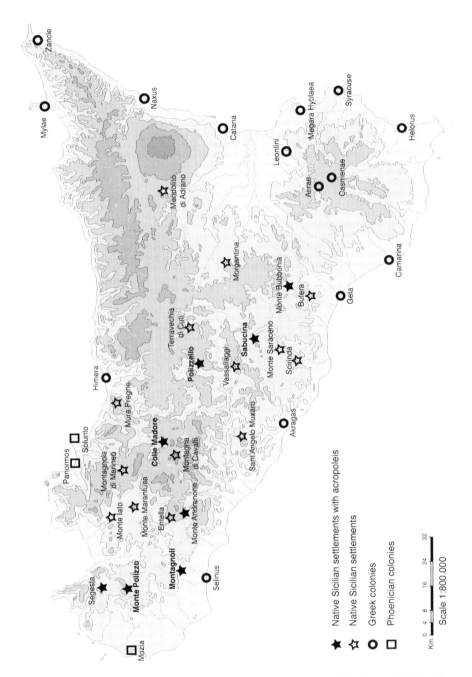

Figure 1.1 Map of Sicily showing the main native settlements of the first half of the first millennium BCE, the main acropoleis and Greek and Phoenician colonies.

Source: Image provided by the author.

The forgotten things   15

to restrictive or esoteric practices and others to ancillary practices, such as the storage of food or objects used in these ceremonies (Ferrer 2012). At the same time, the considerable presence of open spaces, where auxiliary structures such as altars, hearths, or pits were located, indicates that the ritual activities carried out in these areas were probably visually accessible to a wide audience (Ferrer 2012).

Material evidence from the acropoleis bears witness to a great variety of ritual practices, ranging from the emphasis on deer hunting at Monte Polizzo (Morris *et al.* 2002), to metal production at Colle Madore (Vassallo 1999), to the accentuation of the warrior group in the latest levels (sixth century BCE) of Polizzello (De Miro 1988). Despite this considerable diversity, in all of these settings and throughout their occupation, three highly ritualized practices have been repeatedly documented: the cleaning of these spaces, as suggested by the few finds in these places (Ferrer 2012, 394–8), votive deposition, and collective commensality. These three activities do not represent a novelty within the Sicilian ritual tradition; all of them have been documented in communal ritual places located at settlements dated in the precolonial period, for example, in La Muculufa (Holloway *et al.* 1990); in Madre Chiesa di Gaffe (Castellana 2000) or the first levels of Polizzello (Tanasi 2009).

In sum, the geographical and architectonical features of these places, as well as the successive celebrations carried out in them, make the acropoleis crucial spaces of local interaction inside the settlements. They were meeting points, but also, due to their visibility, they were places of mnemonic reference for all those who lived in or even only visited these centers. The continued execution of communal feastings in these settings converted the acropoleis into arenas where social solidarity was promoted and group identity was forged among all those who participated in these events (Ferrer 2012, 2013). The heterogeneity of the participants, however, their different experiences and social and cultural identifications, also turn the acropoleis into arenas where the various power relations that existed within these communities were built, negotiated, and reified (Ferrer 2012, 2013).

Feasting the community: Drinking and eating on the acropoleis

In the last few years, several archaeological studies conducted from different theoretical and methodological perspectives have argued for the sociocultural importance of feasting practices (among others: Dietler 1990; Gumerman 1997; Hamilakis 1998; Dietler and Hayden 2001; Pauketat *et al.* 2002; Bray 2003; Halstead and Barrett 2004; Jennings *et al.* 2005; Swenson 2006; Twiss 2008; Hayden and Villeneuve 2011; Ferrer 2013). All of these studies assume that feasts are a universal phenomenon imbued with a community's ideology wherein social identities are established and altered. These studies conceive of feasting as a key factor in the negotiation and maintenance of social order as well as in processes of social change. Practices of collective commensality are understood as arenas where both social competition and integration are produced simultaneously. As Dietler (2001, 77) has pointed out, "Feasts conceived sincerely by the participants as harmonious

16 *Meritxell Ferrer*

celebrations of community identity are simultaneously arenas for manipulation and the acquisition of prestige, social credit and the various forms of influence [. . .] that social capital entails."

Most of these studies argue that the power of feasting derives precisely from its extraordinariness, in particular the presence of a larger number of banqueters and a differential consumption of food and drink, both in quantity and quality (Dietler 1990; Gumerman 1997; Dietler and Hayden 2001; Pauketat *et al.* 2002; Bray 2003; Jennings *et al.* 2005; Hayden and Villeneuve 2011). This perspective based on exceptionality isolates feasting practices from daily meals. In spite of this usual stress on the exceptionality, in this particular context I assume that the importance of the feast lies precisely in the social and symbolic dimension of food, as well as in the close relationship and the continuity that exists between these collective practices and quotidian meals.

As other studies have suggested, food ingested both in "ordinary" and "extraordinary" consumption practices participates actively in the processes of constructing and representing identity – both collective and individual – and power. Several studies in diverse disciplines stress how food, as happens in feasting, acts in these processes in a dual way. On the one hand, food is involved in the construction of social and political relations characterized by equality, cohesion, or solidarity, i.e. everyone eats meat from the same animal or food from the same pot. On the other hand, feasting works in the creation, legitimation, and representation of social and political relations based on difference, i.e. in the order in which participations are served, the amount and type of food they receive (Appadurai 1981; Goody 1984; Bourdieu 1988; Caplan 1997; Counihan and Van Esterik 1997; Counihan 1999; Scholliers 2001; from an archaeological perspective: Hamilakis 1998; Halstead and Barrett 2004; Smith 2006; Delgado 2008, 2010; Ferrer 2013). Moreover, the different context in which both actions are performed, whether at home or in communal events, and their different social and political purposes, converts them into arenas where collective temporalities – that is, cycles of time shared by all the community – are constructed as well as disrupted and punctuated, allowing the creation of different social memories as well as "forgettings" (Hamilakis 2008, 15–16).

Similarly, the act of eating has ritual aspects. To eat is a highly formalized and repetitive practice that is informed by symbols, independent of the specific context where it is carried out, whether in the everyday of the household group or eventual communal ceremonies. Thus eating shares some of the features that in recent scholarship have been interpreted as inherent to any ritual act (Bell 1992; Barrett 1994; Brück 1999; Bradley 2005). In this sense, feasts carried out in the acropoleis must be interpreted as an emphasis or ritualization of a daily practice widely known to all the members of the community, involving an extrapolation to larger social structures of the social and power dynamics at work in the daily meals carried out in households (see, for example: Douglas 1975; Weismantel 1989; Bradley 2005; Delgado 2008, 2010; Delgado and Ferrer 2011a).

The existence of continuity between feasts and daily meals finds its archaeological confirmation in the fact that most of the material culture recorded in these ceremonial settings was highly similar to the material documented in the contemporary household contexts. In other words, in both arenas the same kinds of vessels (tableware, cooking ware, and domestic storage containers), whether local (coarse, plain, or decorated by being incised, impressed, and painted) or imported (mainly of Greek manufacture), have been recorded. Besides this similarity, the difference of grade that exists between both contexts, as well as the dominant presence of a material culture related to food – its storage, preparation, service, and, especially, its consumption – recorded in the acropoleis, suggests the strong relevance that feasting practices had in the successive celebrations carried out in this communal ritual settings.

Consuming alcohol and meat on the acropoleis

Most of the materials from the acropoleis refer to consumption practices, in particular to drinking paraphernalia. Among these vases was found a considerable number of closed receptacles dedicated to serving liquids, especially jugs mostly of local production. But among the ceramics related to drinking there is an absolute predominance of open shapes devoted to consumption, particularly cups and bowls of local production, to which were added, from the second half of the seventh century BCE, a certain number of Greek imports, both of metropolitan and colonial production (Ferrer 2013).

This pattern, documented in all Sicilian acropoleis, is perfectly illustrated at Polizzello throughout the life of the settlement. During the early occupation of its acropolis, specifically, in the use-level of the North Building (first half of the ninth century), open vases – cups and bowls both simple and carenated – represent 75 percent of all the ceramics identified in this space (Palermo *et al.* 2009, 51). In a later period, 17 pits from the last use-level of Structure B (*c.* 600–550 BCE) show again a clear predominance of drinking paraphernalia: service and, mainly, consumption vessels were documented in almost all of them (Tanasi 2009, 34–43).

Along with the material related to drinking, other elements associated specifically with solid and semi-solid food, such as cooking wares, grill hooks, and faunal data, have also been documented on the acropoleis, although in less quantity. Despite their recurring presence, it is worth pointing out that they have had little influence on the traditional scholarly narratives concerning the Sicilian acropoleis. This is especially the case for cooking ware and its association to daily practices and, in particular, to feminine agency. In fact, in these accounts, feasting has been inferred only through drinking paraphernalia and alcoholic consumption. This practice of ignoring everything that goes beyond beverage consumption derives not only from the considerable volume of material related to drinking from these spaces but principally from the importance that usually has been given to alcoholic consumption. In particular, we refer to alcohol's connotation as "extraordinary" food related to prestige and status, to the establishment and maintenance of a direct association between this beverage and the masculine sphere, and, above all, to its traditional association with the importation of products specifically Greek (Hodos 2000, 2009; Domínguez Monedero 2010).

18   *Meritxell Ferrer*

Along with these drinking practices, in these ceremonies the consumption of food was also very important. Although this consumption has been documented through two kinds of sources that refer to two different kinds of food (meat and porridge), more attention has been given to the first one. As is the case with alcoholic beverages, greater attention is given to meat consumption, at the expense of other kinds of food also consumed at the acropoleis, because it is considered "extraordinary" and is associated with the male sphere.

The consumption of meat is inferred in communal ceremonies by grill hooks and faunal remains. Despite the current absence of a detailed faunal analysis from each Sicilian acropolis, the available data from Monte Polizzo (Hnatiuk 2003) allow us to consider this practice. If we compare the faunal recording from Monte Polizzo's acropolis with that documented in the contemporary domestic contexts of the same settlement, in particular House 1 and 2 (Mühlenbock 2008), we observe that both contexts present the same variety of species. However, the proportions of each species differ completely between the two contexts. In the two houses we see a predominance of domestic animals, which represent almost the totality of the fauna identified in these spaces (House 1: 96 percent; House 2: 97.7 percent), while wild animals have a small presence (House 1: 2.6 percent; House 2: 2.1 percent). On the acropolis, this pattern is completely inverted, with a clear predominance of wild animals, mainly deer, representing 51 percent of the acropolis's faunal register (Zone A: 39.7 percent; Zone B: 84.4 percent), while domestic animals only represent 15 percent of the total. Despite the small presence of domestic animals on the acropolis, the relative proportions among them coincide completely with what is observed in the domestic contexts, ovicaprids being the most attested animals, followed by bovines, and then pigs (Fig. 1.2).

Another interesting feature of these faunal remains is the partial representation of the animal. Most of the remains documented on the acropolis at Monte Polizzo come from the head and the extremities, mainly hoofs or legs, the presence of long bones being scant relative both to the foreparts and hindquarters of the animal. This pattern indicates a virtual absence of remains of the more edible animal parts, which have more caloric and nutritional value, and this suggests that the activities related to animal sacrifice and dismembering, and probably also cooking, predominated on the acropoleis. However, meat consumption on a large scale seems to have taken place outside the central area of the acropoleis, either in the domestic contexts or the open areas adjacent to these settings, where that segment of the audience which lacked access to the main platform during the celebration of the ceremonies could be situated (Ferrer 2013).

This faunal pattern reveals one behavior that partially differs from that inferred from drinking practices. Unlike the ceramic record, which points directly to collective consumption in these settings, the faunal remains documented on the acropoleis – at least in Monte Polizzo, but probably also in Polizzello and Colle Madore – suggest that meat consumption was less localized. But, despite this difference, the act of sharing the same animal would have had the same effects as collective drinking: both would have built a sense of community and both

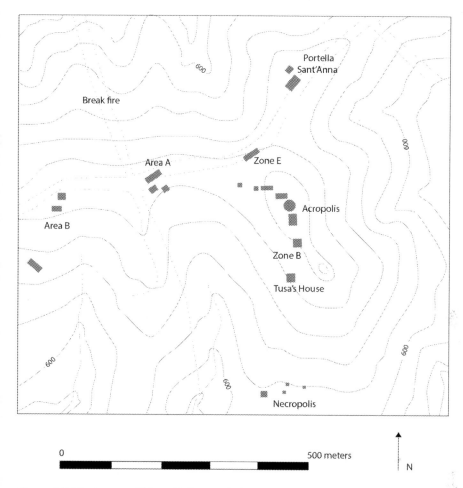

Figure 1.2 Planimetry of Monte Polizzo pointing out their domestic and ritual areas.
Source: After Morris *et al.* (2002, fig. 3). Courtesy of Ian Morris.

would have created, displayed, and legitimized the social and power dynamics that existed within it. Additionally, the translation of these practices and their effects to other spaces would have introduced new areas of the settlement into the construction of this community and its collective memory, while the consumption of the same animals on the acropoleis and in houses stressed the continuities between daily and ritual meals. This continuity suggests that in the communal celebrations on the acropoleis not only men had the ability to act but also, as happened in the domestic realm, women and men actively participated in them (Ferrer 2012, 2013).

20 Meritxell Ferrer

Porridges on the acropoleis: Humble foods and the centrality of women

The existence of close bonds between households and acropoleis, but also the active participation of some women in these communal ceremonies, is stressed when we analyze the second type of food eaten in these communal ceremonies: liquid or semi-solid foods cooked in pots. Although the presence of cookware is not widespread in the acropoleis, it is worth noting that it is documented at all stages in the life of all of them. Cooking ware represents 22.92 percent of all the ceramics on the acropolis of Monte Polizzo (percentage extracted from Morris and Tusa 2004: table 1), and cooking wares have also been recorded on the acropolis of Polizzello (Panvini *et al.* 2009) and in structure 7 of Montagnoli (Castellana 1990, 1992).

The most common type of cookware documented on the acropoleis, as in domestic contexts, is the *pignatta*. This is a handmade pot of coarse clay, with a tronco-conic body of more or less oblique walls, a completely flat bottom and the addition of two or four clay lumps as handles (Fig. 1.3). Its extensive documentation in native Sicilian domestic contexts suggests that it was the most common cooking vessel used by local people throughout the first millennium BCE and well into the medieval period (Isler 1995, 56–8). The *pignatte* represent 69 percent of cooking ware in Monte Maranfusa's domestic contexts (Valentino 2003, 255). They are the most common cooking vessels documented in the four houses published from Monte Polizzo (Mühlenbock 2008); *pignatte* have also been found in Monte Iato (Russenberger 2010), Cozzo Mususino (Tamburello 1969), Morgantina (Leighton 1993, 171) and Montagnola di Ramacca (Albanese and Procelli 1988–89, 126). The extreme simplicity and formal diversity displayed by the *pignatte* suggest that these vessels may have been produced within the domestic sphere by members of the household group who took care of the daily cooking, that is, by some of the women of the household.

Bioarchaeological data from Sicilian native contexts of the first millennium BCE are scarce. The data suggest, however, that cereals, mainly barley and wheat, and to a lesser extent faro and rye, were the main alimentary resources for native Sicilian communities (Spigo 1981; McConnell 1996; Stika 2002; Stika *et al.* 2008). The preeminence of cereals in the native Sicilian diet, together with the very morphology of the *pignatte* and their frequent presence in domestic areas clearly associated with hearths and/or mills suggests that these pots were mainly used in the preparation of cereal porridges. Indeed, cereal porridges cooked in *pignatte* were most likely a key staple of the daily diet of the native Sicilian people throughout the first millennium BCE.

The continued presence of *pignatte* on the acropoleis, their high degree of formal diversity, and the fact that most of them show evidence of having been well-used suggest that some members of the community who participated in the successive communal events performed in these ritual settings may have brought their own cook pots to these ceremonies. This possibility becomes more plausible when we compare the size and volume of the *pignatte* documented in domestic contexts with those recorded on the acropoleis – an analysis that can currently only be carried out

Figure 1.3 At the top of the figure some *pignatte* from the acropolis of Monte Polizzo. At the bottom some *pignatte* from domestic contexts of Monte Maranfusa.

Source: Top: Ferrer (2012, fig. 8.18); bottom: after Valentino (2003, fig. 220). Courtesy of Francesca Spatafora.

22   *Meritxell Ferrer*

for Monte Polizzo, as it is the only site where its acropolis (Morris *et al.* 2002, 2003; Morris and Tusa 2004) and some of its domestic contexts (Mühlenbock 2008) have been published. Most of the *pignatte* documented in its domestic contexts have a diameter that ranges between 13 and 34 cm (Mühlenbock 2008, 85). The same pattern appears on the acropolis of Monte Polizzo, where *pignatte* fragments whose diameters can be measured present similar measurements, with diameters that generally range between 12 and 36 cm. Specifically, of the 69 *pignatte* measured in this acropolis, 64 have a diameter that fits perfectly within the pattern documented in its domestic contexts (92.25 percent), with only five larger pots (7.25 percent). These larger *pignatte* present a diameter that ranges between 42 and 48 cm. Their production and use could be considered as exceptional, mostly related to these communal celebrations. The very close resemblance between the *pignatte* found in both contexts – domestic and ritual – as well as the evidence that they had been used before suggests that the *pignatte* used in communal celebrations may have been brought from the homes themselves. Specifically, these objects were probably brought to the acropolis by the same individuals who used them daily in their households, that is, by the women who regularly cooked for their household groups.

This idea seems to be reinforced when we consider two possible dump areas related to this acropolis and the successive ceremonies carried out in it. The first of these areas is located in Zone E, a natural slope 50 meters northwest of the acropolis. Its stratigraphy presents a continued sequence of depositions from the mid-seventh century to the beginning of the fifth century BCE, a time-span that coincides with the main phases of the use of this acropolis. The association of this dump with the acropolis is suggested by the close proximity of the spaces, the temporal coincidence in periods of use, and the similarity in materials, both from a typological and from a proportional perspective (Morris *et al.* 2002; Cooper 2007). Most of the materials recorded in this dump are ceramics – mainly fine ware of local and imported production as well as cookware, including a large number of *pignatte,* representing between 28 percent and 42 percent of all recorded ceramics (Cooper 2007, 42–3). Additionally, metallic objects, such as personal ornamentations, i.e. fibulae, pins, or beads, as well as tools, such as iron knives, and faunal remains, have been recorded (Cooper 2007). The second dump is located in Zone B, only five meters southeast from the higher point of the acropolis. This deposit, with a maximum width of 5.5 meters and with 0.5 meters of depth at its central point, dates from the third quarter of the sixth century BCE. Unlike the dump in Zone E, only a very limited amount of local and imported fine ceramics was found, along with cookware and metallic objects. Nevertheless, a considerable volume of charcoal, ashes, faunal remains and fragmented big storage containers – especially *pithoi* (domestic storage containers) of local production – has been found (Morris *et al.* 2002) (see Fig. 1.2).

Although both dumps seem to contain most of the debris from the successive ceremonies carried out in this acropolis, the dissimilarity in the materials recorded in each one indicates that they could have been used for different purposes. In this sense, most of the materials recorded in the dump in Zone B seem to be related to

The forgotten things   23

the possessions of the acropolis and, by extension, of the community as a whole, while those documented in the dump in Zone E – mainly drinking vessels and cookware – could be personal or household belongings provided by those who participated in these ceremonies (Ferrer 2012, 405). The possibility that some of the participants in these communal ceremonies provided some vessels normally used in their daily lives highlights the bonds that were established between the domestic and the ritual spheres in these celebrations. Furthermore, the use of these vessels stresses the importance of the house in the development of these communal celebrations and, by extension, in the construction of a sense of community and the power relationships created, contested, and legitimized through it. It also evidences the importance of some women in these processes that affect both their homes and their communities. Indeed, through the act of providing and cooking with some of the pots used in their everyday lives to feed their families in communal celebrations, these women were extrapolating their central role as nourishers and carers of their households to wider social structures.

The distribution of *pignatte* on the acropoleis has a rather homogenous pattern. Most *pignatte* have been recorded in clear association with hearths or in pits related to them. This pattern suggests that, while some of the porridges consumed in these communal ceremonies may have been cooked at home and then brought to the acropoleis, most of them were cooked in these ritual spaces during the celebration of these communal events. The cooking of everyday meals in communal ceremonies would have emphasized the bonds that were established between ritual events and the domestic sphere, that is, the daily life of these settlements, during these celebrations. Just as with the ingestion of wine or meat, the shared consumption of porridges, widely known by everyone for being the basis of their daily diet, in communal events would have constructed and ordered a sense of community. It would also have emphasized and realized (in material terms) the active participation of various households groups in the constitution of their communities. The consumption of staple food in these exceptional events implies that the boundaries of the various households that make up these communities had been crossed and that the communities had been joined, physically and symbolically. The construction of this web that brought all households of the settlement together is perfectly exemplified by the larger *pignatte* recorded in the acropoleis. The capacity of these pots far exceeds the everyday needs of a household group and thus would have allowed other members of the community that were not members of the familial group to eat together. Eating the same porridge from the same pots would have strengthened the bonds of solidarity woven in these ceremonies, while simultaneously establishing and legitimizing the social hierarchies and power dynamics that existed within the community.

Furthermore, the consumption of porridges implied that the construction of a sense of community and the realization in material terms of its membership was not something ephemeral, exclusively limited to the celebration of a ritual event. Unlike the ingestion of meat, the use in these ceremonies of a staple food – such as cereal porridges – known and accessible to all who resided in these settlements represented a daily reminder of membership in the community as well as of the

24   *Meritxell Ferrer*

power relationships that existed within it and that were negotiated and contested during the events celebrated in the acropoleis. The cooking of porridges during these celebrations would have turned women into central actors in these ritual events and, by extension, in the building of a sense of community and of the power dynamics that would have been created, negotiated, and realized in material terms within it. These women would not have been simple passive observers of the dynamics of their settlement. They cooked one of the main foods that were eaten in these celebrations, and they possibly also managed, distributed it, and served it to participants.

As was the case with the household, the act of sharing the same food with the entire community meant that these women would have weaved bonds of solidarity among the different actors that participated in these ceremonies. As such, they would have reinforced the idea of social cohesion and brought everyone together in spite of their differences. With the act of serving, however, these same women would also have established social identifications and hierarchies that distinguished participants, as well as the power relations that existed among them – for instance, by serving some participants before others or by serving differently sized portions.

The centrality of these women in their households and in the community can be clearly seen in Montagnola di Marineo. In this settlement, a ritual deposit associated with its city wall has been documented (Fig. 1.4). The deposit is mostly made up of armor elements of a Greek type: two greaves, three helmets, some metallic elements associated with a horse saddle, and what is probably a shield. Secondly, there is a considerable amount of local and Greek ceramics related to drinking practices. There are also two small pendants, a small bronze axe, and a ram in bone. Finally, there is a jar with the remains of two small ovicaprids. These materials were deposited directly on the soil, close to a small stone altar that was clearly associated with a hearth and to a *pignatta* of considerable dimensions (Spatafora 1997, 2000).

This ritual ensemble seems to allude to the celebration of a ritual ceremony related to a shared space, namely, the wall. This ceremony was linked to martial elements and, by extension, to the male sphere, and to the consumption of alcoholic beverages and food, this latter represented mainly by the *pignatta*. The presence of this pot yet again brings into focus the active participation of some women in ritual celebrations associated with the community, as well as their centrality in these events.

Indeed, the importance of staples such as cereal porridges prepared by women in these celebratory contexts suggests that the importance that women had within the household was transferred to a wider political sphere through collective ceremonies. By preparing and sharing food, women would have consolidated themselves as active members of the community and realized in material terms their centrality in its creation and the power relationships that existed within it, while at the same time reinforcing the position and authority of their own household within the community.

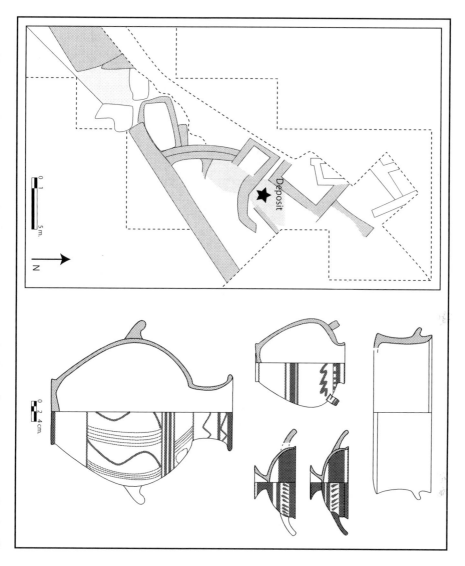

Figure 1.4 Planimetry of Montagnola di Marineo's city wall showing the localization of its votive deposit and some of the ceramics recorded in it.

Source: After Spatafora (1997, fig. 6 and 7; 2000, tav. 174). Courtesy of Francesca Spatafora.

Conclusions

The presence of objects strongly associated with the feminine sphere, such as *pignatte* and other cooking ware, on the acropoleis not only indicates the attendance of some women in successive communal ceremonies carried out in these spaces.

26   *Meritxell Ferrer*

The use of daily objects in the development of one of the most important and recurrent ritual practices in these communal celebrations, such as the feasts, also stresses the ability of some women to act publicly and effectively in the development of these ceremonies. By cooking and serving their cereal porridges to the participants of these communal ceremonies, these women reinforced and realized in material terms their active participation and their centrality in the construction and representation of an idea of equality, social cohesion, and solidarity shared by all participants and, by extension, by the whole community. The manner, however, in which women served porridge, that is, the sequence and amount of porridge they distributed, also legitimized and visualized social distinctions and power relationships inherent to these communities. Yet, unlike the exceptional consumption of meat or wine, the ingestion of the most common everyday meals cooked by these women in these celebrations allowed the social dynamics constructed in these periodic ceremonies to be transposed to the daily lives of participants. As such, every time participants ate, smelt, or tasted these porridges, they would remember their membership in these communities as well as their position in the social and power hierarchies that existed within them. Similarly, it is crucial to highlight that the importance of these women in these communal celebrations emerged from their fundamental role in the economic, social, and affective development of the different household groups that formed these communities. In fact, through the actions they performed in these ritual celebrations, women extrapolated their centrality in their households to wider social structures. This move serves to stress the continuity between daily life and the ritual sphere in this Sicilian world. In sum, although these women have been long been forgotten in the scholarly Sicilian narrative and in the publications of the archaeological record from Sicily, the detailed analysis of some objects strongly associated with their daily tasks in ritual communal contexts allows us to recover the ritual competence of Sicilian women of the first millennium BCE in the development not only of their households but also in their communities.

Note

1   The study presented in this chapter has been funded by Agència de Gestió d'Ajuts Universitaris i de Recerca (AGAUR), in particular by its postdoctoral fellowship Beatriu de Pinós.

Works consulted

Albanese Procelli, R. M. and Enrico Procelli. 1988–89. "Ramacca (Catania). Saggi di scavo nelle contrade Castellito e Montagna negli anni 1978, 1981 e 1982." *Notizie degli Scavi di Antichità* 42–3: 7–150.

Appadurai, Arjun. 1981. "Gastro-Politics in Hindu South Asia." *American Ethnologist* 3: 484–511.

Barrett, John. 1994. *Fragments from Antiquity: An Archaeology of Social Life 2900–1200 BC.* Oxford: Blackwell.

Bell, Catherine. 1992. *Ritual Theory, Ritual Practice.* New York: Oxford University Press.

The forgotten things 27

Bourdieu, Pierre. 1980. *La Sens Pratique.* Paris: Éditions de Minuit.

Bourdieu, Pierre. 1988. *La Distinction: Critique Sociale du Jugement.* Paris: Éditions de Minuit.

Bradley, Richard. 2005. *Ritual and Domestic Life in Prehistoric Europe.* London: Routledge.

Bray, Tamara. ed. 2003. *The Archaeology and Politics of Food and Feasting in Early States and Empires.* New York: Kluver Acad./Plenum.

Brück, Joana. 1999. "Ritual and Rationality: Some Problems of Interpretation in European Archaeology." *Journal of European Archaeology* 2: 313–44.

Burford, Alison. 1961. "Temple Building at Segesta." *Classical Quarterly* 11: 87–93.

Caplan, Pat. 1997 "Approaches to the Study of Food, Health and Identity." In *Food, Health and Identity*, edited by Pat Caplan, 1–31. London: Routledge.

Castellana, Giusseppe. 1990. "L'insediamento di Montagnoli nei pressi di Selinunte: un contributo per la conoscenza delle poblazions anelleniche lungo il corso finale del Belice." In *Gli Elimi e l'area elima. Atti del seminario di studi*, edited by Giuseppe Nenci, 325–33. Palermo: Archivo Storico Siciliano.

Castellana, Giusseppe. 1992. "Nuovi dati su scavi condotti nel versante orientale del Basso Belice en el bacino finale del Platani." In *Giornate Internazionali di Studi sull'area elima (Gibellina 19–22 Settembre 1991)*, edited by Giuseppe Nenci, 191–202. Pisa-Gibellina: Scuola Normale Superiore di Pisa.

Castellana, Giusseppe. 2000. *La Cultura del medio bronzo nell'agrigentino ed i rapporti con il mondo miceneo.* Palermo: Regione Siciliana – Beni Culturali.

Cooper, Jeanette. 2007. *Traditions in Profile: A Chronological Sequence of Western Sicilian Ceramics (7th–6th centuries* BCE*).* Unpublished PhD dissertation, State University of New York, Buffalo.

Counihan, Carole. 1999. *The Anthropology of Food and Body: Gender, Meaning and Power.* New York: Routledge.

Counihan, Carole and Penny Van Esterik. eds. 1997. *Food and Culture: A Reader.* London: Routledge.

Cuozzo, Mariassunta. 2003. *Reinventando la Tradizione. Immaginario Sociale, Ideologie e Rappresentazione nelle Necropoli Orientalizzanti di Pontecagnano.* Paestum-Salerno: Pandemos.

Delgado, Ana. 2008. "Alimentos, poder e identidad en las comunidades fenicias occidentales." *Cuadernos de prehistoria y arqueología de la Universidad de Granada* 18: 163–88.

Delgado, Ana. 2010. "De las cocinas coloniales y otras historias silenciadas: domesticidad, subalternidad e hibridación en las colonias fenicias occidentales." *Saguntum-extra* 9: 27–42.

Delgado, Ana and Meritxell Ferrer. 2007. "Alimentos para los muertos. Mujeres, rituales funerarios e identidades coloniales." *Treballs d'Arqueologia* 13: 29–63.

Delgado, Ana and Meritxell Ferrer. 2011a. "Life and Death in Ancient Colonies: Domesticity, Material Culture and Sexual Politics in the Western Phoenician World, 8th–6th Centuries BC." In *The Archaeology of Colonialism: Intimate Encounters and Sexual Effects*, edited by Barbara Voss and Eleanor Cassella, 195–213. Cambridge: Cambridge University Press.

Delgado, Ana and Meritxell Ferrer. 2011b. "Representing Communities in Heterogeneous Worlds: Staple Foods and Ritual Practices in the Phoenician Diaspora." In *Guess Who's Coming to Dinner: Feasting Rituals in the Prehistoric Societies of Europe and the Near East*, edited by Gonzalo Aranda, Margarita Sánchez Romero and Sandra Montón, 184–203. London: Oxbow Books.

28   *Meritxell Ferrer*

De Miro, Ernesto. 1988. "Polizzello, centro de la Sicania." *Quaderni dell'Istituto di Archeologia della Facoltà di lettere e filosofia della Università di Messina* 3: 25–42.

Dietler, Michael. 1990. "Driven by the Drink: The Role of Drinking in the Political Economy and the Case of Early Iron Age France." *Journal of Anthropological Archaeology* 9: 352–406.

Dietler, Michael. 2001. "Theorizing the Feast: Rituals of Consumption, Commensal Politics, and Power in African Contexts." In *Feasts: Anthropological and Ethnographic Perspectives on Food, Politics and Power*, edited by Michael Dietler and Brian Hayden, 65–114. Washington: Smithsonian Institution Press.

Dietler, Michael and Brian Hayden. eds. 2001. *Feasts: Anthropological and Ethnographic Perspectives on Food, Politics and Power*. Washington: Smithsonian Institution Press.

Domínguez Monedero, Adolfo. 2010. "Dos religiones en contacto en ambiente colonial: Griegos y no Griegos en la Sicilia antigua." *Polifemo* 10: 131–84.

Douglas, Mary. 1975. "Deciphering a Meal." In *Implicit Meanings: Selected Essays in Anthropology*, edited by Mary Douglas, 231–50. London: Routledge.

Ferrer, Meritxell. 2010. "La (re-)creación de una memoria: la materialización de un 'sentido de lugar' en la Sicilia occidental, ss. VIII–V a.C." *Bollettino di Archaeologia On-line, volume speciale*: 43–52.

Ferrer, Meritxell. 2012. *Acrópolis sicilianas: rituales, comunidades y poderes (ss. X–V a.C.)*. Unpublished PhD dissertation. Pompeu Fabra University-IUHJVV, Barcelona. Internet Edition: http://www.tdx.cat/handle/10803/83650

Ferrer, Meritxell. 2013. "Feasting the Community: Ritual and Power on the Sicilian Acropolei (10th – 6th Centuries BC)." *Journal of Mediterranean Archaeology* 26: 211–34.

Gleba, M. 2008. *Textile Production in Pre-Roman Italy.* Oxford: Oxbow Books.

Goody, Jack. 1984. *Cooking, Cuisine and Class: A Study in Comparative Sociology.* Cambridge: Cambridge University Press.

Guidi, Alessandro. 1996. "Processual and Post-Processual Trends in Italian Archaeology." In *Theoretical and Methodological Problems: Colloquium I: The Debate on Function and Meaning in Prehistoric Archaeology: Processual Versus Post Processual Archaeology in the 90s*, edited by Amilcare Bietti, Alberto Cazella, Ian Johnson and Albertus Voorrips, 29–36. Forlì: A.B.A.C.O.

Gumerman, George. 1997. "Food and Complex Societies." *Journal of Archaeological Method and Theory* 4: 105–39.

Guzzone, C. (2009). "I santuari". In *Sabucina, 50 anni di studi e ricerche archeologiche*, edited by R. Panvini. Palermo: Regione Siciliana–Beni Culturali.

Halstead, Paul and John Barrett. eds. 2004. *Food, Cuisine and Society in Prehistoric Greece*. Oxford: Oxbow.

Hamilakis, Yannis. 1998. "Eating the Dead: Mortuary Feasting and the Politics of Memory in the Aegean Bronze Age Societies." In *Cemetery and Society in the Aegean Bronze Age*, edited by Keith Branigan, 115–32. Sheffield: Sheffield University Press.

Hamilakis, Yannis. 2008. "Time, Performance, and the Production of a Mnemonic Record: From Feasting to an Archaeology of Eating and Drinking." In *DAIS: The Aegean Feast*, edited by Louise Hitchcock, Robert Laffineur and Janice Crowley, 3–20. Liège: Université de Liège.

Hayden, Brian and Suzanne Villeneuve. 2011. "A Century of Feasting Studies." *Annual Review of Anthropology* 40: 433–49.

Hnatiuk, T. (2003). "Preliminary faunal report on the Acropolis of Monte Polizzo." *Memoirs of the American Academy in Rome* 48: 76–9.

The forgotten things   29

Hodos, Tamar. 1999. "Intermarriage in the Western Greek Colonies." *Oxford Journal of Archaeology* 18: 61–78.

Hodos, Tamar. 2000. "Wine Wares in Protohistoric Eastern Sicily." In *Ancient Sicily: Archaeology and History from Aeneas to Augustus*, edited by Christopher Smith and John Serrati, 41–54. Edinburgh: Edinburgh University Press.

Hodos, Tamar. 2006. *Local Responses to Colonization in the Iron Age Mediterranean.* London: Routledge.

Hodos, T. 2009. "Colonial Engagements in the Global Mediterranean Iron Age." *Cambridge Archaeological Journal* 19: 221–41.

Holloway, R. R., Martha S. Joukowsky and Susan Lukesh. 1990. "La Muculufa, the Early Bronze Age Sanctuary: The Early Bronze Age Village." *Revue des Archeologues et Historiens d'Art de Louvain* 23: 11–68.

Humphrey, Caroline and James Laidlaw. 1994. *The Archetypal Actions of Ritual: A Theory of Ritual Illustrated by the Jain Rite of Worship.* Oxford: Clarendon.

Isler, Hans Peter. 1995. "Monte Iato." In *Federico e la Sicilia. Dalla Terra a la corona.vol. I*, edited by Carmela A. di Stefano, Antonio Cadei and Maria Andaloro, 121–50. Palermo: Lombardi.

Jennings, Justin, Katheleen Antrobus, Sam Atencio, Erin Glavich, Rebeca Johnson, German Loffler and Christine Liu. 2005. "Drinking Beer in a Blissful Mood: Alcohol Production, Operational Chains, and Feasting in the Ancient World." *Current Anthropology* 46: 275–303.

Leighton, Robert. 1993. *The Protohistoric Settlement on the Cittadella: Morgantina Studies IV*. Princeton: Princeton University Press.

Leighton, Robert. 1999. *Sicily before History: An Archaeological Survey from the Paleolithic to the Iron Age.* Ithaca: Cornell University Press.

McConnell, Brian. 1996. *Archaeologia in Pietralunga.* Catania: Regione Siciliana.

Morris, Ian, Emma Blake, Trinity Jackman, Brien Garnard and Sebastiano Tusa. 2003. "Stanford University Excavations on the Acropolis of Monte Polizzo, Sicily, III: Preliminary Report on the 2002 Season." *Memoirs of the American Academy in Rome* 48: 243–315.

Morris, Ian, Emma Blake, Trinity Jackman and Sebastiano Tusa. 2002. "Stanford University Excavations on the Acropolis of Monte Polizzo, Sicily, II: Preliminary Report on the 2001 Season." *Memoirs of the American Academy in Rome* 47: 153–98.

Morris, Ian and Sebastiano Tusa. 2004. "Scavi sull'acropoli di Monte Polizzo (TP), 2000–2003." *Sicilia Archeologica* 37: 277–97.

Mühlenbock, Christian. 2008. *Fragments from a Mountain Society: Tradition, Innovation and Interaction at Monte Polizzo, Sicily.* Göteborg: Gotac Series C.

Palermo, Dario, Davide Tanasi and Eleanora Pappalardo. 2009. "Polizzello. Le origini del Santuario". In *EIΣ AKPA. Insediamenti di altura in Sicilia dalla Preistoria al III sec. a.C. Atti del V Convegno di Studi (Caltanissetta, 1–11 maggio 2008)*, edited by Marina Congiu, Calogero Micchè and Simona Modeo, 53–85. Palermo: Salvatore Sciascia Editore.

Panvini, Rosalba, Carla Guzzone and Dario Palermo. eds. 2009. *Polizzello. Scavi dell 2004 nell'area del santuario arcaico dell'acropoli.* Palermo: Regione Siciliana.

Pauketat, Timothy, Lucretia Kelly, Gayle Fritz, Neal Lopinot, Scott Elias and Eve Hargrave. 2002. "The Residues of Feasting and Public Ritual at Early Cahokia." *American Antiquity* 67: 257–79.

Perego, Elisa. 2011. "Engendered Actions: Agency and Ritual in Pre-Roman Veneto." In *Ritual Dynamics in the Ancient Mediterranean: Agency, Emotion, Gender, Representation*, edited by Angelos Chaniotis, 17–41. Stuttgart: Franz Steiner Verlag.

30 *Meritxell Ferrer*

Péré-Noguès, Sandra. 2008. "Recherches autor des 'marqueurs funéraires' à travers l'exemple de quelques sépultures féminines de la nécropole du Fusco (Syracuse)." *Pallas* 76: 151–71.

Robb, John. 1997. "Female Beauty and Male Violence in Early Italian Society." In *Naked Truths: Women, Sexuality, and Gender in Classical Art and Archaeology*, edited by Ann Olga Koloski-Ostrow and Claire Lyons, 43–65. London: Routledge.

Russenberger, Christopher. 2010. "Monte Iato (PA): ultime testimonianze di una cultura indigena attorno al 300 a.C." *Bolletino di Archaeologia Online, Volume Speciale*: 12–22.

Scholliers, Peter. 2001. *Food, Drink and Identity: Cooking, Eating, and Drinking in Europe since the Middle Ages*. Oxford: Berg.

Shepherd, Gillian. 1999. "Fibulae and Females: Intermarriage in the Western Greek Colonies and the Evidence from the Cemeteries." In *Ancient Greeks East and West*, edited by Gocha Tsetskhladze, 267–300. Leiden: Brill.

Smith, Monica. 2006. "The Archaeology of Food Preference." *American Anthropologist* 108: 480–93.

Spatafora, Francesca. 1997. "La Montagnola di Marineo. Campagna di scavi 1996." *Kokalos* 43–4: 703–19.

Spatafora, Francesca. 2000. "Indegini, Punici e greci in età arcaica e tardo-arcaica sulla Montagnola di Marineo e nella Valle dell'Eleuterio." In *Terze Giornate Internazionali di Studi sull'Area Elima*, edited by Giuseppe Nenci, 895–918. Pisa: Scuola Normale di Pisa.

Spatafora, Francesca. 2003. *Monte Maranfusa, un insediamento nella media Valle del Belice: l'abitato indigeno*. Palermo: Regione Siciliana.

Spigo, Umberto. 1981. "Ricerche a Monte San Mauro, Francavilla di Sicilia, Acireale, Adrano, Lentini, Solarino." *Kokalos* 26–7: 771–95.

Stika, Hans Peter. 2002. "Preliminary Report on the First Analysis of Macrobotanical Remains from Monte Polizzo." *Memoirs of the American Academy in Rome* 47: 87–91.

Stika, Hans Peter, Andrew Heiss and Barbara Zach. 2008. "Plant Remains from the Early Iron Age in Western Sicily: Differences in Subsistence Strategies of Greek and Elymian Sites." V*egetation History and Archeobotany* 17: 139–48.

Swenson, Edward. 2006. "Competitive Feasting, Religious Pluralism, and Decentralized Power in the Late Moche Period." In *Andean Archaeology III: North and South*, edited by William H. Isbell and Helaine Silverman, 112–41. New York: Springer/Plenum Press.

Tamburello, Ida. 1969. "Una classe di vasi arcaici da Palermo." *Archeologia Classica* 21: 270–6.

Tanasi, Davide. 2009. "L'acropoli di Polizzello tra le fine del X e gli inizi dell'VIII secolo a.C." In *ΕΙΣ ΑΚΡΑ. Insediamenti di altura in Sicilia dalla Preistoria al III sec. a.C. Atti del V Convegno di Studi (Caltanissetta, 10–11 maggio 2008)*, edited by Marina Congiu, Calogero Micchè and Simona Modeo, 49–59. Palermo: Salvatore Sciascia Editore.

Twiss, Katheryn. 2008. "Transformations in an Early Agricultural Society: Feasting in the Southern Levantine Pre-Pottery Neolithic." *Journal of Anthropological Archaeology* 27: 418–42.

Valentino, Matteo. 2003. "La ceramica da fuoco e da cucina." In *Monte Maranfusa. Un insediamenti nella media Valle del Belice*, edited by Francesca Spatafora, 255–68. Palermo: Regione Siciliana.

Vassallo, Stefano. 1999. *Colle Madore: un casi di ellenizzazione in terra sicana*. Palermo: Regione Siciliana.

The forgotten things 31

Weismantel, Mary. 1989. *Food, Gender and Poverty in the Ecuadorian Andes.* Philadelphia: University of Pennsylvania Press.

Whitehouse, Ruth. 2001. "Exploring Gender in Prehistoric Italy." *Papers of the British School at Rome* 69: 49–96.

Whitehouse, Ruth. 2013. "Gender in Central Mediterranean Prehistory." In *A Companion to Gender Prehistory*, edited by Diane Bolger, 480–501. Chichester: Willey-Blackwell.

2 Materiality and ritual competence

Insights from women's prayer typology in Homer

Andromache Karanika

Introduction

Rituals are discursive practices that involve formalization of language, a sense of repetition, and channeling of specific actions, during which the ordinary is rendered extraordinary, and, as such, they embody, as Stanley J. Tambiah famously put it, the "logic of persuasion" (Tambiah 1979, 148). They are part of community and cultural discourse and involve agency. The practitioners of rituals are the ones who act in often codified and prescribed ways. But how does one know what to do, how to act, what to say? In other words, how is ritual competence acquired, manifested and, perhaps, how is its efficacy or success measured? Recent ritual competence theory points to the fact that ritual functions like language. Just like language it produces patterns, and just like linguistic competence it is a form of tacit if not intuitive knowledge one acquires through a variety of means and in a broad spectrum of time and space. It extends beyond one's lifetime, involves the lifetime of smaller or greater communities, and becomes cultural capital. Once acquired, just like linguistic users, ritual users are not always conscious or totally in control of the deep structures. And just like language, ritual can create meaning, forge communities, and navigate life changes. There are several advantages in using linguistic theory and modes to talk about ritual competence, as there are similarities between the two: some patterns of action or thought are ingrained or learned in innocent ways, but on its own ritual can become a tool of power, social control, means of survival, a concrete way to negotiate personal and cultural relations. Language and ritual are forms of symbolic cultural systems, meaning they are relatively restricted in their use and transmission. Explicit instruction is usually absent, and competence comes the way one learns to speak; "ritual competence is like grammar, most of us learn to speak before we can articulate rules of grammar" (Grimes 2013, 308). Ritual is increasingly analyzed as a linguistic system of communication;, like language, it is a generative and primary system of communication; and the rules of its codification are only secondary knowledge, if it reaches the conscious level at all.

One of the earliest and most ubiquitous forms of ritual discourse is prayer, a platform most fertile to apply to a linguistic way of thinking to understand the ramifications of competence in the way it is practiced, as manifested in a full

Materiality and ritual competence   33

narrative frame. Early Greek epic poetry presents *effective* and *non-effective* prayers, and through an analysis of the narrative details we can explore understandings of prayer as part of a linguistic system, of things one must do, say, or avoid from the viewpoint of its practitioners, their audiences, or cultural worlds. Just like deciphering a language from fragments, prayer fragments or representations in text can give valuable information about hidden rules and ideologies regarding practice. Prayers use multiform language that extends beyond just words and involves action, gestures, and positioning of the body in a specific place, time, and fashion. Often involving a verbal aspect that addresses the divine (broadly conceived), it extends beyond the verbal element through accompanying postures of body, material offerings in a temple, or simply physical manifestations such as libations or offerings of scent that create a multisensual experience. Moreover, a prayer is the ritual to persuade *par excellence*, usually celebrating a divinity and, often, asking for something. A prayer can never be a *solo* performance: prayers are cultural products, are rendered in usually crystallized language, involve a level of stylization in their practice, and invoke explicitly or implicitly a culturally postulated superhuman agency, as E. Thomas Lawson and Robert N. McCauley have put it (Lawson and McCauley 1990).

The early Greek epic examples of prayer are a great showcase study of a type of language that is open to all; namely, it is not restricted to a "priestly" cast. Anyone from the leader of the army to the herdsman, kings, queens, and servants, elite and non-elite, men and women, can utter prayers in public or private settings. In the early Greek epic world, prayer is a clearly marked type of performance in Homeric speech. Homeric prayer has indeed received significant scholarly attention; while a number of studies have focused on the typology of prayer in early Greek literature and its stylization as a speech act, in the greater nexus of narrative direction and reciprocity patterns, a perspective that analyzes synchronic views on ritual competence has been largely unexplored (Kitts 2005; Lateiner 1997; Letoublon 2011; Morrison 1991; Muellner 1976). The Homeric poems present eloquent scenarios for ritual acts that constitute successful as well as failed attempts to accomplish the intended outcome.

In the following, I consider, in particular, female prayers and their stylization in Homeric speech, seeking to analyze further the underlying ideology that is reflected and received in later receptions of these scenes of women's prayers. Let me clarify: by "underlying" ideology, I mean what kind of cultural frame is inherited and set upon a formal act of prayer, which then defines the outcome of this prayer, and what kind of codification is passed inherently and perhaps not consciously. I also want to see what distinctive lessons we learn about female prayers as language, how they are transmitted and used, and what specifically gendered cognitive process is passed with them. Moreover, the few female prayers in Homeric poetry provide a fertile analytical framework of ritual as a linguistic system that its practitioners use. As a general premise, I posit that stylized speeches are indeed modeled on actual speech genres, in historic use. The fact that Homeric prayers, just like any speech act, are placed as part of a larger narrative has significant advantages as we try to discern the cultural underpinnings in the background of those

34 *Andromache Karanika*

stylized prayers and explore how ancient minds thought of ritual competence by analyzing the type scenes that overtly mark prayers as effective or not. Reading prayer as a ritual act and, as such, the manifestation of a linguistic transaction, the Homeric text gives us the opportunity to analyze in more depth scenes that underline not just prayer as a verbal performance, but, as mentioned already, a performance that extends beyond the verbal and includes physical activity, specific gestures, and types of offerings that create a vibrant communication pattern, as reflected in the text.

Defining prayer as an address from a mortal to a god, where the words of the request are given in direct speech (and not looking at indirect speech), we find the kernel of prayer in usually an imperative verb, a "request" for intercession: e.g. "Break Diomedes' spear," or "Let not the sun go down until I have hurled headlong the fortress of Priam blazing." There are 30 such prayers in Homer, 20 in the *Iliad* and 10 in the *Odyssey* (Morrison 1991, 147). Of those, mortal women utter only three, one in the *Iliad* and two in the *Odyssey,* all of which are rich examples for a typology of female prayer in Homer. I begin with the first instances from the *Odyssey* (one prayer by Penelope and another by disguised Athena as a variant), then move to a collective female prayer in the *Iliad*, and conclude with the last instance of a more private form of prayer that resembles a curse from the *Odyssey*.

The materiality of prayer: A view of ritual competence in the *Odyssey*

In recent ritual competence theory, Harvey Whitehouse talks about modes of religiosity and argues that we have two types that reflect different modes of transmission of ritual competence: *doctrinal* (which relies on doctrines, repetition, checking of orthodoxy of rituals, etc., scripted memory) and the *imagistic*, which relies on single and traumatic events stored in episodic memory that function as "flashbulb" memory, with the two modes often occurring together (Whitehouse 2004). Whitehouse, from the perspective of anthropology and cognitive sciences, seeks to explain how rituals are remembered and passed on. Explicit instruction is juxtaposed to implicit memory making. In other words, on the one hand, an explicit mode makes individuals aware of what and how to do things (in ritual as well as in other spheres), thereby granting them an awareness of their competence. Implicit memory, on the other hand, allows individuals to perform a ritual without conscious awareness of its rules (or even their capacity and attention to following them). While the first tends to characterize larger communities where intense and repetitive teaching channels ritual behavior, the latter tends to be associated with a smaller scale of practice. This framework proves particularly fertile when applied to the Homeric instances, where a combination of the *doctrinal* and *imagistic* is refracted in the text.

In Book 4, after Penelope has realized that her son is away from home, she addresses her maids in a lament-like discourse (4.718–41). As any lament is about negotiating transitions in life, in this lament-like speech, Penelope remembers

Materiality and ritual competence 35

Odysseus and then seeks a plan of action. She creates a narrative circle that unites the absent husband who left in the distant past with the absent son whose absence she has just realized and whose journey she was unable to undo. While Penelope asks for her trusted gardener, Dolios, someone given to her by her own father, to summon her father-in-law to take the role of the lamenter in front of the suitors in suggestively associative language (as the servant has a name associated with the idea of deceit, reflecting Penelope's own trick), it is the loyal nurse Eurykleia who will bring the ritual solution. Eurykleia states: "I will not hide my counsel (*mythos*) from you" (4.744). In an authoritative way, as the word *mythos* suggests, Eurykleia reveals in her speech to Penelope (4.43–757) that she indeed knew that Telemachus was gone and that she had taken an oath not to reveal anything before the twelfth day (Martin 1989; Pournara Karydas 1998). She then moves on to give specific ritual instructions to her mistress (4.742–57): first she needs to bathe, then take clean clothing, and then pray to Athena for her son's safety (4.750–7). The doctrinal aspect of ritual competence is portrayed in Eurykleia's speech, an older woman addressing a younger woman, an expert servant whose epistemic spectrum exceeds that of Penelope, the queen of the house; not only does she know what has been going on in the palace with regard to Telemachus and his departure, she also presents a plan to Penelope instructing her what to do. Interestingly, in this passage the reference to the oath with its commitment that Eurykleia made toward Telemachus is brought into conjunction with the authoritative language of ritual instruction and etiquette. This is the moment when Penelope is soothed in her lament and moves on to pray to Athena, as told. Yet the lines show that the doctrinal part that comes as a reminder from Eurykleia is augmented with more activity: Penelope does everything that her loyal old maid instructed her but also places sacrificial grains in a basket, as a ritual offering before she utters her prayer.

> Thus spoke Eurykleia and lulled Penelope's laments and made her tears stop. Penelope then bathed and, taking clean clothes, went to her chamber upstairs with her maids, filled a basket with sacrificial grains, and prayed to Athena.
> (Hom. *Od.* 4.758–61)[1]

Penelope follows traditional practice in her activity right before the prayer to Athena. Like language, she just knows what and how she must do things. Just as formulaic diction is adapted as repeated, so formulaic action is augmented or adapted as necessary. Cognitively, Eurykleia gave simply a reminding cue, a *hypomnesis,* of what Penelope needed to do, and Penelope follows and does more. The idea of *hypomnesis*, the reminding cue, is central to anything that has to do with prayer. No prayer stands on its own. Instead, it is constructed on an already existing edifice of relations with the divinity. Memory needs to be mobilized as a central factor in creating a favorable ambiance, and as such it constructs the space of former prayers or ritual acts. In this case, Penelope reminds Athena of Odysseus' sacrifices before formulating her request in the imperative, "save my dear son" (4.765).

36 *Andromache Karanika*

> Hear me, Atrytone, child of aegis-bearing Zeus! If ever-resourceful Odysseus burned the fat thighs of a heifer or sheep to honor you in his palace, remember these now, save my dear son for me, and ward off from him the evil and arrogant suitors. Thus she spoke and followed with ululation, and the goddess heard her prayer. But in the shadowy hall the suitors broke into uproar; one of the arrogant young men spoke like this, "It seems as if our much-courted queen is preparing a wedding and that she doesn't have a clue that her son's death has been arranged."
>
> (Hom. *Od.* 4.762–71)

It is a twofold request, one that asks for saving and another that has a clearly apotropaic movement, to guard Telemachus from the suitors (4.766). The prayer is topped off with the appropriate ululation, a ritual cry that comes often in moments of sacrifice, representing the release of extreme emotional tension in specific moments. As Laura McClure remarked, "like lamentation, this speech genre may be considered a socially constructive utterance executed on behalf of the larger community" (McClure 1999, 52). The individual *ololyge* (ululation) of the queen is matched by the goddess's hearing of her prayer (4.767) and the collective uproar that follows by the suitors, who completely misread it. It was not only the goddess that heard the female ululation, but also the suitors, with whom there is no other direct communication. The communicative pattern of the sense of hearing is multiform. The goddess *hears* the prayer (4.767), whereas the suitors' reaction (with no explicit reference to the sense of hearing on their part) is a wrong one. Ululation can often be found in nuptial or victory contexts. One of the suitors, on hearing the ululation, as we can infer from the text, expresses the thought that indeed the queen is preparing a marriage while they plot death for her son, until Antinous reproaches them and asks for silence (4.776).

The narrative describes a complete and effective prayer, one instructed by an older woman to a younger married woman, carried out fully by the younger woman, and positively received by a goddess. The narrative concludes with Penelope's ritual cry and also suggests the conceited and twisted reception of this prayer by the collective body of suitors. Multiple perspectives are given in this scene that throw more light on how the language of prayer works: Penelope is reminded about how she is to act and does so in a more complete way out of her own accord, showing full mastery of her ritual duty, whereas the suitors prove themselves to have the wrong perspective.

Uproar from the suitors followed by a request for silence also shows the dynamics of the soundscape of the passage. The text oscillates from dialogue to prayer to ritual ululation for the practitioner of prayer to uproar and then request for silence from the suitors as the side audience of a ritual cry, in a schema where there is no communication between the two worlds, the female of Penelope and the male of the suitors. Penelope remains upstairs, worried about her son, in a way that exemplifies the mother's anxiety. She abstains from food and drink: "She was lying there without food, not having tasted any food or drink" (4.787). This is the same line used of the goddess Demeter (*Hom. Hymn Dem.* 200), when she was desperate

Materiality and ritual competence   37

in her quest for her daughter. It shows a crystallized way of expressing female anxiety with a maternal aspect. Penelope knew how to act for her prayer, what to offer the goddess, what to say, and how she should act following Eurykleia's earlier instruction. She follows the offering of the basket with sacrificial grains with an utterance that aims to connect her addressee with her own past. Her request to the goddess to save her son is her response to her reminder to the goddess of Odysseus' earlier offerings.

The doctrinal aspect transmitted by Eurykleia to Penelope is augmented by the *imagistic* aspect of the offering of sacrificial grains in a basket, as the material locus that prepares the utterance of prayer in language that connects the past with the present and future. In fact, if, as said before, rituals and prayers are about the logic of persuasion, the most persuasive power is based on earlier action. It is not a simple *do ut des* in the present or the future, but one intertwined in the relation between practitioner and addressee in the projection of time of the past before asking something about the present and future. The imperatives "save" and "ward off" come as expected outcomes of argumentation and not as mere requests and are part of an elaborate weaving of ritual action showing female competence at different levels, from the old nurse Eurykleia to queen Penelope. Penelope's prayer builds from another, older woman's admonition to her and is delivered in front of other women. The first is an imperative for positive action (save), whereas the second is an apotropaic moment (ward off). Penelope is part of a network of women of different ages and statuses; like them, she follows an utterance with an activity, placing barley grains in a basket. Such activities take place automatically, without much thought. Nor are we told anything about the meaning of this offering.

Competence in ritual can become an act of social economy for survival: one knows that one needs to feed a child to help her or him grow and, often, doing it does not always mean constantly thinking about it, its significance, or its meaning. What matters is to do it and do it well, and it is something that happens almost automatically; it is part of an essential grammar of survival. Penelope's offering of barley grains, as accompaniment to a mother's prayer to express a request for her son's safety, resembles the mother's offering of food, out of which multiple meanings could be constructed as a ritual act is modeled on a daily maternal task. There is a type of action by memory that is being enacted here, and one that expresses itself with material terms. These terms were not dictated, as the nurse Eurykleia did not tell Penelope exactly what to do. She only gave the grieving queen the initial "trigger" of what she needed to do, and Penelope followed, by offering first the basket with sacrificial grains and then uttering her prayer. The grain becomes the material locus of a ritual offering, without which the prayer would not have been properly uttered. The Homeric text here is an open show-and-tell case of cognitive processes behind ritual behavior.

In the beginning of the *Odyssey* (3.36–69), Athena, disguised as Mentor in Pylos, also performs a prayer to Poseidon, which she brings to completion. Peisistratos, son of Nestor, is the one who speaks to Mentor (disguised Athena), after pouring wine in a golden cup, and asks him to pray to Poseidon. The emphasis is

38   *Andromache Karanika*

less on gender here and more on age. After he offers instruction on how to perform the appropriate prayer, Peisistratos offers a golden cup to Mentor/Athena rather than to Telemachus, whom, he notes, is young like himself and should thus be served second (3.42–50). The instruction is followed by a simple gesture: the cup of wine is placed into the hand of the guest/disguised Athena, who rejoices that she is the first to receive the golden cup, which after her prayer (3.55–61) will be passed to Telemachus, who will perform his own prayer. In just a few lines (ll. 40–66), there are six references to the cup (ll. 41, 46, 51, 53, 63) as it goes around and becomes the material locus of transmission for the prayer. The prayer is not just an utterance; it begins and continues only due to the simple gesture of passing the cup from one hand to the other. The golden cup is the necessary link that will trigger and help the moment continue. It is the central vessel for a libation and the offering of liquid, without which no utterance could either begin or be complete. Peisistratos first commands the disguised Athena to utter the prayer while giving specific instructions about the libations and the passing of the cup from one person to the other as the locus of a transaction between mortal and divine. In other words, the Homeric text not only gives us the text of Athena's prayer but the circumscribed parameters of how this utterance must be enacted. The presence of the object is a catalyst in how the scene unfolds, the focus and central locus of the performance, or what one could call the material aspect, which will remain even after the speech act will be completed. The cup is not an offering, as is the case with the dedication of the woven fabric by the Trojan women, but is part of a parallel ritual language of physicality that exemplifies the passing of the cup from one to another as a gestural prelude, accompaniment, and conclusion of the speech act of prayer. This material aspect is crucial in all the scenes. The barley basket, seen in the previous scene, the golden cup here, or a woven fabric, as we shall see, are not just inanimate objects but material bearers of a power to shape the way the scenes are circumscribed.

When a prayer goes wrong: Materiality and ritual incompetence in the *Iliad*

While the text in both these instances is clear in telling us what the outcome of the prayer is, as Athena listened to Penelope's prayer in the first example and, in the second, Athena completes her own prayer, things are quite different in the next scene under consideration: this has a moment of ritual incompetence that I will try to highlight. In *Iliad* Book 6, when, at the request of Hector, the Trojan women dedicate the most beautiful *peplos* of the palace to Athena (combining sacrifice, ululation, and dedication), their prayer is famously rejected by the goddess. This scene has been interpreted mostly from the point of view of the narrative, the women's prayer being a pretext that brought Hector inside Troy (Morrison 1991). It is indeed expected by audiences who know the outcome of the war that Athena, who supports the Achaian side, will reject the prayer. Moreover, it has been too conveniently read as a foreshadowing of events. Still, this is the only moment of a prayer's utter failure (cf. Agamemnon's prayer in Book 2 of the *Iliad* that is not

Materiality and ritual competence 39

immediately completed, which is quite different). The women's prayer, enacted by a priestess, the only female officiant in Homer, is sealed in the narrative as an utter failure, since the goddess rejected the offering. Let us look at the details of the narrative first in order to see where the ritual error is as we explore the ritual logic that audiences were supposed to grasp.

Hector comes into Troy and meets his mother, who asks him to pray and pour a libation to Zeus (6.254–62). Hector does not want to do that with hands that are still filthy with blood and dirt and asks her to gather the older women, go to the shrine of Athena, and offer the best robe, the one dearest to her. He asks her to dedicate it to Athena as well as pledging that they will make a sacrifice of heifers, if the goddess will hold back Diomedes the son of Tydeus from Troy (6.270–85). The queen-mother goes to the chamber where all the embroidery lies and fetches the most beautiful *peplos*, one that was the handiwork of Sidonian women. Paris himself had brought this back from Sidon, on the same trip that carried back Helen. This was the finest piece of embroidery in the palace, and the largest, and was "shining like a star" (6.288–95).

Theano, who has been made a priestess of Athena by the Trojans, dedicates the robe to the goddess, and the whole ritual is described. The women perform the prescribed ululation while lifting their hands in an ensemble, and the priestess utters the prayer in which she asks to break the spear of Diomedes and have him fall before the Scaean gates, so that they will sacrifice to the goddess the heifers (6.305–10). From a certain perspective, as Morrison has argued, the Trojan priestess Theano inappropriately supplicates Athena for the defeat of Achaian Diomedes, going above and beyond Hector's initial request and making a contingent offer. It is possible that we have an innovation in a type scene of prayer. While one would expect the repetition of Hector's request as part of Theano's prayer, Athena's priestess transfers in her prayer not just what Hector asked but, even more, what he wished.[2] In his earlier request addressed to his mother, Hector uttered the wish for Diomedes (6. 281–2) that "the earth would open wide open for him at once." While Hector reveals his emotional world by expressing a curse practically, Theano goes further by including this as part of her prayer and making it the basis of her contingent offer (let Diomedes fall, so that we sacrifice). In many other instances we have such "contingent" offers of sacrifice as part of a negotiation/ persuasive tactic. But there is more going on here, since the initial prayer is accompanied by the offering of a robe.

While we have no description of the robe, the narrative presents an important detail charged with meaning. The *peplos* was made not by the Trojan women but by captive Sidonian women and was brought to Troy by Paris when he brought Helen. Yet despite the textile's splendor (6.295), the sacrificial offering, and the appropriate accompanying ululation, Athena rejects the prayer. The Trojan women commit a grave ritual error, a *faux pas*, something that the audience of the epic performance would comprehend. The work they dedicate to the goddess is not their own but that of others. In other words, they offer a hugely problematic trigger point and material object, flawed from its genesis and making (Karanika 2014; Scheid and Svenbro 1996). A more positivist and superficial reading of this text might

40 *Andromache Karanika*

highlight that this is a moment of danger because the Trojan women cannot start weaving an elaborate *peplos* and must make do with the best available garment. In such a reading, the value and beauty of the *peplos* they choose, not its problematic status, would be emphasized. But there is more to this scene: it underlines deeper thinking about the underlying ritual competence that the performers of the ritual fail to show. Homer presents the Trojan women using, in this moment of acute danger, the wrong material trigger. We have a full show of ritual language that ancient audiences of oral epic could understand.

Maker and product are not easy to separate in Homer (Scheid and Svenbro 1996, 17–18 with *Odyssey* 4.238–98). Thus, when the Trojan women go inside the chamber to fetch a *peplos* and can neither bring one of their own making nor make one for the occasion, their offering of the work of others, and what is more, of women slaves, is a *faux pas*. The offering is the material anchor of the entire scene, and as such it is the trigger of the ritual, which will mobilize the prayer to the goddess. The Homeric text pays special attention to the description of the object's affect (shining like a star) and its origin. Objects have their own memory, and it is through this memory that they become ritual agents. Objects have also their own life, which is interwoven with that of their makers. The fate of the women who wove the fabric is transferred to the old women of Troy who offer it.

Ritual memory is built upon paradigmatic action in narratives about divinity. Athena, patron goddess of women's work and a renowned weaver herself, would never accept such a gift. The idea that ritual objects are commissioned for specific events is found in various cultures around the world. Ritual offerings are not commodities but individualized markers of a community's or a person's work; they become a material record of that event. Beyond the objective value and the intended aim of an offering to a goddess, dedicatory items have an exchange value that any gift has as part of a very complex social nexus, from which the divine sphere is not excluded. Dedicating a robe for the adornment of a god's statue is not only a ritual but also a political reference; the making of the robe is an important ritual act that bears political meanings, which is why ritual details, such as the families the weavers should be from, are precisely circumscribed. Thus, any implicit narrative about the fabric's past is emblematic of its efficacy in ritual use. The Athenians of Classical times seem to have been especially alert to an underlying ideology that connected the making of an offering with its importance. The Panathenaia cult required that aristocratic young Athenian women be the exclusive makers of one of the most venerated ritual offerings to the city's goddess. The Iliadic narrative suggests a deep connection between the object's present use and its makers' past, which leaves a permanent stamp on it.

The festival of the Panathenaia is a manifestation of the importance of weaving in the Athenian civic honor system. Maidens who worked with wool and took part in the city's procession were honored at their father's request by a public decree (*IG* II² 1034). Later ritual emphasized not simply that the best woven garment had to adorn the goddess' statue but, more importantly, that the best woven garment is one that came from the hands of Athenian women who followed ritually prescribed parameters. The making of the *peplos* and the investiture of Athena's statue

Materiality and ritual competence 41

comprised a central theme and act of the festival. With its many threads joining in a unified, perfect fabric, weaving represents an analogy for Athenian history and the political existence of Athens. Weaving was a metaphor and an activity whose central focus was joining many threads into a sturdy garment; in this respect, weaving recalled Athens' foundational hero Theseus, who united the various hamlets of Attica. Thus it could be said that women's work was central to the ritual activity and civic life of Athens in Classical times. Athena Polias could only be invested with a robe that Athenian women from elite families made with their own hands. Joseph Scheid and Jesper Svenbro note that in the festivities surrounding this event, the offering of weaving to the goddess's statue was accompanied by sacrificial offerings of animals, furnished obligatorily by the city, its colonies, and its allies. This aligning of the ritual weaving with sacrificial offerings represented a conscious attempt to celebrate and perpetuate the ideology of social and political unity. The mythic past surrounding the myths of Theseus as the first king and the historical present as represented in colonies and allies' cities were united in crafting the ideology of victory.

The city's artistic production and program commemorated the work of the *arrhephoroi*. Statues of *arrhephoroi* were erected in commemoration on the acropolis, and there is evidence that at least one *arrhephoros* bore the same name as the Trojan priestess in *Iliad* 6, Theano (*IG* II² 3634) – although this could be a mere coincidence.

The Great Panathenaia, during which the *peplos* was carried to the acropolis connected the act of offering with the crucial act of making of the offering. In this festival, a mythic and epic ideology centered on Athena was connected with the ritual and civic practices of fifth-century Athens, where weaving was a metaphor not only for craft and speech making but also for political unity, especially in Classical times. When, in Aristophanes' play of the same name, Lysistrata speaks of cleansing the city after polluting war, for example, she uses the image of wool processing – washing the fleece, removing the sheep dung, carding, and all the necessary preparation for making cloth (Ar. *Lys.* 565–86). Combing the fleece becomes a process analogous to the dissolution of the war (and to removing politically "impure" elements) in her proposals. The processing of wool, the preparation of cloth, and the weaving of a fine new cloak is a metaphor for what she proposes to achieve, namely civic and imperial unity after two decades of war between Athens and Sparta.

The city offered its patron goddess a cloth woven by the hands of its elite, producing the cloth that depicted Athena's victory in the Gigantomachy, and marking the offering as a symbol of victory and supremacy; thus the *peplos* was not simply an inanimate object but a tangible symbol of the goddess's supremacy and, by extension, her city's. Fabric preparation and political processes were interwoven metaphorically in ancient Greek political thought. Tangible and material terms expressed political decision-making and action. The city's fabric, its unity and welfare, was not an abstract notion. The inclusion of female work as the materialized metaphor added to the concrete formulation of ideas on political unity but with direct counterparts in the city's ritual activities, as the display of female

42   *Andromache Karanika*

weaving was prominent in the public arena in one of the most important civic and ritual settings.

Contemporary ritual theorists argue that people are more likely to remember stories that violate the norms (Barrett and Trigg 2014), which is exactly what we have in Book 6 of the *Iliad*, a story about ritual errors. From a cognitive perspective, such stories are worth remembering but not too taxing to keep in memory. The only openly failed prayer in Homer, which also happens to be a collective and female prayer, is from the cognitive perspective, an "imagistic" type of ritual transmission, one that includes a trauma in episodic memory, and a trauma needs a material aspect, which is no other than the intricate handiwork of the wrong hands. It is significant that in this episode the only doctrinal part came from a male hero, Hector, who had asked his mother to pray and given instructions about how this prayer should be accompanied by the offering of the best and dearest robe in the palace, with burnt offerings (a detail that points to the sense of scent), and animal sacrifice (6.269–82). But the Trojan women show incompetence and lack of awareness of the deeper structures of their activities around the material offering of the robe.

Conclusion

Ritual competence is highlighted in the Homeric poems by concrete references to material offerings or accompanying acts. A female prayer scene that underscores some of the earlier points made in this chapter comes from *Odyssey* 20. After Odysseus, still dressed as a beggar hiding his true identity, returns to his home, a "feeble" woman prays to Zeus asking for a sign that will resolve the situation of the suitors' presence at Odysseus's palace. The desired sign comes from a woman who has been assigned the task of grinding. In this early account, the task of grinding is performed by a group of women. What is noteworthy, however, is the ritual moment: this woman performs alone at night, when the others are asleep.

> Then a word of omen came from within the house, from a woman who was grinding at the mill nearby, where the mills of the shepherd of the people were. At these mills 12 women were grinding barley and wheat, the marrow of men. Now the others were sleeping, after they were done with grinding, but this woman alone had not yet ceased, for she was the most feeble of all. She stopped her mill and she spoke a word, a sign for the king: "Father Zeus, you who are lord over gods and men, that was a truly loud thunder coming from the starry sky, yet there is nowhere any cloud. You are revealing this as a sign to someone. Make now, for me the poor woman that I am, make what I say come true: let this be the last day the suitors have their desirable feast at Odysseus' palace. They who have weakened my limbs with painful labor, as I made barley meal, may this be the last time they dine." Thus she spoke, and divine Odysseus rejoiced at the words of omen that he heard!
>
> (Hom. *Od.* 20.105–20)

Materiality and ritual competence   43

This episode occurs at a moment of crisis and differs substantially from the previous female prayers. While the previous female prayers are prayers from a defensive position, the grinding older woman is aggressive, asking for the suitors' deaths in ways that make this prayer seem like a curse. Moreover, while she remains as part of the group, none of the other women participate in the prayer act, nor does any doctrinal aspect come to the surface. Age is again a factor: like Eurykleia earlier, the older woman is associated with the knowledge of how to perform ritual and make a ritual request. Prayer seeks the resolution of the crisis by foreshadowing an event favorable to the protagonist. Moreover, while there is apparently some gender segregation in this atmosphere of secrecy, the *Odyssey* suggests that female ritual activity was situated in dynamic interaction with male action. Grinding not only validates the female speech act but is seen as an important element in the utterance of the woman's prayer, portrayed through Odysseus' perspective as a *kledon* (Lateiner 2005). Odysseus overheard it and took the women's prayer/curse as an omen for what would follow. The act of crushing the barley acquires a symbolic extension that empowers the utterance and, through it, changes the course of action, and as such, it is presented as a magical act (especially given the space and time of the prayer). There is no offering here, but the activity evolves around the materiality of an element that changes its substance through grinding. The prayer translates in words what the hands were doing; as the barley is ground and reduced to a different entity, so are the suitors' lives expected to be crushed. Action and utterance coincide, the one triggering the other, in a circle that is intended to result in action by the god. The mill acquires an extended power to act tangibly upon reality. Homer gives us a glimpse of the cognitive aspect behind word and action: the mill becomes the material trigger for the kind of prayer, as well as an analogous image for what and how to pray in this instance about the enemy.

Ritual offerings or tools of work at the moment of utterance are not innate objects, but they become agents. They become a material record of that event but as such also circumscribe the parameters necessary to ensure efficacy in the practitioner's mind. Cognitively, they are the necessary triggers to ensure that ritual action will move on completely and competently. As I have argued, ritual competence has a material focus, often an object, and is also framed by material gestures and actions that go far beyond the specifics of the ritual at hand. Instead, any ritual action is part of long-established practices about how one should do things and how one should not. Poetic narrative preserves moments of physicality by lingering on an image of an artifact, a libation cup, a woven garment, a basket, as a kind of an "archaeological" vestige for the ritual language beyond the verbal aspect. Literary representations, and especially those in oral literature, could have a lasting effect in the way they mark competence or the images they use to delineate incompetence.

The female Homeric prayer is staged within a narrative that echoes the doctrinal aspect, one absorbed by an older woman in all instances, but performed not simply as utterance but as part of an ensemble of activities. In all instances, the prayer is anchored around the physicality of a material focal point, part of an accompanying gestural language that includes an offering or activities around the utterance, such

44 *Andromache Karanika*

as the offering of a robe, placing of sacrificial grains in a basket, passing of a cup in the scene of the disguised goddess, or grinding. Ritual competence is less about what to say during a prayer and more about what to do and how to act. The Homeric text preserves the reference to objects and the choreography of body language around prayers, highlighting the imagistic aspect that extends the merely verbal. Competence in performing a prayer is not simply measured by what one says but even more by the totality of ritual activity around prayers. The physical object at the center of each scene serves as the condensed image of knowledge that passes into collective memory. Deeper ritual competence is what ultimately reaffirms a prayer as effective or nullifies it as ineffective. In a nexus of activities that extends the parameters of the specific place and time of a prayer, it draws from a common core of conscious or unconscious knowledge about how to perform ritual prayer. The ultimate test lies not just around words but extends to a fuller participation of the senses, which includes physical deeds and material objects.

Notes

1 Prose translations of the Odyssey and Iliad passages are mine.
2 Morrison (1991, 152–6) argues that Theano's failure at prayer constitutes Homer's ad hoc innovation to a traditional pattern and scene.

Works consulted

Adkins, A.W.H. 1969. "Euchomai, Eychole and *Euchos* in Homer." *Classical Quarterly* 19: 20–33.

Barrett, Justin L. and Roger Trigg. 2014. *The Roots of Religion: Exploring the Cognitive Science of Religion*. Surrey: Ashgate.

Bassi, Karen. 2005. "Things of the Past: Objects and Time in Greek Narrative." *Arethusa* 38: 1–32.

Bell, Catherine. 1997. *Ritual: Perspectives and Dimensions*. New York: Oxford University Press.

Cohen, Beth, ed. 1995. *The Distaff Side: Representing the Female in Homer's "Odyssey."* Oxford: Oxford University Press.

Depew, Mary. 1997. "Reading Greek Prayers." *Classical Antiquity* 16.2: 229–58.

Grimes, Ronald L. 2013. *The Craft of Ritual Studies*. Oxford: Oxford University Press.

Hüsken, Ute, ed. 2007. *When Rituals Go Wrong: Mistakes, Failure and the Dynamics of Ritual*. Leiden: Brill.

Karanika, Andromache. 2001. "Memories of the Poetic Discourse in Athena's Cult Practices." In *Athena in the Classical World*, edited by Susan Deacy and Alexandra Villing, 277–91. Leiden: Brill.

———. 2014. *Voices at Work: Women, Performance and Gender in Ancient Greece*. Baltimore: Johns Hopkins University Press.

Kitts, Margo. 2005. *Sanctified Violence in Homeric Society: Oath-Making Rituals in the Iliad*. Cambridge: Cambridge University Press.

Lateiner, Donald. 1995. "Ominous Accidental Utterances in Classical Historiography." *Greek, Roman and Byzantine Studies* 45: 35–57.

———. 1997. "Homeric Prayer." *Arethusa* 30.2: 241–72.

Materiality and ritual competence   45

———. 2005. "Signifying Names and Other Ominous Accidental References in Classical Historiography." *Greek Roman and Byzantine Studies* 45: 35–57.

Lawson, E. Thomas and Robert N. McCauley. 1990. *Rethinking Religion: Connecting Cognition and Culture*. Cambridge: Cambridge University Press.

Letoublon, Francoise. 2011. "Speech and Gesture in Rituals of Supplication and Prayer in Homer." In *Ritual Dynamics in the Ancient Mediterranean: Agency, Emotion, Gender, Reception*, edited by Angelos Chaniotis, 291–311. Stuttgart: Steiner Verlag.

Lyons, Deborah. 2012. *Dangerous Gifts: Gender and Exchange in Ancient Greece*. Austin, TX: University of Texas Press.

Martin, Richard P. 1989. *The Language of Heroes: Speech and Performance in the "Iliad."* Ithaca, NY: Cornell University Press.

McClure, Laura. 1999. *Spoken Like a Woman: Speech and Gender in Athenian Drama*. Princeton, NJ: Princeton University Press.

Minchin, Elizabeth. 2001. *Homer and the Resources of Memory: Some Applications of Cognitive Theory to the "Iliad" and the "Odyssey."* Oxford: Oxford University Press.

Morrison, James V. 1991. "The Function and Context of Homeric Prayers: A Narrative Perspective." *Hermes* 119: 145–57.

Mueller, Melissa. 2007. "Penelope and the Poetics of Remembering." *Arethusa* 40: 337–62.

Muellner, Leonard C. 1976. *The Meaning of Homeric Eukhomai through Its Formulas*. Innsbruck: Innsbrucker Beiträge zur Sprachwissenschaft.

Murnaghan, Sheila. 1987. *Disguise and Recognition in the Odyssey*. Princeton, NJ: Princeton University Press.

Parca, Maryline and Angeliki Tzanetou, eds. 2007. *Finding Persephone: Women's Rituals in Context*. Bloomington: Indiana University Press.

Pournara Karydas, Helen. 1998. *Eurykleia and Her Successors: Female Figures of Authority in Greek Poetics*. Lanham: Rowman and Littlefield.

Scheid, Joseph and Jesper Svenbro. 1996. *The Craft of Zeus: Myths of Weaving and Fabric*. Translated by Carol Volk. Cambridge, MA: Harvard University Press.

Staal, Frits. 1979. "The Meaninglessness of Ritual." *Numen* 26.1: 2–22.

Stehle, Eva. 2005. "Prayer and Curse in Aeschylus' Seven Against Thebes." *Classical Philology* 100.2: 101–22.

Tambiah, Stanley J. 1979. "A Performative Approach to Ritual." *Proceedings of the British Academy* 65: 113–66.

———. 1985. *Culture, Thought, and Social Action: An Anthropological Perspective*. Cambridge, MA: Harvard University Press.

Weinbaum, Batya. 2001. "Lament Ritual Transformed into Literature: Positing Women's Prayer as Cornerstone in Western Classical Literature." *The Journal of American Folklore* 114.451: 20–39.

Whitehouse, Harvey. 2004. *Modes of Religiosity: A Cognitive Theory of Religious Transmission* (Cognitive Science of Religion). Walnut Creek, CA: AltaMira Press.

3 Power through textiles

Women as ritual performers in ancient Greece

Cecilie Brøns

Introduction

Studies of ancient Greek religion tend to leave out an important category of votive offerings: textiles. This is a consequence of two factors: the underestimation of the importance of textiles in modern scholarship and the near absence of textiles themselves in the archaeological record. Exceptional climatic conditions such as freezing, waterlogging, or desiccation – conditions which are not prevalent in the ancient Mediterranean – account for the few textiles that are preserved (Gleba and Mannering 2012, 2). There are therefore few preserved textile remains from ancient Greece, and these rare examples are almost exclusively from burials (Spantidaki and Moulhérat 2012). Furthermore, when textiles are recovered it is either in the form of small fragments or in the form of so-called pseudomorphs, i.e. they are in a mineralized state caused by the chemical interaction with metal objects (Moulhérat and Spantidaki 2009a, 2009b).

Consequently, there is little research on the role and importance of textiles in rituals and how these influence our understanding of women in Greek religion. This chapter attempts to shed light on this particular gap in our knowledge by investigating some of the evidence for the dedication and use of textiles in sanctuaries in order to clarify women's role in ritual and dedicatory practices. Among the themes to be addressed are the role of textiles in Greek society, the relationship between women and textile dedications in religious contexts, and how the ritual use of textiles for dressing the gods leads to new insights about the sensual, sensory side of religion – touch in particular. This chapter first examines the evidence for textiles in temples and then, using theories of embodiment and agency, especially as formulated by Alfred Gell, considers how women were ritual agents who used textiles to interact with cult images and hence the gods themselves.

Dedicating textiles in Greek sanctuaries

The study of textile dedications in sanctuaries presents obvious challenges, inasmuch as the textiles themselves have not survived and other sources of information must be found for their study. One such potential source is literary and epigraphic evidence. For example, Homer describes the offering of a garment to a deity in the

Power through textiles   47

Iliad, when Hecabe goes to the Temple of Athena in order to give the goddess the largest and most beautiful *peplos* in her house, which Theano, Athena's priestess, places on the knees of the cult statue (*Iliad* 6.287–304; also discussed by Andromache Karanika and Laurie O'Higgins in this volume). As far as the epigraphic record is concerned, the so-called temple inventories, in particular, have great potential to increase our knowledge of the dedication of textiles to various deities.

The term "temple inventories" generally refers to lists of votive offerings that were kept in temple treasuries. They have been found over large parts of the Greek world and span a rather long period, from the fifth century BCE to the second century CE (Scott 2011, 240). A large majority of inventories with references to textiles belong to the Hellenistic period, while a few can be dated to the late Classical period. Some temple inventories record large numbers of different types of textiles that were considered valuable and important enough to be recorded. A large majority of inventories that include textiles are for female deities, especially Artemis, but also Demeter, Hera, and Athena (Brøns 2015). Three are of special interest to this chapter because they also record the names of the donors of the textiles. These are the Brauron clothing catalogues, an inventory of a temple of Demeter and Kore from Tanagra, and a temple inventory from Thebes.

The inventories from the sanctuary of Artemis Brauronia on the Athenian acropolis are among the central documents for the study of Greek clothing and its use as offerings (*IG* II² 1514–30; translated in Cleland 2005). The inventories consist of 13 fragments originally belonging to six separate *stelai* and record offerings made to Artemis. According to the traditional interpretation of these lists, they record dedications made at the sanctuary of Brauron, and it has been argued that the same records were inscribed and displayed both at Brauron and at Athens (Dillon 2002, 19). Most of these documents, though mentioned briefly in Ioannis Papadimitriou's reports of the excavations, remain unpublished; Dina Peppas-Delmousou offers some commentary on them (Papadimitriou 1956, 1957; Peppas-Delmousou 1988). Inscriptions found in the sanctuary complex at Brauron in the area of the cave (Ekroth 2003, 80; Papadimitriou 1956, 27–8, 1957, 21–2) are said to be identical to those recovered on the Athenian acropolis (*IG* II² 1517, 1524, 1529). As preserved, they pertain to dedications made in the years 349/8 to 336/5 BCE (Cleland 2005, 1).

The catalogues list a great number of garments, many of which are described as colored, decorated, luxurious, fine, and so on. The names of the donors indicate that women were the primary – almost exclusive – donors of these garments. Among those described with complete names in the catalogue, 118 are female donors; the complete names of males are the names of archons, which are listed to provide an indication of when the inventory was made, and thus they are not donors of garments. In addition, there are many fragmented names of dedicants, of which all appear to be female.

Robin Osborne has performed a prosopographical analysis of the 125 names listed in the Brauron catalogues, which provides valuable information about the women who made dedications to Artemis (Osborne 1985). In many cases, only the

48 *Cecilie Brøns*

first name is recorded, without the name of the husband or father or the name of the deme of origin; the absence of this additional information may indicate the extent of women's activity and its importance in this sanctuary. We know too little about these female names to be able to reach significant conclusions, but Osborne does note that some of the names appear to be aristocratic (Osborne 1985, 158). Of the 125 names, only 16 include the name of the husband or father and are thus traceable. Seven of these 16 women belong to families otherwise known through inscriptions (Osborne 1985, 159 provides a complete list of these references). All of these women come from the more distant of the demes represented, and the fact that they all lived at a considerable distance from Brauron suggests, as Nancy Demand observes, that the garments were not casual offerings made by visitors stopping by the sanctuary (Demand 1994, 90), and thus demonstrate Brauron's regional importance. Most important, however, is the fact that all of these women were of very high social status (Vikela 2008, 86). This lends support to another point that can be inferred from the inventories: the expensive nature of many of the offerings suggests that donors were most often elite, or at least well-off, individuals (Dillon 2002, 22).

A marble *stele* from Tanagra, dating to the second half of the third century BCE, provides further information about the offering of textiles in sanctuaries. The *stele* has inscriptions on both sides (for the complete Greek text, see Reinach 1899; Roller 1989, 100–8). Side A bears an inscription with a sacred regulation concerning a sanctuary of Demeter and Kore at Tanagra, and it is reasonable to assume that side B also relates to this sanctuary. Below the regulation on side A is a list of women who contributed financially to the construction of the temple, while side B carries an inventory of individuals who donated garments to the sanctuary. Every entry records the name of the donor and the type of garment given. The inscription records several donors, the large majority of whom are women; only one male makes a dedication, and this is on behalf of a woman.

A marble slab from the first half or middle of the third century BCE, probably from the sanctuary of the Kabeiroi located 8 km west of Thebes, bears an inscription with an inventory list (*IG* VII. 2421, Roesch 1985, 74). The inscription is fragmented, and the right and bottom parts are missing. The inventory records garments dedicated to a deity whose name is not preserved, but according to Günther (1988, 232 n. 97) it could possibly be Artemis Eukleia, who was venerated in Boiotia. The inscription records several garments donated in the sanctuary exclusively by women.

The temple inventories from Brauron, Tanagra, and Thebes establish that it was primarily women who donated textiles in sanctuaries of female deities – even if names of donors are often omitted on inventories and the name of one male dedicant appears on an inventory from the Parthenon. Iconographic evidence too suggests that women were the dedicants and handlers of textiles in ritual contexts, although depictions of this particular act are rare, and in fact, only four examples are so far known. The first and earliest example of a depiction of a textile dedication is a Boiotian relief *pithos* (storage jar) dated to the seventh century BCE (Fig. 3.1). The scene on the neck of the *pithos* depicts five women walking in

Figure 3.1 Boiotian relief *pithos*, seventh century BCE.
Photograph: © Museum of Fine Arts, Boston, inv. no.99.506.

procession toward the left. All five women are clad in garments that reach to their feet and are decorated with circular, rosette-like patterns; the woman leading the procession also wears a decorated mantle and carries a long staff that may indicate her status as a priestess. The vase is fragmented, but at least two women each carry a square object with exactly the same patterns as those on their own garments. The repetition of the pattern makes it reasonable to conclude that the objects they carry are folded textiles. It has been suggested that the scene represents a mythical or epic scene of Hecabe or the priestess Theano and the Trojan women carrying textiles to be dedicated to Athena *(LIMC* iv 'Hekabe', no. 12; Caskey 1976, 33), although the Homeric interpretation is now rarely advanced (Burgess 2001, 226, n. 162). The scene may depict women walking toward a sanctuary with offerings of textiles – although the textiles could also be wedding or burial gifts.

A votive relief dated to the end of the fourth century BCE, recovered at Echinos in central Greece, depicts a scene that takes place in a temple, as the two framing pillars and a peristyle indicate (Dillon 2002, 231). To the far right stands a goddess with a long torch in her right hand, and before her is an altar, in front of which is a small male figure holding a sacrificial victim. Behind him stands a young woman holding out an infant toward the goddess, and behind her is a smaller woman or girl. Finally, to the far left stands a tall woman with a mantle over her head. But, most interestingly, on the wall behind the worshippers hang several clothing items – votive offerings to the goddess residing in the temple. The relief is usually interpreted as a thank-offering to a goddess (Artemis or Demeter) for a successful childbirth and for the continued protection of the child (Dakoronia and Gounaropoulou 1992, 218).

Women not only dedicated textiles but also appear to have been the ones who handled them in sanctuaries. This is attested by a group of votive terracottas from the Doric Greek colony of Lokroi Epizephyrioi in Southern Italy. At the sanctuary of Persephone, a large number of mold-made votive *pinakes* (plaques/tablets), dated to the first half of the fifth century BCE, decorated in relief with different scenes of cult activities and mythological narratives was uncovered (Dillon 2002, 222; MacLachlan 1995, 218, and see Bonnie MacLachlan's chapter in this volume). According to Helmut Prückner, three groups of scenes involve textiles: the storage of textiles, the transport of textiles, and the dedication of textiles (Prückner 1968, 39). Scenes of textile storage usually depict a woman placing a folded textile in a chest (Fig. 3.2) (Prückner type 14–15). These scenes take place

Figure 3.2 Woman placing a folded textile in a chest. Pinax from Lokris, *c.* 500–450 BCE.

Source: National Museum of Reggio Calabria, inv. no. 2866, 57414, 61251.© Soprintendenza Archeologica della Calabria.

indoors, since there is furniture, and different items – such as *kalathoi* (wool baskets), mirrors, *kantharoi,* and *lekythoi* (jugs) can be seen hanging on the wall. The scenery has been interpreted as a sanctuary, although it could also be a representation of the female quarters of a private household. The ritual nature of the event depicted, however, is clear due to the *pinakes'* ritual function as votives deposited in a sanctuary and the depiction of goddesses on the related specimens (MacLachlan 1995, 214).

Scenes of textile transport can be divided into two main types: processions interpreted as *peplophoria,* which is the ritual carrying of a textile, possibly a *peplos,* and women carrying a folded textile on a sort of tray balanced on the head ("*Gewandprozession*") (Prückner types 16–28). The *peplophoria* scenes usually depict about four women walking in procession and carrying a large textile (Fig. 3.3). The procession is either led or followed by a differently dressed woman with a mantle covering her hair who carries a lustration bowl and an aspersion rod. She is usually interpreted as a priestess (Dillon 2002, 227; MacLachlan 1995, 213; Prückner 1968, 42). In rare instances, the robe is not carried by women, but by men (Dillon 2002, 227), perhaps in a ritual honoring a goddess or in a procession connected with a marriage ceremony (MacLachlan 1995, 213). Occasionally, the women carrying folded textiles on their heads are also accompanied by a priestess with a bowl and aspersion rod. Scenes related to the textile dedications often depict a woman standing in front of a seated goddess. A table with offerings on which a

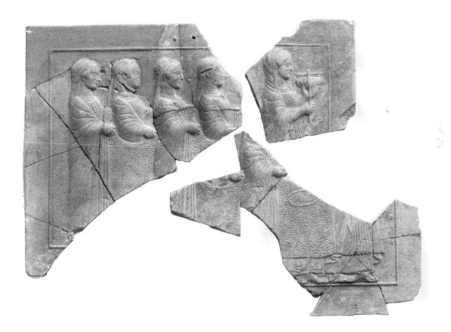

Figure 3.3 Peplophoria. *Pinax* from Lokris, *c.* 500–450 BCE.

Source: National Museum of Reggio Calabria, inv. no. 57482. © Soprintendenza Archeologica della Calabria.

52   Cecilie Brøns

folded piece of textile has been placed often appears between the two figures (Prückner type 29). It has been suggested that the scene depicts Persephone receiving the *peplos* during the *peplophoria* (MacLachlan 1995, 215). These three types of votive plaques thus testify to the different ritual uses of textiles and their dedication by women in sanctuaries.

Yet the most famous example of the dedication and ritual use of a garment does not involve women, but a man: the east frieze of the Parthenon (438–432 BCE). The central scene depicts a ceremony involving five figures and a folded cloth. The generally accepted view is that it depicts the *peplos* for Athena that was escorted to the acropolis during the great Panathenaic procession (Blundell and Williamson 1998, 59; Neils 2001, 173; Sourvinou-Inwood 2011, 284. For alternative interpretations, see e.g. Connelly 2014; Jeppesen 2007). The man holding the cloth could be the *archon basileus*, the chief religious officer of Athens. It has been suggested that the scene illustrates the handing over of the *peplos* to the *Praxiergidai*, an Athenian clan that had the right and duty to maintain the statue's garments (Barber 1992, 113). This depiction shows us that no matter how dominant women appear to be as dedicants and handlers of textiles in ritual contexts, these activities were not exclusive to them, and men were also involved in ritual acts involving textiles.

A note on who produced the *peploi* is in place here: The Great Panathenaia occurred every four years, and the Lesser Panathenaia was held on the three off years. The dominant view is that two different *peploi* are reflected in the sources, one offered annually and a *peplos* woven by professional weavers every fourth year at the Great Panathenaia (Barber 1992, 113; Mansfield 1985, esp. 5–7, 16–17, 51, 55). A section of Zenobios' *Proverbs* (1.56) dated to the second century CE states that the first Panathenaic *peplos* was fabricated by two Cypriot men, Helikon and his father Akesas, whom Athenaios also mentions, who were renowned weavers (Ath. 2.30). This has led to the assumption that the Panathenaic *peplos* was always produced by men, while the small annual *peplos* was made by Athenian women (e.g. Barber 1992, 113, 117; Stamatopoulou 2012, 75). Yet there is nothing in the sources to indicate that this was actually the case, and the remaining literary and epigraphic sources solely mention women as the producers of the *peploi* (Brøns 2014, appendix 1).

In ancient Greece, textile production was usually associated with the female sphere, and it is often argued that a Greek woman spent most of her time and energy producing textiles for her household (Håland 2004, 168–70; Reeder 1995, 200; Sebesta 2002, 127). Textiles were thus considered to be synonymous with the domesticity of civilised life (Reeder 1995, 200). The quintessential skill that Greek men required in a wife – besides the ability to provide offspring – was woolworking, and the acquisition of textile skills appears to have been a prerequisite for marriage (Sebesta 2002, 126–7). The ability to work wool was so fundamental in a wife that Xenophon, in his treatise on household management, takes for granted that a bride will have mastered all the relevant skills before her marriage (Xen. *Oec.* 7.6; Sebesta 2002, 126). This association of textile production with women is supported by the depiction of this activity in Greek vase-painting: only

Power through textiles   53

women are depicted, most often spinning. They are seldom weaving or engaged in other stages of textile production (Larson Lovén 2013).

Textiles could, however, be produced both at home and in workshops. Yet the scarcity of sources that refer to women – at least of higher social status – selling the textiles that they had produced suggests that this scenario of selling home-produced textiles was out of the ordinary (see Xen. *Mem.* 2.7.7–12). This is an important point in connection with the dedication of textiles, since it could mean that women most probably produced the dedicated garments at home rather than purchasing them at a shop or stall before or while visiting the sanctuary – although this possibility cannot be excluded. So although one should of course be wary of making the assumption that the producers of textiles also control their distribution (Schneider and Weiner 1991, 21), the evidence suggests that women were the primary dedicants of textiles that were most probably their own products.

No matter their size or their producers, textiles were not just any type of votive offering. On the contrary, recent research has proved the immense value of ancient textiles, competing in worth with items made of precious metals. Textiles were valuable because every step of their production from obtaining and preparing fibers to spinning, setting up the loom, and weaving took immense time. For example, with regard to wool, sheep needed to be cut or plucked, and then their wool had to be washed, sorted, and combed before it could be spun (Andersson Strand 2012). Imported fibers or fabrics, silk for example, were very expensive, as were the dyes, such as the famous shellfish purple made from specific species of murexes or the dyes obtained from kermes insects or the famous saffron-dyes. All these dyes were very time consuming to produce because enormous amounts of raw material had to be collected and processed before they were used to dye textiles (Cardon 2007). Finally, embroidery with gold thread or attached ornaments made textiles even more valuable (Gleba 2008). Thus textiles were often prestige items and could represent great wealth. Indeed, those donated by women in the sanctuaries were often not simple, home-made votive offerings but represented an enormous amount of work and immense value. This illustrates the role of women as important contributors to the wealth of the sanctuaries and benefactors in their religious economy.

These textile dedications were not random but were primarily given to female deities, especially Artemis, but also Athena, Demeter, and Hera. This pattern suggests that women dedicated textiles to female goddesses who were most likely to secure their transition through the life events of puberty, marriage, and childbirth. From a more practical perspective, these offerings functioned as a means of ensuring the survival of the woman and the newborn child and thus of the continuity of the family lineage. Incorrect performance of the dedicatory rites could result in infertility or death. This means that these dedications served to maintain the health and survival not only of the woman herself, but also of the entire *oikos*, on which society was based. By extension, the textile offerings contributed to the maintenance of society, which depended on the birth of new citizens, and thus secured the well-being and survival of the polis (Blundell and Williamson 1998, 27). In this way, the household as well as the city were dependent on female fertility – a

54   *Cecilie Brøns*

reality that is reflected in the fact that, at Athens, the community provided the sanctuary in which the family placed its offerings (Morgan 2007, 306).

Women's dedications of textiles were therefore not insignificant or concerned with only one individual but rather were important on a civic level. Women were associated with the private sphere, but their religious practices affected the public standing of the *oikos* and its relationship to society as a whole. In this way, women had what Victoria Sabetai calls "a cultic citizenship" (Sabetai 2008, 289). The position of women in ancient Greek society has thus been considered something of a paradox, inasmuch as women's reproductive capacity placed them at the center of the *oikos* and the polis because neither could survive without them (e.g. Ar. *Lys.* 650–1). But at the same time women were marginalized in a social and political sense since they were defined by their relationships with men and were inferior in status to men (Morgan 2007, 309). In producing and dedicating textiles, women tied family, city, and gods together in a religious economy necessary for the survival of all three.

Dressing the gods

Textiles were not just offerings of high value and importance but were also used as implements in specific rituals. Most notably, textiles were used to dress cult images. Inventories record a god or goddess who "has", i.e. own, garments, garments that were "wrapped around" statues or have dress-fasteners suggesting that they were worn by statues.

The Brauron catalogues describe different cult statues in the sanctuary. The catalogues mention an "old (seated) statue" (*toi hedei toi archaioi*) (*IG* II² 1514.34–9), a "(seated) statue" (*toi hedei*) (*IG* II² 1514.22–3), and the "stone (seated) statue" (*to lithinon hedos*) (*IG* II² 1514.27–8), which possibly, but not necessarily, are one and the same. The catalogue also mentions an "upright statue" (*toi agalmati toi orthoi*) (*IG* II² 1514.42–3). Because these terms occur in the same inscription, they may refer to several different statues. Other inscriptions record a "statue" (*agalma*) (*IG* II² 1523.27–9; 1524B.204–6, 215–16.224), a "standing statue" (*toi agalmati toi hestekoti*) (*IG* II² 1524B.207), and an "upright statue" (*agalma to orthon*) (*IG* II² 1522.28–9). The statues termed *hedoi* (possibly seated) are described in connection with various garments: there are a Tarentine garment (*tarantinon*) (*IG* II² 1514.37), two wraps (*IG* II² 1514.34–6), and an embroidered garment (*IG* II² 1514.38) around the old (seated) statue; an Amorgian *chiton* (*chiton amorginon*) (*IG* II² 1514.22–3) around the (seated) statue; and a white *himation* (mantle) with purple border around the (seated) stone statue (*IG* II² 1514.27–8). Another inscription also records something around the statue (*IG* II² 1524B.224) and around the old (seated) statue (*IG* II² 1524B.227), but the text specifying the type of garment is not preserved. There is a patterned *chitoniskos* around the upright statue (*IG* II² 1514.42–3), and another inscription records that the upright statue has something – perhaps the double-layered, saffron-dyed garment (*krokotos*) recorded immediately before (*IG* II² 1522.28–9). Finally, there is also a record of the statue (*to agalma*, and thus unknown exactly which one) having a *kandys*, a coat with sleeves

Power through textiles 55

originally of Persian origin (*IG* II² 1523.27–8). There is thus evidence of at least two different cult statues being dressed, one seated and one upright. Different terms are used to describe this phenomenon: either the garments are placed "around" (*peri*) the statues or the statue "has" (*ekhei*) garments. A rather wide variety of garments is used to dress the statues: *tarantinon, chiton, himation, chitoniskos,* and *kandys*.

A marble *stele* that can be dated to 346/45 BCE, bearing an inscription with an inventory of the sanctuary of Hera, was recovered from the Heraion on Samos (Ohly 1953, 46–8; *SEG* 45.1163, *SEG* 47.1314; Shipley 1987, 157). The inventory demonstrates that the statue of Hera was dressed in costly raiment, and numerous ceremonial garments and materials are listed as "belonging to" the goddess. Hera was originally the sole deity of the sanctuary, but later other gods appeared on the scene. For example, the inventory lists two statues of Hermes, one of which is thought to have stood in the temple of Aphrodite. The inventory gives a long list of different textiles donated in the sanctuary. In contrast to, for example, the inventory from Tanagra, there is no record of gender for either garments or donors, and only one donor is named – a man by the name of Diogenes. The inventory of the Heraion on Samos describes "the goddess" (Hera) as having *(ekhei)* a *mitre* (a belted girdle or snood to tie up women's hair) (Ohly 1953, no.11). The inventory also records a *proslemma* (a type of wrap or shawl) with purple edges "belonging to the goddess," possibly indicating that a statue of Hera wore this garment and that a *sindon* (fine cloth/linen) was spread before the goddess, i.e. her statue. Later in the inventory, it is recorded that, under Thrasyanax, the goddess had *chitones*; under Hippodamas, the goddess had two *chitones*; and, finally, when Demetrios was archon, the goddess had two *chitones*. According to the inventory, other statues in the Heraion also wore garments: "the Euangelis" – probably a third statue of Hera (Mansfield 1985, 484) – had one of the seven veils and the so-called "Goddess at the back" had a white *himation*. According to O'Brien (1993, 29), "the goddess" is the earlier wooden cult image, while the "Goddess at the back" is a more recent sixth-century BCE statue. The inventory also records that the statue of Hermes had one of the 38 *chitones* and one of the 48 *himatia*, and that the statue of Hermes in the temple of Aphrodite had two of these *himatia*. The inventory thus establishes that both the statue of Hera and that of Hermes were likely to have been dressed in real garments.

Finally, several of the inscriptions from Delos record that a number of cult images were dressed in real garments. Thus, the statue of Artemis is described, in 146/5 BCE, as being clothed in a purple garment interwoven/plaited with gold (*ID* 1442B, ll. 54–6; Mansfield 1985, 475–7). Earlier, in 279 BCE, the statue is reported to have had simply a woolen garment (*IG* XI, 2 161B.62). The statue of Leto seems to have been wearing a purple mantle in 269/8 BCE, since purple dye is twice reported to have been bought specifically for her *himation* (*IG* XI, 2 203A.73 and *IG* XI, 2 204.75–6). In 156/5 BCE, the wooden statue of the goddess is described as wearing a linen *chiton*, a linen wrap, and a pair of shoes or half-boots (*ID* 1417A, l.100–3), and an inscription from 140/39 BCE records the presence of Leto's *chiton,* gold diadem, and linen cloth/garment (*othonion*), along with a belt with

56   Cecilie Brøns

inwoven gold (*ID* 1450A.200–1). The inventory of 155 BCE records the *chitoniskos* of Leto, which could indicate that her statue wore it. Furthermore, the inscription records that something – perhaps the statue of Leto – was "in" a linen cloth/ garment (*othonion*) that featured a purple-edged circle with decoration in gold thread and was bound with a belt interwoven with gold. The inscription also records the presence of dress-fasteners at the shoulders, which are a further indication that the garment was placed on a statue (Mansfield 1985, 478–9; *ID* 1428, II.53–8). In the Heraion, moreover, there was a linen cloth/garment (*othonion*) for Hera (296 and 250 BCE: *IG* XI, 2 154A.21–2; 287A.120–1), and the inventory of 155/4 BCE records that two statues (*agalmata*) were clothed in linen (Mansfield 1985, 482; *ID* 1417A, II.22). Finally, it is possible that the statue of Dionysos also wore a garment. According to an inventory of 141/0 BCE, it had a *chiton* that belonged previously to the goddess Artemis (Mansfield 1985, 480; *ID* 1444Aa.38). Furthermore, *ID* 1442B.54–6 report that the old garment of Artemis was put on the statue of Dionysos.

The ritual use of textiles to dress the cult images is also attested in iconography. When, however, it comes to depictions of cult statues in vase-painting, it is gener- ally very difficult to ascertain whether the garments of the cult images are painted on and/or sculpted or whether they were meant to represent actual garments used to dress the images. A group of vases, usually termed "Lenaia vases," can help in this regard, since they represent without a doubt a cult statue dressed in real gar- ments. The Lenaia was an annual winter festival in Athens in honor of Dionysos Lenaios. *Lenaia* probably comes from *lenai*, which is another name for the mae- nads (Simon 1983, 100). The Lenaia vases consist of a group of approximately 100 Athens-produced vases that depict maenads, perhaps at the Lenaia or at the Anthesteria, a festival of the new wine held in the spring (Neils 2008, 247). Some of these vases bear a representation of a cult statue of Dionysos Lenaios as their central motif. This particular cult statue took the form of a column or pillar draped with garments and had a bearded mask occasionally adorned with twigs (Simon 1983, 100). On some of the vases, a table with textiles is placed in front of the image – perhaps offerings to the god (e.g. British Museum, inv. 1843, 1103.32, E452; Louvre, inv. G407). Usually, the attendants of the god are female, either maenads or female devotees.

The act of clothing cult images was an important responsibility assigned to particular individuals. Many female deities had official wardrobe mistresses who changed the clothes of images when necessary and appropriate. The dressing and adornment of statues appears – at least at some sanctuaries and cults – to have been managed by officials and subject to regulations, in order to ensure that the practice was correctly observed, as well as to give the impression that images were in need of regular attention and maintenance (Weddle 2010, 54). There were regulations and traditions that determined how the image ought to be dressed and who could perform this task. The latter point was perhaps considered to be especially impor- tant, because those who dressed the statue naturally had to remove the previous garment and would therefore essentially see the image "naked." Those responsible for these intimate interactions appear to have been officially categorized in the religious terminology and in some sanctuaries were called *kosmophoroi* (Weddle 2010, 53–4). The term comes from *kosmos*, which can be translated as "adornment" or "adorning." Another term connected with the official duty of dressing cult statues is the priestly title *stolizon* or *stolistes*, which can be translated as "rober" (Vidman 1970, 62). The word is employed in several inscriptions, e.g. on statues and a herm, all in the sanctuary of Isis. The majority date to the second century CE (*IG* II/III² 4771, 4772, 3564, 3644, 4818). There are other related titles in the written record. One is the *hypostoloi*, who were probably assistants of the *stolistes* (robers). The term is recorded in two inscriptions from the third century BCE and 117 BCE (*IG* XII, suppl. 571 and *IG* IX, 2 1107b). Another title for staff that dress a cult statue at Argos is *gerairades*, who are defined as "those who dress the statue of Athena at Argos" (Hesychios, *s.v. gererades;* LSJ *s.v. geraira*: priestesses of Athena at Argos; Robertson 1996, 51).

The *Praxiergidai*, who are mentioned in relation to the sanctuary of Athena on the Athenian acropolis, are also important in this connection. They were an Athenian clan whose members were responsible for keeping the *xoanon* (the old wooden statue of Athena) and its garments clean, that is, washing the statue and its garments, an activity that took place during the Plynteria festival (Dillon 2002, 133–4; Robertson 1996, 48–52; Sourvinou-Inwood 2011, 135–224). Members of the *Praxiergidai* also placed the new *peplos* upon the statue at the annual Panathenaia (Mansfield 1985, 366). There were some cult personnel titles that were probably filled by members of this clan. These include the *Loutrides* ("bather-women"; Hesychios, *s.v. loutrides*; Photios, *s.v. loutrides*), who bathed the statue of Athena; the *Plyntrides* (washer/laundry-women), who washed the statue's garments; and probably also the *Kataniptes* (washer), who probably cleaned and washed the whole statue and its garments throughout the year (Mansfield 1985, 367–8; Sourvinou-Inwood 2011, 265).

In sum, rich evidence for the dressing of cult images in textiles demonstrates that this ritual act was not left to coincidence but often was a preserve for specific cultic personnel. We do not know for certain, however, whether these cultic personnel were men or women, since the sources are silent in this respect. Yet, in consideration of the fact that women were the primary dedicants of textiles (and also the ones who produced them) and that the recipients were primarily – almost exclusively – female deities, it would appear that women were highly represented among the persons performing this task.

Textiles and the anthropology of touch

Epigraphic and iconographic evidence indicates that women were not only largely responsible for producing and dedicating garments to goddesses but also dressed the gods. Scholars often assume that the acts of handling textiles in a sanctuary as well as washing and dressing its cult statues were not especially important but part of simple maintenance (Mansfield 1985, 442; Romano 1980). Yet this was not the case. In this respect, Gell's ideas on idolatry are illuminating, for he argues that in the context of idolatry, the idol is not simply a depiction of the god but the body

58   *Cecilie Brøns*

of the god in artefact-form (Gell 1998, 99). In other words, something can be both a representation and part of something such as a deity (Gell 1998, 106). He further argues, "if appearances of things are material parts of things, then the kind of leverage which one obtains over a person or thing by having access to their image is comparable, or really identical, to the leverage which can be obtained by having access to some physical part of them" (Gell 1998, 105). In this view, a worshipper's access to a cult image could imply some sort over power it. Yet cult images are not merely objects that can be manipulated.

Gell considers the question of external and internal conceptions of agency in order to make sense of the relationship between worshipper and cult image. The external (or practical) aspects of agency attribution are formed by outer actions or conditions such as language, practices, routines, rules, etc. and are more related to the body, while the internal concept of agency attribution is more closely related to inner aspects of the mind (Gell 1998, 126–7). According to Gell, the simplest solution to the question of idolatry is an "external" theory of agency, since idols are social others to the extent that, and because, they obey the rules laid down for idols as co-present others (gods) in idol-form. So although idols may not produce much visible behavior, they may be very "active" invisibly (Gell 1998, 128). The externalist theory of attributing agency is easily applicable to the cult of idols in ancient Greece. The washing and dressing of the images of the gods imposed agency on them by making them "patients" in social exchanges, which necessarily implies and confers agency. As claimed by Gell, there is no make-believe about such performances: they would be pointless if they did not induce agency in social others in human form. These acts are not symbolic because there was no alternative way to dress the gods. Thus, the acts of dressing a cult image were real, practical services performed for divine social others in image-form, not symbolic acts (Gell 1998, 134–5). In sum, according to Gell, the essence of idolatry is that it permits real physical interactions to take place between persons and divinities (Gell 1998, 135).

How did the ancient Greeks conceptualize their cult images? Did they think they represented or embodied the gods? Since it is clear from the evidence that the Greeks did interact with the cult images (e.g. by washing and dressing them), it seems to me that there is no doubt that the Greeks somehow thought of the cult images as embodying divinity, although this topic has been much debated. Richard Gordon, for example, suggests that the statues are neither completely inanimate nor completely alive. He argues that if "living" is broken down into its denotations: breath, sight, feelings, movement, skin-sheen, and facial expression, and in so far as one or two of these denotations may be taken as sufficient evidence of life, then ancient statues were alive, although the whole inventory is never present (Gordon 1979, 10). Thus, since ancient statues, such as the ones by Daidalos, could move of themselves in spite of being inanimate, it is clear that sculpture (and perhaps other artefacts) were seen as neither inert matter nor as humans or animals but required a special classification (Gordon 1979, 8). In sum, according to Gordon, "people believed simultaneously that statues were gods and that they were not" (Gordon 1979, 16). Whether the statues, however, were considered animate or only

Power through textiles 59

partly animate does not argue against the idea that they were considered to be some form of embodiment of a god. Furthermore, as argued by David Freedberg, people do not interact with cult images just out of habit: "they do so because all such acts are symptoms of a relationship between image and respondent that is clearly predicated on the attribution of powers which transcend the purely material aspect of the object" (Freedberg 1989, 91). Ancient Greek cult images appear to have been treated and addressed in ways that indicates that they housed power. *Xoana* (early wooden cult images) were thought to possess special powers, sometimes being believed to be dangerous, and able to inflict blindness, madness, or sterility on their viewers (Petrovic 2010, 210; Pausanias 3.16.7–11). Approaching them was therefore not without risks. Covering them in textiles could thus also have the practical function of protecting the viewers from such disasters or injuries. This also illustrates that these cult statues were believed to somehow have the capacity to act (Mitchell 2010, 266). There is, however, possibly also an element of co-dependency. Although statues are relationally capable of being more powerful than devotees since they have supernatural power, devotees potentially have power over statues in terms of their care, restoration, and regeneration (Whitehead 2013, 184).

The preceding discussion on the dressing of cult images leads to six further points on the potential functions of textiles in ritual. First, when textiles were placed around the cult image, they literally came in touch with the deity represented and in this way became like a second skin (Baert 2007, 242). Thus, textiles were potentially the closest thing to the god or goddess, thereby automatically becoming something special. Second, textiles have certain properties that make them a particularly useful medium in ritual. For example, they are portable and flexible and therefore can be wrapped around an image, such as a large cult statue. This leads to the third point, which is the ability of textiles to shape and transform what they surround. This ability can change the expression and thus the message of the cult image to the observing worshipper. The addition of a garment or a piece of textile can thus be used to alter the content it enwraps, to manipulate its perception by others, and to provide a surface with which to contain or convey emotions. In this way, dressing may involve not only physical transformations but also psychological and symbolic transformations of objects, places, and people – in this case cult images (Douny and Harris 2014, 6). This is very important, since textiles were the only medium available to do this in antiquity, with the possible exception of the jewelry embellishments, which can, however, be considered part of dress.

A fourth and related point is the interchangeability of textiles. In contrast to permanent forms of adornment or decoration, such as, for example, the sculpted dress of a bronze or stone statue, textiles were impermanent. They could be used to dress the cult image to signal specific occasions, perhaps by employing specific garment types, colors, dress arrangements, or textiles with certain patterns or figurative decoration. At the end of a particular occasion, the textiles could be removed and/or replaced with other textiles. In this way, textiles may have served as a means of creating an impression that the cult image was transformable and changeable; this practice also speaks to the usefulness of textiles as a dynamic means of communication.

60   *Cecilie Brøns*

A fifth point is the ability of textiles to communicate identity. That dress was employed as a means of communicating and signaling aspects of identity has long been established in scholarship. In the case of human beings, the addition and removal of clothing allows different aspects of the person to be revealed and concealed according to the situation. Clothing can thus materialize aspects of a person, whether these are aesthetic, economic, or moral values or other qualities such as charisma, power, or gender (Douny and Harris 2014, 24). This was so for cult images, too, for which the adding or removing of specific textiles or clothing items could signal specific properties or aspects of the divinity in question.

The sixth and final point is the functionality of textiles as a mediator between the sacred and the profane. Textiles are often said to mediate between the personal and the social, for which reason it has been argued that they can also be used to define the liminal passage toward sanctity (Rudy 2007, 22), and since textiles can mediate between categories such as the physical and the visionary, it can be argued that they can also denote the borders between the sacred and the secular (Rudy 2007, 35). Conversely, textiles can also construct boundaries to create interfaces not only between objects, subjects, and the world (Douny and Harris 2014, 4) but also between the sacred and the secular.

This leads to further considerations of the possibilities inherent in the use of textiles in ritual. Ancient textiles could carry detailed figure scenes, illustrating stories of myth and the glorious past, as for example the *peplos* of Athena on the acropolis, which according to literary sources carried scenes of the Gigantomachy. This figurative decoration means that it was possible, quite literally, to read clothing based on the stories illustrated on them. Such figurative messages could transform the bodies/cult images that they clothed (Warr 2010, 15), thus providing the viewer with further clues as to how to understand the images, contextualize them, and possibly approach them. This, in connection with their ability to be in direct touch with the cult image, makes them an obvious choice as for example a propagandistic measure – like a giant picture book for all visitors to the sanctuary to see, readable by all, whether literate or not.

Conclusion: The power of touch

Sensual religion is the religious expressions that can be touched, felt, smelled, etc. The idea of sensual religion, however, is problematic to modern minds due to the fact that (modern) conceptions of religion are often defined in terms of transcendence or metaphysics. Therefore religious objects (such as cult images) are often defined as symbols or representations (Whitehead 2013, 117). Yet as shown here, Greek cult appears to have been different in that cult images were somehow understood as embodying the deity. This is highly important in relation to interactions between human beings and cult images, since this implies that being close to the cult image allowed worshippers to be close to the deity. By touching the image, one would actually, by proxy, touch the deity. But what does that mean to our understanding of the interaction between Greek cult images and the ancients?

Power through textiles   61

Whether or not a statue can be touched and physically interacted with has an impact on the role that it plays contextually (Whitehead 2013, 145). This means that the way in which the statue is displayed and whether or not it is physically accessible to worshippers plays a significant role in understanding how performances and interactions with such statues took place. Unfortunately, we do not always know whether the ancient Greek cult images were placed in ways that made them accessible to the visitor or whether such close encounters were reserved for specific persons or cultic personnel (Hewitt 1909, 84). Even when the bases for the original cult images are found *in situ*, it cannot be ascertained whether this spot was accessible to worshippers, since being allowed into the temple does not necessarily imply that one was allowed close enough to the cult image to touch it.

This leads back to the cultic personnel who dressed and/or washed the cult images, since they were those closest to the cult images, sometimes even seeing them "naked," which made dressing the cult image a significant point of interaction. As Laurence Douny and Susanna Harris argue, undressing is not simply the reversal of dressing: "the act of unwrapping is significant in itself and has its own outcomes. Unwrapping may refer to either a physical or a conceptual revelation whereby knowledge is gained or secrecy exposed. The removal of wrappings and their application elsewhere may be a device to accumulate and store the power of their contents" (Douny and Harris 2014, 3–4; see also Gell 1993, 89). Therefore, these individuals were, because of this privilege, possibly among the most important cultic personnel. Yet, modern perceptions of gender and ecclesiastical hierarchies, in which washing and dressing are women's tasks and thus, by extension, not as important as men's tasks, such as sacrificing a bull, seem to have obscured the import and meaning of dressing cult statues. In an ancient context for which epigraphic and iconographic sources provide invaluable evidence, however, women can be seen to be significant contributors to the economy of the sanctuaries through their production and dedication of textiles. Additionally, this chapter has established that, through the materiality of their textile offerings and the uses to which they were put, women were intimate with cult images and thus with the gods themselves. In this view, both women and cult images had ritual agency.

Works consulted

Andersson Strand, Eva. 2012. "The Textile Chaine Opératoire: Using a Multidisciplinary Approach to Textile Archaeology with a Focus on the Ancient Near East." *Paléorient*: 38.1–2: 21–40.

Baert, Barbara. 2007. "Mantle, Fur, Pallium: Veiling and Unveiling in the Martyrdom of Agnes of Rome." In *Weaving, Veiling, and Dressing. Textiles and Their Metaphors in the Late Middle Ages*, edited by Kathryn Rudy and Barbara Baert, 215–38. Turnhout: Brepols Publishers.

Barber, Elisabeth. 1992. "The Peplos of Athena." In *Goddess and Polis: The Panathenaic Festival in Ancient Athens*, edited by Jenifer Neils, 103–18. Princeton: Princeton University Press.

Blundell, Sue and Margaret Williamson. 1998. *The Sacred and the Feminine in Ancient Greece*. New York: Routledge.

62 Cecilie Brøns

Brøns, Cecilie. 2014. *Gods and Garments: Textiles in Greek Sanctuaries from the 7th to the 1st Centuries BC*. PhD diss., University of Copenhagen.

Brøns, Cecilie. 2015. "Textiles and Temple Inventories: Detecting an Invisible Votive Tradition in Greek Sanctuaries in the Second Half of the 1st Millennium BC." In *Tradition: Transmission of Culture in the Ancient World, Acta Hyperborea* 14, edited by Jane Fejfer, Annette Rathje and Mette Moltesen, 43–83. Copenhagen: Museum Tusculanum Press.

Burgess, Jonathan S. 2001. *The Tradition of the Trojan War in Homer and the Epic Cycle*. Baltimore: Johns Hopkins University Press.

Cardon, Dominique. 2007. *Natural Dyes: Sources, Tradition, Technology and Science*. London: Archetype.

Caskey, Miriam Erwin. 1976. "Notes on Relief Pithoi of the Tenian-Boiotian Group." *AJA* 80.1: 19–41.

Cleland, Liza. 2005. *The Brauron Clothing Catalogues: Text, Analysis, Glossary and Translation*. Oxford: British Archaeological Reports.

Connelly, Joan Breton. 2014. *The Parthenon Enigma: A New Understanding of the World's Most Iconic Building and the People Who Made It*. New York: Knopf.

Dakoronia, Fanouria and Loukretia Gounaropoulou. 1992. "Artemiskult auf einem Weihrelief aus Achinos bei Lamia." *Mitteilungen des Deutschen Archäologischen Instituts, Athenische Abteilung* 107: 217–27.

Demand, Nancy. 1994. *Birth, Death, and Motherhood in Classical Greece*. Baltimore and London: Johns Hopkins University Press.

Dillon, Matthew. 2002. *Girls and Women in Classical Greek Religion*. London and New York: Routledge.

Douny, Laurence and Susanna Harris. 2014. "Wrapping and Unwrapping, Concepts and Approaches." In *Wrapping and Unwrapping Material Culture, Archaeological and Anthropological Perspectives*, edited by Laurence Douny and Susanna Harris, 15–40. Walnut Creek: Left Coast Press.

Ekroth, Gunnel. 2003. "Inventing Iphigeneia? On Euripides and the Cultic Construction of Brauron." *Kernos* 16: 59–118.

Freedberg, David. 1989. *The Power of Images: Studies in the History and Theory of Response*. Chicago: University of Chicago Press.

Gell, Alfred. 1993. *Wrapping in Images*. Oxford: Clarendon Press.

Gell, Alfred. 1998. *Art and Agency: An Anthropological Theory*. Oxford: Clarendon Press.

Gleba, Margarita. 2008. "*Auratae Vestes*: Gold Textiles in the Ancient Mediterranean." In *Purpureae Vestes II*, edited by Carmen Alfaro Giner and Lilian Karali, 61–77. Valencia: Universitat de València.

Gleba, Margarita and Ulla Mannering. 2012. *Textiles and Textile Production in Europe from Prehistory to AD 400*. Oxford: Oxbow Books.

Gordon, Richard L. 1979. "The Real and the Imaginary: Production and Religion in the Graeco-Roman World." *Art History* 2.1: 5–34.

Günther, Wolfgang. 1988. "Vieux et inutilisable dans un inventaire inédit de Milet." In *Comptes et inventaires dans la cité grecque*, edited by Denis Knoepfler, 215–37. Geneva: Université de Neuchâtel, Faculté des lettres.

Håland, Evy Johanne. 2004. "Athena's Peplos: Weaving as a Core Female Activity in Ancient and Modern Greece." *Cosmos* 20: 155–82.

Hewitt, Joseph William. 1909. "Major Restrictions on Access to Greek Temples." *TAPA* 40: 83–91.

Jeppesen, Kristian. 2007. "A Fresh Approach to the Problems of the Parthenon Frieze." *Proceedings of the Danish Institute at Athens* 5: 101–72.

Larson Lovén, Lena. 2013. "Female Work and Identity in Roman Textile Production and Trade: A Methodological Discussion." In *Making Textiles in Pre-Roman and Roman Times: People, Places, Identities*, edited by Margarita Gleba and Judith Pázstókai-Szeôke, 109–25. Oxford: Oxbow.

MacLachlan, Bonnie. 1995. "Love, War and the Goddess in First-Century Locri." *The Ancient World* 25–6: 205–23.

Mansfield, John. 1985. *The Robe of Athena and the Panathenaic Peplos*. PhD diss., University of California, Berkeley.

Mitchell, Jon P. 2010. "Performing Statues." In *Religion and Material Culture: The Matter of Belief*, edited by David Morgan, 262–76. New York: Routledge.

Morgan, Janett. 2007. "Women, Religion, and the Home." In *A Companion to Greek Religion*, edited by Daniel Ogden, 297–310. Malden, MA: Blackwell.

Moulhérat, Christophe and Giouli Spantidaki. 2009a. "Cloth from Kastelli Chania." *Arachne* 3: 8–15.

Moulhérat, Christophe and Giouli Spantidaki. 2009b. "Archaeological Textiles from Salamis: A Preliminary Presentation." *Arachne* 3: 16–29.

Neils, Jenifer. 2001. *The Parthenon Frieze*. Cambridge: Cambridge University Press.

Neils, Jenifer. 2008. "Adonia to Thesmophoria: Women and Athenian Festivals." In *Worshipping Women: Ritual and Reality in Classical Athens*, edited by Nikolaos Kaltsas and Alan Shapiro, 242–65. New York: Alexander S. Onassis Public Benefit Foundation.

O'Brien, Joan V. 1993. *The Transformation of Hera: A Study of Ritual, Hero, and the Goddess in the Iliad*. Lanham, MD: Rowman and Littlefield.

Ohly, Dieter. 1953. "Die Göttin und ihre Basis." *AM* 68: 24–50.

Osborne, Robin. 1985. *Demos: The Discovery of Classical Attika*. Cambridge: Cambridge University Press.

Papadimitriou, Ioannis. 1956. "Brauron." *Ergon* 1956: 25–31.

Papadimitriou, Ioannis. 1957. "Brauron." *Ergon* 1957: 20–4.

Peppas-Delmousou, Dina. 1988. "Autour des inventaires de Brauron." In *Comptes et inventaires dans la cité Grecque. Actes du colloque international d'epigraphie tenu á Neuchâtel du 23 au 26 septembre 1986 en l'honneur de Jacques Tréheux*, edited by Denis Knoepfler, 323–46. Geneva: Université de Neuchâtel, Faculté des lettres.

Petrovic, Ivana. 2010. "The Life Story of a Cult Statue as an Allegory: Kallimachos' Hermes Perpheraios." In *Divine Images and Human Imaginations in Ancient Greece and Rome*, edited by Joannis Mylonopoulos, 205–24. Leiden: Brill.

Prückner, Helmut. 1968. *Die Lokrischen Tonreliefs*. Mainz am Rhein: P. von Zabern.

Reeder, Ellen D. 1995. *Pandora: Women in Classical Greece*. Baltimore: Trustees of the Walters Art Gallery in association with Princeton University Press.

Reinach, Théodore. 1899. "Un temple élevé par les femmes de Tanagra." *REG* 12: 53–115.

Robertson, Noel. 1996. "Athena's Shrines and Festivals." In *Worshipping Athena: Panathenaia and Parthenon*, edited by Jenifer Neils, 27–77. Madison: University of Wisconsin Press.

Roesch, P. 1985. "Les femmes et la fortune en Béotie." In *La femme dans le monde Méditerranéen*, edited by Anne-Marie Vérilhac, Claude Vial and Laurence Darmezin, 71–84. Lyon: Maison de l'Orient.

Roller, Duane W. 1989. *Tanagran Studies I: Sources and Documents on Tanagra in Boiotia*. Amsterdam: J. C. Gieben.

Romano, Irene B. 1980. *Early Greek Cult Images*. PhD diss.; Philadelphia: University of Pennsylvania.

64 *Cecilie Brøns*

Rudy, Kathryn M. 2007. "Introduction: Miraculous Textiles in Exempla and Images from the Low Countries." In *Weaving, Veiling, and Dressing: Textiles and Their Metaphors in the Late Middle Ages*, edited by Kathryn M. Rudy and Barbara Baert, 1–36. Turnhout: Brepols.

Sabetai, Victoria. 2008. "Women's Ritual Roles in the Cycle of Life." In *Worshipping Women: Ritual and Reality in Classical Athens*, edited by Nikolaos Kaltsas and Alan Shapiro, 289–333. New York: Onassis Foundation.

Schneider, Jane and Annette B. Weiner. 1991. *Introduction to Cloth and Human Experience*, edited by Jane Schneider and Annette B. Weiner, 1–29. Washington: Smithsonian Institution Press.

Scott, Michael. 2011. "Displaying Lists of What Is (Not) on Display: The Uses of Inventories in Greek Sanctuaries." In *Current Approaches to Religion in Ancient Greece. Papers Presented at a Symposium at the Swedish Institute at Athens, 17–19 April 2008*, edited by Matthew Haysom and Jenny Wallensten, 239–52. Stockholm: Svenska Institutet i Athen.

Sebesta, Judith Lynn. 2002. "Visions of Gleaming Textiles and a Clay Core: Textiles, Greek Women, and Pandora." In *Women's Dress in the Ancient Greek World*, edited by Lloyd Llewellyn-Jones, 125–42. London: Duckworth.

Shipley, Graham. 1987. *A History of Samos 800–188 BC*. Oxford: Clarendon Press.

Simon, Erica. 1983. *Festivals of Attica: An Archaeological Commentary*. Madison: University of Wisconsin Press.

Sourvinou-Inwood, Christiane. 2011. *Athenian Myths and Festivals: Aglauros, Erechtheus, Plynteria, Panathenaia, Dionysia*. Oxford: Oxford University Press.

Spantidaki, Stella and Christophe Moulhérat. 2012. "Greece." In *Textiles and Textile Production in Europe*, edited by Margarita Gleba and Ulla Mannering, 185–202. Oxford: Oxbow Books.

Stamatopoulou, Zoe. 2012. "Weaving Titans for Athena: Euripides and the Panathenaic Peplos (*HEC*. 466–74 and *IT* 218–24)." *Classical Quarterly* 62.1: 72–80.

Vidman, Ladislav. 1970. *Isis und Sarapis bei den Griechen und Römern*. Berlin: De Gruyter.

Vikela, Evgenia. 2008. "The Worship of Artemis in Attica: Cult Places, Rites, Iconography." In *Worshipping Women: Ritual and Reality in Classical Athens*, edited by Nikolaos Kaltsas and Alan Shapiro, 79–105. New York: Alexander S. Onassis Public Benefit Foundation.

Warr, Cordelia. 2010. *Dressing for Heaven: Religious Clothing in Italy, 1215–1545*. Manchester and New York: Manchester University Press.

Weddle, Polly. 2010. *Touching the Gods: Physical Interaction with Cult Statues in the Roman World*. PhD diss., Durham University, Durham, UK.

Whitehead, Amy. 2013. *Religious Statues and Personhood: Testing the Role of Materiality*. London: Bloomsbury Academic.

4 Silent attendants
Terracotta statues and death rituals in Canosa

Tiziana D'Angelo and Maya Muratov

Introduction

In the Classical world, death rituals were a means of healing for both the family of the deceased and the community that suffered the loss of one of their members, and therefore their correct performance was vital to guarantee private as well as public regeneration of the community. Administering some of these rituals was one of the major responsibilities that women had in antiquity, whether that involved mourning or praying for the deceased, taking care of the corpse, or visiting and bringing offerings to the grave. This chapter discusses a unique *corpus* of Hellenistic half-life size terracotta statues of young women from tombs at the Daunian site of Canosa, in south-eastern Italy (Fig. 4.1), in order to elucidate the role that Italic women played within the funerary sphere.[1]

Modern scholarship on the Canosan statues has so far concentrated mostly on technical issues and the history of the collecting of the statues, whereas this chapter aims to adopt a broader approach and shift attention to the ritual function of these artifacts. In the first part of the chapter, we discuss some important aspects of the manufacture of these terracotta statues as well as the archaeological and sociocultural contexts in which they were produced. A proposed study of the statues' iconographic typologies, materials, and technical features leads to a reassessment of their complex role within the funerary process. By placing them within a broader context of South Italian and Mediterranean funerary art, this chapter argues that the terracotta statues found inside some of the Canosan tombs were not, as has always been assumed, grave goods *per se* and that they did not serve to express and celebrate the socioeconomic status of the deceased. Rather, they had a public, ceremonial, and practical function: they represented pubescent girls and were employed as actors in funerary rites, where they served to accompany the cortège and perform some crucial tasks of the death rituals in front of the community. This premise allows us to treat the statues as material evidence reflecting the public roles played by adolescent girls within the context of the social, cultural, and ritual changes that took place in Daunia in the course of the third century BCE.

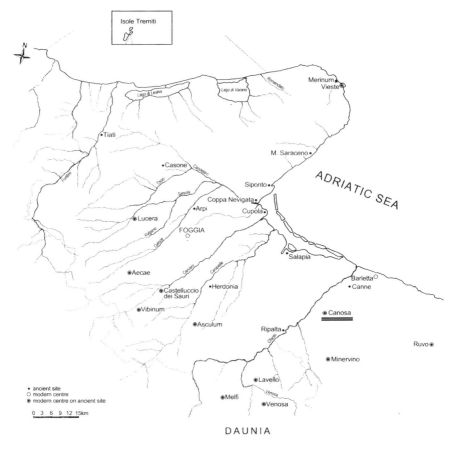

Figure 4.1 Map of Daunia, south-eastern Italy.
Source: After Colivicchi (2011, fig. 7.1).

Technique and iconography

The Apulian town of Canosa became an important economic center, especially after the coming of the Romans into the area in the late fourth century BCE; its privileged geographic position, directly on the future *Via Traiana*, significantly added to its economic growth (Rinuy *et al.* 1978, 142). It has been established that local ceramic workshops produced objects intended exclusively for the funerary realm: red-figure vases, polychrome vases with plastic decoration, and *thymiateria* (incense burners) (Rinuy *et al.* 1978, 141–2; van der Wielen-van Ommeren 1986; van der Wielen-van Ommeren 1988). Currently, about 48 terracotta statues of young women from Canosa are known from public and private collections around the world (Jeammet 2003a, 281–92). The figures range in height from 0.6 m to

Silent attendants 67

about 1 m (see Figs. 4.2–4.5). As some of them have been restored, often inaccurately, in the late eighteenth and nineteenth centuries, we focus here on the figures that are better preserved in order to minimize the possibility of dealing with erroneous much later reconstructions (Jeammet and Nadalini 1997).

In the past 20 years, conservation work on some of the Canosan statues prompted their careful examination, which resulted in a reassessment of their manufacture and the publication of studies that focus on methods of their production (Jeammet and Nadalini 1997; van der Wielen-van Ommeren 1999; Jeammet 2003a; Costello and Klausmeyer 2014). It has been determined that these statues were manufactured by using two techniques: they were mostly hand-modeled, with some mold-made elements (Jeammet 2003a, 258–60; Costello and Klausmeyer 2014). A conical tubular construction built with horizontal superimposed strips of clay served as a base for each statue. Openings for head and arms were left on a tip and on the sides of a cone, respectively (Jeammet 2003a, 259, fig. 1). A rectangular opening in the back of some statues, often understood as a vent, has been shown to have had a different practical use: these must have been assembly windows, and it was through them that separately made head and arms were attached to the bodies (Jeammet 2003a, 258; Costello and Klausmeyer 2014, 379). Besides, since the figures were hollow and always open at the bottom, there simply was no need for a vent. There are, however, some figures that do not have an opening at the back – in which case head and arms must have been attached through the open bottom.

The arms were made out of thin slabs of rolled clay (Costello and Klausmeyer 2014, 380, fig. 4); additional details, such as hands and fingers, were modeled by hand (Jeammet 2003a, 260; Costello and Klausmeyer 2014, 380). The elaborate *chitones* (tunics) and *himatia* (mantles) of the figures were hand-modeled from strips and thin rolls of clay vertically attached to a conical base and then smoothed out and worked with a variety of tools to achieve a continuous surface with pleated effect (Jeammet 2003a, 260; Costello and Klausmeyer 2014, 380, fig. 5). In some cases, certain relief parts of the figures, such as breasts or slightly bent knees, were shaped by the craftsmen by slightly pushing the clay core out from within (Jeammet 2003a, 258; Costello and Klausmeyer 2014, 380). The feet, partially visible underneath the gowns, were also hand-built (Costello and Klausmeyer 2014, 380–1, fig. 8). Necks were made of rolled slabs of clay and connected molded heads to bodies. The heads were the only part of the statues manufactured in bivalve molds, and Jeammet determined that only five molds were used to produce the heads of all existing statues (Jeammet 2003a, 260–1, n. 20, 262). Pupils, lips, other minute details, as well as locks of hair or braids, were modeled by hand and tools and attached prior to firing (Costello and Klausmeyer 2014, 379).

A curious feature of these statues are two or three circular holes about 1.5 cm in diameter cut through in the lower part of a figure prior to firing (see Figs. 4.3–4.5); the usual configuration is one in front and two in the back. This feature – crucial to our interpretation of the statues' function – will be addressed later. After firing, the statues were covered with white kaolin slip and then brightly painted (Costello and Klausmeyer 2014, 380–1); traces of polychromy survive on several

68 *Tiziana D'Angelo and Maya Muratov*

statues (see Fig. 4.5), which would have once looked quite striking (e.g. Malibu, J. Paul Getty Museum, inv. 85.AD.76.3; Basel, Antikenmuseum Basel und Sammlung Ludwig, inv. BS 329; for chemical analysis of remains of paint, Costello and Klausmeyer 2014, 381–3).

First attempts to categorize the figures based on iconographic features such as dress and then to further subdivide them based on hairdo were undertaken by Frederike van der Wielen-van Ommeren (1999). In her influential and to date most complete technical and stylistic study of the Canosan statues, Violaine Jeammet groups the figures based on the type of dress each statue wears (Jeammet 2003a). She then introduces several subgroups that take into consideration specific details of the dress and arrangement of hair, and believes that such criteria might help to distinguish between different workshops and perhaps even single out individual artisans (Jeammet 2003a, 260). The iconographic and stylistic classification proposed by Jeammet is necessary for exploring the issue of workshops and production of the Canosan figures. Our objectives here are different. We are looking into the possible explanations of the statues' functions and are treating them as indicative of the roles undertaken by contemporary women during local funerary rites.

There have also been attempts to interpret the difference in figures' hairstyles and dress as indicative of different age groups (van der Wielen-van Ommeren 1999, 48–53; cf. also Mazzei 1992, 201; Corrente 2015, 461–2). While van der Wielen-van Ommeren identifies the statues wearing only a *chiton* as "young girls" and the ones wearing both *chiton* and *himation* as married women (van der Wielen-van Ommeren 1999, 52–3), our iconographic analysis leads us to identify all of them as unmarried pubescent girls, approximately between the age of 11 and 15. Looking at garments, we notice that none of the statues are veiled, which marks their girlhood status (Kalaitzi 2010, 334; Beaumont 2012, 32). Three main groups with several subgroups are recognized. The first group is comprised of figures wearing only a *chiton* belted just below the chest, with a long *apoptygma* (overfold) (see Figs 4.2–4.4; cf. Jeammet 2003a, 261–7). This outfit, beneath which "budding breasts" are visible, indicates that the statues represent pubescent girls who have reached physical maturity and the ability to bear children. In fact, in Classical Greece adolescent females, i.e. *parthenoi*, were usually represented with developing breasts and wearing only a *chiton* with highly visible overgirding (Lawton 2007, 56; Beaumont 2012, 31–2; see also Lee 2015, 44, 106). This slightly revealing attire alluded to their attractiveness and reflected their liminal status as sexually mature, though still unmarried, women (Lawton 2007, 55–6). Figures in the second group wear a short *himation* over a *chiton*, with the bottom of the *apoptygma* showing underneath (Jeammet 2003a, 267–9). The third group is similar, but the *himation* becomes longer (see Fig. 4.5; cf. Jeammet 2003a, 269–71). While the long *apoptygma* and the lack of veil indicate that we are still dealing with unmarried women, the use of *epiblemata* (overgarments) could denote a different category within female adolescence. The mantle was possibly used to obscure partly the form of the mature female body (Lee 2015, 106) and might point to a special ritual role that pubescent girls took up at some point before marriage. Similar practices are known in Greece in the late fifth and fourth

Silent attendants 69

centuries BCE, when several gradations of age representations can be observed for the *parthenoi* (Beaumont 2012, 37). In particular, artistic evidence shows that the *kanephoroi*, maidens honoured with heading the ritual festival procession, began to sport a special mantle draped over their shoulders and arms (Roccos 2000; Lawton 2007, 55–6; Beaumont 2012, 32–3).

The identification of all the statues as belonging to this special age group, i.e. pubescent unmarried women, is corroborated also by the several types of hairstyles which are known across the various iconographic subgroups. The fact that all the statues have long and uncovered hair confirms, once again, that we are dealing with unmarried women. Those without a *himation* have either hair brushed backwards with wavy locks arranged in the back and on the shoulders (Fig. 4.2), or hair well-combed and tied at the back of the head (Figs. 4.3–4.4). Statues with a

Figure 4.2 Terracotta statue of a maiden, from Canosa.

Source: Naples, Museo Archeologico Nazionale, CS 105. Photo courtesy of Ministero dei Beni e delle Attività Culturali e del Turismo – Soprintendenza per i Beni Archeologici di Napoli.

Figure 4.3 Terracotta statue of a maiden, from Canosa.
Source: Copenhagen, Ny Carlsberg Glyptotek, 422. Photo courtesy of Ny Carlsberg Glyptotek.

himation either sport long hair which falls freely about the head and shoulders, or more often long hair restrained in a braid or arranged in a sleek triangular formation on the back (Fig. 4.5). These hairstyles are common in Greek sculpture and vase painting and have been associated specifically with pubescent girls (Kalaitzi 2010, 334; Beaumont 2012, 30).

The representation of maidens entering the public sphere through ritual activity is particularly significant in a South Italian funerary context, as the transition from girlhood to womanhood might allude to the passage from life to death and rebirth, in line with Pythagorean and Orphic beliefs that were popular in Apulia in the late Classical and Hellenistic periods (Todisco 2006, 32–40). In addition to hairstyle and clothing, we believe that it is crucial to distinguish the figures based on their

Figure 4.4 Terracotta statue of a maiden, from Canosa.
Source: Collection of Cliff Schorer, on long-term loan to the Worcester Art Museum. Photo courtesy of Worcester Art Museum.

gestures. Although it has been recognized that the arms of the Canosan figures are placed in different positions (van der Wielen-van Ommeren 1999; Jeammet 2003a, 257) and their gestures are traditionally and rather parenthetically described as expressing either mourning or prayer, no attempt to separate them based on this criterion had been made. All 48 figures can be divided into four groups. The most common position is that of the raised forearms (Fig. 4.5). Statues of this type are characterized by rather disproportionate hands. This is a very important feature, which will be addressed in detail later in the discussion of local beliefs and funerary iconography. A second group is represented by just a couple of surviving examples: figures extend their hands forward and hold them in front with palms

Figure 4.5 Terracotta statue of a maiden, from Canosa.
Source: Basel, Antikenmuseum Basel und Sammlung Ludwig, BS 330. Photo courtesy of Antikenmuseum Basel und Sammlung Ludwig.

down (Fig. 4.4). A third group is characterized by the arms folded on the chest (Fig. 4.2). The fourth group features one hand raised and touching the chin or a cheek, whereas the other arm is held horizontally across the body (Fig. 4.3). In antiquity, gestures were understood as *schemata*, shared elements of visual expression that could be transferred and used in different ritual contexts (Catoni 2005). They constitute a nonverbal means of communicating and therefore are an important element of social performance (Thomas 1991, 3), the main focus of this chapter.

One of the most distinctive features that characterized the production of funerary terracotta statues in Canosa is that they were not conceived of as individual artifacts, but they seem to have been arranged, used, and deposited in sets of three or four (and consequently six and eight). These statues belong to the same category as the terracotta vessels and figurines that were intentionally and exclusively produced for funerary purposes. Their relatively large size and a particular technical feature – the holes in the bottom – set them aside, however, from the rest of the grave assemblage and lead to a re-evaluation of their function within the archaeological context of the burials.

The statues and their context

The Daunian civilization flourished between the ninth and third centuries BCE in northern Apulia (Fig. 4.1). The structure of the society was based on a delicate balance between the elite, mostly represented by wealthy landowners, and the rest of the community, comprised mainly of peasants (de Juliis 1984, 137–84; Corrente 2012, 272; Lippolis 2012, 307). During the fourth and third centuries BCE, the major Daunian centers, including Canosa, were dominated by clans of aristocrats who exercised power on a local and regional level (de Juliis 1992a, 136–41; Corrente 2012, 271–300; Lippolis 2012, 301–23). These were the groups who most probably commissioned the tombs where the terracotta statues were found.

The history of these tombs has been an uninterrupted sequence of discoveries, losses, and rediscoveries. When the architect Carlo Bonucci, in charge of overseeing the excavations promoted by the *Real Museo Borbonico*, visited the necropolis of Canosa, he described it as "an Italic labyrinth without any other parallel" ("un labirinto italico di cui non si ha finora nessun'altro esempio": Ruggiero 1888, 551); he also drafted a plan which, unfortunately, is now lost (Ruggiero 1888, 551–4; Cassano 1996, 109; Corrente 2005a, 101–4). The tombs were not concentrated in a specific area but were scattered across the urban and extra-urban territory. They were usually placed along major roads connecting the city to its countryside and to other regional centers (Mazzei and Lippolis 1984, 187–90; cf. Lamboley 1982; Cassano and Corrente 1992, 147; de Juliis 1992b, 143–4; Lippolis 2012, 308–9), thereby making the strength and power of the urban elite visible to anyone coming to or leaving from the city. These wealthy underground tombs were cut into the tufa bedrock and were covered with a flat, two-faced, or vaulted ceiling. Many of them had a monumental façade decorated with painted friezes (Tinè Bertocchi 1964, 15–32; Steingräber 2008), and their plan could vary significantly (Mazzei and Lippolis 1984, 190–6; Cassano and Corrente 1992, 145–8). The entrance was preceded by an inclined or stepped *dromos*, a corridor leading directly into a funerary chamber or into a vestibule that gave access to multiple burial chambers. They were built in the late fourth or the third century BCE, and they were in use until the second or first century BCE. Their underground location should not mislead us to believe that these tombs were completely invisible after the funerals: for example, the façade of the Lagrasta II Hypogaeum most probably had two stories, and the upper one would have been visible even after the tomb was backfilled (Cassano 1992, 206–7, 219–20; Cassano 1996, 131).

While there is no doubt that the statues in question come from these aristocratic burials, the information regarding their find spots and original conditions is scanty and uncertain, as most of the tombs were discovered in the eighteenth century and

74   *Tiziana D'Angelo and Maya Muratov*

were not methodically excavated. They were often accidentally unearthed by local landowners, who collected the most precious grave goods before reporting the discovery to the authorities, so that the grave assemblages were sold or dispersed without being properly recorded (Cassano 1996, 108–9). Occasionally, the finds were sketched and documented and were later sent to museums, as occurred in the case of the three Lagrasta tombs (Cassano 1992, 206–24; Milanese 1996, 143–7). Even the information recorded during the excavations, however, often disappeared in the following decades (Macchioro 1911, 159). The actual monuments were sometimes reburied and forgotten until the second half of the twentieth century. The Scocchera B Hypogaeum, which was found in Canosa in 1895, was only partly excavated, and after being backfilled it was thought to be lost for about a century until it was accidentally rediscovered in 1974 (de Juliis 1992d, 231). Something similar happened for the Tomb of the Gold Ornaments, which was unearthed in 1928, then "lost," and finally discovered again in 1971 (Corrente 1992, 337–45). Recent studies manage to shed some light on the archaeological contexts of some of the terracotta statues, which now can be confidently associated with four tombs: the Barbarossa Hypogaeum, the Lagrasta I Hypogaeum, the Scocchera B Hypogaeum, and the Tomb of the Gold Ornaments.

Three or four statues, approximately 1 m. tall, were found in the Barbarossa Hypogaeum in 1828 (Naples, Museo Archeologico Nazionale, inv. 22296, 22246, 22247. Gerhard 1829, 183; Lombardi 1832, 285–9, n. 4; Mazzei 1992, 199–201; Cassano 1996, 150–1; Jeammet 2003a, 278). The tomb contained multiple burials and was in use between the late fourth and the second century BCE. Upon its discovery by Sabino Barbarossa, the finds were distributed among the mayor of Canosa, a judge, and other notable citizens; the female statues appear to have been sent to the Royal Museum of Naples a few years later. Their exact identification, however, is still a subject of discussion (Mazzei 1992, 199–201; Cassano 1996, 150–1; Jeammet 2003a, 278, n. 55).

The Lagrasta I Hypogaeum was discovered in 1843 and archive documents mention a partly restored statue purchased by the Royal Museum of Naples from the canon Basta in 1854 (Milanese 1996, 143–7; Jeammet 2003a, 279, n. 57: according to Jeammet, this statue could be identified with Naples, Museo Archeologico Nazionale, inv. 22296). Eight other statues were found in the Scocchera B Hypogaeum when it was accidentally unearthed in 1895 (Oliver 1968, 19; de Juliis 1992d, 231–7). In a report published a year later, Salvatore Cozzi drafted a list of the objects that were discovered in the tomb, although for most of them he could not specify the exact find spot (Cozzi 1896, 493–4). Among the numerous finds, which included ceramic vessels, glass, jewelry, and terracotta plaques, the largest objects were eight female statues. According to Cozzi's report, they all were 1 m in height and all wore only a *chiton* (Cozzi 1896, 495). Three of them have been identified by Oliver with statues that are now in the collections of the Museo Provinciale in Bari (inv. 455), Musée départemental des Antiquités in Rouen (inv. 1965), and Nationalmuseet in Copenhagen (inv. 4995; Oliver 1968, 16, 19). As Jeammet rightly pointed out, however, the Bari statue, which wears a *himation* over a *chiton*, does not match the description given by Cozzi (Jeammet 2003a, 276–7).

The tomb has been dated between the late third and the first half of the second century BCE (Oliver 1969, 9–16; de Juliis *et al.* 1986, 454). Lastly, three or four female terracotta figures, approximately 0.9 m. tall, were found in the Tomb of the Gold Ornaments, which was excavated in 1928 and can be dated to the late third century BCE (Bartoccini 1935; de Juliis *et al.* 1986, 450–2; Corrente 1992, 337–45). Unfortunately, the grave assemblage was immediately divided into two groups, thus creating confusion as to where each object was originally found. According to Bartoccini's description, the terracotta figures were dressed in a *himation* over a *chiton* with a long *apoptygma* (Bartoccini 1935, 230; de Juliis *et al.* 1986, 446; Corrente 1992, 345; Jeammet 2003a, 277–8). One of the figures has been tentatively identified by Corrente with a statue currently in the collection of the Museo Civico in Canosa (Corrente 1992, 345, n. 58). Jeammet has convincingly argued that a typologically distinctive subgroup comprising four statues (with short *himation*) might be associated with this tomb. These statues, including one from Canosa and one from Bari (traditionally, yet erroneously, associated with the Scocchera B Hypogaeum), perfectly match Bartoccini's description (Jeammet 2003a, 278).

Although these brief and often somewhat ambiguous reports cannot be used to recreate securely archeological contexts for the figures, two patterns become apparent: first, the statues were placed in tombs in sets of three or four (Oliver 1968, 19; Mazzei 1992, 201); second, the statues from each set shared certain iconographic similarities. These important points will become better defined later in the chapter, when the Canosan figures are analyzed within their broader ritual and cultural framework. Even with the particular archaeological contexts of the statues irremediably affected by the unscrupulous practices of the eighteenth- and nineteenth-century excavations, analysis of the available local archaeological and historical data provides enough grounds to venture a reconstruction of a cultic milieu in which these figures were manufactured and used.

Women and funerary rites in South Italy

In the societies of the ancient Mediterranean, women played an integral role in the funerary rites. Their involvement into these rituals in mainland Greece in general and Athens in particular was authorized by the community and therefore must have been a social norm (Stears 1998; Dillon 2002, 268–92; Tsanetou 2007, 4, 7–8). Judging, however, from the Geometric, Archaic, and Classical representations of various stages of mourning and funerals (Garland 2001 [1985], 23–31), gestures of men and women seem to have been standardized, albeit differently from each other, which presupposes specific roles in the ceremonies (Stears 1998, 115). Although it is often assumed that much is known about the roles Athenian women played during funerals, this information is based on a synthesis of scattered sources from rather different time periods, such as Classical tragedies, fourth-century BCE speeches, Byzantine compilations of earlier sources, depictions on Archaic and Classical painted pottery, and actual archaeological evidence (Stears 1998, 113). It is traditionally assumed that women were prominent in the funerary sphere: they dealt with the corpse before and after the *prothesis* (laying out of the dead body), mourned the deceased in a rather conspicuous way, accompanied the funerary cortège while lamenting, and visited the tomb afterwards (Alexiou 1974; Stears 1998, 116–17, 124).

76 *Tiziana D'Angelo and Maya Muratov*

In South Italian contexts, because of a lack of literary evidence (Shepherd 2012, 220), one is forced to rely exclusively on archaeological evidence: wall paintings, funerary stelai, pottery, and terracotta statues, which are the focus of this chapter. Can we speak of a more or less "standardized" set of rites, as was the case in Attica (Stears 1998, 114)? While representations of mourning women rarely occurred in Hellenistic terracotta figurines (Kleiner 1984; Higgins 1986; Uhlenbrock 1990; Graepler 1997; Jeammet 2007; Jeammet 2010a, 124–5), this iconography enjoyed great popularity in contemporary South Italian funerary art, especially tomb painting (Huber 2001, 178–96).

A large number of fourth- and third-century BCE aristocratic tombs from Lucania and Apulia were decorated with funerary processions or *prothesis* scenes (Tinè Bertocchi 1964, 15–19; Pontrandolfo and Rouveret 1992, 48–52; Steingräber 2008, 185–91; Corrente 2012, 294, fig. 22). Adult women were often represented tending to the corpse and lamenting energetically, touching their forehead or beating their chests (e.g. Pontrandolfo and Rouveret 1992, 213, fig. 3, 214, fig. 1; Huber 2001, 187–8), whereas young women were mostly featured in funerary processions. It is especially this latter group that shares strong iconographic similarities with the Canosan statues. Two young women are depicted on the north wall of Tomb 58 from the necropolis of Andriuolo at Paestum, and their facial expressions and gestures clearly indicate mourning (Pontrandolfo and Rouveret 1992, 149, fig. 2, 152, fig. 1). Both of them are wearing a *chiton* with two vertical stripes in the middle, a detail which characterizes the depiction of indigenous women across Southern Italy and which occurs also on several Canosan statues (Fig. 4.5) (Ferruzza-Giacommara 1993, 71, n. 2). As we have seen, this clothing style may refer to adolescent girls. One of the girls has her arms crossed on her chest, as with some of the Canosan statues (Fig. 4.2; see also Paris, Louvre, inv. Cp4311, Cp4312; cf. the wall paintings of Tomb 8 and Tomb 30 from the necropolis of Andriuolo at Paestum. Pontrandolfo and Rouveret 1992, 165, fig. 3, 167, figs. 1–2). The painted decoration of Tomb 113 from the necropolis of Spinazzo at Paestum features two young women on a chariot taking part in a funerary procession (Rouveret and Pontrandolfo 1985, 124). In hairstyle and clothing, they closely resemble the group of Canosan figures that we have identified as pubescent girls (Fig. 4.2; see also Copenhagen, Nationalmuseet, inv. 4995; London, British Museum, inv. 73.8–20.528; Paris, Louvre, inv. Cp4311, Cp4312; Rouen, Musée départemental des Antiquités, inv. 1965; Worcester, Worcester Art Museum, inv. 1927.45): they are wearing a *chiton* girded below the chest with two vertical stripes, and long braids are falling over their shoulders. Last, two young women depicted in Tomb IX from the necropolis of Laghetto wear a *chiton* and lift both arms up toward the sky (Pontrandolfo and Rouveret 1992, 221, figs. 1–2). Their posture and restrained facial expression, with sealed lips, correspond to those of many Canosan statues (e.g. Malibu, J. Paul Getty Museum, inv. 85.AD.76.1–4; Bari, Museo Provinciale, inv. 455; Naples, Museo Archeologico Nazionale, inv. 22246, 22247, 22296).

Moving on to the Canosan tombs, in the painted frieze that decorated the façade of the Sant'Aloia Hypogaeum (Fig. 4.6) and the entrance to one of the funerary chambers of the Cerberus Hypogaeum, a *deductio ad inferos* (journey to the

Figure 4.6 Wall painting depicting a journey to the Underworld, from the façade of the Sant'Aloia Hypogaeum, Canosa, first half of the third century BCE.

Source: Canosa di Puglia, Museo Archeologico di Palazzo Sinesi. Photo courtesy of Ministero dei Beni e delle Attività Culturali e del Turismo – Soprintendenza Archeologica della Puglia.

78   Tiziana D'Angelo and Maya Muratov

Underworld) is represented in the left part of the scene, while two young women are standing to the right (Sant'Aloia Hypogaeum: Tinè Bertocchi 1964, 16–19, figs. 1–2; de Juliis 1992e, 346. Cerberus Hypogaeum: de Juliis 1992f, 348–9; Steingräber 2008, 189–90, fig. 11). These two figures, which have been rightly interpreted as mourning women and possibly members of the deceased's family (de Juliis 1992e, 346; de Juliis 1992f, 348; cf. van der Wielen-van Ommeren 1999, 50), are remarkably similar to some of the terracotta statues (Fig. 4.5): they are wearing a *himation* over a *chiton* and their hair is parted in the middle and seems to be tied in the back; both features are shared by the Canosan statues and indicate that wearers are unmarried adolescent maidens. The attention to iconographic details such as clothing, hairstyle, and postures suggests a degree of realistic accuracy (cf. Corrente 2003, 133).

These examples show that adolescent unmarried women played a crucial and well-defined role in the performance of funerary rituals in South Italy. This is especially important because death rites in Classical antiquity were associated primarily with adult women (Stears 1998). While they were usually not in charge of tending to a dead body, pubescent girls appear to have been essential during the funerary procession, where they engaged in prayers and controlled manifestations of grief. Their social and biological status as women who have not yet experienced marriage and childbirth made them incapable of ritual pollution, but thanks to their liminal condition they were suitable to mark the deceased's transition from life to death and then rebirth, thus guaranteeing them a safe journey from the world of the living to the Underworld.

Bridging two worlds

Scholars have traditionally identified the Canosan terracotta statues either as mourners or *orantes*, that is, praying women (de Juliis *et al.* 1986, 454; Ferruzza-Giacommara 1993, 71; Jeammet 2003a; Jeammet 2010b, 222; cf. van der Wielen-van Ommeren 1999).[2] Our analysis of their gestures and facial expressions, however, reveals that it is misleading to introduce such a sharp distinction. The Canosan figures are consistently represented in a tidy state, with no indication of uncontrolled or emotionally exhausting wailing. None of them strikes her head, rends her hair, or beats her chest, all of which were common ways of representing lamenting women in Mediterranean art (Alexiou 1974; Stears 1998, 13–127; Dillon 2002, 276–82). The only example that has one hand on her head is unpublished, and its present whereabouts are unknown. It survives only in a photograph, but the arm in question is the result of an incorrect restoration. It was supposed to be half-stretched upwards (Jeammet 2003a, 266, fig. 6; 284, nos. 13–14). The figures' hair is not disheveled or falling over their faces and their mouths are not open to suggest that they are performing a lamentation. With this can be compared a fourth-century BCE terracotta statue of similar size from Tanagra, which has her mouth open in an attitude of lamentation (Paris, Louvre, inv. MNB 1008; Jeammet 2010a, 124, no. 92). On the one hand, this behavior is appropriate to restrained and self-controlled girls of marriageable age (Kalaitzi 2010, 334). On the other hand,

Silent attendants 79

it is in line with contemporary Orphic and Pythagorean doctrines popular in Magna Graecia, which prohibited weeping, lamenting, and similar behavior during funerals (Iamb. *VP* 234; Todisco 2006, 40). The emphasis is almost entirely placed on the representation of the hands, and this particular iconographic element can potentially clarify the function of these statues.

As has been already discussed, the Canosan figures could be divided into four main groups based on the position of the arms. In many exemplars (Fig. 4.5), the hands are also slightly disproportionate in size (see also Bari, Museo Provinciale, inv. 455; Basel, Antikenmuseum Basel und Sammlung Ludwig, inv. BS 329; San Antonio, San Antonio Museum of Art, inv. 95.18.2; Malibu, J. Paul Getty Museum, inv. 85.AD.76.1-4). This feature should not be dismissed, and it cannot be explained exclusively, or at all, as the result of technical difficulties or incompetence of the artisans. Interestingly, while it does not occur in Hellenistic figurines from South Italy (Graepler 1997, 198–226; Graepler 2010, 218–19; Lippolis 2010, 216–17), it is observed in the female figurines attached to some of the polychrome Canosan *askoi* (Mazzei and Lippolis 1984, 209, fig. 250; van der Wielen-van Ommeren 1986, 222–3, figs. 5 and 7; Ferruzza-Giacommara 1993, 80, fig. 11; de Juliis 1997, 142, no. 162; Corrente 2003, 119, fig. 68, 121, fig. 70). In fact, oversized hands appear to belong to the Daunian artistic tradition and should be directly associated with the funerary sphere. Thousands of anthropomorphic funerary stelai, dated to the Archaic period, were found in Daunian sites (de Juliis 1984, 153–5; Nava 1992, 131–5; D'Ercole 2000, 327–49; Nava, ed. 2011). The stelai were decorated on all four sides with incisions and low reliefs, and the only parts of the body to be consistently emphasized were the hands. The Daunian *ollae*, funerary vessels which became particularly popular in the late fourth century BCE, were characterized by hand protomes, a curious iconographic feature that seems to continue this local tradition (de Juliis 1991; van der Wielen-van Ommeren 1992, 472, no. 27; 523, fig. 4). This evidence confirms the ritual importance that was attributed to hands in Daunian funerary rituals, and it leads us to argue that the unusual size of the hands of most Canosan statues served as a visual device to express in an immediate and straightforward way the specific ritual action that the figures were engaging in.

The most common ancient *schemata* associated with mourning and lamentation practices, e.g. one arm brought to the head (Catoni 2005, 182–7), are not adopted for the Canosan statues. The figures with arms crossed on the chest (Fig. 4.2; see also Paris, Louvre, inv. Cp4311, Cp4312) and those with the right hand to the chin and the left arm folded on the waist (Fig. 4.3) are the only ones to be immediately recognizable as mourners, as these gestures unequivocally convey sorrow and grief (see also Worcester, Worcester Art Museum, inv. 1927.45. Copenhagen, Ny Carlsberg Glyptotek, H.I.N. 422. Paris, Petit Palais, inv. Dut. 198 A; cf. the small figurine that decorates a globular *askos* from Canosa: London, British Museum, inv. D 181). These, however, represent only a relatively small portion of the overall number of surviving statues. The most popular iconographic type shows a woman lifting both arms in the air and turning the palms upwards (Fig. 4.5). We argue that this *schema*, which was also adopted for some of the small figurines on the *askoi*

80 *Tiziana D'Angelo and Maya Muratov*

and which has been interpreted as a gesture of lamentation (Jeammet 2003a, 261; cf. van der Wielen-van Ommeren 1999, 52–3), is only indirectly connected with the funerary sphere. It is a typical gesture of praying, and more specifically it refers to the "upwards" prayers, i.e. the prayers to invoke the ouranic gods.

In Greek religion, for this type of prayer, one had to stand up with arms raised toward the sky or to stretch one arm forwards (Furley 2010, 127–8). Literary evidence also indicates that in Classical Greece it was mostly women who prayed to the gods with both arms lifted toward the sky (Aesch. *Prom.* 1002–6; Catoni 2005, 181–2). In the context of ancestor-cult or in invocations to the chthonic gods, one might stretch one hand out, with the palm directed down into the earth (Felton 2010, 90).[3] This gesture, which is apotropaic in nature, characterizes a small group of Canosan statues that has so far puzzled scholars and that includes a statue from the Ny Carlsberg Glyptotek in Copenhagen (H.I.N. 419) and one recently acquired by a private collector in the United States and currently on long-term loan to the Worcester Art Museum (Fig. 4.4). While both statues are partly damaged, it is clear that the arms were half-stretched downwards and that at least one was also stretched forward. The statue from the private collection also has the right hand with the palm turned down, toward the ground.

We interpret these figures as women invoking the dead or chthonic deities, i.e. Hades, Demeter, and Persephone, who were traditionally seen as representing death and renewal. In Greek religion, Demeter played an important role as protector of the dead (Simon 1969, 91). These deities gained increasing importance in Canosa during the third and second centuries BCE, as shown by a growing interest in funerary iconography related to the Underworld (Corrente 2003, 117–24; Colivicchi 2011, 113–14; Corrente 2015; see also Lippolis 1995). The painted decoration on the Catarinella *askos*, a third-century BCE Canosan vase found at Lavello/*Forentum*, features a funerary ceremony unfolding between two large female heads surrounded by funerary and ouranic symbols, which have been interpreted as allusions to the worlds of the living and of the dead (Bottini and Tagliente 1990, 220–36; see also van der Wielen-van Ommeren 1999, 51; Di Fazio 2009, 205–14).

The production of bottomless funerary vessels (Rossi and van der Wielen-van Ommeren 1983, 112; van der Wielen-van Ommeren 1992, 480–1, no. 76; cf. also Giuliani 1999, 43–4), mainly *askoi*, kraters, and *loutrophoroi* (vessels with an elongated neck and two handles used in ritual ceremonies), suggests that libations were also performed directly onto the ground, possibly in order to establish a connection with the deceased and the gods below. In addition, recent studies on third-century BCE Canosan elite burials have pointed to evidence of some rites of purification of the tomb that were celebrated following semi-cremation of the deceased (de Juliis 1992c, 149; Corrente 2003, 109–10). In this case, *askoi* and amphorae containing wine or water were possibly used to put out the fire of the pyre and were then deposited at the entrance to the funerary chambers.

In a funerary context, invoking the ouranic and chthonic gods during the *ekphora* (funeral procession) or in the course of libation and sacrifice rituals would have been a necessary procedure in order to guarantee the safe transition of the deceased

Silent attendants 81

from the world of the living to the Underworld. As pointed out by Felton, "ceremonies of worship for ouranic and chthonic deities reflected the contrasts of light and dark, living and dead, above and below the earth" (Felton 2010, 90). The gods were not omnipresent; in fact, they could not be at several places at the same time, and individuals and communities had to compete for their attention (Burkert 1985, 74; Chaniotis 2009, 199–200). Reassurance that the gods were attentive and inclined to bestow their blessings was particularly important at times when a community was grieving for the passage of one of their own to the Underworld. There were numerous ways to draw gods to a particular locale, such as a tomb. Dressing up, gathering sacrificial animals, preparing a feast, performing hymns, all of these were aimed at inviting the gods to be present. Additional appeals that might have been considered more "tangible" from the gods' point of view were the smells of wine during libations and of burning incense (Chaniotis 2009, 200–1). Furthermore, invocations and prayers were thought to be highly effective and could be performed not only at the burial site but also during the *ekphora*. Thus, we propose that the Canosan statues, with their gestures, were meant to attract the attention of the gods and to bridge and at the same time sever the ties between the world of the living and that of the dead, which was the ultimate purpose of any funerary ceremony.

Funerary "drama"

Analysis of the iconographic features of the statues prompted us to reconsider their function in connection with rituals carried out at the tomb. We also suggest that their participation in the funerary rites might extend to the public procession that led toward the grave. In this regard, it is necessary to revisit that particular technical feature of the Canosan statues – the small holes (usually three) consistently pierced in the hems of their *chitones* (Figs 4.3–4.5). Certainly not decorative, these perforations must have served some practical purpose. Interestingly, this feature has either been generally ignored by scholarship or was parenthetically explained as a possible device through which the statues were fastened to a base of some sort (van der Wielen-van Ommeren 1999, 45), perhaps during transportation or during funerary processions (Costello and Klausmeyer 2014, 379; Dodson and Jeammet 2014, 19). The latter explanation is compelling, and we would like to explore the implications that this technical detail adds to our understanding of the function and meaning of these figures, which were, we would argue, an integral part of the funerary cortège.

Processions or ritual movements of a quantity of people from one particular locale to another, often along specifically designated paths, were rather ubiquitous in the Greek world from at least the Late Bronze Age onwards (True *et al.* 2004; Weilhartner 2013; see also Kavoulaki 1999, 296, n. 16). The procession usually formed part of a greater ritual (Mylonopoulos 2006, 103–4) and was an essential component of one of the major *rites de passage*, i.e. funerals (Kavoulaki 2005; Kavoulaki 2011, 135–6). In addition to providing some connectivity between an *oikos* (left by the deceased) and a tomb (which from now on would become the

82   *Tiziana D'Angelo and Maya Muratov*

focal point where one would go to communicate with his/her soul), a funerary procession was also a performance of sorts, "in front of the eyes of a beholder, be that self, an invisible supernatural entity, or a human collectivity" (Kavoulaki 1999, 294; on processions as connectors of spaces, see Mylonopoulos 2006, 103–9).

Recent scholarship has shown that while aspects of theatricality have always been present in ancient Mediterranean societies (Chaniotis 1997; Kavoulaki 1999; Chaniotis 2006; Pilz 2011; Chaniotis 2013), they reached their peak in the Hellenistic period and that the Hellenistic world had in fact become a "society of 'onlookers'" (Chaniotis 1997, 223–4, 252). Funerary processions, often regarded as performances by the ancients themselves, were purposefully designed cultural paradigms with their own regulations, with practically no room left for "the spontaneity of the participants" (Chaniotis 1997, 246; Chaniotis 2013, 34–5). We submit that the Canosan figures in fact served as actors – participants in the drama of the *ekphora*.

Probably attached to wheeled platforms, they actually moved along with human participants. These platforms might have been drawn by donkeys or mules, but they also could have been light enough to be pulled by humans (for numerous examples of statues often transported in various processions: see Broder 2008, with literature). To corroborate this hypothesis, references could be made to some iconographic and contextual parallels from earlier periods. A curious representation on both sides of a ninth-century BCE *pithos* (storage container) from Crete depicts a female figure (usually interpreted as a representation of *Pothnia Theron*, "Mistress of the Animals") on a small wheeled platform. That "device" has been interpreted either as an abbreviated image of a chariot (Coldstream 1984, 97) or as visual indication that the goddess, presiding over "the creatures of the air and sea, and over the fruits of the earth" (Coldstream 1984, 95; Jeammet 2003b, 33), has the ability to bring on change of seasons (for more in depth discussion of this iconography, see Jeammet 2003b, 32–3). Regardless of this figure's identity, such early visual reference to a personage (perhaps even a statue?) placed on a wheeled platform is of great importance here. Furthermore, there exist other representations of figures (most probably living humans, not statues) on wheeled moving carts taking part in an *ekphora* (e.g. an Attic Late Geometric amphora, attributed to the Dipylon Painter, *c.* 750 BCE, Athens, National Archaeological Museum, inv. 803). A seventh-century BCE Attic terracotta model from a burial at Vari (Fig. 4.7), where a bier surrounded by mourners stands on a four-wheeled cart, perhaps provides the closest visual analogy to our understanding of a possible use of the statues in processions. We do not suggest that the Canosan figures were placed on a cart next to or around a body, as in these examples. They could have been fastened to either small individual platforms or larger ones that could accommodate several statues (Fig. 4.8). The Canosan figures had to be easily transported to a burial site and then wheeled through a *dromos* into a tomb, where the funerary "drama" continued – with libations, funerary banquet, and purification rites (on these rites, see Fabbri *et al.* 2000–1; Corrente 2003, 109–10; Corrente 2005b, 71–2).

Figure 4.7 Terracotta group depicting an *ekphora*, from a burial in Vari, first half of the seventh century BCE, Athens, National Archaeological Museum, 26747.

Source: After Kurtz and Boardman (1971, 47, fig. 16).

Figure 4.8 Reconstruction drawing of a set of Canosan terracotta statues on a wheeled platform.

Drawing by Aleksandra Man'kovskaya.

84   Tiziana D'Angelo and Maya Muratov

Between Hellenization and Romanization:
The statues as ritual attendants

This interpretation is in line with the cultural and ritual changes which were introduced in Daunia from the early third century BCE (Corrente 2003, 94–124; Colivicchi 2011; Corrente 2012, 294; Lippolis 2012, 305–7), when the Romans began to gain political and military control over the Greek and native populations in Southeast Italy. The archaeological and artistic evidence from Daunia demonstrates that this period was marked by the development of a new ritual language more focused on funerary and eschatological themes (Corrente 2003, 117–23; Colivicchi 2011, 113–15). Red-figure pottery decorated with Greek mythological scenes rapidly disappeared from the Daunian tombs and was replaced with new classes of materials, largely inspired by the local tradition. These included polychrome pottery with plastic and relief decoration, terracotta figurines, tomb paintings, and reliefs (Colivicchi 2011, 113–14). The hypogaea built in Canosa during the second half of the fourth century BCE continued to be used throughout the Hellenistic period, thus showing that the ruling class remained essentially unchanged (Mazzei and Lippolis 1984, 191; Torelli 1999, 107; Lippolis 2012). The political and social circumstances, however, required the local elites to develop new strategies of self-representation (Colivicchi 2011, 121). The production of large terracotta statues should be understood as part of this broader local phenomenon.

Thus far, scholars have looked at these statues as grave goods, objects that were dedicated to the deceased and deposited inside the tombs as ritual offerings. To a certain extent, they have been considered simply as oversized terracotta figurines, thus having a similar ritual function as those grave goods (Corrente 2003, 131–3; Jeammet 2010b, 222). Terracotta figurines spread in South Italy from the second half of the fourth century BCE to the end of the third. They come mostly from the Greek *poleis* of Tarentum, Naples, and Syracuse, where they were dedicated in votive and especially funerary contexts (Graepler 1997; Lippolis 2001; 2005; Graepler 2010; Lippolis 2010). Their iconographies developed through time and comprise deities, dancers, maenads, and nude or veiled women. This body of evidence, however, does not include praying or mourning female figures (only one example has been found in Hypogaeum 5 in via Settembrini, a second-century BCE tomb in Canosa, but the arms are missing, so that her identification as a praying/mourning figure is not certain: Corrente 2003, 132–3). The majority of the Apulian statuettes were found in graves of children or adolescents, who died prematurely before reaching adulthood. It has also been argued that these grave goods were gender specific, as most of them were deposited in female burials (Graepler 1997, 237–42; Graepler 2010, 219). While a similar hypothesis has been proposed for the Canosan figures (Corrente 2003, 132–3; Jeammet 2003a, 280), it finds no confirmation in the archaeological and archival evidence available: the larger statues might have derived from Tarentine prototypes, but their ritual function was certainly different from that of the Greek figurines.

Both the *askoi* decorated with mourning/praying female figurines and the larger figures were introduced in Canosan tombs to replace the large red-figure kraters

Silent attendants   85

of Greek tradition. The *askoi* did not serve as grave goods but were part of the ritual equipment and were used for libations, funerary banquets, and purification rituals (Fabbri *et al.* 2000–1; Corrente 2003, 109–10, 134–5; Fabbri and Osanna 2005; Colivicchi 2011, 117). We propose that the larger statues were used in similar contexts. They moved in funerary processions and then were present during the rituals carried out in front of the tomb. It is quite possible that they were considered to be participants in these rituals. This implies that the statues were not related to the gender of the deceased, as has often been assumed, but that they simply refer to funerary practices that were traditionally administered by pre-adult women. Thus, we argue that their role was not passive (grave offering) but active in that they served to accompany women during various stages of the funerary ceremony. Our interpretation turns these figures from ritual objects into ritual agents whose presence and role are crucial for the performance of the death rituals. At the end of the funeral, they were left inside the tomb along with the rest of the ritual equipment. Since the tombs were periodically reopened to host new depositions, a given set of statues might have also been reused for multiple funerary ceremonies. While local women acted as "temporary" mourners during the ceremony, the statues could function as "permanent" attendants. In fact, rather than simply mourning the deceased perpetually, we suggest that the statues, used in procession as well as in the funerary chamber, actively contributed to maintaining the connection between the living and the dead, even after the tomb was sealed. After all, in Classical antiquity the cult of the dead was based on the belief that the dead remained present at the grave and could watch over the living. At the same time, the visits performed by relatives to the gravesite were meant to reinstate the connection with the deceased (Felton 2010, 88).

Why did it become necessary for the Canosan elites to incorporate these terracotta attendants into their death rituals? And what does this new practice reveal about the role played by young women in the indigenous societies of Apulia? Although lack of reliable archaeological documentation for several of the Canosan tombs excavated in the nineteenth century prevents us from drawing any conclusive inference, two key points deserve further analysis: first, these figures were meant to accompany women during the funerary processions and the commemoration of the deceased; second, when compared with earlier or contemporaneous representations of female mourners in South Italy and Greece, their gestures appear far more restrained, bearing no sign of wailing or lamentation. This might indicate a concern with limiting or regulating the involvement of women in the funerary ceremony, with possible connections with Orphic or Pythagorean rituals. Lamenting women were dangerous when "out of hand," but they were still essential to the funerary rites.

Ever since the sixth century BCE, funerary legislation in Greece imposed restrictions on the participation and behavior of women during funerals. In the fifth century BCE, on the island of Keos, the deceased had to be carried to the burial site in silence and no woman was allowed to participate in the *ekphora* (Dillon 2002, 272–3). These regulations increased in the course of the fourth century BCE under Demetrios of Phaleron, when the figure of the *gynaikonomos*, whose main concern

86 *Tiziana D'Angelo and Maya Muratov*

was of overseeing the behavior of women at funerals and religious festivals, was introduced (Dillon 2002, 290–1). These regulations are attested and confirmed by a change in iconography that led to the practical disappearance of mourning women in art (Dillon 2002, 288). The influence of these Greek practices in Italy during the Republican period is confirmed by Cicero (*Laws* 2.23.59; 2.24.60), who claims that the Roman funerary legislation was modeled on the Solonian one and that women were not allowed to engage in loud and violent lamentation.

Considering the strong cultural influence that Tarentum and the Macedonian world had on Canosa in the course of the fourth century BCE and that the city became a *civitas foederata* in 318 BCE (Livy 9.20.4; 9.20.7–8; Torelli 1995, 141–58; Torelli 1999, 89–118; see also Marchi 2008, 269–70; Fronda 2010, 13–37), it is possible that similar regulations were introduced there as well, perhaps as part of the radical changes in the funerary ritual that are documented in the early third century BCE. During this transitional phase the statues might have served both to limit the presence of women to what was strictly necessary and at the same time to provide an appropriate model of how women attending the funerals should behave. This, however, remains only a hypothesis, as the archaeological evidence from the Canosan tombs is at the moment too fragmentary to allow for a reconstruction of these details of the funeral.

Nonetheless, it is clear that the terracotta statues represented a ritual "experiment" which lasted for about two generations and that their production gradually ended without spreading to other sites in Daunia. Funerary traditions tended to be conservative in the ancient world, but the late third and second centuries BCE in Canosa witnessed major changes in the urban planning of the city, burial customs, and forms of cult. On the one hand, the composition of the grave assemblages and the sculptural and painted decoration of the Daunian tombs testify to a development of new funerary behavior and a gradual shift in the models of self-representation employed by the local elites (Colivicchi 2011, 122–5). On the other hand, the architecture of the Temple of San Leucio reflects the adoption of exclusively Roman cultural models (Torelli 1999, 108–9). These changes have been associated with the flourishing of philo-Roman aristocracy in Canosa and the development of the Roman ideal of *urbanitas* in Southern Italy after the Hannibalic War (Torelli 1999, 107–8; Fronda 2010, 95–9; Colivicchi 2011, 123–7). The disappearance of the large terracotta statues from the Canosan tombs should be considered within this historical, cultural, and ritual process of Romanization of Daunia.

Conclusion

In conclusion, the Canosan terracotta figures offer precious insights into the local funerary traditions and allow us to reconstruct some of the roles played by indigenous young women of South Italy in the administration of death rituals. The analysis of the archaeological context of these statues and of their technical and iconographic features has led to a reassessment of their meaning and ritual function and has shed light on their role as active participants in the funeral. Their production, which lasted for about two generations, should be understood as part of the ritual changes introduced in Daunia in the early third century BCE. Unlike Greek terracotta figurines, these larger statues were used as proper ritual equipment during various stages of the funerary process: we argued that they were wheeled in procession through the city and to the tomb, where they served as attendants in the mourning rituals. Their clothing and hairstyles identify them as pubescent girls. Allusions to age group and initiation rituals within a funerary context were known in South Italy and could be linked to the liminal status of the deceased and the idea of death as a rite of passage within the cycle of life-death-rebirth. The statues' facial expressions betray controlled grief, while postures and gestures only marginally refer to practices of lamentation. The comparison with earlier and contemporaneous depictions of women in Greek and South Italian funerary art leads us to suggest that the majority of the statues are shown as praying, as though they were in charge of propitiating the ouranic or chthonic gods. Thus, we propose that their use was primarily connected with the performance of libations or purification rituals in honor of the dead, which were usually carried out by female professional mourners or family members of the deceased in the *dromos* or the tomb's vestibule. At the end of the ceremony, the statues were left inside the tomb, where they served to maintain a connection between the living and the dead and were possibly reused for later ceremonies.

The cultural or social reasons behind the use of these figures are not entirely clear. One possibility is that their function extended beyond the funeral. During the funeral they served as attendants to the real mourners, whereas after the ceremony they turned into perpetual attendants of the deceased. It remains uncertain whether their use was also meant to limit an unnecessary presence of women during part of the funerary ceremony, in line with laws that were being passed at the time both in Greece and Italy. If their function was so important from a social and religious point of view, why did they disappear from the Canosan tombs within a century? We suggest that this was connected with major cultural and ritual changes introduced in the city as a result of the accelerating process of Romanization of Daunia in the late third and second centuries BCE. The use of these "silent attendants" within the funerary ceremonies of the Canosan elites provides an accurate reflection of the ritual behavior of young women in Hellenistic Daunia and of their essential role in strengthening the identity and social cohesion of the local community.

Notes

1 We are very grateful to Lisa Maurizio, Matthew Dillon, and Esther Eidinow for a terrific opportunity to present this research in its initial stage at a conference at Bates College in 2014. Various colleagues at the conference contributed to a fruitful discussion, and Professor M. Harari read and provided insightful comments on a later draft. We would also like to thank the Worcester Art Museum, and especially Dr. Paula Artal-Isbrand, for organizing in 2013 an exhibit and a symposium dedicated exclusively to the Canosan statues, "*Orantes*: Ancient Statues from South Italy." That was a wonderful occasion for Tiziana D'Angelo to share the results of her research on the archaeological and cultural context of the Canosan statues.

88 *Tiziana D'Angelo and Maya Muratov*

2 In a symposium held at the Worcester Art Museum on 25 October 2013, V. Jeammet discussed this particular question once more in a presentation titled: "Female statues of Canosa: *Orants* or mourners?" While she did not reach a definitive answer to this complex problem, she pointed out the strong allusions that these statues make to mourning practices. A partly different interpretation was proposed by van der Wielen-van Ommeren (1999), who argued that the statues should be identified as mourners, offerers, and dancers.
3 Prayer or invocation to the chthonic deities is possibly illustrated on one side of the Hagia Triada sarcophagus: Preziosi and Hitchcock 1999, 179, fig. 118.

Works consulted

Alexiou, Margaret. 1974. *The Ritual Lament in Greek Tradition.* Cambridge: Cambridge University Press.

Bartoccini, Renato. 1935. "La Tomba degli Ori di Canosa." *Japigia* 6: 225–62.

Beaumont, Leslie A. 2012. *Childhood in Ancient Athens: Iconography and Social History.* London and New York: Routledge.

Bottini, Angelo, and Marcello Tagliente. 1990. "Due casi di acculturazione del mondo indigeno della Basilicata." *Parola del Passato* 45: 206–31.

Broder, Philipe-Alexandre. 2008. "La manipulation des images dans les processions en Grèce ancienne." In *Image et Religion dans l'Antiquité Gréco-Romaine*, edited by Sylvia Etienne, Dominique Jaillard, Natacha Lubtchansky, and Claude Pouzadoux, 121–34. Collection du Centre Jean Bérard, 28. Naples: Le Centre Jean Bérard.

Burkert, Walter. 1985. *Greek Religion*, translated by John Raffan. Cambridge, MA: Harvard University Press.

Cassano, Raffaella. 1992. "Ipogei Lagrasta." In Cassano, ed. 1992, 203–24.

———. Ed. 1992. *Principi, imperatori, vescovi. Duemila anni di storia a Canosa.* Venice: Marsilio.

———. 1996. "Ruvo, Canosa e Egnazia negli scavi dell'Ottocento." In *I Greci in Occidente. La Magna Grecia nelle collezioni del Museo Archeologico di Napoli*, edited by Silvia Cassani, 108–13. Naples: Electa.

———, and Marisa Corrente. 1992. "La necropoli." In Cassano, ed. 1992, 145–8.

Catoni, Maria Luisa. 2005. *Schemata. Comunicazione non verbale nella Grecia antica.* Pisa: Edizioni della Normale.

Chaniotis, Angelos. 1997. "Theatricality Beyond the Theater: Staging Public Life in the Hellenistic World." In *De la scène aux gradins. Théâtre et representations dramatiques après Alexandre le Grand*, edited by Brigitte Le Guen, 219–60. Pallas 47. Toulouse: Presses Universitaires du Mirail.

———. 2006. "Rituals between Norms and Emotions: Rituals as Shared Experience and Memory." In *Ritual and Communication in the Graeco-Roman World*, edited by Eftychia Stavrianopoulou, 211–38. Kernos, Supplément 16. Liège: Centre International d'Étude de la Religion Grecque Antique.

———. 2009. "Acclamation as a Form of Religious Communication." In *Die Religion des Imperium Romanum: Koine und Konfrontationen*, edited by Hubert Cancik and Jorg Rupke, 199–218. Tübingen: Mohr Siebeck.

———. 2013. "Processions in Hellenistic Cities: Contemporary Discourses and Ritual Dynamics." In *Cults, Creeds and Identities in the Greek City after the Classical Age*, edited by Richard Alston, Onno M. van Nijf, and Christina G. Williamson, 21–48. Leuven: Peeters.

Coldstream, J. Nicholas. 1984. "A Protogeometric Nature Goddess from Knossos." *BICS* 31: 93–104.

Colivicchi, Fabio. 2011. "The Long Good-Bye: The Local Élites of Daunia between Continuity and Change (3rd–1st c. BCE)." In *Local Cultures of South Italy and Sicily in the Late Republican Period: Between Hellenism and Rome*, edited by Fabio Colivicchi, 112–37. JRA Supplementary Series 83. Portsmouth: Journal of Roman Archaeology.

Corrente, Marisa. 1992. "La Tomba degli Ori." In Cassano, ed. 1992, 337–45.

———. 2003. *Canusium. L'Ipogeo dei Serpenti Piumati.* Canosa di Puglia: Serimed.

———. 2005a. "L'attività di Bonucci a Canosa." In *Magna Graecia: archeologia di un sapere,* edited by Salvatore Settis and Maria Cecilia Parra, 101–7. Milan: Electa.

———. 2005b. "Produzione e circolazione della ceramica a figure rosse a Canosa e nel territorio: i dati delle scoperte." In *La céramique apulienne. Bilan et perspectives,* Actes de la Table Ronde organisée par l'École française de Rome en collaboration avec la Soprintendenza per i Beni Archeologici della Puglia et le Centre Jean Bérard de Naples (Naples, 30 November–2 December, 2000), edited by Martine Denoyelle, Enzo Lippolis, Marina Mazzei, and Claude Pouzadoux, 59–76. Naples: Le Centre Jean Bérard.

———. 2012. "Nascita e sviluppo dell'aristocrazia daunia." *Scienze dell'Antichità* 18: 271–300.

———. 2015. "*Descensus ad inferos*: Taming (Easily) the Monsters in the Daunian Pictorial Tradition: The Exorcism of the Underworld and the Representation of Opposite Boundaries." *Academic Journal of Interdisciplinary Studies* 4.1: 457–68.

Costello, Susan D., and Paul Klausmeyer. 2014. "A Re-United Pair: The Conservation, Technical Study, and Ethical Decision Involved in Exhibiting Two Terracotta Orante From Canosa." *Studies in Conservation* 59.6: 322–90.

Cozzi, Salvatore. 1896. "Canosa di Puglia." *Notizie degli scavi di antichità* 1896: 491–5.

De Juliis, Ettore M. 1984. "L'età del Ferro." In *La Daunia antica dalla preistoria all'altomedioevo,* edited by Marina Mazzei, 137–84. Milan: Electa.

———. 1991. "L'olla daunia con labbro ad imbuto: origine, forma e sviluppo." *Archeologia Classica* 43: 893–913.

———. 1992a. "L'apogeo dei principes." In Cassano, ed. 1992, 136–42.

———. 1992b. "L'assetto urbano." In Cassano, ed. 1992, 143–4.

———. 1992c. "Alcuni aspetti del rituale funerario." In Cassano, ed. 1992, 149.

———. 1992d. "Ipogeo Scocchera B." In Cassano, ed. 1992, 231–7.

———. 1992e. "Ipogeo di Sant'Aloia." In Cassano, ed. 1992, 346–7.

———. 1992f. "Ipogeo del Cerbero." In Cassano, ed. 1992, 348–9.

———. 1997. *Mille anni di ceramica in Puglia.* Bari: Edipuglia.

———, Alessio Arcangelo, and Maurizio Di Puolo. 1986. *Les Ors hellénistiques de Tarente.* Milan: Arnoldo Mondadori.

D'Ercole, Maria Cecilia. 2000. "Immagini dell'Adriatico arcaico. Su alcuni temi iconografici delle stele daunie." *Ostraka* 9: 327–49.

Di Fazio, Massimiliano. 2009. "Morte e pianto rituale. Il caso dell'askos "Catarinella"." In *Icone del mondo antico. Un seminario di storia delle immagini,* edited by Maurizio Harari, Silvia Paltineri, and Mirella T. A. Robino, 205–14. Rome: «L'Erma» di Bretschneider.

Dillon, Matthew. 2002. *Girls and Women in Classical Greek Religion.* London and New York: Routledge.

Dodson, Kari, and Violaine Jeammet. 2014. "Symposium Report: Clay Statues from Canosa." *Newsletter for the Association of Coroplastic Studies* 11: 18–20.

Fabbri, Marco, Marina Mazzei, and Massimo Osanna. 2000–1. "Sacrificio e banchetto funebre nella Daunia preromana: l'area sacra di Ausculum." *Siris* 3: 23–106.

Fabbri, Marco, and Massimo Osanna. 2005. "Aspetti del sacro nel mondo apulo: rituali di abbandono tra area sacra e abitato nell'antica Ausculum." In *Lo spazio del rito: santuari*

90 *Tiziana D'Angelo and Maya Muratov*

e culti in Italia meridionale tra indigeni e Greci, edited by Maria Luisa Nava and Massimo Osanna, 215–33. Bari: Edipuglia.

Felton, Debbie. 2010. "The Dead." In *A Companion to Greek Religion*, edited by Daniel Ogden, 86–99. Oxford and Malden, MA: Blackwell.

Ferruzza-Giacommara, Maria Lucia. 1993. "Quattro statue in terracotta provenienti da Canosa." In *Studia Varia from the J. Paul Getty Museum* 1, edited by Marion True and Kenneth Hamma, 71–82. Malibu: J. Paul Getty Museum.

Fronda, Michael P. 2010. *Between Rome and Carthage: Southern Italy during the Second Punic War*. Cambridge: Cambridge University Press.

Furley, William D. 2010. "Prayers and Hymns." In *A Companion to Greek Religion*, edited by Daniel Ogden, 117–31. Oxford and Malden, MA: Blackwell.

Garland, Robert. 2001 [1985]. *The Greek Way of Death*. Second Edition. Ithaca: Cornell University Press.

Gerhard, O. 1829. "Varietà sepolcrali della Magna Grecia." *Bollettino dell'Instituto di Corrispondenza Archeologica* 1: 181–92.

Giuliani, Luca. 1999. "Contenuto narrativo e significato allegorico nell'iconografia della ceramica apula." In *Im Spiegel des Mythos. Bilderwelt und Lebenswelt / Lo specchio del mito. Immaginario e realtà*, edited by Francesco de Angelis and Susanne Muth, 43–51. Wiesbaden: L. Reichert.

Graepler, Daniel. 1997. *Tonfiguren im Grab*. Munich: Biering & Brinkmann.

———. 2010. "Tanagras as Funeral Offerings: The Examples of Tarentum." In Jeammet, ed. 2010, 218–21.

Higgins, Reynold. 1986. *Tanagra and the Figurines*. London: Trefoil Books.

Huber, Ingeborg. 2001. *Die Ikonographie der Trauer in der Griechischen Kunst*. Mannheim and Möhnesee: Bibliopolis.

Jeammet, Violaine. 2003a. "Quelques particularités de la production des pleureuses canosines en terre cuite." *RA* 2: 255–92.

———. 2003b. *Idoles-cloches de Béotie*. Paris: Réunion des Musées nationaux.

———. 2007. *Tanagras: de l'objet de collection à l'objet archéologique*. Paris: Picard.

———. 2010a. "Tanagran and Theban Workshops." In Jeammet, ed. 2010, 111–31.

———. 2010b. "Canosa: A Blend of Greek and Local Traditions." In Jeammet, ed. 2010, 222–5.

———. Ed. 2010. *Tanagras: Figurines for Life and Eternity: The Musée du Louvre's Collection of Greek Figurines*. Valencia: Fundacion Bancaja.

———, and Gianpaolo Nadalini. 1997. "Restauration et étude technique de deux'orantes' de Canosa." *Revue du Louvre* 4: 69–76.

Kalaitzi, Myrina. 2010. "The Representation of Children on Classical and Hellenistic Tombstones from Ancient Macedonia." In *L'enfant et la mort dans l'antiquité I. Nouvelles researches dans les nécropoles grecques. Le signalement des tombes des enfants*, edited by Anne-Marie Guimier-Sorbets and Yvette Morizot, 327–46. Paris: de Boccard.

Kavoulaki, Athena. 1999. "Processional Performance and the Democratic Polis." In *Performance Culture and Athenian Democracy*, edited by Simon Goldhill and Robin Osborne, 293–320. Cambridge: Cambridge University Press.

———. 2005. "Crossing Communal Space: The Classical *Ekphora*, 'Public' and 'Private'." In *Idia kai dèmostia: Les cadres "privés" et "publiques" de la religion grecque antique*, edited by Véronique Dasen and Marcel Piérart, 129–45. Kernos, Supplément 15. Liège: Centre International d'Étude de la Religion Grecque.

———. 2011. "Observations on the Meaning and Practice of Greek *Pompe*." In *Current Approaches to Religion in Ancient Greece*, edited by Matthew Haysom and Jenny Wallensten, 134–50. Stockholm: Svenska institutet i Athen.

Kleiner, Gerhard. 1984. *Tanagrafiguren: Untersuchungen zur hellenistischen Kunst und Geschichte*. Berlin: De Gruyter.

Kurtz, Donna C., and John Boardman. 1971. *Greek Burial Customs*. London and Southampton: Thames and Hudson.

Lamboley, Jean-Luc. 1982. "Les hypogées indigène apuliens." *MEFRA* 94.1: 91–148.

Lawton, Carol L. 2007. "Children in Classical Attic Votive Reliefs." In *Constructions of Childhood in Ancient Greece and Italy*, edited by Ada Cohen and Jeremy B. Rutter, 41–60. Princeton: ASCSA Publications.

Lee, Mireille M. 2015. *Body, Dress, and Identity in Ancient Greece*. New York: Cambridge University Press.

Lippolis, Enzo. 1995. "Le porte degli inferi." In *Arpi. L'Ipogeo della Medusa e la necropoli*, edited by Marina Mazzei, 315–32. Bari: Edipuglia.

———. 2001. "Culto e iconografie della coroplastica votiva. Problemi interpretativi a Taranto e nel mondo greco." *MEFRA* 113: 225–55.

———. 2005. "Pratica rituale e coroplastica votiva a Taranto." In *Lo Spazio del Rito. Santuari e culti in Italia meridionale tra indigeni e greci*. Atti delle giornate di studio (Matera, 28–29 giugno 2002), edited by Maria Luisa Nava and Massimo Osanna, 91–102. Bari: Edipuglia.

———. 2010. "Votive Tanagra figurines in South Italy." In Jeammet, ed. 2010, 216–17.

———. 2012. "Cultura e manifestazione dell'aristocrazia canosina." *Scienze dell'Antichità* 18: 301–23.

Lombardi, A. 1832. "Memoria sul sepolcro trovato a Canosa nel dicembre 1826." *Annali dell'Instituto di Corrispondenza Archeologica* 4: 285–9.

Macchioro, Vittorio. 1911. *Curiosità canosine*. Martina Franca: Apulia.

Marchi, Maria Luisa. 2008. "Dall'abitato alla città. La romanizzazione della Daunia attraverso l'evoluzione dei sistemi insediativi." In *Storia e archeologia della Daunia. In ricordo di Marina Mazzei*. Atti delle giornate di studio (Foggia, 19–21 maggio 2005), edited by Giuliano Volpe, Maria José Strazzulla, and Danilo Leone, 267–86. Bari: Edipuglia.

Mazzei, Marina. 1992. "Ipogeo Barbarossa." In Cassano, ed. 1992, 197–202.

———, and Enzo Lippolis. 1984. "Dall'ellenizzazione all'età tardorepubblicana." In *La Daunia antica dalla preistoria all'alto medioevo*, edited by Marina Mazzei, 185–252. Milan: Electa.

Milanese, Andrea. 1996. "La scoperta dell'ipogeo Lagrasta del 1843 a Canosa e i materiali immessi nel Museo di Napoli." In *I Greci in Occidente. La Magna Grecia nelle collezioni del Museo Archeologico di Napoli*, edited by Stefano De Caro, Mariarosaria Borriello, and Silvia Cassani, 143–7. Naples: Electa.

Mylonopoulos, Joannis. 2006. "Greek Sanctuaries as Places of Communication through Ritual." In *Ritual and Communication in the Graeco-Roman World*, edited by Eftychia Starianopoulou, 69–110. Kernos, Supplément 16. Liège: Centre International d'Étude de la Religion Grecque.

Nava, Maria Luisa. 1992. "Le stele della Daunia." In Cassano, ed. 1992, 131–5.

———. Ed. 2011. *Stele daunie da Trinitapoli*. Foggia: Claudio Grenzi.

Oliver, Andrew Jr. 1968. *The Reconstruction of Two Apulian Tomb Groups*. Bern: Francke.

———. 1969. "A Gold-Glass Fragment in the Metropolitan Museum of Art." *Journal of Glass Studies* 11: 9–16.

92 *Tiziana D'Angelo and Maya Muratov*

Pilz, Oliver. 2011. "The Performative Aspect of Greek Ritual: The Case of the Athenian *Oschophoria.*" In *Current Approaches to Religion in Ancient Greece*, edited by Matthew Haysom and Jenny Wallensten, 151–67. Stockholm: Svenska institutet i Athen.

Pontrandolfo, Angela, and Agnès Rouveret. 1992. *Le tombe dipinte di Paestum.* Modena: Franco Cosimo Panini.

Preziosi, Donald, and Louise A. Hitchcock. 1999. *Aegean Art and Architecture.* Oxford: Oxford University Press.

Rinuy, Anne, Frederike van der Wielen, Peter Hartmann, and François Schweizer. 1978. "Céramique insolite de l'Italie du sud: Les vases hellénistiques de Canosa." *Genava* 26: 141–68.

Roccos, Linda Jones. 2000. "Back-Mantle and Peplos: The Special Costume of Greek Maidens in Fourth-Century Funerary and Votive Reliefs." *Hesperia* 69.2: 235–65.

Rossi, Luisa, and Frederike van der Wielen-van Ommeren. 1983. *Canosa II.* Bari: Dedalo.

Rouveret, Agnès, and Angela Pontrandolfo. 1985. "Pittura funeraria in Lucania e in Campania. Puntualizzazioni cronologiche e proposte di lettura." In *Ricerche di pittura ellenistica: lettura e interpretazione della produzione pittorica dal IV secolo a.C. all'ellenismo*, 91–130. Quaderni dei Dialoghi di Archeologia 1. Rome: Edizioni Quasar.

Ruggiero, Michele. 1888. *Degli scavi di antichità nelle province di terraferma dell'antico regno di Napoli dal 1743 al 1876.* Naples: Tipografia di Vincenzo Morano.

Shepherd, Gillian. 2012. "Women in Magna Graecia." In *A Companion to Women in the Ancient World*, edited by Sharon L. James and Sheila Dillon, 215–28. Malden, MA: Wiley-Blackwell.

Simon, Erika. 1969. *Die Götter der Griechen.* Munich: Hirmer.

Stears, Karen. 1998. "Death Becomes Her: Gender and Athenian Death Ritual." In *The Sacred and the Feminine in Ancient Greece*, edited by Sue Blundell and Margaret Williamson, 113–27. London and New York: Routledge.

Steingräber, Stephan. 2008. "La pittura funeraria della Daunia." In *Storia e archeologia della Daunia*, edited by Giuliano Volpe, Maria José Strazzulla, and Danilo Leone, 183–93. Bari: Edipuglia.

Thomas, Keith. 1991. "Introduction." In *A Cultural History of Gesture*, edited by Jan Bremmer and Herman Roodenberg, 1–14. Ithaca: Cornell University Press.

Tinè Bertocchi, Franca. 1964. *La pittura funeraria apula.* Naples: Gaetano Macchiaroli.

Todisco, Luigi. 2006. *Pittura e ceramica figurata tra Grecia, Magna Grecia e Sicilia.* Rome and Bari: La Biblioteca.

Torelli, Mario. 1995. *Studies in the Romanization of Italy*, edited and translated by Helena Fracchia and Maurizio Gualtieri. Edmonton: The University of Alberta Press.

———. 1999. *Tota Italia: Essays in the Cultural Formation of Roman Italy.* Oxford: Oxford University Press.

True, Marion, Jens Daehner, Janet B. Grossman, and Kenneth D. S. Lapatin. 2004. "Processions." In *Thesaurus cultus et rituum antiquorum* I, edited by Bertrand Jaeger, 1–20. Los Angeles: J. Paul Getty Museum and Basel: Fondation pour le Lexicon Iconographicum Mythologiae Classicae.

Tsanetou, Angeliki. 2007. "Ritual and Gender: Critical Perspectives." In *Finding Persephone: Women's Rituals in the Ancient Mediterranean*, edited by Maryline Parca and Angeliki Tsanetou, 3–26. Bloomington: Indiana University Press.

Uhlenbrock, Jaimee P. Ed. 1990. *The Coroplast's Art: Greek Terracottas of the Hellenistic World.* New Rochelle: Aristide D. Caratzas.

Van der Wielen-van Ommeren, Frederike. 1986. "Vases with Polychrome and Plastic Decoration from Canosa." In *Italian Iron Age Artefacts in the British Museum*, edited by Judith Swaddling, 215–26. London: British Museum Publications.

———. 1988. "La céramique hellénistique de Canosa: technique de fabrication." In *Proceedings of the 3rd Symposium on Ancient Greek and Related Pottery, Copenhagen, August 31–September 4, 1987*, edited by Jette Christiansen and Torben Melander, 665–73. Copenhagen: Nationalmuseet (Ny Carlsberg Glyptotek, Thorvaldsens Museum).

———. 1992. "La ceramica a decorazione policroma e plastica." In Cassano, ed. 1992, 520–9.

———. 1999. "'Orantes' canosines." In *Genève et l'Italie* III, *Mélanges publiés à l'occasion du 80e anniversaire de la Société genevoise d'études italiennes*, edited by Angela Kahn-Laginestra, 43–65. Genève: Société genevoise d'études italiennes.

Weilhartner, Jörg. 2013. "Textual Evidence for Aegean Late Bronze Age Ritual Processions." *Opuscula: Annual of the Swedish Institutes at Athens and Rome* 6: 151–73.

Part II
Authority and transmission

5 Shared meters and meanings

Delphic oracles and women's lament

Lisa Maurizio

Introduction

As Telemachus is bidding farewell to Menelaos and Helen in Homer's *Odyssey*, an eagle flies overhead. Peisistratos, Telemachus' companion, asks Menelaos if the eagle's flight signals a message from the gods for them. Before Menelaos can answer, Helen responds, "Listen to me! I will prophesy how the gods put this in my spirit and how I think it will be accomplished" (*Odyssey* 15.173–4).[1] Helen's use of the future tense in "I will prophesy" (*manteusomai*) points to the prophecy that she is in the middle of articulating. The use of the future tense for verbs describing the actions or speech of a performer, such as singing, praising, cursing, dancing, supplicating, and binding, whether in paeans, hymns, tragic choral odes, *parthenaea*, curses, and charms, refers to the present performance, not a future one (Calame 1995; Faraone 1995). Such "performative futures" are often accompanied by the first-person pronoun, the adverb *nun*, and/or deictic pronouns that emphasize the here and now of performance (Faraone 1995, 3). Helen's use of the performative future, "I will prophesy," fits this typology well: she uses the first-person pronoun twice as she commands those around her to listen to her prophecy.

Helen's mantic ability has been ascribed to different aspects of her character. Most recently, Richard P. Martin has convincingly explained it as a consequence of her presentation in epic tradition as a "paradigmatic lamenter" (Martin 2008, 124). Drawing on Nadia Seremetakis's ethnographic study of women's laments in Inner Mani, a peninsula off the southern coast of Greece, in which she argues that "cosmology and fate enter the social domain as fragments in improvised mourning songs, dreaming, and exhumation of the dead" (Seremetakis 1991, 2), Martin argues that Helen is a lamenter and a prophetess, or more precisely she is a prophetess because she is a lamenter (Martin 2008, 124). Indeed, both ancient and modern laments point forward as well as backward in time as a solo mourner describes her hopes and fears about the future without the deceased. Such future ruminations in laments gain potency from their ritual setting. Following Seremetakis (1991, 121), Martin notes that laments are antiphonal not for aesthetic reasons but because the chorus, by repeating the solo lamenter's words, transforms them. Once heard by the community at the gravesite (or funeral pyre) and the funeral cortege, her words, amplified by chorus and community, become part of the *social world* and

98 *Lisa Maurizio*

acquire the status of juridical truth (Martin 2008, 125). Whatever a solo mourner may anticipate, then, is granted a solemnity and social currency that funerary ritual conventions bestow on it. More than this, the finality of death and the mourners' suffering confers a finality to laments, captured in Seremetakis's book title "the last word," that cannot be undone, any more than death can be reversed. In this way, lament shades into prophecy, a process for which *kledons*, the kindred cousins of prophecies, offer a parallel. *Kledons* are chance utterances that are believed to predict, perhaps even cause to happen, the meaning that a listener ascribes to them. Thus, *kledons* are a type of predicative speech; they occupy an intermediate space between expressing a sentiment, usually about the future, and a prophecy (Hirvonenk 1969, Peradotto 1969, Latiener 2005, Maurizio 2013). So too do laments.

In his ethnographic study of modern Greek laments by a young woman in Glendi, Crete, Michael Herzfeld, for example, writes that "Greek laments often have prospective thrust" in so far as the lamenter often imagines the impact of the loss of a male protector, whether father, husband, brother, or more expansively the men of her destroyed city (Herzfeld 1993, 244). Indeed, the modern Greek word for lament, *miroloya*, or "words of fate" as Herzfeld translates, suggests that laments do not express "passive resignation to the inevitable" but are used instrumentally by the lamenter to protest or secure a better future. Herzfeld observes that in the lament of the young Cretan woman he observed, she conflated marriage with death and a potential groom with her deceased father. Death is frequently a metaphor for marriage in ancient Greek literature and religion, most notably in the *Homeric Hymn to Demeter* and the Mysteries of Demeter at Eleusis. To the extent that this metaphor was perceived by listeners to be imbued with traditional language, the Cretan woman's lament acquired a solemnity that she could not otherwise command. It gave credence to her implicit claim to act effectively, despite her social station, in the community subsequent to the funeral. As Herzfeld argues, the young woman lamented in ways that "anticipated" her subsequent actions to secure a husband for her sister and herself despite the many social disadvantages that her father's death imposed. Herzfeld is careful to distinguish her lament from prophecy: she did not "prophesy this sequence of events through her lamentations" and "this was not a prophecy" (Herzfeld 1993, 251, 252). Nonetheless, he notes that she used the future tense in her lament and looked forward in time rather than to the past and to telling stories about her deceased father. Here, as in the case of Helen in the epic tradition and in Seremetakis' study of laments from Inner Mani, prophetic fragments, anticipatory glimpses of what the future may hold, are a part of laments. Their utterance during funerary rituals, especially if followed by a chorus of singers, stamps them with a ritual force that renders them potent and true, that is, prophetic, even if Classical scholars have only recently recognized this aspect of laments, largely through ethnographic studies of women's funerary songs and actions in contemporary Greece.

The prophetic aspect of Delphic oracles attributed to the Pythia, the title given to women who served as Apollo's priestesses at Delphi, has never been in doubt for obvious reasons. Delphic oracles were linked to the divinatory ritual at Delphi;

Shared meters and meanings 99

their prophetic import comes from listeners' beliefs that their origins are Apollo. Perhaps for this reason, the particular features of Delphi oracles that would have been recognized as indicating their prophetic cast, beyond their renowned ambiguity, have remained less studied. Yet oracles contain generic markers of prophetic or inspired speech. In one oracle, for example, the Pythia, like Helen, uses the performative future "I will prophesy" (*manteusomai*) in the same position in a hexameter oracle (fourth foot) when she pronounces an oracle to the Lykourgos of Sparta, who consults Delphi seeking laws for his city (PW 29: Hdt. 1.65.2 and PW 216: Diod. Sic. 7.12). The Pythia greets Lykourgos as "dear to Zeus and all the gods who have homes on Olympus" and then states, "I am undecided about whether I will prophesy (*manteusomai*) to you as a god or as a man." The Pythia and the "paradigmatic lamenter" Helen's use of *manteusomai* hints that women's laments and the Pythia's oracles have affinities with one another that, if collected and examined, may shed light on key issues in the study of laments and Delphic oracles.

To my knowledge, women's laments and the Pythia's oracles have not been brought together for study. Both types of verses fall under the general rubric of women's poetic competence in ancient Greece, an area of study greatly aided by recent scholarship on women's song culture in ancient Greece. Andromache Karanika's study of women's work songs lays the foundation for imagining the range of songs in ancient Greece that women would regularly have sung as they labored at the loom or grinding stone (Karanika 2014, and her contribution in this volume). Her work contributes to ongoing scholarly attention to the performance settings, oral composition, and generic conventions of laments that Margaret Alexiou's groundbreaking study of this genre initiated (Alexiou 1974 (2002)). Building on this growing body of scholarship, this chapter suggests that there are several stylistic features common to Delphic oracles in hexameter verse and the few laments represented in direct quotation in Homer's *Iliad* and *Odyssey* and in Euripides' tragedy *Andromache*. These shared features include meter, emphatic use of first–person pronouns and possessives, and performative futures or presents as well as praise or blame. The presence of these features in both genres draws together two seemingly disparate questions in the study of laments and Delphic oracles, namely why prepared laments, the place of laments, and the number and familial connection of lamenters to the deceased were legally restricted throughout Greece during the sixth and seventh centuries BCE and whether or not the Pythias composed verse oracles at Delphi.

Scholarly opinions on the legal restrictions on women's laments, though they differ in emphasis, are agreed that this legislation attempted to secure greater communal harmony. The means by which legal restrictions achieved this goal are variously described: they curtailed aristocratic displays of power, or inhibited any incitements toward revenge, or transferred allegiance from family to state (achieved in Athens through the development of mourning rituals such as the Adonia, the Eleusinian Mysteries, and public commemoration of the war dead), or diminished the risks of ritual pollution or inhibited any unnecessary expenditure of private wealth that might otherwise go to the state (Garland 1989; Derderian 2001, 69

100   *Lisa Maurizio*

offer surveys of the scholarship on this topic with bibliography). The prophetic aspects of women's laments described here suggest an additional reason for this legislation.

While no scholars question that women composed laments at funerals (Alexiou 2002 [1974]; Holst-Warhaft 1995; Nagy 2010) and that laments, although some-times performed by men, were a "female–dominated genre" (Tsagalis 2004, 8), whether the Pythias composed verse oracles at Delphi continues to inspire debate. The view that duplicitous shrine personnel issued oracles as they attended a bab-bling Pythia no longer has any currency in scholarship (Johnston 2008, 56; Clay 2009, 8–9; Flower 2009, 216–22; Stoneman 2011, 39), though the Pythias's ability to versify has been assumed – or denied – on the grounds that women were not "educated" in a manner that would enable them to compose verses (Amandry 1950, 168; Parke and Wormell 1956, vol. I, 33; Bowden 2005, 16 and 33). This study of the shared features in Delphic oracles and women's laments suggests that women, particularly during the seventh through fifth centuries BCE, when oral poetry was a primary means of communication, were competent (or in the words of the debate, sufficiently "educated") to compose *both* laments in verse and ora-cles in verse. From this perspective, it seems not simply plausible, but highly likely, that the Pythias composed verse oracles and that the words of female lamenters were perceived as ominous as well as sorrowful, and therefore worthy of restriction.

Verse oracles

Of the 600 or so oracles attributed to Delphi, roughly 175 are in hexameter verse (collected without commentary by Andersen 1987). The few studies of this subset of oracles as a genre of oral poetry tend to pass over the historical and divinatory aspects of Delphi in favor of studying the characteristics – dialect, prosody, and formulae – that verse oracles share with Homer and Hesiod. Wallace E. MacLeod took up the question of the oral composition of verse oracles in a study that remains a touchstone for all subsequent inquiries into verse oracles (1961, 325). Deploying techniques used to study the oral compositions of Homer and Hesiod, MacLeod counted the formulae in the first verse oracle in Parke and Wormell's collection (1956, PW1: Ion Hist. (*FHG* II, 51) *fr.* 17 and Mnaseas (*FHG* III, 157) *fr.* 50). He concluded that the high number of formulae shared by this oracle with Homer and Hesiod indicated that most verse oracles were orally composed. To explain their oral composition, MacLeod proposed that local freelance bards at Delphi put the Pythias's utterances into verse because the erudition and versifying abilities typical of oracles were, he assumed, beyond the scope of a "peasant" woman and neces-sarily required a "long apprenticeship" (1961, 321). Further MacLeod argued that Delphic oracles were part of a local Phokian school of oral poetry that was distinct from Hesiod's Boiotian didactic tradition or Homer's Ionic epic tradition.

MacLeod's nod to the local origins of oracles echoes Heinrich Ludolf Ahrens' claim that Delphic verse oracles were the origin of Hesiod's Doricisms – a claim that inspired August Fick to publish a "Delphic" edition of the *Theogony* (Davies

Shared meters and meanings 101

1964, 138). M. L. West (1966, 80) also posited that "a residue of dialect forms for which no Homeric parallel is to be found" that is "especially Aeolic and West Greek" in Hesiod may be the result of Delphic influence. Even so, the dialect of Delphic oracles along with a Phokian school of oral poetry has remained peripheral to subsequent studies of oracles as a genre of hexameter oral poetry – one revived by L. E. Rossi (1981), who also argued oracles were orally composed. Following Rossi's study, J. A. Fernandez-Delgado catalogued the formulae, meter, prosody, and proverbial sentiments that verse oracles share with Hesiod (1986). Contrary to MacLeod, Fernandez-Delgado concluded that these shared features indicate that oracles comprise a "continental poetic tradition of a didactic type, clearly different from other traditions," but not distinctly Phokian or West-Greek. In a series of articles, Jesús M. Nieto Ibánez, comparing the formulae, meter, and prosody of Delphic oracles to the verses of Homer and Hesiod, argued that they have affinities with *both* Hesiod and Homer (1988, 1989, 1990). Additionally, Nieto Ibánez observed that although Delphic oracles pertaining to events in the Archaic period are found in works that span some 1,000 years from the Archaic period to the fourth century CE, they do not change over time. That is, these oracles exhibit the metrical and prosodic characteristics of archaic hexameters, not the hexameters of later literate authors such as Kallimachos, Apollonios, Nikandros, or Nonnos. The consistency in oracles over time may confirm Michael Flower's claim that Delphic oracles were written down more quickly and preserved with greater care than other forms of oral poetry (Flower 2009, 218). Taken together, these studies do not offer any evidence that suggests the Pythias, rather than other temple attendants, composed Delphic oracles. Nonetheless, these studies demonstrate that verse oracles share a sufficient number of formulae with Homer and Hesiod to conclude that they were orally composed. This chapter, then, takes all verse oracles, regardless of the date of the works in which they are recorded, as oral compositions for the purposes of comparison with laments.

Elegiac funerary laments

From a range of visual material, references to women's lament, and representations of women singing laments in Greek literature, the content and meter of funerary laments must be deduced. One representation of a woman singing lament in a tragedy, namely Andromache's lament in Euripides' play of the same name, offers compelling evidence that ritual laments were in elegiac verse. At the play's beginning, Andromache, speaking in iambic trimeters, proclaims that she will fill the air with lamentation, to which her life is now devoted (93). As she begins to mourn the destruction of Troy and the death of Hector, trimeters become elegiac couplets (103–16). Andromache's use of elegiac verse combined with references to mournful songs and funerary epigrams in elegiac verse led Denys Page to conclude that funerary laments deployed elegiac verse (1936).[2] Yet, the use of elegiac verse in a variety of poems with a far broader array of topics than death, such as personal reminiscences, gnomic utterances, war, and politics, performed at private symposia or civic occasions (West 1974; Bowie 1986) by solo performers or by choruses,

102   *Lisa Maurizio*

sometimes sung to an *aulos* and at other times spoken, has made the use of elegiac verse in women's funerary laments seem tenuous. The recent publication of a number of poems in elegiac meter that have consolatory themes or were sung over the dead (Simonides Elegy *fr.* 22; the Plateaea elegy, an elegiac epitaph on a *polyandrion* in Ambracia [*SEG* 44.463]), however, have made Page's claim that funerary laments deployed elegiac meter all but certain (Tsagalis 2004; Faraone 2008; Garner 2011; Nagy 2010, Budelmann and Power 2013, 13). Thus, Gregory Nagy's claim that Andromache's verses recall "a real lament as really sung by women" (2010, 32–3) pertains largely to her use of elegiac meter. Such "real" laments were sung at three moments at a funeral: when the body was laid out and ritually cleaned in a house (*prothesis*); when a procession of mourners accompanied the body to the gravesite (*ekphora*); and at the graveside. The tripartite structure in literary representations of laments may pertain to these three ritual moments (Alexiou 1974; Faraone 2008, who observes a five-couplet stanzaic form in elegiac poems, does not limit his study to funerary elegies) and further suggests the ritual underpinnings of elegy that Nagy seeks to demonstrate. If Andromache's lament has any affinities with elegies performed by men at symposia or public festivals, this is because such elegies, as Nagy describes them, were "decontextualized," "masculinized," "professionalized," and "stylized" adaptations of women's laments. For women first developed elegy through their ritual singing over the dead, and men then contributed to the genre by developing topics appropriate to the venues in which they performed elegies (Nagy 2010). For the purposes of this chapter, the priority of women in the development of elegy is less important than the fact that women composed and sang laments in elegiac verse to mourn the dead (Alexiou 1974; Tsagalis 2004; Faraone 2008; Dué 2009; Nagy 2010).

Andromache's few lines comprise the only literary representation of a woman's ritual lament in elegiac verse. Yet her verses are not the only evidence available for this chapter. Elegiac meter has close metrical similarities to hexameter. Elegy is "a variation upon the heroic hexameter in the direction of lyric" (Hardie quoted in Bowra 1938, 3), a relationship that Nagy's definition seeks to highlight: "the genre of elegy is marked by the hexameter combined with pentameter" (Nagy 2010; see also Barnes 1979, 1995). Tyrtaeus's elegiac poem *Eunomia* offers a case study of the relationship between hexameter and elegy as defined by Nagy and is particularly apt for this chapter because it incorporates a hexameter Delphic oracle (PW 21: Plut. *Lyc.* 6). First recited in civic Spartan festivals during Tyrtaeus' life and then in sympotic competitions by Spartan soldiers on military campaigns (D'Alessio 2009), this one elegiac poem was choral or monodic depending on its performance venue – a fact that suggests the different performance styles and venues that make the elegiac genre difficult to define (Budelmann and Power 2013) or, phrased somewhat differently, that indicate that the elegiac genre had a "capacity for performing the functions of forms that belong to other genres" (Nagy 2010). In Trytaeus' poem elegiac pentameters "only supplement the meanings of the quoted oracular hexameters" (Nagy 2010) – a view that is likely given that few Delphic oracles were in iambic and elegiac verse (Parke 1945, 64). Thus Tyrtaeus's

Shared meters and meanings 103

poem performs the function of an oracle. The following is a modified translation from Nagy 2010.

> Having heard Phoebus, from Pytho to home they carried
> Prophecies of the god and words that would be accomplished:
> *God-honored kings will oversee deliberations,*
> To whom the beautiful city of Sparta is a care,
> *And the elders by virtue of their age, and then the men in the community,*
> Answering with straight words,
> *Will speak well and perform just acts,*
> And not offer any crooked plan for the city,
> *And victory and prosperity will attend all the people.*
> So Phoebus pronounced these matters to the city.

Trytaeus' elegy demonstrates the fluidity between elegiac verse and (oracular) hexameter. Because of the similarities between hexameters and elegiacs, laments included in Homer's epics, necessarily in hexameter, offer a corpus of literary representations of women's laments that can meaningfully compared to Delphic oracles.

Homer refers to two types of lament (*threnos* and *goos*), when Priam returns to Troy with the body of his slain son Hector (*Iliad* 24.719–25). Hector's family calls upon singers (*aoidous*) described as "leaders of laments" (*threnoi*) to attend his corpse. Women surrounding these singers also lament Hector (*threnon*) and groan (*stonoessan*) when Andromache, Hector's wife, begins performing her lament, called a *goos*. This passage offers key evidence for the distinction drawn between *threnoi* and *goos* (Tsagalis 2004, chapter 1). *Threnoi* are laments sung by professional singers (*aoidoi*), most likely male, perhaps to a flute (*aulos*). These may precede *gooi* and are antiphonal. *Gooi* refer to the laments of kin, most often female, performed over a corpse or in anticipation of the death of kin. They too are antiphonal: a solo performance of a *goos* is followed by a choral refrain and dancing by a larger group of kin and/or community. Because choruses join both female kin who lead *gooi* and professional singers who lead *threnoi*, the distinction between *threnoi* and *gooi* ought not to be drawn too sharply (Swift 2010, 302). Indeed, by the fifth century the Homeric distinction between *gooi* and *threnoi* has disappeared. Moreover, in the *Iliad* or *Odyssey*, no laments labeled as *threnoi* are represented with direct quotation – the word *threnos* is used once in each poem (the Iliadic passage cited here and *Odyssey* 24.60) – though several laments, some labeled *gooi* and some not labeled with either word, are represented with direct speech (Tsagalis 2004, chapter 1). Since there is no way to assess any qualitative differences between these two types of laments, Tsagalis classifies laments in Homer's *Iliad* not simply by the appearance of the word *goos* but also by introductory and closing formulae (2004, chapter 2). These are 4.155–82 (Agamemnon); 6.407–39 (Andromache); 18.52–64 (Thetis); 18.324–42 (Achilles); 19.287–300 (Briseis); 19.315–37 (Achilles); 22.416–28 (Priam); 22.431–6 (Hekabe);

104   *Lisa Maurizio*

22.477–514 (Andromache); 24.725–745 (Andromache); 24.748–59 (Hekabe); 24.762–75 (Helen).

This group of hexameter laments in Homer's epics offers the best evidence for women's elegiac funerary laments and thus provides material with which to explore the connection between oracular hexameters and women's laments. Even so, there are no formulaic similarities between this collection of laments as defined by Tsagalis and Delphic verse oracles. Indeed, Andromache's lament in the *Iliad* shares almost no formulae with the *Iliad* (Derderian 2001). Nonetheless, Homeric laments and verse oracles do exhibit a number of shared features, namely performative futures (or presents), the emphatic use of first-person pronouns and adjectives, deitics, and praise and blame. These features have received no scholarly attention because they have little relevance to the Pythia's predictions, in the case of Delphic oracles, and, except for praise and blame of the deceased, to deceased in the case of laments. Yet they are significant for marking the speeches in which they occur as ritual performances that have prophetic aspects. In the following, I explore how these features suggest the affinities between Delphic oracles and laments and thereby offer new ways to address questions concerning the authorship of oracles and the restrictions on laments.

The oracular "I"

When an "I" appears in a Delphic oracle, it poses certain questions: to whom does this "I" refer? Apollo or the Pythia inspired by Apollo? Are these two possibilities distinct from one another in the understanding of original audiences? In some instances, the first-person of an oracle refers exclusively to Apollo. For example, in his interrogation of oral sources about why the land of Epidauros is dear to Asklepios, Pausanias quotes a Delphic oracle given to Apollophanes of Arkadia. Apollophanes asks Delphi if Asklepios is the son of Apollo and Arsinoe. The Pythia directly addresses Asklepios with a vocative, despite the fact that he is not in the divinatory consultation. She then states that Koronis bore Asklepios having mixed in love "with me" that is, Apollo, not the Pythia (PW 276: Paus. 2.26.7). These features – an absent Asklepios is addressed by his divine father Apollo as the Pythia speaks – might indicate that the story is best treated as a fiction that bears no meaningful connection to a historical divinatory consultation at Delphi. Yet Parke and Wormell offer a plausible historical setting for the oracle – "after the refounding of Messene, and at a time when the Arkadians were in close relations with the new state" – and consider it genuine, i.e. likely to have taken place. Fontenrose, on the other hand, rejects this scenario, reasoning that the Pythia would not deny Asklepios' connection to Messene through Arsinoe (as Apollophanes hopes to demonstrate by means of his consultation at Delphi) and thereby provoke Apollophanes' displeasure (Fontenrose 1978, 342 [Q226]). Apart from the question of a possible historical setting for this oracle, it is one of the few verse oracles where an oracle's first-person pronoun refers exclusively to Apollo (see also PW 154 and 379, where the Pythia refers to "my father" in reference to Zeus, indicating that Apollo is speaking). Conversely, there are few verse oracles where

Shared meters and meanings   105

Apollo is referred to in the third person and thereby consistently distinguished from the Pythia (PW 334, 363, 416, 443, 492), as in the following example. To Battos, the legendary founder of Kyrene, the Pythia says, "Battos, you come here about your voice. King Phoibos Apollo sends you to Libya, rich in flocks, as its founder" (PW 39: Hdt. 4.155.3 with PW 71: Diod. Sic. 8.29).

Most often the "I" in an oracle is far more ambiguous, referring neither to Apollo or the Pythia but to both; it also functions dramatically as well as ritually (Faraone 1995). How the Pythia's "I" was understood ritually is suggested by the use of the first-person pronoun by the poet Homer to refer to himself. John Garcia has recently argued that when Homer uses first-person pronouns, they indicate "ritual speech," that is a type of speech used alongside certain types of ritual behavior, both of which are linked in some way to the divine and distinguished from ordinary speech by listeners (Garcia 2002, 41). Referring to the work of cognitive linguist Pascal Boyer, who argues that ritual speech must be understood not only in terms of content or traits (i.e. invariance, repetition, etc.) but primarily in terms of "the representations that people make about the value and content of the discourses in which they partake," Garcia considers the performative context of Homer's use of the first-person pronoun (Garcia 2002, 49) at the rare moments when he introduces himself into his song and acknowledges the limits of his poetic powers. When Homer is trying to describe the especially intense fighting of Greek and Trojans, he says, "it is difficult for me (*me*) to pronounce all these things (*tauta*) like a god" (*Iliad* 12.176). In this instance "the narrator intrudes his personality only to abandon it; the accurate telling is the work of an eyewitness" (Garcia 2002, 52). The use of the first-person pronoun, then, does not assert the poet's knowledge or poetic abilities so much as suggest his or her limits, for this "I" emerges at the moment that the Muses or god are named as the sources of knowledge. The "I" indicates that the poet is in relation with the divine, who vouches for what follows (though this is implied not stated). The Pythia shares with Homer and other poets an "I" that does not necessarily indicate that Apollo is speaking through her, or assert her individuality or powers, but instead marks her relationship with the divine, one that is recognized by listeners.

The seeming paradox of this "I" is further highlighted by the use of the deictic "these things." In Homer, the demonstrative pronoun "this" (*houtos*) most often occurs in the speech of characters. It is rarely used by the narrator, as in *Iliad* 12.176, because a deictic pronoun "points to what is really there, here and now" (Bakker 1999, 6). When the narrator of the poem uses the demonstrative, it brings the oral performance of the poem into the recorded text, or, stated conversely, "the remote reality of the epic tale 'intrudes' into the immediate reality of the performance" of the poet through his use of the demonstrative (Bakker 1999, 8). For Bakker, the demonstrative "creates a special human bond between the poet and his audience." In almost all of the examples of the poet's use of the demonstrative pronoun that Bakker cites (*Iliad* 2.484–7 and 760 as well as Hesiod *Theogony* 22–5, 112–14), the poet makes specific reference to being inspired by the Muses or god and, significantly, uses first-person pronouns. The combination of a first-person pronoun, a demonstrative pronoun, and a reference to divine inspiration

106　*Lisa Maurizio*

suggests not only that the poet is bringing the epic past into the here and now of performance but also that the poet is beginning to see before his eyes a *tableau vivant* and that the vividness of his perceptions is so great that it almost overwhelms any capacity to narrate it. In these instances, then, the poet's "I" marks reliance or communication with the divine for the information thus conveyed. The poet's "I" is, in Garcia's words, "multidimensional," "dialogic," or "emergent," i.e. it comes into a fullness of being during performance. It is neither the god speaking directly through the poet nor the poet in full control of his poetic facilities. It implies a self whose boundaries are fluid and whose speech consequently has authority because this "I" is recognized by its listeners as being in conversation with the divine – a situation for which Aeschylus' description of Kassandra's prophecies in the *Agamemnon* offers a parallel.

Throughout Kassandra's interaction with the chorus, she uses the first-person pronoun, for example, when she addresses Apollo – "where have you led me?" (1088) – and in moments of high emotion – "I, I" (1257). She uses the demonstrative pronoun "this" (*hode*) to refer to her prophecies (1095), the house of Atreus behind her (1102), the future murder of Agamemnon (1110), and the vision entering into her sight (1114). After she then enjoins the chorus to look (1126) and promises that she will speak more clearly (1178), she describes a chorus and then two boys on *this* house (1186 and 1227). The two boys are Thyestes' sons, and the vision is of a past event. Aeschylus's depiction of Kassandra lends weight to the idea that Homer's use of both first-person pronouns and deictics coupled with references to the gods recalls, as Garcia suggests, a ritual performance wherein speaker and audience subscribe to and generate the conventions that mark divinatory speech as a dialogue between mortal and god. Kassandra's "I" may best be called an oracular "I." This oracular "I" appears in many of the Pythia's verse oracles.

A series of verse oracles pertaining to the founding of Kroton contain the oracular "I." When Myskellos of Rhipai asks about children, the Pythia replies that, ". . . Far–darter Apollo loves you and will give you children; but he orders you to found Kroton, a great city in beautiful fields" (PW 43: Diod. Sic. 8.17). Surprised by this response, Myskellos asks where he might find Kroton. The Pythia then uses the first-person pronoun, yet the boundaries between the Pythia and Apollo are not sustained (PW 44: Diod. Sic. 8.17).

> Far–darter Apollo himself (*autos*) points this out; pay attention.
> This here is the unplowed Taphian land; here (*hede*) is Chalkis;
> (*hede*) here too is the holy land of the Kouretes.
> Here (*haide*) are the Echinades. The vast sea is on the left.
> I say that you cannot miss the Lakinian heights
> Nor can you miss holy Krimisa, nor the river Aisaros.

"I say" is a performative present that describes the Pythia's ritual speech. The Pythia is the "I" in the first-person verb "I say" (*phemi*), though it would make little sense to argue that her words are wholly her own. After ordering Myskellos

Shared meters and meanings 107

to pay attention, she uses demonstratives to describe where he must go. Like Kassandra, the Pythia's use of three deictics suggests that what she describes to Myskellos is before her eyes. Thus, the Pythia is speaking and seeing with Apollo; neither can be or ought to be wholly disentangled from one another in the ritual performance. The Pythia uses what might best be described as the oracular "I."

The most dynamic oracular "I" occurs in the first Delphic oracle of Herodotos' *Histories*. The Pythia responds to envoys of the Lydian king Kroisos, who have been instructed to ask at various oracular shrines about Kroisos' activities (Hdt. 1.47; PW 52). When the Pythia is asked about the king's strange activities, she responds in meter with an emphatic "I know the number of the sands and measures of the ocean . . ." (*oida d'ego*). The ability to count large amounts is evidence of prophetic skills; thus the "I" must refer to the Pythia in conversation with Apollo. When the Pythia then goes on to say that the smell of turtle reaches "*my* senses" again the conflation of Apollo and the Pythia is implied. The smell reaches both Pythia and Apollo, or reaches the Pythia because of Apollo. Like the vision of the location of Kroton, the odor of Kroisos' cooking is described by the Pythia as though it is before her. More accurately, the setting of the divinatory ritual allows the "I" of the Pythia's utterance to be understood as an oracular "I."[3]

Laments in Homer's *Iliad* often contain an "I" that is seemingly oracular. When Menelaos is wounded, Agamemnon performs a lament in which his companions then join (4.155–82). Taking Menelaos's hand, Agamemnon addresses him directly, much as the Pythia addresses clients directly, and rues his decision to make an oath with the Trojans, i.e the situation that led to Menelaos's injury. He then states, "*I* know *this* well in my heart and mind: there will be a day when holy Troy is destroyed." Notably, Hector repeats these two lines in his response to Andromache's anticipatory lament for him (6.447–8). Agamemnon refers to Zeus, who will be responsible for Troy's destruction, before concluding that "these things (*tade*) will not be unfulfilled." Here, Agamemnon's "I," like the "I" of many a lamenter, is an oracular "I." The emphatic use of the first-person pronoun or first-person verbs coupled with predictions in the future tense also appear in Thetis' anticipatory lament over Achilles (18.59–60) and Achilles's lament over Patroklos's corpse (18.330–3). In all of these instances, the lamenter's words acquire a solemnity and a status like the oracles of the Pythia during a divinatory ritual. That status derives not so much from content as from stylistic features used in a ritualistic, if not ritual setting (i.e. lamenters standing over an ailing if not dead body). The "I" of lamenters may be less an assertion of identity than an imitation of the oracular "I" with its implied claims to communion with a god and the ability to predict the future. This combination of style and setting comprises a "representation" that ancient listeners hold about prophetic or efficacious language. Thus, listeners would not consider the lamenter's description of the future a mere flight of fancy. It necessarily is ominous, spoken in such a way in such a setting that it is perceived or understood to be prophetic. In such a context, any praise or blame of the deceased that a lamenter utters becomes freighted with the solemnity of ritual and the quality of truth. All laments contain an evaluation of the deceased.

108   *Lisa Maurizio*

Curiously the Pythia also praises and blames her clients. Here too, then, is another affinity between laments and oracles.

Praise and blame

Laments often begin with a "praising address" to the dead, such as Achilles' words to Patroklos "dearest of friends" (*Il.* 19.315), and conclude with the praise of the deceased, thereby creating a ring composition (Tsagalis 2004, 28–34). Andromache's last lament for Hector in the *Iliad* (24.725–45) exemplifies this pattern: her address to Hector (725–33) is followed by a narrative section (732–40) in which she describes her and her son Astyanax's future and concludes with an address to Hector (741–5) (Tsagalis 2004, 46). Her lament also contains many of the stylistic elements that laments and oracles share such as a performative present (727), repeated and emphatic use of the first-person pronoun and adjective (727, 732, 742, 743, 744), and deictics (727, 731). It also showcases how these features transform a lament into prophecy during performance and how praise of the deceased at the start and conclusion of a lament can often become blame, thereby transforming the lamenter's portrayal of the deceased from a personal feeling to the deceased's fate, as the memory of the deceased is determined by the lamenter's "last word."

The narrative section of Andromache's lament is primarily devoted to her anticipation of the consequences of Hector's death upon her, her son Astyanax, and all of Troy; the future tense is used frequently (728, 729, 731, 733, and 735). Andromache states that Troy will fall and that its women will be taken on ships to Greece. She imagines that Astyanax may follow her and the other women but then describes with greater confidence that some Greek soldier whose relative Hector has killed will throw Astyanax from the walls. This fate is not entirely unique to Astyanax; it appears on two vases, one late Geometric vase and one pithos from the seventh century, the first of which most likely does not refer to Astyanax (Richardson 1993, 354). In other words, Andromache offers a plausible vision of the likely fates of women and children at Troy's destruction. Even so, dangers attend describing these fates aloud, if listeners take seriously the power of words not simply to anticipate the future but to determine it, as *kledons* were imagined to do. Andromache conjoins her bitter sorrow over Hector's death and the fall of Troy so that her lament renders one past event (Hector's death) and one future event (the fall of Troy) indissoluble. At the end of her lament, Andromache's brief praise of Hector – he was "not kind" on the battlefield – is replaced by blame for the silence of his final hour: "You spoke no word of great import *to me*, which I might remember as I cry throughout my nights and days" (741–5). Andromache implies that she has been left bereft of the smallest comfort, for which Hector is responsible, and implies that he is responsible for her future and the fall of Troy. As the chorus of lamenters around her cry out, they echo her sentiments, her (minimal) praise of Hector and her plausible, even generic, picture of the fate of Troy and its residents. Their antiphonal response lends legitimacy to Andromache's words and imbues them with a communal authority they would not otherwise have. Thus within the

Shared meters and meanings 109

ritual context of the funeral ritual, a woman's voice, her summation of the deceased, whether praise or blame, however idiosyncratic it may be, enters into communal discourse and thus becomes part of the communal memory of the deceased. More pointedly, a mourner's prerogative to imagine the future, to praise or blame the deceased, combined with stylistic devices, as enumerated here, gives a lament a prophetic cast. This prophetic cast may vary in degree: a lament may become a prophecy if it shares a significant number of stylistic devices with oracles, or it may be understood as a *kledon*, an utterance that may be perceived by listeners to be ominous.

The Pythia sometimes praises or blames clients when she addresses them. In most instances praise accompanies predictions of favorable circumstances and blame accompanies predictions of dire outcomes. Blame is more frequent than praise. The Pythia tells the men of Aigion that they are so lowly they cannot be compared to other Greeks (PW1); she calls Kleisthenes of Sikyon a stone thrower, i.e. a soldier with no weapons (*leuster*: PW 24); she calls Kroisos "very naïve" (*mega nepie*: PW 55), the Athenians wretched (*meleoi*: PW 94). She orders some clients out of her temple (PW 4 and 575).[4] The few oracles in iambic verse, as may be expected, often contain abuse (for examples, see Parke 1945). On the other hand, she addresses Eetion, the tyrant of Korinth, as "very honored" (*polutitmon*: PW 6). She calls Kypselos, tyrant of Korinth, "fortunate" (*olbios*: PW 8), and the men of Sybaris blessed (*eudaimon* PW 73).[5] The prerogative of the Pythia to address those who enter her shrine in any way she chooses befits her ritual station during the divinatory ritual at Delphi. Such a prerogative was available to women within the confines of lament until legislation restricted women's lamentation and mourning of the dead.

Conclusion

It is surely correct that cities throughout Greece curtailed women's mourning because of its potential for social and political disruption. But I want to argue that the affinities between laments and prophecies were just as likely a factor. First, it is worth noting that whether and how women's laments in the *Iliad* support or challenge the poem's ideological framework continues to be debated. Homeric laments are understood as comporting with and reinforcing Homeric values through praise of the deceased (Dué 2002), even predating and thus influencing Homeric values (Weinbaum 2001), or critiquing Homeric values by speaking about the deceased in terms that mirror the boasts of enemies of the war dead (Derderian 2001) or by blaming the deceased (Holst–Warhaft 1995; Perkell 2008). Perhaps the only conclusion to be drawn by these various interpretations of the import of women's laments is that what women could or might say in a lament was not entirely constrained by generic and ritual forms. Funerary rituals granted women a licit and public voice with which to describe the deceased and seal his memory, and hence his fate, for future generations and to anticipate the future, predicting it or causing it through her performance, if her words were imagined to comprise a *kledon*. In other words, it was the "prophetic thrust" of women's

110 *Lisa Maurizio*

laments that made them dangerous in a familial as well as a social or political setting. Legislation curtailing women's speech, then, was a curtailment of women's prerogative to speak publicly in a ritual setting in which their words – punctuated by the emphatic use of the first-person pronoun or adjective, deitics, and praise and blame and repeated by those around them – gained solemnity and became tinged with, or indeed were understood as, prophecy. It is no wonder that only Euripides offers any glimpse into the rhythm and pulse of women's funerary performances in Andromache's few elegiac verses. Women's elegiac laments were not replicated in tragedy because introducing a living ritual tradition on stage with no modification might threaten to break the aesthetic texture of the play – and might suggest male reliance on, if not competition with or comparison to, female artistry. Only distantly, or belatedly, did epigrams on funeral stelae deploy female elegiac verses, wherein their verses were abbreviated, professionalized, and masculinized because men's copy books and carving dictated most features of their form and content (Derderian 2001; Tsagalis 2008; Garner 2011).

If we turn to Delphic oracles, we find a similar process of masculinization and professionalization. We think of oracles as coming from the divinatory session at Delphi, and of course they did originate there. Yet they were often performed on other ritual and social occasions in the city-states that sought them, by ambassadors in assemblies and by poets who included them in their verses. These various oracular performances, which were then recorded in writing, are best understood in terms of what Hans Joachim Gehrke has called "intentional history," namely "history as an expression of a group's self-perception . . . where one finds that elements of self-categorization relevant for collective identity are regularly projected into the past or that older traditions are reinterpreted in their light" (Gehrke 2010, 16–17). In this way, Delphic oracles became historical narratives as men professionalized, stylized, masculinized, adopted, adapted, imitated, and committed the Pythia's verses to writing. The oral origins of oracles and the means of their transmission make it reasonable to argue that there is no written record of the Pythia's oracles (nor the *Iliad* of Homer for that matter) and that many Delphic oracles may have been constructed by local poets in and for their city-states (Maurizio 1997; Giangiulio 2001, 2010; Luraghi 2014). But this is an entirely different argument from positing that women were uneducated and thus unable to orally compose verses at a divinatory consultation at Delphi. I want to argue that the meters, stylistic devices, and prerogatives to praise and blame shared by verse oracles and women's funerary laments suggest that the Pythias were indeed competent to compose verses. If the Pythia "would seem to have been an uneducated peasant woman" (Parke 1945, 65), the burden of proof is on the holder of such a view to explain why and how a such a woman in ancient Greece could have been "uneducated" with respect to composing oral songs in hexameters or elegiacs. After all, a "peasant" woman's main occupation was to tend hearth, grindstone, loom, child, or deceased, and to sing songs while doing so. A Delphian woman chosen to serve in Apollo's temple would have acquired ritual and poetic competence necessary for her post, and this included composing verse oracles.

Shared meters and meanings   111

Notes

1 All translations are the author's unless otherwise indicated.
2 Page also argued that the Dorian dialect of Andromache's lament suggests that the origin of elegiac laments was in the Peloponnese. Yet, because *sung* passages in tragedy are in the Dorian dialect, Page's suggestion has remained unpersuasive. Recently, Budelmann and Power (2013) have rejected a strict dichotomy between spoken and sung elegy: the placement of Andromache's elegiac lament between her spoken iambics and the chorus' lyrical song suggests that it, along with elegies more generally, occupies an intermediate position that Budelmann and Power consider "spoken song." One implication of their argument is that the Dorian alphas in Andromache's lament may not be there because choral lyric in tragedy used the Dorian dialect but because, as Page first argued, songs in elegiac verse, including laments, developed first in the Peloponnese. While no scholarly consensus exists for such Doric origins, renewed attention to this question (Nobili 2011) and more pointedly to Dorian origins of occasional verses in hexameter sung by women (Levaniouk 2008) hint at a women's song tradition that yet may come into scholarly focus – one that shares dialectical features with West Greek/Dorian, the local dialect of Delphi.
3 Other oracles with an oracular "I" are: PW 17, 25, 41, 42, 45, 47, 52, 68, 69, 74, 95. 99, 100, 129, 130, 173, 206, 225, 230, 231, 233, 242, 243, 247, 254, 282, 311, 316, 329, 334, 338, 363, 366, 374, 424, 433, 443, 447, 487, 492, 537. These oracles contain a first-person verb or a first-person pronoun that refers to both Apollo and the Pythia.
4 For examples of abusive addresses, see PW 41, 55, 74, 106, 235, 245, 381, 514.
5 For examples of praise, see PW 29, 45, 88, 92, 206, 420, 469.

Works consulted

Alexiou, Margaret. 2002 [1974]. *The Ritual Lament in Greek Tradition*, edited by D. Yatromanolakis and P. Lanham, MD: Rowman and Littlefield Publishers.

Amandry, Pierre. 1950. *La Mantique Apollinienne a Delphes: Essai Sur Le Fonctionnement De L'Oracle.* Paris: de Bocard.

Andersen, Lene. 1987. *Studies of Oracular Voice: Concordance to Delphic Responses in Hexameter Verse.* Copenhagen: Munksgaard.

Bakker, E. 1999. "Homeric OUTOS and the Poetics od Diexis." *Classical Philology* 94: 1–19.

Barnes, H. R. 1979. "Enjambement and Oral Composition." *The American Philological Association* 109: 1–10.

———. 1995. "The Structure of the Elegiac Hexameter: A Comparison of the Structure of Elegiac and Stichic Hexameter Verse." In *Struttura e storia dell'esametro Greco, 2 vols. Studi di metrica classica 10*, edited by M. Fantuzzi and R. Pretagostini, 135–62. Rome: Gruppo editoriale internazionale.

Bowden, Hugh. 2005. *Classical Athens and the Delphic Oracle: Divination and Democracy.* Cambridge, UK: Cambridge University Press.

Bowie, E. L. 1986. "Early Greek Elegy, Symposium and Public Festival." *Journal of Hellenic Studies* 106: 13–35.

Bowra, Cecil Maurice. 1938. *Early Greek Elegists.* Cambridge, MA: Harvard University Press.

Budelmann, F. and Power, T. 2013. "The Inbetweenness of Sympotic Elegy." *The Journal of Hellenic Studies* 133: 1–19.

Calame, Claude. 1995. "From Choral Poetry to Tragic Stasimon: The Enactment of Women's Song." *Arion* 3: 136–54.

112 *Lisa Maurizio*

Clay, Jenny Strauss. 2009. "The Silence of the Pythia." In *Apolline Politics and Poetics*, edited by Lucia Athanassaki, Richard P. Martin, and John F. Miller, 5–16. Athens: The European Cultural Centre of Delphi.

D'Alessio, G.B. 2009. "Defining Local Identities in Greek Lyric Poetry." In *Wandering Poets in Ancient Greek Culture: Travel, Locality and Pan–Hellenism*, edited by Ian Rutherford and Richard Hunter, 137–67. Cambridge, UK: Cambridge University Press.

Davies, Anna Morpurgo. 1964. "'Doric' Features in the Language of Hesiod." *Glotta* 42.3–4: 138–65.

Delgado, J.A. Fernandez. 1986. *Los Oraculos y Hesiodo.* Extremadura: Universidad de Extremadura.

Derderian, Katherine. 2001. *Leaving Words to Remember: Greek Mourning and the Advent of Literacy*. Mnemosyne Supplement 209. Leiden: Brill.

Dué, Casey. 2002. *Homeric Variations on Lament by Briseis*. Lanham, MD: Rowman and Littlefield Publishers.

———. 2009. *The Captive Women's Lament in Greek Tragedy.* Austin, TX: University of Texas Press.

Faraone, Christopher. 1995. "The 'Performative Future' in Three Hellenistic Incantations and Theocritus' Second *Idyll.*" *Classical Philology* 90: 901–15.

———. 2008. *The Stanzaic Architecture of Early Greek Elegy.* Oxford: Oxford University Press.

Flower, Michael A. 2009. *The Seer in Ancient Greece*. Berkeley and Los Angeles: University of California Press.

Fontenrose, Joseph. 1978. *The Delphic Oracle.* Berkeley and Los Angeles: University of California Press.

Garcia, J. 2002. "Ritual Speech in Early Greek Song." In *Epea and Grammata: Oral and Written Communication in Ancient Greece. Volume 4: Mnemosyne Supplement 230*, edited by I. Worthington and J. M. Foley, 29–53. Leiden: Brill.

Garland, R. 1989. "The Well Ordered Corpse: An Investigation into the Motives behind Greek Funerary Legislation." *Bulletin of the Institute of Classical Studies* 36: 1–15.

Garner, Robert Scott. 2011. *Traditional Elegy: The Interplay of Meter, Tradition and Context in Early Greek Poetry*. Oxford: Oxford University Press.

Gehrke, Hans–Joachim. 2010. "Greek Representations of the Past." In *Intentional History: Spinning Time in Ancient Greece*, edited by Lin Foxhall, Hans–Joachim Gehrke, and Nino Luraghi, 15–34. Stuttgart: Franz Steiner Verlag.

Giangiulio, Maurizio. 2001. "Constructing the Past: Colonial Traditions and the Writing of History: The Case of Cyrene." In *The Historian's Craft in the Age of Herodotus*, edited by Nino Laraghi, 116–37. Oxford: Oxford University Press.

———. 2010. "Collective Identities, Imagined Past, and Delphi." In *Intentional History: Spinning Time in Ancient Greece*, edited by Lin Foxhall, Hans–Joachim Gehrke, and Nino Luraghi, 121–36. Stuttgart: Franz Steiner Verlag.

Herzfeld, M. 1993. "In Defiance of Destiny: The Management of Time and Gender at a Cretan Funeral." *American Ethnologist* 20: 241–55.

Hirvonenk, K. 1969. "Cledonomancy and the Grinding Slave, *Odyssey* 20.91–121." *Arctos* 6: 5–21.

Holst–Warhaft, Gail. 1995. *Dangerous Voices: Women's Laments and Greek Literature.* New York and London: Routledge Press.

Ibanez, J.M. Nieto. 1988. "Fórmulas Homéricas y Lenguaje Oracular." *Minerva* 2: 33–46.

———. 1989. "Estudio Estadístico del Hexámetro de los oráculos de Delfos." *Revue: Informatique et Statistique dans les Sciences humaines* 25: 139–55.

Shared meters and meanings 113

———. 1990. "La Prosodia del Hexametro Delphico." *Minerva* 4: 53–73.

Johnston, Sarah Iles. 2008. *Ancient Greek Divination*. Malden, MA: Wiley-Blackwell.

Karanika, Andromache. 2014. *Voices at Work: Women, Performance and Labor in Ancient Greece*. Baltimore, MD: Johns Hopkins University Press.

Latiener, Donald. 2005. "Signifying Names and Other Ominous Accidental Utterances in Classical Historiography." *GRBS* 45: 35–57.

Levaniouk, Olga. 2008. "Lament and Hymenaios in Erinna's *Distaff*." In *Lament: Studies in the Ancient Mediterranean and Beyond*, edited by Ann Suter, 200–32. Oxford: Oxford University Press.

Loraux, Nicole. 1998. *Mothers in Mourning*. Ithaca, NY: Cornell University Press.

Luraghi, Nino. 2014. "Oracoli esametrici nelle Storie di Erodoto: Appunti per un bilancio provvisorio." *Seminari Romani di Cultura Greca* 3–2: 233–56.

Martin, Richard P. 2008. "Keens from the Absent Chorus: Troy to Ulster." In *Lament: Studies in the Ancient Mediterranean and Beyond*, edited by Ann Suter, 118–38. Oxford: Oxford University Press.

Maurizio, Lisa. 1997. "Delphic Oracles as Oral Performances: Authenticity and Historical Evidence." *Cl. Ant.* 16: 308–34.

———. 2013. "Interpretative Strategies for Delphic Oracles and Kledons: Prophecy Falsification and Individualism." In *Divination in the Ancient World: Religious Options and the Individual*, edited by Veit Rosenberger, 61–79. Stuttgart: Franz Steiner Verlag.

McClure, Laura. 1999. *Spoken Like a Woman: Speech and Gender in Athenian Drama*. Princeton: Princeton University Press.

McLeod, Wallace. 1961. "Oral Bards at Delphi." *The American Philological Association* 92: 317–25.

Muich, Rebecca. 2010–2011. "Focalized and Embedded Speech in Andromache's Iliadic Laments." *ICS* 35–6: 1–24.

Nagy, G. 2010. "Ancient Greek Elegy." In *The Oxford Handbook of the Elegy*, edited by Karen Weisman, 13–42. Oxford: Oxford University Press.

Nobili, C. 2011. "Threnodic Elegy in Sparta." *GRBS* 5: 26–48.

Page, D.L. 1936. "The Elegiacs in Euripides *Andromache*." In *Greek Poetry and Life: Essays Presented to Gilbert Murray on his Seventieth Birthday*, edited by Cyril Bailey, 206–30. Oxford: Oxford University Press.

Parke, H.W. 1945. "The Use of Other than Hexameter Verse in Delphic Oracles." *Hermathena* 65: 58–66.

———. 1981. "Apollo and the Muses, or Prophecy in Greek Verse." *Hermathena* 130–131: 99–112.

Parke, H.W. and Wormell, D.E.W. 1956. *Delphic Oracle, 2 Volumes*. Oxford: Basil Blackwell.

Peradotto, J. 1969. "Cledonomancy in the *Oresteia*." *American Journal of Philology* 90: 1–21.

Perkell, Christine. 2008. "Reading the Laments of *Iliad* 24." In *Lament: Studies in the Ancient Mediterranean and Beyond*, edited by Ann Suter, 93–118. Oxford: Oxford University Press.

Richardson, N. 1993. *The* Iliad*: A Commentary. Vol 6. Books 21–24*. Cambridge: Cambridge University Press.

Rossi, L.E. 1981. "Gli oracoli come documento d'improvvisazione." In *I poemi epici rapsodici non omerici e la tradizione orale*, edited by Carlo Brillante, Mario Cantilena, and Carlo Odo Pavese, 203–30. Padua: Antenore.

Seremetakis, C. Nadia. 1991. *The Last Word: Women, Death, and Divination in Inner Mani*. Chicago, IL: University of Chicago Press.

114 *Lisa Maurizio*

Shapiro, Alan. 1991. "The Iconography of Mourning in Athenian Art." *AJArch.* 95: 629–56.

Stears, Karen. 2008. "Death Becomes Her: Gender and Athenian Death Ritual." In *Lament: Studies in the Ancient Mediterranean and Beyond*, edited by Ann Suter, 139–55. Oxford: Oxford University Press.

Stoneman, R. 2011. *The Ancient Oracles: Making Gods Speak.* New Haven: Yale University Press.

Swift, L. 2010. *The Hidden Chorus: Echoes of Genre in Tragic Lyric.* Oxford: Oxford University Press.

Tsagalis, Christos C. 2004. *Epic Grief: Personal Laments in Homer's Iliad.* Berlin and New York: Walter de Gruyter.

———. 2008. *Inscribing Sorrow: Fourth-Century Attic Funerary Epigrams.* Berlin and New York: Walter de Gruyter.

Weinbaum, Batya. 2001. "Lament Ritual Transformed into Literature." *Journal of American Folklore* 114: 20–39.

West, M. L. 1966. *Theogony: Edited with Prolegomena and Commentary.* Oxford: Clarendon Press.

———. 1974. *Studies in Greek Elegy and Iambus.* Berlin and New York: Walter de Gruyter.

6 Priestess and polis in Euripides' *Iphigeneia in Tauris*

Laura McClure

Introduction

Euripides' *Iphigeneia in Tauris* (*IT*) is the only extant tragedy to feature a priestess as its protagonist. As such, the play is deeply engaged with religion. References to formal and traditional ritual practices, such as prayer, supplication, and sacrifice, as well as nuptial and funerary ritual, abound. *Iphigeneia in Tauris* also includes three distinct aetiologies related to actual or imagined Athenian cultic practice. The first explains the origins of the custom of drinking from individual cups in the Athenian festival of the Choes as an attempt to avoid Orestes' pollution from matricide (Eur. *IT* 947–60). In the second, Athena instructs Orestes to found a cult at Halai, where the sacred image of Taurian Artemis will be set up in its precinct and honored with a new, nonpolluting rite of bloodshed in commemoration of the Taurian cult of human sacrifice (1446–61). Finally, Iphigeneia is to be installed as a priestess of Artemis at nearby Brauron and will become the subject of another cult. She will be posthumously honored with a tomb and will receive dedications of clothing for women who have died in childbirth (1462–7).

From the perspective of Greek religion, Iphigeneia will be deified and receive a cult (Sourvinou-Inwood 2003, 36). No other female character in an extant tragedy formally receives this honor within Attica (Wolff 1992, 320; Sourvinou-Inwood 2003, 174; Hall 2013, 30). Although much has been written about ritual in the play, especially about the aetiologies (Wolff 1992; Dunn 2000), not enough attention has been given to the form and function of Iphigeneia's religious authority and its relation to the polis. This chapter will look in detail at how the sacred duties performed by Iphigeneia, especially her control of ritual space and performance of ritual procedure, afford her unprecedented scope for action within the play, endowing her with

116 *Laura McClure*

extraordinary power over the Taurian community and foreshadowing her role as a founder of a cult in the Athenian polis. Her ritual competence suggests how Athenian women may have influenced their communities and possibly even acted autonomously within a religious framework.

Produced around 413 BCE, *Iphigeneia in Tauris* is a play of mixed reversal, variously identified as a tragicomedy, a romantic tragedy, an escape play, and even a form of satyr drama (Burnett 1971, 71–2; Sansone 1976, 292). The plot exemplifies the structural complexity of the genre in its use of exotic setting, foreign characters, mythic innovation, recognition, and happy ending. To summarize briefly: although believed to have died at Aulis, Iphigeneia has been rescued by Artemis and installed as her priestess in the land of Tauris on the Black Sea. Her brother, Orestes, is improbably driven there by Apollo to steal the cult image of the goddess and return it to Greece and so put an end to his matricide-induced madness. Just prior to his arrival, Iphigeneia reports a dream that an earthquake has destroyed the ancestral palace and left just one pillar standing. She interprets it to mean her brother has died, a conclusion that delays the recognition of the siblings and leads to his near death at her hands. Once the recognition is accomplished, the reunited pair contrives to steal the cult image of the goddess by convincing the barbarian king, Thoas, that both it and the putative victims require purification with seawater. This deception allows Iphigeneia, Orestes, and Pylades to escape to the ship with the statue. At the last minute, a sudden wind threatens to wash them back to Tauris, necessitating the intervention of Athena, who orders Thoas not to pursue the fugitives and instructs Orestes and Iphigeneia to found two new cults in Attica, one at Halai and the other at Brauron (1438–69).

Despite this singular portrayal of a female protagonist who outwits a powerful king to save herself and her brother, not to mention founding a new Attic cult, critics have tended to downplay Iphigeneia's authority and agency. Wolff views the establishment of her cult as a curtailment of her power rather than as an expression of it, in contrast to Orestes, who survives mortal risk to achieve heroic success (Wolff 1992, 330). Zeitlin argues that her cultic association with death in childbirth represents in symbolic terms her arrested development, "having failed to reach motherhood, she will then be the witness of other women's failures" (Zeitlin 2006, 217). Tzanetou and Cole similarly argue that Iphigeneia cannot escape her problematic past and successfully reintegrate within her community because she is unable to complete the female rites of passage overseen by Artemis (Tzanetou 1999–2000, 204; Cole 2004, 220–1). In contrast, Hall views Iphigeneia as a heroine and stresses the positive results of her quest, the public recognition of "women's contribution to the city-state in the production both of children and textiles, in the performance of motherhood and ritual" (Hall 2013, 30). Building on the latter point, I will show first how Iphigeneia's ritual competence is articulated in the Taurian polis and then examine how it facilitates the escape and the foundation of a new cult. Finally, I will situate this ritual activity in the context of Iphigeneia's worship at Aulis and its implications for the role of women in the Athenian polis.

Women, religion, and the polis

It is by now a commonplace of Classical scholarship that although women were excluded from political participation in the Athenian polis, they actively engaged in religious activities and thus possessed a form of "cultic citizenship" (Parker 2011, 241). Athenian men and women experienced relative equality in the performance of ritual acts such as sacrifice, prayer, dedication, and processions, whether as part of household worship or public festivals. Religious activity dominated the Athenian political calendar: 170 festival days were set aside for the worship of a particular deity, while over 2,000 cults existed in Attica alone. Women participated in around 85 percent of all religious activities and were in charge of more than 40 major cults (Blok 2001, 112, 114; Connelly 2007, 276). If we agree with Connor's assertion that "radical separation between sacred and secular does not directly apply to Athenian society," it stands to reason that women also actively contributed to and even influenced the political life of the polis in their capacity as religious agents (Connor 1988, 184; Blok 2004).

Athenian drama offers a rich resource for understanding these activities because of its extensive use of female characters, all of whom perform rituals, whether large or small, on behalf of household or polis. Oft-cited examples such as Aristophanes' *Lysistrata* (638–48) and Euripides' *Melanippe Captive* (*TGrF* 5.1 F494.12–22) attest to female cultic activities as a source of authority and influence in the community. These ritual representations are embedded within the polis ideology of tragedy and as such serve to reinforce civic – although not necessarily democratic – values and social norms, especially with regard to gender (Griffin 1998; Rhodes 2003). Richard Seaford, for instance, argues that tragedy stages perversions of domestic ritual, such as sacrifice, wedding, and funeral, to assert the authority of the polis during a critical period of state formation (Seaford 1995, xiv). More recently, Barbara Goff has investigated women's ritual practice in Greek tragedy in order to uncover how historical women may have exerted influence and autonomy in the Classical city as well as to show how the genre used women's ritual to articulate sociopolitical anxieties (Goff 2004, 295). Tragedy's ritual discourse is therefore deeply intertwined with what Christiane Sourvinou-Inwood has called "polis religion," which she argues provided the fundamental framework for all religious activity (Sourvinou-Inwood 2000, 19–20). Recent critiques have rightly emphasized the limited scope of control exercised by the polis over religious activities (Garland 1984, 75; Aleshire 1994, 10; Cole 2004; Eidinow 2011; Kindt 2012). Nonetheless, it remains a useful concept for understanding the religious framework of Euripides' *Iphigeneia in Tauris*, especially given that Iphigeneia serves as the priestess of an imaginary polis religion and uses her responsibilities and duties to bring about the rescue of the victims and the goddess (Connelly 2007, 197–219; Parker 2011, 53–6; Cole 2004, 122–36).

Priestess of Taurian Artemis

The ritual world of *Iphigeneia in Tauris* evokes real-life rituals, such as prayer, lamentation, and purification, and yet organizes them around the disturbing

118   *Laura McClure*

demand for human sacrifice. Artemis is identified with this practice in the very first lines of the play as Iphigeneia recounts her slaughter at Aulis (8). Mandated by the city, the Taurian custom of human sacrifice predates her arrival there (38). Although a foreigner "without polis" (220), Iphigeneia nonetheless administers a form of polis religion on behalf of the Taurians (464, 595). She does so unwillingly (595) and with little enthusiasm, rejecting the belief that Artemis herself actually requires human victims. Instead, she blames the custom on the local inhabitants who, she argues, project their own homicidal tendencies onto the goddess, "I think that the people here, because of their violent nature, attribute this sorry business to her" (389–90; see Platnauer 1938, 92–3; Sourvinou-Inwood 2003, 33–4).

Iphigeneia is a living witness to the horror of human sacrifice, and the trauma of her own near death at Aulis serves as the defining moment of her history (cf. 211–17, 358–60, 563–5, 770, 783–5, 852–61; cf. 338–9 (chorus); Strachan 1976). She equates the cult at Tauris with the memory of Aulis (358). The language of the play further develops the linguistic parallels between the two places: Iphigeneia's purification of sacrificial victims (*chernibes*, 58 and *passim*) recalls her nuptial bath at Aulis (*chernibon*, 861), while as priestess (*hierean*, 34) in charge of the Taurian cult, she performs the same sacrificial role as her father (*hiereus*, 360). Without an origin myth or clear purpose, Artemis' rites appear to have meaning only to Iphigeneia in that they continually remind her of her past, "I cannot forget those former troubles" (361). In remembering Aulis, Iphigeneia proves her loyalty to the goddess who rescued her from death, while her escape represents a betrayal, a "forgetting" of the original benefaction (1419). The memory of trauma will become an essential component of Iphigeneia's worship at Brauron in the form of dedications for women who have died in childbirth.

Iphigeneia's ritual competency

Although powerless to change the grim requirement of the barbarian cult, Iphigeneia can and does use her control of ritual procedure and sacred space to effect her return to Greece and the rescue of both her brother and the goddess. This section will look first at the ways in which Iphigeneia's duties directly reflect aspects of female sacred service in the Athenian polis and then consider how these are refracted through the foreign cult. Before turning to the escape plan, let us look more closely at how Iphigeneia's status as priestess endows her with religious authority and ritual control over the sanctuary of Taurian Artemis. Many of Iphigeneia's religious activities conform to Beate Dignas' description of the work of priests and priestesses:

> to perform or assist in public or private sacrifice, to maintain order and respect for the sacred laws, to organize the religious festivals, to look after the cult

Priestess and polis in Iphigeneia   119

statue and the relevant cult-buildings, and also to check on the revenues and expenditures of the sanctuary.

(Dignas 2002, 33)

Her main tasks are to direct the cultic ceremonies of sacrifice, particularly preparatory purification, and the care of the sacred precinct and cult image. Although they were prominent public figures, priestesses did not normally exert authority beyond the boundaries of their sanctuaries (Garland 1984, 75–6). Iphigeneia clearly oversteps these bounds by dictating a new ritual procedure in order to facilitate the theft of temple property, a crime that carried the death penalty and precluded burial within the boundaries of Attica (Xen. *Hell.* 1.7.22; *Mem.* 1.2.62; Isoc. 20.6; see Garland 1984, 79).

As the priestess in charge of a civic deity, Iphigeneia perhaps evoked for the audience the priestess of Athena Polias. Since this position comprised the highest-ranking and most visible priesthood in Athens, it would have been familiar to everyone in the Classical polis (Garland 1984, 86, 91–4; Kron 1996, 140). Moreover, she likely supervised the purification rituals central to the annual festival of the Plynteria (Deubner 1932, 17–22; Parke 1977, 152–5; Parker 1983, 26–8; Garland 1984, 77). Held at the end of Thargelion, the Plynteria entailed the cleaning of the temple and cult image of Athena. Members of the Praxiergidai *genos* removed the clothing from the ancient wooden object, veiled it and then performed secret rites (Plut. *Alc.* 34.1). The statue was then taken from the temple and carried in a procession down to the sea, where it was washed. Since the veiling of the image represented "a kind of absence" (Parker 2011, 186), the day was regarded as highly inauspicious. Temples were closed (Pollux 8.41), and individuals avoided undertaking any serious enterprise (Xen. *Hell.* 1.4.12). Alcibiades had the misfortune to return to Athens for the last time on this unlucky day, whereupon the goddess greeted him with hostility, appearing to, "cover her face and keep him at a distance from herself" (Plut. *Alc.* 2).

Iphigeneia's deception involves many of the same actions: a cult object that closes its eyes, its removal from the temple by the priestess who carries it in a procession through the city streets, veiling – albeit of the captives and king, not of the image – secret rites, and purification with seawater (Sourvinou-Inwood 2003, 302–3). It is also noteworthy that Athena, rather than Artemis, intervenes at the end of the play, giving instructions for the foundation of a new cult that will be overseen and controlled by Athens.

The keys to the temple

Like those of historical priestesses, Iphigeneia's sacred duties at Tauris closely resemble female household tasks in that she is largely charged with supervising the temple, which is described as a domestic space (Cole 2004, 113; Goff 2004, 47–8, 51–61; Connelly 2007, 5; Parker 2011, 95, 98, 113, 242, n. 47). Both she and the goddess reside within what is interchangeably called a *domos* and an *anaktoron* (65–6). The assimilation of sacred space to the household is further seen

120   *Laura McClure*

in Iphigeneia's role as its gate-keeper (1153) and key carrier (131). Possession of the key symbolizes her access to, and control of, the restricted inner space of the temple in which treasures are stored, including the image of the goddess. It also replicates the role of the Greek wife, who looked after the keys of the storeroom, where family valuables were kept. For example, Penelope wields the curved bronze key to the storeroom containing the household's treasures (Hom. *Od.* 21.6, 47). Other examples include Io, who holds the key to the temple of Hera (Aesch. *Supp.* 291), and Athena, who alone knows the whereabouts of the keys to the house where Zeus' thunderbolt is stored (Aesch. *Eum.* 827). In Greek art, the temple key is the primary iconographic signifier of priestly status for females, while for males it is the sacrificial knife (see Dillon 2002, 80–3; Connelly 2007, 14, 92–3; Parker 2011, 50; Bremmer 2013, 91, n. 20).

As the supervisor of the sanctuary and the holder of the temple key, Iphigeneia has access to a space forbidden to other mortals and the authority to determine who may or may not enter it (Garland 1984, 76). Moreover, Iphigeneia lacks a male guardian, further signaling her ability to operate semi-independently, as did real-life Athenian priestesses. According to Uta Kron (1996, 141), Athenian priestesses did not require a *kyrios* to act in legal matters: she cites the case filed by the priestess of Demeter against a male colleague for impiously performing a sacrifice ([Dem.] 59.115–17; Ath. 13.594b).

The cult statue

Even more important than her control of the temple entrance is Iphigeneia's direct contact with the cult image, which only she is authorized to touch (1045). The care of this object was especially important in priesthoods reserved for maidens, such as those surrounding Artemis. These priesthoods often involved the maintenance of portable cult statues that were perceived as living entities rather than as mere representations (Schnapp 1988; Cole 2004, 200; Connelly 2007, 39). Such a statue required shelter, clothing, cleaning, and sustenance, all of which the priestesses provided. It typically occupied the secure interior of the temple into which entry was restricted only to cult personnel: hence the requirement of a key carrier. Once installed inside the temple, the statue often became the focus of worship, adorned with special garments and taken out for processions (the dressing of cult images is discussed in detail in this volume by Cecilia Brøns; Kindt 2012, 43–4). The innermost recess of the temple not only safeguarded the image from theft, as in our play, but also served to protect individuals from coming into contact with its awesome power. Plutarch reports that when the cult statue of Artemis at Pellene was removed from the temple as part of a procession, it aroused such dread that the participants averted their gaze out of fear (Cole 2004, 200; Bremmer 2013, 97–8):

> But the Pellenians say that the *bretas* of the goddess usually stands untouched, and that whenever it is removed by the priestess and carried forth from the

Priestess and polis in Iphigeneia   121

temple, no one looks directly at it, but all turn their gaze away; for not only to mortals is it a horrible and unpleasant sight, but also the trees past which it is carried become barren and miscarry their fruit.

(Plut. *Arat.* 32.2)

Susan Cole speculates that respect for the power and danger of such threatening deities resulted in myths of foreign origins and their association with unsettled areas, as depicted in our play (Cole 2004, 203). The task of caring for the cult image inside the temple – usually performed by women in cults of Artemis – also meant that a certain amount of female religious activity occurred in secret, out of the public view. This prerogative will prove indispensable to the success of Iphigeneia's escape plan.

As the object of Orestes' fervent quest, the cult statue of Artemis is mentioned almost 30 times within the course of the play, whether as a *xoanon*, *agalma*, or *bretas* (on these terms, see Cropp 2000, 179–80). The term *xoanon* (1359), used only here in Euripides' surviving work, would have suggested to the contemporary audience an ancient, carved wooden image, much like the sacrosanct *agalma* of Athena Polias, described by Pausanias as "the holiest thing of all" (Paus. 1.26.6), said to have fallen from heaven. Xenophon refers to the cypress-wood copy of Ephesian Artemis with the same term (Xen. *Anab.* 5.3.12). Orestes similarly describes the figure as carved (*xeston . . . agalma*, 111–12). The term *xestos* can also mean "polished," suggesting a stone icon (Bremmer 2013, 95). Indeed, we are probably to imagine a wooden image easily carried in the arms of Iphigeneia (1158; Bremmer 2013, 95). More frequently, however, the image is called a *bretas* or *agalma*. Although the former suggests an Archaic image, the terms are interchangeable in the play, as evidenced by Thoas' acknowledgement that he will obey Athena's command and allow the statue to leave Tauris: "Let them go to your land with the *agalma* of the goddess and may they successfully set up the *bretas* there" (1480–81). The statue occupies a fixed pedestal in the interior of the temple (1157) and inspires fear in both Iphigeneia (37) and her potential victims (277). Iphigeneia's stewardship of this potentially threatening object gives her authority over the king and citizens of Tauris, since only she can come into contact with it and perform the requisite rites of purification that will effectively neutralize its power.

Another aspect of Iphigeneia's competency derives from close identification with the goddess. In actual religious practice, it was not uncommon for a priestess to be associated with the cult statue of the goddess she served, or perhaps even to dress similarly; for example, funerary *stelai* depict priestesses holding the cult image of a goddess (Burkert 1985, 97–8; Dillon 2002, 81–3, figs 3.2–3; Connelly 2007, 104–15). The use of the term *agalma* for the divine image encourages the view of Iphigeneia as the doublet of Artemis, inasmuch as it recalls her status as "the ornament" of her father's house in Aeschylus' *Agamemnon* (*domon agalma*, 208). The language of the play continually equates the pair: both are called *potnia* ("mistress"; 463, 1123; 533, 1082) and *kore* ("girl"; 402, 114); both were dropped on Tauris from the sky (29–30, 88, 977) and are now objects of rescue (28, 1400,

122   *Laura McClure*

1359). Both are untouchable (*athiktois,* 799; 1045; Wolff 1992, 320; Zeitlin 2006, 201, 2011, 452–3). Both make use of clever arguments (*sophismata*, 380, 1031; Hall 2013, 29). Once heroized, Iphigeneia will receive dedications just like Artemis, only of clothing rather than of human victims (1464–5). Athena further equates girl and goddess when she instructs Orestes to "take the image and your sister and go" (1448). This assimilation may reflect the genesis of Artemis worship at Brauron. Hollinshead proposes that the original cult centered on Iphigeneia, whose name, "strong in birth," points to her origins as a "cave-dwelling goddess of childbirth in which women's garments were dedicated" until her identity gradually merged with Artemis (Hollinshead 1985, 425–6, 428; for Iphigeneia's name as an epithet of Artemis, see Platnauer 1938, ix; Garland 1984, 88).

Purity and sacrifice

In addition to supervising the sanctuary and caring for the cult image, another primary ritual duty of Iphigeneia as priestess is the preparation of victims for sacrifice in her capacity as *thuepolos* (1359; cf. Eur. *Tro.* 330 [Kassandra], *IA* 746 [Kalchas], *El.* 665). At first, it is unclear whether she actually kills the victims herself, a task typically, but not always, assigned to male cultic personnel in animal sacrifice. Uncertainty about Iphigenia's behavior is mirrored in the broader uncertainty about blood sacrifice (Osborne 1993; Dillon 2002, 88, 241–6; Cole 2004, 93, 98–100; Goff 2004, 42; Connelly 2007, 179–90; Parker 2011, 241, n. 45; Bremmer 2013, 92). In the prologue, she says simply, "I sacrifice" (*thuo* 39), which leads her to explain that she only performs the preliminary rites, while those inside do the actual killing (40–1; for the line as an interpolation, see Cropp 2000, 175). This ambiguity builds dramatic suspense, raising the possibility that the girl might unwittingly kill her brother before she recognizes him. Similarly, when Orestes asks in the recognition scene who will sacrifice him (617), she states that she will (*ego*, 618). In response to his surprise that a woman will perform the sacrifice (621), Iphigeneia then quickly clarifies that she will only sprinkle water around his head (622). Once the recognition is accomplished, Iphigeneia confirms that she only officiates in the slaughter of strangers (776). Further, Thoas asks whether she has the lustral basins and her sword (*xiphos*) ready (1190). The term *xiphos*, used first in connection with Iphigeneia's own death at Aulis and subsequently with that of Orestes (27, 621, 880, 1190; cf. 1459), hints at the priestess's complicity in ritual violence, although it probably means that she will only provide the instrument of slaughter.

Iphigeneia's main cultic duty therefore is not murder but rather the more customary task of purification, as signified by the terms *chernips* and *hydraino*. As she recounts in her dream: "So I, observing this art of stranger-killing, sprinkled [him] with water, as though about to die" (53–4). Indeed, water was central to Artemis' rites at Brauron, where it was used for rituals of transition, for purification before marriage and after childbirth, and for rituals associated with childrearing (Cole 2004, 191–4; Bremmer 2013, 88). The divine demand for purity is further

Priestess and polis in Iphigeneia   123

seen in the prohibition against allowing individuals polluted by murder, childbirth, or death to approach Artemis' altar (381–4):

> When any of us mortals has contact with bloodshed,
> or even touches childbirth or a corpse with their hands,
> she bans them from her altars, judging them polluted –
> while she herself relishes human sacrifices.

This taboo will provide the rationale for the escape plan, since Orestes, as a matricide, has incurred pollution (*ou kithara*, 1163; *miasma*, 1173) and must therefore be cleansed before he can be sacrificed. Iphigeneia, in contrast, has avoided the pollution of childbirth, thanks to her failed nuptials at Aulis, and remains fixed in a state of perpetual virginity (*agamos ateknos*, 220). She meets the requirements of ritual purity for a priestess of Artemis and, as such, is inviolate, like the cult statue itself; not even her robes are to be touched by a murderer (799).

The other Artemis

The goddess whom Iphigenia serves is a deity almost exclusively preoccupied with murder. The other Artemis, the one who oversees the maturation of girls and the successful delivery of children, is brought into the world of the play by the chorus of captive female worshippers. In contrast to the play's heroine, the members of the chorus have no identity: they are placeless and nameless, with no mythic ancestry or known place of residence, and they are sent to no particular locale when rescued. They come from "horse-rich Hellas" (132) and were purchased expressly to work for the priestess and altars of Tauris after the destruction of their native city (1115–16). The chorus thus has no collective identity except as Greek ritual participants in the foreign sanctuary (Hall 2013, 53). From a mythic perspective, they play the part of an entourage of nymphs to Iphigeneia's Artemis (Hom. *Od.* 6.102–9). Their first words identify their religious function as they urge a ritual silence (123) before addressing a prayer to the goddess (126). They process to the temple on "sacred virgin foot" (130) and then join Iphigeneia in lamentations for Orestes, who is presumed dead (179–80). As ritual slaves (63, 131, 144, 451), they have no capacity for independent action and no authority over the Taurians, in contrast to the priestess they serve.

Like Iphigeneia, they reject the barbarian practice of human sacrifice, condemning it as contrary to religious norms (*oukh hosias*, 464). In this respect, they reinforce a Hellenic, perhaps even Athenian, perception of Artemis. Their songs interject a Greek worldview through their memories of home, most of which revolve around the rituals of maidenhood (Cropp 2000, 41). Perhaps because of their role as worshippers of Artemis "the choral goddess par excellence," they frequently call attention to their participation in choral performance (Kowalzig 2013, 183). They yearn for their home and a return to the choral performances of their polis (453–5), and happily recall their girlhood dancing at weddings, where they advertised their beauty and eligibility (1143–52; see Cropp 2000, 243).

124 *Laura McClure*

Through their memories, the chorus continually affirms Athenian cultic norms for women against the savage practices of the Taurians. Central to their odes is the role of Artemis in female life. They frequently return to the spaces associated with the goddess: Eurotas, Sparta, and her birthplace in Delos (Hall 2013, 55). They call upon Artemis in her function as Birth-Bringer or Lochia (cf. Eur. *Supp*. 958; *LIMC* ii 'Artemis', no. 721a; Cropp 2000, 51, 240), expressing their desire to participate in her choral performances at Delos (1097–8; cf. *Hom. Hymn* 3.146–50; Eur. *Hec.* 463–5; Callim. *Hymn* 4. 279, 304–6; see also Cropp 2000, 240).

Their evocation of Artemis Lochia highlights their own deprivations of marriage and children while at the same time affirming her importance in the female life cycle, foreshadowing the capacity in which she will be worshipped at Brauron. The chorus thus stresses Artemis' non-Taurian aspects, particularly her role in ensuring the reproductive capacity of the community's women, the health of its children, and the ritual cycle that marked the stages of the reproductive process, as well as indicating what will be the nature of her worship at Brauron (Cole 2004, 209).

Ritual deception

Now that we have examined the forms of Iphigeneia's ritual competence and the two faces of Artemis, let us look at how Iphigeneia deploys her sacred duties to formulate and implement the escape plan. Given that Artemis' temple is staffed almost entirely by foreign cultic personnel, it is not surprising that the Taurians do not seem to have a firm grasp of their own polis religion. Indeed, to judge by the herdsman's account of the arrival of strangers on Tauris, they cannot easily distinguish god from mortal, since he at first mistakes Orestes and Pylades for deities (*daimones*, 267; cf. *agalmata*, 273).

By portraying the Taurians as stereotypical barbarians, easily duped and unfamiliar with Greek myth and custom, the herdsman's speech foreshadows the rescue stratagem, which hinges on the ignorance and gullibility of the king for its success. Iphigeneia, in contrast, is represented as stereotypically Greek and feminine in her cleverness. The king remarks, "Hellas raised her to be wise" (1180) and later praises her foresight (*promethia*, 1201) in dealing with the potential contamination of Artemis' statue. Iphigeneia's "ingenious solution" (1029), the washing of the statue in seawater, prompts Orestes to exclaim, "Women are clever at coming up with schemes!" (1031). The female penchant for duplicity combined with the ritual authority of the priestess ensures the success of the stratagem. When reporting the disappearance of the captives, the messenger resorts to another tragic generalization: "how untrustworthy is the female race!" (1298).

By engineering and carrying out a fraudulent ritual performance that nonetheless contains elements of actual religious practice, Iphigeneia's actions fit with the play's general pattern of ritual deception (Hartigan 1986; Wright 2005, 213–14). With a similar trick, Odysseus lured Iphigeneia to Aulis on the pretext of marriage to Achilles (24). This cunning treachery, repeatedly

Priestess and polis in Iphigeneia   125

described as a *dolos* (371, 539, 859), in turn leads to the erroneous performance of nuptial and funerary rites, inciting Clytemnestra to provide a nuptial bath (818) for a wedding that never happens and in turn to accept a lock of hair as a funerary offering for a spurious death (819–21). The dream reported in the prologue (41–60) similarly leads to ritual error in that it falsely convinces the girl that her brother is dead, causing her to perform unnecessary lamentations on his behalf (143–251).

But the greatest act of ritual duplicity belongs to Artemis, when she interrupts the sacrifice of Iphigeneia, stealing her away to Tauris (27), and yet does not disclose the girl's actual fate, thereby setting in motion a string of violent intrafamilial murders. In using the treachery of Odysseus (1316, 1355) to steal the statue (1359) and return home alive, Iphigeneia thus reenacts and reverses the original deception at Aulis.

The use and abuse of ritual

In addition to her cunning, Iphigeneia's control of sacred space and objects, supervision of the sacrificial victims, and knowledge of correct ritual procedures in her capacity as priestess of the Taurian cult are indispensable to the success of the escape stratagem. Once captured, the victims, as the property of the goddess, are considered holy (469) and therefore subject to the authority of the priestess (Bremmer 2013, 94). Iphigeneia has the power to determine whether they comply with Artemis' demand for purity, as well as what will happen to their bodies after death (630–5).

Unlike real-life priestesses, she also has the autonomy to determine correct ritual procedure and to dictate it to the community. So she will proclaim that it is not right to sacrifice Orestes and Pylades to the goddess in their contaminated condition (1035). Whereas Iphigeneia had earlier spoken of purifying Orestes in preparation for his sacrifice (705), she will now use his pollution incurred from matricide (1037) as a pretext for transferring the captives to the shore, where they will be cleansed with sea water (1039). Other scholars have argued that the fake ritual actually provides the real purification of Orestes (Wolff 1992, 317; Goff 2004, 339). The cult image must also be cleansed, on the grounds that it has also come into contact with the polluted Orestes (1041). She then employs her cultic prerogative regarding the *agalma* in service of the plan: as the only person permitted to touch the cult image, only she has the authority to remove it from the temple. Her manipulation of Taurian ritual further requires the complicity of the chorus, whom she exhorts to stay silent, "for we are women: a race friendly to one another and most steadfast at protecting our common interests" (1061–2). Although female complicity is a common Euripidean trope, the generalization stresses the unity of the female cultic context under Artemis. Iphigeneia concludes her account of the plan with a prayer to Artemis for a second deliverance from death (1082–3).

The ultimate test of Iphigeneia's religious authority comes with the arrival of Thoas at line 1152. His shock at the sight of the *agalma* outside the temple, lifted "from a base that must not be disturbed" (1157; cf. 1176, 1201), immediately calls

126 *Laura McClure*

attention to her autonomy. Her demand that the king stay outside the temple further demonstrates her control of sacred space even as it prevents him from having direct knowledge of events within it (1159). Instead, he must rely on Iphigeneia's explanation, which she shrinks from narrating on the grounds that it is potentially polluting, "I spit it away" (1161).

The justification for her intervention is the preservation of the purity of the goddess, as evidenced by the repeated use of *katharos* and cognates in this scene. Of the 10 instances of the term in the play, nine relate to the escape plan, and six occur in the exchange between Iphigeneia and Thoas (cf. 1037, 1163, 1191, 1216, 1221, 1225, 1231). When brought into sight of the victims, the *bretas* of its own accord "turned away, backwards in its place" (1165) and shut its eyes (1167) to avoid their pollution. When Thoas asks what is to be done, Iphigeneia states that it is necessary to respect established law (1189). The *nomos*, of course, is not Taurian but invented on the spot, incorporating familiar aspects of Athenian religious practice. Iphigeneia explains that both the cult image and the victims must be cleansed with seawater before the sacrifice can be performed, evoking the ritual of the Plynteria. This mock purification must take place not near the temple but at a remote spot along the shore, well out of the sight of the Taurians (1197).

Although fraudulent, many of the elements of the procedure would have been familiar to the contemporary audience. The reaction of the image of Artemis to the victims recalls the anecdote about the confrontation of the cult statue of Athena and Alcibiades during the Plynteria: whereas Artemis turns around and closes her eyes, Athena veiled herself and kept herself at a distance (Plut. *Alc.* 34.2). The removal of the statue from the temple in a public procession further evokes the purification of the statue of Athena Polias at the festival of the Plynteria and its attendant procession, as discussed earlier. References to the adornment of the goddess (1223), purification with animal blood (1223), torches (1224), and other measures to bring about purification (1225) would have also been familiar ritual activities (Sourvinou-Inwood 2003, 301).

The collective fear of incurring pollution, not only from physical contact with the strangers but also from viewing them and the cult object, further contributes to the success of the escape plot. Like the residents of Pellene during the procession described earlier, they do not want to look upon the dangerous sacred image directly. Just as she closes her eyes in the presence of the victims, so, too, the Taurian people must not view the source of pollution. Because Thoas shrinks from viewing "unmentionable things" (1198), he allows the transfer of the *bretas* from the temple to the shore. Iphigeneia mandates that no one is to come in sight of the victims (1212) but instead should remain at home (1210; cf. 1227–9). She further instructs the king to cover his eyes with his garments when the strangers are brought out of the temple (1218).

This idea of covering has connections to pollution elsewhere, both as a means of preventing the pollution of natural elements (cf. Eur. *HF* 1159–62, 1203–4, Soph. *OT* 1424–8; Parker 1983, 293, 309–17) and as a way to isolate the polluted individual from the community (Bremmer 2013, 96). This religious attitude works to Iphigeneia's advantage, for it keeps the Taurians in the dark as to

Priestess and polis in Iphigeneia   127

the movements of the victims. Finally, the fear of inadvertently "seeing what they should not" (1342) prevents the king's attendants from intervening in the purification procedure despite their mounting suspicion. By skillfully manipulating the Taurians' fear of coming into contact with pollution through the faculty of sight, Iphigeneia ensures that no one except herself, Orestes, and Pylades will witness the mock ritual and that her duplicity will not be detected until all are safely aboard ship.

A new polis for Artemis

We have seen how Iphigeneia's plan succeeds due to her deceptive manipulation of ritual procedures, her control of sacred space, her bond with the chorus, and the ignorance and fear of the Taurians. Her status and authority as priestess of a polis religion further contribute to the favorable outcome. She addresses her ritual instructions not only to Thoas but to the whole polis (1209). Especially at risk, she cautions, are citizens preparing for initiation or fulfilling a vow of purity, those about to marry, and pregnant women (1226–9). Her attention to the welfare of the community elicits praise from Thoas, who exclaims, "You are taking good care of the polis!" (1212). Indeed, her precautions elicit the admiration of the entire city (1214). Despite her civic authority, Iphigeneia believes Tauris is the wrong polis for Artemis (1086–8):

> But gladly leave this barbarian land
> for Athens. It is not right for you to dwell here,
> when it is possible for you to inhabit a prosperous polis.

Here Iphigeneia prays not only for her own rescue but establishes herself as a founder of a new cult of Artemis in Athens, the only other place termed a polis in the play. There both the goddess and the girl will participate in a far more civilized form of polis religion, one that lacks the component of human sacrifice, as decreed by Athena (1462–7):

> You, Iphigeneia, are to serve the goddess as key carrier in the sacred terraces of Brauron. There you will also be buried when you die, and they will dedicate to you fine-textured clothing as a gift, which the women who have died in childbirth leave behind in their houses.

The aetiology for Iphigeneia's cult, while fictive, represents the culmination of the play's positive depiction of women's ritual competence. Iphigeneia will continue to minister to Artemis in her capacity as priestess and key carrier, and then she will enjoy a form of divinity as a reward for her unfailing ritual service to the goddess: the tomb that lacked a body at Argos after the sacrifice at Aulis now will hold her remains at Brauron. Moreover, she will serve the Artemis celebrated by the chorus in her capacity as the guardian of women's reproductive capability. Like the trauma of Iphigeneia's near death at Aulis, so, too, the suffering of mothers who die in

128 *Laura McClure*

childbirth will be remembered, but in the form of the dedication of clothing, which stresses their contributions to the polis through the production of textiles and children. As Cole observes, "women who died in childbirth had to be remembered, even compensated, for the life they had lost" (Cole 2004, 219). In the translation of Artemis from Tauris to Brauron, the girl and the goddess become part of a much larger and democratized system of polis religion.

Conclusion

Priestesses seem to have been much in the air in Athens during the last two decades of the fifth century BCE. Four Euripidean plays produced in rapid succession between 415 and 412 – *Troades, Ion, Iphigeneia in Tauris*, and *Helen* – all significantly involve priestesses, whereas none are found in the poet's earlier tragedies, including among the extant fragments (Hamilton 1985, 53). Moreover, it is now widely accepted that Aristophanes' *Lysistrata,* produced in 411 BCE, modeled two of its characters on contemporary priestesses. The character of Myrrhine appears to have been based on the same-name priestess of Athena Nike (Clairmont 1979), while Lysistrata probably evoked the priestess of Athena Polias named Lysimache, who may still have been alive when the play was performed (Lewis 1955; Dillon 2002, 75, 86, 87, 92; Parker 2011, 20, 50).

Although the reasons for this sudden interest in staging priestesses are unclear, it points at the very least to the high regard in which such women were held and their capacity for exercising authority in the Classical polis. As Euripides' portrait of Iphigeneia suggests, priestesses possessed professional knowledge and duties that set them apart from other members of the community. Their identification with the deity and access to sacred space and cult objects invested them with special power and may have allowed opportunities for autonomous action. While few women could aspire to serve in this capacity, they nonetheless regularly contributed to the state as religious agents, whose individual and collective ritual activities rendered them shareholders in the political life of the Athenian state.

Works consulted

Aleshire, Susan. 1994. "Towards a Definition of 'State Cult' for Ancient Athens." In *Ancient Greek Cult Practice from the Epigraphical Evidence*, edited by Robin Hägg, 9–16. Stockholm: P. Åström.

Blok, Josine. 2001. "Virtual Voices: Toward a Choreography of Women's Speech in Classical Athens." In *Making Silence Speak: Women's Voices in Greek Literature and Society*, edited by André Lardinois and Laura McClure, 95–116. Princeton: Princeton University Press.

———. 2004. "Recht und Ritus der Polis: Zu Bürgerstatus und Geschlechterverhältnissen im klassichen Athen." *Historische Zeitschrift* 278: 1–28.

Bremmer, Jan. 2013. "Human Sacrifice in Euripides' *Iphigeneia in Tauris*: Greek and Barbarian." In *Human Sacrifice: Cross-Cultural Perspectives and Representations*, edited by Pierre Bonnechere and Renaud Gagné, 87–100. Liège: Presses universitaires de Liège.

Priestess and polis in Iphigeneia 129

Burkert, Walter. 1985. *Greek Religion: Archaic and Classical*. Trans. J. Raffan. Cambridge MA: Harvard University Press.

Burnett, Anne. 1971. *Catastrophe Survived: Euripides' Plays of Mixed Reversal*. Oxford: Clarendon Press.

Clairmont, C. 1979. "The Lekythos of Myrrhine." In *Studies in Classical Art and Archaeology*, edited by G. Günter and M. Moore. Locust Valley, NJ: J. J. Augustin.

Cole, Susan G. 2004. *Landscapes, Gender, and Ritual Space: The Ancient Greek Experience*. Berkeley: University of California Press.

Connelly, Joan. 2007. *Portrait of a Priestess: Women and Ritual in Ancient Greece*. Princeton: Princeton University Press.

Connor, Robert. 1988. "'Sacred' and 'Secular': Ἱερὰ καὶ Ὅσια and the Classical Athenian Concept of the State." *Ancient Society* 19: 161–88.

Cropp, Martin. 2000. *Euripides: Iphigeneia in Tauris*. Warminster: Aris & Phillips.

Deubner, L. 1932. *Attische Feste*. Berlin: H. Keller.

Dignas, Beate. 2002. *Economy of the Sacred in Hellenistic and Roman Asia*. Oxford: Oxford University Press.

Dillon, Matthew P. J. 1997. *Pilgrims and Pilgrimage in Ancient Greece*. London: Routledge.

———. 2002. *Girls and Women in Classical Greek Religion*. London and New York: Routledge.

Dunn, Francis. 2000. "Euripidean Aetiologies." *CB* 76: 3–28.

Eidinow, Esther. 2011. "Networks and Narratives: A Model for Ancient Greek Religion." *Kernos* 24: 9–38.

Garland, Robert. 1984. "Religious Authority in Archaic and Classical Athens." *Annual of the British School at Athens* 79: 75–123.

Goff, Barbara. 2004. *Citizen Bacchae: Women's Ritual Practice in Ancient Greece*. Berkeley: University of California Press.

Griffin, Jasper. 1998. "The Social Function of Attic Tragedy." *Classical Quarterly* 48: 39–61.

Hall, Edith. 2013. *Adventures with Iphigeneia in Tauris: A Cultural History of Euripides' Black Sea Tragedy*. Oxford: Oxford University Press.

Hamilton, Richard. 1985. "Euripidean Priests." *Harvard Studies in Classical Philology* 89: 53–73.

Hartigan, Kim. 1986. "Salvation Via Deceit: A New Look at *Iphigeneia in Tauris*." *Eranos* 84: 119–25.

Hollinshead, Mary. 1985. "Against Iphigeneia's *adyton* at Three Mainland Temples." *American Journal of Archaeology* 89: 419–40.

Kindt, Julia. 2012. *Rethinking Greek Religion*. Cambridge: Cambridge University Press.

Kowalzig, Barbara. 2013. "Transcultural Chorality: *Iphigeneia in Tauris* and Athenian Imperial Economics in a Polytheistic World." In *Choral Mediations in Greek Tragedy*, edited by Renaud Gagné and Marianne Hopman, 178–210. Cambridge: Cambridge University Press.

Kron, Uta. 1996. "Priesthoods, Dedications, and Euergetism: What Part Did Religion Play in the Political and Social Status of Greek Women?" In *Religion and Power in the Ancient Greek World*, edited by Pontus Hellström and Brita Alroth, 139–82. Uppsala: Acta Universitatis Upsaliensis.

Lewis, David. 1955. "Notes on Attic Inscriptions (II): XXIII. Who Was Lysistrata?" *Annual of the British School at Athens* 50: 1–36.

Linders, Tullia. 1972. *Studies in the Treasure Records of Artemis Brauronia Found in Athens*. Lund: P. Åström.

130 *Laura McClure*

Osborne, Robin. 1993. "Women and Sacrifice in Classical Greece." *Classical Quarterly* 43: 392–405.

Parke, H. W. 1977. *Festivals of the Athenians.* Ithaca, NY: Cornell University Press.

Parker, Robert. 1983. *Miasma: Pollution and Purification in Early Greek Religion.* Oxford: Clarendon Press.

———. 2005. *Polytheism and Society at Athens.* Oxford: Oxford University Press.

———. 2011. *On Greek Religion.* Ithaca: Cornell University Press.

Platnauer, M. 1938. *Euripides Iphigeneia in Tauris.* Oxford: Clarendon Press.

Rhodes, Peter J. 2003. "Nothing to do with Democracy: Athenian Drama and the *Polis.*" *Journal of Hellenic Studies* 123: 104–19.

Sansone, David. 1976. "The Sacrifice Motif in Euripides' *IT.*" *Transactions of the American Philological Association* 105: 283–95.

Schnapp, Alain. 1988. "Why the Greeks Needed Images." In *Proceedings of the Third Symposium on Ancient Greek and Related Pottery*, edited by J. Chistiansen and T. Melander, 568–74. Copenhagen, NY: Carlsberg Glyptotek.

Seaford, Richard. 1995. *Reciprocity and Ritual: Homer and Tragedy in the Developing City-State.* Oxford: Clarendon Press.

———. 2003. *Tragedy and Athenian Religion.* Lanham: Lexington Books.

Sourvinou-Inwood, C. 2000. "What is Polis Religion?" In *Oxford Readings in Greek Religion*, edited by R. Buxton, 13–37. Oxford: Oxford University Press.

Strachan, J. 1976. "Iphigeneia and Human Sacrifice in Euripides' *Iphigeneia Taurica.*" *Classical Philology* 71: 131–40.

Tzanetou, Angeliki. 1999–2000. "Almost Dying, Dying Twice: Ritual and Audience in Euripides' *Iphigeneia in Tauris.*" *Illinois Classical Studies* 24–25: 199–216.

Wolff, Christian. 1992. "*Iphigeneia among the Taurians:* Aetiology, Ritual, and Myth." *Classical Antiquity* 11: 308–34.

Wright, Matthew. 2005. *Euripides' Escape Tragedies.* Oxford: Oxford University Press.

Zeitlin, Froma. 2006. "Redeeming Matricide? Euripides Rereads the *Oresteia.*" In *The Soul of Tragedy: Essays on Athenian Drama*, edited by Victoria Pedrick and Steven M. Oberhelman, 199–206. Chicago: University of Chicago Press.

———. 2011. "Sacrifices Holy and Unholy in Euripides' *Iphigeneia in Tauris.*" In *Dans le laboratoire de l'historien de religions: Mélanges offerts a Philippe Borgeaud*, edited by Francesca Prescindi and Youri Volokhine, 449–66. Geneva: Labor et fides.

7 Owners of their own bodies

Women's magical knowledge and reproduction in Greek inscriptions

Irene Salvo

Introduction

This chapter explores epigraphic evidence attesting what ancient Greek women knew about the use of magic for controlling fertility.[1] Compared with the literary texts, epigraphy displays a wider array of social interactions in which women were leading protagonists. While undoubtedly there are challenges involved in working with such sources, inscriptions, when available, are crucial for better understanding the active female contribution to family health care. Yet scholars interested in ancient women and medicine have not fully explored Greek inscriptions, particularly those on curse tablets and amulets. Although inscriptions such as the oracular tablets from Dodona, the healing miracle stories from Epidauros, and the dedications from the sanctuary of Artemis Brauronia at Athens have been considered together with the Hippocratic treatises (Flemming 2013, 581–8), curse tablets and amulets remain confined to the desks of historians of religions. Yet these two genres of documents can contribute significantly to the scholarly search for evidence of women's knowledge of reproduction as expressed in healing rituals.

The choice of curse tablets and amulets causes an inevitable enlargement of the chronological and geographical limits of the enquiry. Indeed, the dates of the curses and amulets selected for this chapter span over the first four centuries CE and are from different areas of the ancient Greek-speaking world, from mainland Greece to Asia Minor. Furthermore, two methodological questions immediately emerge: can we distinguish "magic" from "religion"? And in what sense can we separate "religious" practices from "medical" therapies? A single chapter is not enough to explore these issues at length (see, among many others, Lanata 1967; Versnel 1991; Gordon 1995; Dasen 2011, 73 n. 1). I will only mention that in antiquity, at a sociocultural level, the realms of magic, religion, and medicine were strictly interconnected. Medical anthropologists have examined how the experience of disease is informed by social inequality, relationships of domination, and factors such as economy and poverty, while anthropologists have defined "ritual" as a performative action and/or utterance whose efficacy in transforming realities is guaranteed by the performance of the ritual itself (Tambiah 1985). In particular, rituals are considered crucial in the process of shaping social identities and relationships, as well as in the affirmation of social power and hierarchies. The healing

132   *Irene Salvo*

rituals found on amulets and curse tablets, then, can be more fruitfully studied when medical anthropology and a performative approach to ritual are integrated (Sax 2004).

This chapter combines insights gained from both strands of anthropological literature in its exploration of how women used curse tablets and amulets for addressing their medical needs and for defining their social identity. The emphasis will be on women as knowledgeable of their own bodies and as ritually competent rather than on women viewed exclusively as mothers. It asks: do curse tablets and amulets provide evidence for women's knowledge about sexual reproduction? Were women independent from men when they made decisions about their reproductive needs and ritual cures? Do curse tablets and amulets offer a picture different from that of ancient medical writings? Or did women's knowledge as it appears on curse tablets and amulets then get adopted in medical practice and enter the Hippocratic corpus? After a careful review of evidence, this chapter returns to these questions in its conclusion.

Cursing the womb: Reproduction and aggressive magic

Throughout antiquity, pregnancy and childbirth were considered not only physically but also ritually dangerous phases (see Parker 1983, 48–66, and in Roman religion, see Lennon 2014, 58–61). In order to enhance protection in this critical moment, ancient Greek women exploited religion and magic, invoking divine help and performing magical rites in a number of ways. The power of ritual actions was often combined with pharmacology and herbal medicine, although the efficacy of these methods is a topic of scholarly debate (see recently Totelin 2009, 214–24). Furthermore, the idea that the womb was a live and independent organ within a woman's body (see, for example, Pl. *Tim.* 91c; *PGM* VII.260–71) meant that its activities could be controlled through rituals and treatments.

In the realm of reproductive rituals, the supernatural agent could be called upon for both protective and aggressive aims. A recently published text opens new perspectives on aggressive magical practices around fertility. It is a curse written on a lead tablet and comes from the sanctuary of Demeter and Kore in Korinth. Korinth, destroyed in 146 BCE, was refounded after 44 BCE as a new Roman *colonia*; the sanctuary stayed a place of worship until the end of the fourth century CE (Stroud 2014, 189). The sanctuary buildings were altered in the Roman period, but the cult maintained its Greek origins, although it was integrated into the Imperial religious context (Bookidis 2005, 162f.). Seventeen inscribed lead tablets in standard Attic or *koine* standard, with occasional doricisms, and one in Latin, have been found (Stroud 2013, 81–157). They are dated to the Roman period, around the first and second century CE. In six tablets the victim is a woman, while three have female authorship.

Ten of the excavated tablets have been found clustered around four low stone bases in the southern end of a room, called by the excavators the Building of the Tablets. Fragments of lamps, incense burners, and small vessels found together with the lead tablets suggested to the excavators that incense, lighting, and libation

Owners of their own bodies 133

ceremonies accompanied the oral recitation of spells and the deposition of the tablets. The ritual activity in this room seems to have been mainly nocturnal (see Stroud 2013, 138–53, for a detailed description of the archaeological context of the tablets). One of the most interesting texts from the Building of the Tablets is a curse written against a woman, Karpime Babbia. Two other curses were directed against the same woman (Stroud 2013, nos. 123 and 124), and since the handwriting presents some similarities, perhaps one person dedicated them all (Stroud 2013, 103). In the following text, the author, most probably a woman, asks fertility for herself and destruction for Karpime Babbia:

125 Παραθίτομα[ι] καὶ καταθί[το]μα[ι] Καρπί-
        μην Βαβίαν στεφανηπλόκον Μοίραις Π-
        ραξιδίκαισς ὅπως ἐγδεικ[ής]ωσι τὰς ὕβρ{ι}εις,
4   Ἑρμῇ Χθονίῳ, Γῇ, Γῆς παισίν, [ὅ]πως κατεργά-
        σων‹τ›αι καὶ διεργάσωνται ψ[υ]χὴν αὐτῆς κα-
        ὶ νοῦ‹ν› αὐτῆς [καὶ] φρένες ν
        Καρπίμης Βαβίας σ‹τ›εφανη[π]λόκου. ὁρκίζ-
8   ω σε καὶ ἐναρῶμαί σε καὶ ἐνεύχομαί σ-
        ‹σ›οι, Ἑρμῇ Χθόνιε, τὰ μεγάλα *vacat 0.05m*
126 ὀ[νύ]ματα τῆς Ἀνάνκης ΝΕΒΕΖΑΠ
        ΑΔΑΙΕΙΣΕΝ[.]ΓΕΙΒΗΩΗΕΡΑ κάρπισαί
12   με, τὸ μέγα ὄν[υ]μα τὸ ἐπάνανκον, ὃ οὐκ εὐ-
        χερῶς ὀνθμάζεται, ἄν μὴ ἐπὶ μεγάλαις ἀν-
        ανκαίαι‹ς›, ΕΥΦΕΡ, μέγα ὄνυμα, κ‹άρ›πισαί με καὶ κα-
        τέργασαι Καρπίμην Βαβίαν στεφ[α]-
16   νηπλόκον ἀπὸ κεφαλῆς μέχρι ἰχνέων
        ἰ‹ς› ἐπιμήν‹ι›ον κατεργασ[ί]αν.

I entrust and consign Karpime Babbia, weaver of garlands, to the Fates who exact justice, so that they may punish her insolent behaviour, to Hermes of the Underworld, to Earth, to the children of Earth, so that they may subdue and completely destroy her soul and heart and her mind and the wits of Karpime Babbia, weaver of garlands. I adjure you and I implore you and I pray to you, Hermes of the Underworld, that the mighty names of Ananke, Nebezapadaieisen [.]geibebeohera, make me fertile; that the mighty name, the one carrying compulsion, which is not named recklessly unless in dire necessity, EUPHER, mighty name, make me fertile and destroy Karpime Babbia, weaver of garlands, from her head to her feet with monthly destruction.

(Stroud 2013, nos 125/126, second half of the first century
to the early second century CE. English translation
modified from Stroud 2013)

The complexity of this document is immediately clear, but I will only discuss a few of the main aspects here. The text was engraved on two tablets rolled up and fastened together by a nail. Both tablets were folded seven times perpendicular to

134   *Irene Salvo*

the lines of text: no. 125 was rolled from left to right, while no. 126 from right to left. The number seven probably held a magical meaning; and the process of folding the tablets seven times was probably an intentional part of the ritual (Stroud 2013, 104, fig. 80). The text seems to fit the category of "prayers for justice," public appeals to a divinity in order to exact vengeance for an offense or injustice suffered by the author of the text (see Versnel 2010 on their differentiation from binding curses, in particular pp. 313–15 on these Korinthian tablets). However, as has been noted, the text combines elements of binding curses and of prayers for justice (Stroud 2014, 197). As Stroud (2013, 114) further observes: "The curse and punishment to be inflicted on Karpime Babbia occupy lines 1–7. Then, with asyndeton, the next seven lines are devoted to the prayer to Hermes Chthonios to the effect that the Great Names make the writer fertile. The text then ends with a four-line injunction to the Great Name, Ouphor, first, in inverse or chiastic order, that the writer be made fertile, and second, that Karpime Babbia suffer total and lasting destruction." If categorizations of the ancient sources are an essential explanatory heuristic tool, each document might present peculiar characteristics that escape the known formula. I think it is worth noting that, while this inscription contains a vindictive prayer for justice, it seems that in addition to the cursing utterance the tablet was deposited as an intended fertility ritual.

The text, however, does not provide many details on the story behind it. In the attempt to guess the events that provoked it, it seems to be unquestionable that the main point at issue was fecundity. The author of the text may have been barren and may have been publicly ridiculed by Karpime Babbia (Versnel 2010, 314; Stroud 2013, 114). It is plausible to imagine a competition between the two women. While Karpime was able to produce offspring and was a serene mother of more than one healthy child, the writer had experienced several reproductive failures. She, then, felt envy for Karpime's fertility and her perfect motherhood. Even if these were not the exact details of the events, the *defigens* felt indeed a strong desire for vengeance, since she was asking for the complete destruction of her rival. The social setting of the Demetriac festival of the *Thesmophoria* probably fueled the rumination of negative emotions in our writer (Salvo 2012). Surrounded by fertile women, mothers, and prospective mothers (Stroud 2013, 112), perhaps she could not bear any more mocking comments on her undefined social identity, being an adult woman without children.

The invocation of the Great Name *Eupher* (line 14) can be linked to the Egyptian spell *Ouphôr*: the different first letter can be interpreted as a spelling mistake, or perhaps it was written differently in the magical handbook from which the author copied the formula (Stroud 2013, no. 125/126, line 14, with Stroud 2013, 112f.). Stroud accepts the interpretation of Moyer and Dielmann, according to whom *Ouphôr* indicates a spell employed for the vivification of the image engraved on a ring representing a divinity (Moyer and Dielmann 2003). *Ouphôr* is a transcription from the Egyptian *wp.t-r*, the "Opening of the Mouth," a ritual that was intended to bring to life mummies, statues, and more generally images in funerary or liturgical ceremonies (Moyer and Dielmann 2003, 49). Following this line of thought, it is tempting to speculate that perhaps the invocation to *Eupher* was

Owners of their own bodies　135

directed at a figurine that the writer molded and deposited together with the tablet, and the spell *Eupher/Ouphôr* was recited in order to vivify the object.

Another detail is worth highlighting. The temporal specification of a "monthly destruction" (l. 17), together with a wish for total annihilation, seems to imply a specific reference to Karpime's womb and her menstrual cycle. The victim might have been afflicted by painful and particularly unpleasant menstrual periods that consequently meant not being able to bear children (Stroud 2013, 114). The Greek word κατεργασία means literally "working up" and is used for food in the sense of "stewing, boiling" (LSJ). The intended destruction might have entailed also an internal "boiling" of the blood caused by a dysfunctional disease. The sensation of boiling blood might be caused by a feverish condition, and, according to Aristotle, physicians recognized the emotion of anger in this symptom (Arist. *De anim.* 403A31). The supposition of a connection between the curse and a specific illness is triggered by the parallel with similar prayers for justice from Knidos (modern Turkey), where one of the punishments invoked by the author of the cursing prayer is an inner "fever" (see e.g. *I. Knidos* 148). Furthermore, it is reasonable to add that the wished-for destruction of Karpime would have been not only physical but also psychological: each month her painful period would also have destroyed her hope for a child, increasing her feeling of longing for a pregnancy that supernatural powers would have impeded.

As noted here, although in curse tablets formulaic expressions often recur, sometimes extra elements personalize the text, defying any modern classification. It is noteworthy that in this document – a prayer for justice – the request to make the author fertile goes beyond a wish for the satisfaction of revenge against a wrongdoer. It reveals the hope and aspiration of this woman to conceive, and the enormous fear of remaining totally sterile in a community of expecting mothers and puerperae. Furthermore, it is interesting to remember that Hippocratic medicine linked the reproductive function to the general health of a woman: sexual intercourse was considered to improve health and pregnancy was a sign of health (Hippoc. *Genit.* 4 = 7.476 Littré; *Mul.* 5 = 8.28 Littré; more references, with previous bibliography, in Totelin 2009, 200; Parker 2012, 121). Therefore, although a woman could have an unfruitful womb and still be healthy (King 2005, 157), infertility was probably seen as affecting the overall well-being of a woman. In this tablet, the invocation of divine helpers had two parallel aims – ruin of the victim and prosperity of the agent – and this structure transforms the curse into a ritual for getting pregnant and regaining health. The fertility ritual probably included the hope of giving birth to a healthy baby, since to conceive was not always enough for giving birth to a baby, as a recipe for a woman who wants to become pregnant *and* to bear children implies (Hippoc. *Superf.* 29 = 8.494 Littré). If we remember that the author of the tablet dedicated not one but three curses, we have an index of how desperate she was: not only how badly she hated Karpime Babbia but also how stressful she found her impaired reproduction. The case of the author of the curse against Karpime Babbia was probably not isolated. As noted by Nasrallah (2012, 125–32), in the Korinth of the first century CE, the mother–child relationship was fragile and often caused anxiety and grief. The city where

136 *Irene Salvo*

the murdered children of Medea were worshipped was experienced in how to cope with the fragility of infants through witchcraft. However, Graeco-Roman magic was not the only solution available. Stroud (2014, 201f.) asks whether the women performing official and non-official rituals in the sanctuary of Demeter and Kore were paying attention to Paul's message and his preaching in the city.

Outside of Korinth, we can find more parallels for spells and oral prayers used in order to aid or impede reproduction. In a famous passage from a Platonic dialogue, Socrates alluded to the power of midwives (*maiai*), who were able to stimulate or lessen labor pains as well as to induce a miscarriage through drugs and incantations (Pl. *Tht.* 149c-d, see on this passage Leitao 2012, 237f.). In telling the story of Hercules' birth, Ovid recalls how the goddess of childbirth, Lucina – following Juno's orders – halted Alcmena's delivery, murmuring spells in a low voice (Ov. *Met.* 9.300f.). Oral incantations were believed to interfere with nature and the body. Galen fiercely criticized the use of similar sung charms for controlling female fertility and reproduction:

> ἐγὼ τοίνυν οὔτε βασιλίσκων οὔτε ἐλεφάντων οὔθ᾽ ἵππων Νειλώων οὔτ᾽ ἄλλου τινὸς οὗ μὴ πεῖραν αὐτὸς ἔχω μνημονεύσω, τῶν δὲ καλουμένων φίλτρων, ἀγωγίμων, ὀνειροπομπῶν τε καὶ μισήτρων, αὐτοῖς γὰρ τοῖς ἐκείνων ὀνόμασιν ἐξεπίτηδες χρῶμαι, τὴν ἀρχὴν ἂν, οὐδ᾽ εἰ πεῖραν ἱκανὴν εἶχον, ἐμνημόνευσα διὰ γραμμάτων, ὥσπερ οὐδὲ τῶν θανασίμων φαρμάκων ἢ τῶν ὡς αὐτοὶ καλοῦσιν παθοποιῶν. ἐκεῖνα μὲν γὰρ αὐτῶν καὶ γελοῖα, καταδῆσαι τοὺς ἀντιδίκους, ὡς μηδὲν ἐπὶ τοῦ δικανικοῦ δυνηθῆναι φθέγξασθαι, ἢ ἐκτρῶσαι ποιῆσαι τὴν κύουσαν, ἢ μηδέποτε συλλαβεῖν, ὅσα τ᾽ ἄλλα τοιαῦτα.

> I will not recall the use of the basilisk nor of parts from the elephants or from the horses of the Upper Nile, nor from something else of which I do not have experience of the risks. Then, about those called philtres, those that attract, induce dreams, trigger hate – on purpose I surveyed their names, although I do not have a sufficient experience of them, I will mention the principles in the treatise, as not lethal remedies or – as they say – remedies that cause bodily diseases. For some of these are even ridiculous, like those supposed to tie up the opposing litigant, so that he will not be able to speak in court, or provoke an abortion on a pregnant woman, or inhibit conception for ever, or do this and that.

> (Gal., *De simpl. medic. temp. ac fac.,* Kühn XII, 251–2)

In this passage, I am uncertain whether Galen is discussing the use of curses or of drugs (Kapparis 2002, 16, 19, 29, 77 translates *philtron* as drugs). Although he is dealing with ingredients and recipes in the initial sentence of the paragraph, the primary meaning of *philtron* is "charm, spell," and Galen defines these charms with adjectives attested for incantations in the magical handbooks. In particular, *agogimos* ("liable to seizure") is the technical term for spells aimed at attracting a reluctant beloved person (see, for example, *PGM* VII.973). *Oneiropompos* ("charm sending dreams") indicates a charm that induces dream-visions or gods and demons that speak in dreams (see, for example, *PGM* VII.2439). A *misetron*,

Owners of their own bodies   137

"charm producing hate," is the opposite of an *agogimos philtron* ("charm producing love") and is a rare term equivalent to μίσηθρον, which has the same meaning and is attested only three times (Luc. *Dial. meret.* 4.5.1; Origen *C. Cels.* 7.69.15; *PGM* III.164 – here it is paired with a dream-sending spell and a *diakopos* ("spell that produces a breach"), a charm that separates two people, often a married couple). Galen continues, condemning the use of these spells in judicial litigations or within the medical sphere, such as in the case of a pregnancy, as, for example, the situation in which Karpime Babbia was attacked. In brief, it seems more plausible that here, with φίλτρα, Galen means curses and incantations rather than drugs.

Other magical procedures for manipulating reproduction

Alongside curses, another popular means for controlling fertility was inscribed amulets, written on small gold, silver, bronze, or copper lamellae, which were rolled up into capsules and hung around the neck. The chronology of these protective magical texts goes from the early first century BCE to the fifth/sixth century CE. Inscribed amulets were probably used together, or in competition with, herbal medicine and plant bioactives (Kotansky 1994, xviii). An example of a gold lamella, dating to the third/fourth century CE and found in a tomb in Nubia, used in a ritual for aiding conception is as follows:

Ἐλθὲ πρὸς ἐμέ, Ἶσις, ὅτι ἐγώ εἰμι Ὄσιρις ὁ ἄρρην, ἀδελφός <σ>ου. Ταῦτα τὰ ὕδατα ἃ προσφέρω, ὕδωρ ἔστι ἱέρακος, στηθυνίων Ἴβεως, ὕδωρ τοῦ Ἀνούβεως ἀδελφόν φθνηθ βεν. Κατὰ νῶτον εἶναι, ἄνοιξόν σου τὴν μήτραν, ἐν ταύτῃ τῇ ὥρᾳ καὶ ἐν <ταύ>τῃ τῇ ῥοπῇ καὶ ἅρπαξον τὸ σπαρὲν ἐν σοὶ ὕδωρ ἐν τῷ σου ὀνόματι, Ἶσι, ἄνασσα, βασίλισσα Τεντύρων, ἤδη, ταχὺ ταχὺ διὰ τὴν δύναμιν ὑμῶν ταχύ.

Come to me, Isis, because I am Osiris your male brother. These are the waters that I present to you: it is the water of the Falcon [Horus], (that) of the little breasts of Ibis, (and) the water of Anubis. Brother Phthnêth ben. Be on your back (and) open your womb in this hour, in this moment, and receive quickly the water seeded in you, in your name Isis, lady, queen of Denderah; now, quickly, quickly; through your power, quickly.

(Kotansky 1994, no. 61; Greek text in normalized
spelling and partly modified English translation
from Kotansky 1994, 362)

The text contains a mythical narrative that involves the figures of Isis and Osiris in order to ensure the opening of the womb and the reception of the semen. Isis, goddess of sexuality and fertility, represents the woman addressed in this spell, while Osiris, brother and husband of Isis, represents the man. The "waters" refer to the male seminal fluid (see Kotansky 1994, 365, with a reference to *PGM* XII.234). In particular, the waters of Anubis were a symbol of life, since he was the god who embalmed Osiris and then contributed to his resurrection. The

138 *Irene Salvo*

injunction to open the womb may have implied a reference to fertility, and the expressions "in this hour, in this moment" may have indicated that the amulet had to be used during the sexual intercourse. It suggests that the woman was wearing the amulet and the man recited the incantation while they were having sex (Kotansky 1994, 367f.).

Magical handbooks offered recipes and incantations also for ending a pregnancy. Historically, there have been few changes in abortion techniques until the last century (Kapparis 2002, 31). In ancient Greek language, there was no perceived difference between a miscarriage and an abortion; the same term could have different meanings depending on the context, and could indicate a spontaneous or voluntary termination as well as the expulsion of a still fetus (see Pepe 2014, 3 with further references). Greek terminology includes, in particular, *diaphthora* and *phthora* (e.g. *IG* II² 1365.22, 1366.7; from *phtheiro*, to destroy), *ambloma* (e.g. Antiph. *Soph.* 148) and *amblosis* (Lys. Fr. 8; both from *amblisko*, to cause a miscarriage), and *ekbolimon* (e.g. Arist. *Hist. an.* 575a.28, from *ekballo*, to expel). Women themselves, midwives, practitioners with medical knowledge, or magicians could procure an abortion through a variety of procedures, some harmless and others dangerous or ineffective (Kapparis 2002, 11). The most accessible way was to swallow drugs and potions made from mixing herbs. These *pharmaka* could have lethal side effects for the mother (Kapparis 2002, 12–19; on recipes for abortifacients, see Hanson 1995b, 298–302; Totelin 2009, 214–19; on the debated evidence on the legal aspects of abortion in the ancient Greek world – especially Athens, see more recently Pepe 2014). Other methods included vaginal suppositories, creams to be applied on the abdomen, strenuous physical exertion or physical violence, and surgical operation for clearing the uterus by dilation and curettage (see Hippoc. *Mul.* 1.78 = 8.178.12–188.24 Littré). Hippocratic writers condemned women using self-help for procuring an abortion, since it was very likely to cause serious lesions in the womb (Hippoc. *Mul.* 1.67 = 8.140 Littré; 1.72 = 8.152.15–21 Littré).

Beside these techniques, ritual means involving supernatural agents were also used. An example is preserved in the Greek magical papyri, where we find these instructions:

> ἀνοιγήτω ἡ φύσις καὶ ἡ μήτρα τῆς δεῖνα, καὶ αἱμασσέσθω νυκτὸς καὶ ἡμέρας.᾽ καὶ τα[ῦτα γρ(άφων)] ἀρ[νείῳ] χρῶ αἵματι καὶ προδί[ω]κε τὰ [πα]ράθε[τα] νυκτὸς γε[9] ιομ[.] πρωτη ηδικησε, καὶ χῶσον παρὰ ῥοῦν ἢ παρὰ . . . δα χα . . . ον ἐν πιττακ[ιδί]ῳ.

> Let the genitals and the womb of her, Ms-so-and-so, be open, and let her become bloody by night and day. And [these things must be written] with menstrual blood, and recite before nightfall, the offerings (?) . . . she wronged first . . . and bury it near a sumac, or near . . . on a tablet.
>
> (*PGM* LXII.76–106, following Aubert 1989,
> 430 n. 14, line 104: αἰσχρῷ αἵματι)

Aubert (1989, 429f.) suggests that the drawing of a semi-crescent might be interpreted as the representation of female genitals – and this charm was probably

Owners of their own bodies   139

read with the intention of opening the womb of a woman, letting the menstrual flux, and perhaps the male seed, flow out of it. The text may be interpreted to be a cure for amenorrhea. However, the mention of some wrongdoing committed by the woman addressed in the charm seems to imply that the purpose was aggressive magic, probably for procuring an abortion (Aubert 1989, 434) or for provoking a constant and sickening menstrual flux. As in the case of the curse against Karpime Babbia, the person that used this text seems to have been motivated by the wish to harm the reproductive function of another person, or more generally to damage a woman's health. Although we do not know with certainty the gender of the user of the spell, it is plausible to suppose that aggressor and victim were both female. Alternatively, a woman could have performed this spell on herself as a contraceptive method (Aubert 1989, 435).

More information about magical rituals for procuring an abortion can be read between the lines of a "confession inscription" from Asia Minor:

> Μηνὶ Ἀρτεμιδώρου Ἀξιοτηνῷ
> *vacat of three lines*
> Συντύχη Θεογένου· εὑρόντος αὐ-
> τῆς Θεογένου τοῦ ἀνδρὸς λιθάριον ὑα-
> 4 κίνθιον, εἶτα κειμένου αὐτοῦ ἐν τῇ οἰκίᾳ
> αὐτῆς ἐκλάπη τὸ λιθάριον, καὶ ζητούσης
> αὐτῆς καὶ βασανιζομένης ἐπεύξατο
> μηνὶ Ἀξιοττηνῷ περὶ αὐτοῦ ἵνα αὐτὴν
> 8 ἱκανοποήσι, καὶ εὑρέθη κατακεκαυμένον
> καὶ ἠφανισμένον, ἐνδεμένον ἐν λινου-
> δίῳ ὑπὸ τοῦ κλέπτου τεθειμένον ἐπὶ
> τὸν τόπον, οὗ ἔκειτο ὁλόκληρον· οὕτως
> 12 τε ἐπιφανεὶς ὁ θεὸς ἐν μιᾷ καὶ τριακοσ-
> τῇ τὴν κλέψασα<ν> καὶ τοῦτο πυήσασα<ν> Ἀπφίαν
> Γλύκωνος οὖσαν παρθένον διέρηξε·
> περι<σ>υρούσης τε αὐτῆς τὴν δύναμιν τοῦ
> 16 θεοῦ διὰ τὸ ἠρωτῆσθαι ὑπὸ τῆς μητρὸς
> τῆς παρθένου, ἵνα σειγήσι, καὶ ὁ θεὸς τοῦ-
> το ἐνεμέσησε, ὅτι οὐκ ἐξεφάντευ-
> σε οὐδὲ ὕψωσε τὸν θεὸν ἡ Συντύχη· διό-
> 20 τι ἐποίησεν αὐτὴν ἐπὶ τέκνου Ἡρακλεί-
> δου ἐτῶν ιγ΄ νέμεσιν ἐπὶ τὸν τόπον αὐτοῦ
> στῆσαι, ὅτι τὸ τῶν ἀνθρώπων μᾶλλον ἐπό-
> ησεν ἢ τοῦ θεοῦ. v Συντύχη Ἀπολλωνίου
> 24 θυγάτηρ καὶ Μελτίνης ἡ προγεγραφοῦ-
> σα τὴν νέμεσιν.

Syntyche, the wife of Theogenes, (made this dedication) to Men Artemidorou Axiottenos. Her husband Theogenes had found a hyacinth stone. Then (later) while the stone was kept in her house it was stolen. As she searched for

140   *Irene Salvo*

it and was being interrogated over it, she prayed to Men Axiottenos to give her satisfaction about it. It was found burned and destroyed, wrapped up in a linen shirt and put back by the thief in the place where it had been kept when it was still undamaged. And so the god having appeared [i.e. shown his power] on the thirty-first day, deflowered Apphia, the daughter of Glykon, who was a virgin and who had stolen the stone and done this. And because she [i.e. Syntyche] completely concealed the power of the god, since the virgin's mother had asked her to keep silent, the god took revenge for this, because Syntyche had not publicized and exalted the god. Therefore he made her set up in his sanctuary this account of the revenge, at the time when he took on her child of thirteen years, Heraklides, because she acted in men's interest rather than in that of the god. It is Syntyche, the daughter of Apollonios and Meltine, who has brought to public knowledge the punishment.

(Petzl 1994, no. 59; perhaps from the area of Kula, Lydia, Asia Minor, ca. 150–250 CE; partly modified English translation from Ogden 2009[2], 243)

The "confession inscriptions" from Lydia and Phrygia were inscribed on stone stelai erected in sanctuaries and date from the first to the third century CE. There is an ongoing discussion on how to label this group of documents: Chaniotis (2012) suggests using the either "records of divine justice" or "records of divine punishment." This is because these texts attest the power of a god who has punished someone for his or her sins. In each case, the writer has interpreted an experience of illness, death, or any damage to his or her property as a divine punishment for known or unknown transgressions. Through the advice and the mediation of a priest, a dream, or an oracular response, the writer of the text determined the reason for this divine response and, confessing his or her guilt publicly, exalted the power of the gods.

In this case, Syntyche dedicated the stele to the praise of the god Men Axiottenos, a local form of the lunar god. After the theft of a precious sapphire gem, she invoked divine help, probably using a prayer for justice. Syntyche prayed to the god to investigate the crime, recover the gemstone, and bring vengeance on the thieves. The god manifested his power and the gemstone was recovered, but it was found in a poor state, burnt and ruined. Syntyche did not reveal the great power of Men, since her friend Glykon, the mother of the thief, a young girl called Apphia, asked her to keep the whole story quiet. Syntyche interpreted the death of her son as the punishment for having asked for divine help but not then having shown her gratitude in public. The marble stele is the result of the final confession.

Why would a young girl, Apphia, have been interested in stealing a gemstone, returning it burnt and damaged after 31 days? Apphia might have used the gemstone in a ritual aimed at solving a gynecological problem, most probably an unwanted pregnancy (Chaniotis 1990). This hypothesis is supported by comparison with other sources, where fumigations with burning stones stimulate the return of the menses. Handbooks on the properties of stones and gems explain that "if a woman exposes her body at its healing fumes, letting them enter into her womb, quickly from it bleeds the black flow" (Orph. *Lith.* 485–91 on the lignite stone,

Owners of their own bodies 141

gagates lithos) and that "when the menstruations of women do not flow, you will grind this stone and you will put it on hot charcoals, then you will say to the woman to walk around it so that the womb will be fumigated with the smoke, and so she will be cleansed with no harm or pain" (Damig. XX additio 3, Halleux and Schamp 1985, 292). The method for purging the womb by fumigation seems to be less dangerous and painful than other techniques.

In addition, the use of linen cloth, as described in Apphia's activities, is also compatible with the performance of a magical rite, as we know from the recipes and the instructions in the Greek magical papyri (Chaniotis 1990, 130, see *PGM* IV.675–676, 1081; VII.359–361; XII 96.313; XXXVI.235–236) and from the archaeological evidence. For example, a 14-week fetus found wrapped in a linen cloth and fastened with a cord was used in magical rites (Kellis, Egypt, late IV CE; Frankfurter 2006, 43). Apphia, then, may have performed a magical operation, waiting 31 days for her next period; but the rite did not work. At this point, she was forced to reveal the pregnancy and the theft. The statement that the god Men deflowered Apphia suggests that the idea of a divine epiphany was exploited in order to conceal a real love affair. It seems likely that the theft was planned by Glykon, the mother of the teenager and the friend of the stone's original owner (cf. Ogden 2009[2], 244: Syntyche's son, Heraklides, might be identified both as the father of the unwanted child and as the thief of the gemstone). The woman knew that her friend Syntyche owned the object, and she may have known how to procure an abortion with that stone. The two women may even have discussed how to perform an abortion, weighing the options, sharing their knowledge, and co-operating. Perhaps, Glykon asked Syntyche to keep the incident silent in order to resort to another more powerful technique, so as to terminate the pregnancy before the news of the daughter's loss of virginity began spreading in the community. Self-medication would have been common, especially in small cities such as this Lydian village, far away from the learned doctors of Athens or Alexandria (on the concentration of surgeries (ἰατρεῖα) in big urban centers see Caliò 2009).

Magic in the birthing chamber: Amuletic gems

Another healing technique for magical rituals as self-medication in the sphere of reproduction consisted in wearing or attaching to the body amulets of various materials. Resorting to amulets for controlling fertility and maternity was probably widespread in major cities as well as in small villages. If in contemporary society we debate the extent of medical control over the birthing process, in the Graeco-Roman world, the question was whether or not to use magical amulets, as we can infer from Soranos of Ephesos (second century CE):

> οὐκ ἀποκωλυτέον δὲ τὴν παράληψιν αὐτῶν· καὶ γὰρ εἰ μηδὲν ἐξ εὐθείας παρέχει τὸ περίαπτον, ἀλλ᾽ οὖν δι᾽ ἐλπίδος εὐθυμοτέραν τὴν κάμνουσαν τάχα παρέξει.

> One must not forbid their use: if the amulet does not have any direct effect, at least giving hope it will soon make the patient more high-spirited.

> (Sor. *Gyn.* III 42)

142   *Irene Salvo*

Beside amulets inscribed on lamellae or tablets, Soranos probably had in mind another popular apotropaic means, that is, gemstone amulets (on magical gems, see, with further bibliography, Bonner 1950; Dasen 2007, 2011, 2014; Faraone 2011). Unfortunately, most of the gems now extant are of unknown provenance, since they come from the antiquarian market. But they were also objects of trade in antiquity, so even when we know of a stone's locality, it may not have been its original provenance. Gemstone amulets could have been used for promoting or preventing conception, for protecting a pregnancy, or for facilitating childbirth. We have Graeco-Egyptian engraved gemstones, which were worn in pendants, rings, or even orally administrated (a small part of the amulet ground and drunk with a liquid). The most common material for amulets used for controlling uterine functions was hematite, a stone that was considered to have antihemorrhagic properties (Blakely 2006, 139–51 provides details on the power of stones and metals in rites of fertility).

Although the extant amulets are dated mainly to the Roman period, scholars think that similar amulets in more perishable materials were common also in the Classical and Hellenistic periods (Hanson 2004, 268; Faraone 2011). However, from the first century CE, the engraving on gemstones became more complex, with long texts, syncretisms between Jewish, Egyptian, Roman, and Greek deities, and *voces magicae* (Bonner 1950, 5f.; Faraone 2011). A group of gemstones bears a recurring design that depicts a kind of round-shaped container with lines underneath, and sometimes divine figures above it, often accompanied by the inscription Ορωριουθ (catalogued in Marino 2010). Scholars agree that this image represents the womb, together with the fallopian tubes and the sinews of the organ. The deities shown in these uterine gems are usually Egyptian and are gods who exercise control over reproduction, such as Isis, guardian of women, and Harpokrates, the divine infant.

The definition of Ορωριουθ is debated, but it was perhaps a supernatural entity protecting generation and birth (Bonner 1950, 85f; Faraone 2011, 56). Furthermore, the symbol of a key is frequently depicted under the vessel-organ: its function was to symbolically enact the opening the womb (promoting conception and birth) or the closing of the womb (aiding contraception and abortion). Perhaps the position of the key indicated the purpose of the amulet, whether it was engraved below the cervix or above the womb, and whether the key handle was pointing upwards or downwards (as in Michel 2004, no. 54.1b; other examples of opposite use of gemstones controlling blood flow in Faraone 2009, 221f.). Sometimes, a deity touches the key so as to indicate the divine power of governing uterine movements. In a red carnelian, Harpokrates' hand is in control of the key (Bonner 1950, no. 141). Another amulet shows an oval pot with a corrugated texture that vividly resembles the look of bodily tissues (Bonner 1950, no. 136). Another amulet, in red jasper, was probably used to encourage rapid birth, since the inscription ἐπὶ ποδία, "onto your little feet," can be read as an order to the child in the womb: he or she had to find the way to come into the world and walk on his/her feet independently from the mother (Bonner 1950, no. 134, translated by Hanson 2004).

Owners of their own bodies   143

The properties of these amulets may have been known not only by professional magicians and physicians but also more generally. Patients' autonomy in the use of amulets seems to be confirmed by a Mesopotamian parallel. A late Babylonian tablet preserves rituals for a woman who is able to conceive but who has faced the disappointment of recurrent miscarriages:

> You thread copper beads, lapis, masculine lonestone, magnetic hematite, and . . . -stone on red (wool). You wind three burls of red-dyed wool. You put (it) on her right hand. (. . .) Make the woman escape the punishments which the caster and castress, the sorcerer and sorceress imposed; cancel (them). May she raise the infants among her male children. (. . .) But I am pregnant and then I do not bring to term what is in my womb.
>
> (*SpTU* no. 248, Uruk, fourth century BCE, extract from lines 1–5, rev. 3–11, rev. 19–25 translated by Scurlock 2002; on this document, see also Couto-Ferreira 2013)

This long text, here only briefly quoted, seems to describe three different but complementary rituals. Without analyzing this document in full detail, three points are especially of interest in comparison with the Greek material. Firstly, a crucial part of the ritual was the production of protective amulets and the use of hematite, a stone whose antihemorrhagic properties were also valued, as we have seen, in the Graeco-Roman world. Secondly, the inability to give birth to a child is attributed to the magical action of an aggressor, a malign force that reminds us of the spell cast against Karpime Babbia. Thirdly, although the woman was not alone in performing the rituals, she seems to be the main agent of the ritual performance. She had an active role in the healing process.

Knowing the body, knowing the formula: Concluding remarks

It is time to draw some conclusions. As scholars agree and sources clearly show, through ritual activities the uterus could be "opened" and "closed" in order to assist or to prevent the performance of its natural functions. The perils around reproduction were contained by the possibility of magically controlling it. The epigraphic texts selected here give us a glimpse of the knowledge possessed by some ancient Greek women about reproductive rituals, which can be defined as rites of a religious or magical nature aimed at solving problems around conception, miscarriage, abortion, and childbirth.

It is difficult, however, to infer unitary conclusions from this material, given that some documents, such as the confession inscriptions, are expressions of a specific time and space, while others – such as the curse tablets and the gemstones – are chronologically and geographically widespread. However, the collected evidence does seem to suggest that women knew how to exploit magical tools and religious worship in order to impede or facilitate reproduction. From these texts it can be imagined how women could have practiced these rituals, with or

144 *Irene Salvo*

without help from male practitioners, doctors, or midwives. In response to the question asked at the beginning of this chapter about the relationship between medical writings and epigraphy, we can observe that, if in the male-authored medical writings the men are those who "plant the seed" and "control the generation of children" (King 1998, 156), these inscriptions in contrast reveal women actively engaged in the manipulation of the birthing process. One might object that magical texts were written by professional magicians, and therefore they do not reflect the personal voice of their clients. However, each single document and its context may present unique elements or specific characteristics that allow us to trace the experience of the ritual agents beyond the formulae of magical handbooks.

It is important to underline that this ritual knowledge was not limited to women. None of these ritual practices was gender-specific, that is, exclusively performed by women or men. Therefore, it would be misleading to label these ritual activities as traditional female-only remedies. However, these documents attest certain gestures, incantations, procedures, and substances that were used by ancient Greek women in the management of gynecological problems. These ritual techniques were probably orally transmitted from mother to daughter or from friend to neighbor and were therapies that some women could use independently from men. The selected inscriptions suggest that this kind of knowledge was probably accessible to a large number of women rather than being limited to "women of experience" or midwives (on these see Hanson 1994; Dean-Jones 1995; King 2013, 180–6). Curse tablets might be deposited during the festival of Demeter and Kore, amulets – made of materials more or less expensive – were a popular purchase, and household objects – such as Sythyche's stone – could be turned into ritual ingredients.

That women managed fertility is not a novelty. What is worth noting is the fact that knowledge of the interaction between magic, ritual, and reproduction provided women with a powerful tool for asserting their influence in society (cf. Stears 1998, 94 on the power exercised by women expert in funerary rituals). Ritual knowledge meant that women could try to exert their will over the natural processes of generation, and in this way they could define their cultural identity as mothers or as independent individuals. From these documents emerges the scale of female agency in the sphere of ritual and society. For example, women casting abortifacient spells were trying to affirm their power and to intervene in the shaping of social relationships. One of the most important social functions – the production of offspring – seems to be managed by women with a good degree of autonomy. The equation between women and fertility might wrongly reflect an image of femininity reduced to motherhood. On the contrary, ritual expertise enhanced the position of women in the community, considering that the performance of the rite itself was deemed sufficient for obtaining a desired result. Women could participate in healing and aggressive rites around the womb, and this competence may have given them the possibility to state their point of view influentially and take decisive action in difficult situations.

Note

1 My research has been supported by a fellowship from the Gerda Henkel Foundation.

Works consulted

Aubert, Jean-Jacques. 1989. "Threatened Wombs: Aspect of Ancient Uterine Magic." *GRBS* 30: 421–49.

Blakely, Sandra. 2006. *Myth, Ritual, and Metallurgy in Ancient Greece and Recent Africa.* Cambridge: Cambridge University Press.

Bonner, Campbell. 1950. *Studies in Magical Amulets Chiefly Graeco-Egyptian.* Ann Arbor: University of Michigan Press.

Bookidis, Nancy. 2005. "Religion in Corinth: 146 BCE to 100 CE." In *Urban Religion in Roman Corinth: Interdisciplinary Approaches*, edited by Daniel N. Schowalter and Steven J. Friesen, 141–64. Cambridge, MA: Harvard University Press.

Caliò, Luigi. 2009. "Cultura medica e urbanizzazione in Grecia tra età classica ed ellenismo. Parte 2." *Parola del Passato* 64: 161–204.

Chaniotis, Angelos. 1990. "Drei kleinasiatische Inschriften zur griechischen Religion." *Epigraphica Anatolica* 15: 127–33.

Chaniotis, Angelos. 2012. "Constructing the Fear of Gods: Epigraphic Evidence from Sanctuaries of Greece and Asia Minor." In *Unveiling Emotions: Sources and Methods for the Study of Emotions in the Greek World*, edited by Angelos Chaniotis, 205–34. Stuttgart: Franz Steiner Verlag.

Couto-Ferreira, M. Érica. 2013. "The River, the Oven, the Garden: Female Body and Fertility in a Late Babylonian Ritual Text." In *Approaching Rituals in Ancient Cultures: Rivista di Studi Orientali, n.s. 86 LXXXVI Suppl. 2*, edited by Claus Ambos and Lorenzo Verderame, 97–116. Pisa and Roma: Fabrizio Serra Editore.

Dakarēs, Soterios, Vokotopoulou, Ioulia, Christidēs, Anastasios Ph. Eds. 2013. *Τα χρηστήρια ελάσματα της Δωδώνης. Των ανασκαφών Δ. Ευαγγελίδη. Τόμος Ι. Επίγραφές 1–2220. Τόμος ΙΙ. Επίγραφές 2221–4216*, edited by Sōtērēs Tselikas and Gēorgiou K. Papadopoulos. Athens: Hē en Athēnais Archaiologikē Hetaireia.

Dasen, Véronique. 2007. "Représenter l'invisible. La vie utérine et l'embryon sur les gemmes magiques." In *L'embryon humain à travers l'histoire: images, savoirs et rites*, edited by Véronique Dasen, 41–64. Gollion: Infolio.

Dasen, Véronique. 2011. "Magic and Medicine: Gems and the Power of Seals." In *Gems of Heaven: Recent Research on Engraved Gemstones in Late Antiquity*, edited by Chris Entwistle and Noel Adams, 69–74. London: The British Museum Research Publication.

Dasen, Véronique. 2014. "Healing Images: Gems and Medicine." *Oxford Journal of Archaeology* 33: 177–91.

Dean-Jones, Lesley. 1995. "*Autopsia, Historia* and What Women Know: The Authority of Women in Hippocratic Gynaecology." In *Knowledge and the Scholarly Medical Traditions*, edited by Don Bates, 41–59. Cambridge: Cambridge University Press.

Faraone, Christopher. 2009. "Does Tantalus Drink the Blood or Not? An Enigmatic Series of Inscribed Hematite Gemstones." In *Antike Mythen: Medien, Transformationen und Konstruktionen*, edited by Ueli Deli and Christine Walde, 248–73. Berlin and New York: Walter de Gruyter.

Faraone, Christopher. 2011. "Text, Image and Medium: The Evolution of Graeco-Roman Magical Gemstones." In *Gems of Heaven: Recent Research on Engraved Gemstones in*

146 *Irene Salvo*

Late Antiquity, edited by Chris Entwistle and Noel Adams, 50–61. London: The British Museum Research Publication.

Flemming, Rebecca. 2013. "The Invention of Infertility in the Classical Greek World." *Bulletin of the History of Medicine* 87: 565–90.

Frankfurter, David. 2006. "Fetus Magic and Sorcery Fears in Roman Egypt." *GRBS* 46: 37–62.

Gaillard-Seux, Patricia. 2008. "Rites magiques néfastes à l'accouchement d'après les sources de l'époque romaine imperiale." In *Femmes en Médecine*, edited by Véronique Boudon-Millot, Véronique Dasen, and Brigitte Maire, 61–73. Paris: de Boccard.

Gordon, Richard. 1995. "The Healing Event in Graeco-Roman Folk-Medicine." In *Ancient Medicine in Its Socio-Cultural Context*, edited by Philip J. van der Eijk, Manfred H.F.J. Horstmanshoff, and Petrus H. Schrijvers, 363–76. Amsterdam: Rodopi.

Gourevitch, Danielle. 1990. "Se marier pour avoir les enfants: le point de vue du médicin." In *Parenté et stratégies familiales dans l'antiquité romaine*, edited by Jean Andreau and John Scheid, 139–51. Rome: Ecole française de Rome.

Halleux, Robert, Schamp, Jacques. Ed. and trans.1985. *Les lapidaires grecs*. Paris: Les Belles Lettres.

Hanson, Ann E. 1994. "A Division of Labor: Roles for Men in Greek and Roman Births." *Thamyris* 1: 157–202.

Hanson, Ann E. 1995a. "Uterine Amulets and Greek Uterine Medicine." *Medicina nei Secoli* 7: 281–99.

Hanson, Ann E. 1995b. "*Paidopoïa*: Metaphors for Conception, Abortion, and Gestation in the *Hippocratic Corpus*." In *Ancient Medicine in its Socio-Cultural Context*, edited by Philip J. van der Eijk, Manfred H.F.J. Horstmanshoff, and Petrus H. Schrijvers, 291–307. Amsterdam: Rodopi.

Hanson, Ann E. 2004. "A Long-Lived "Quick-Birther" (*Okytokion*)." In *Naissance et petite enfance dans l'antiquité*, edited by Véronique Dasen, 265–80. Fribourg and Göttingen: Academie Press.

Kapparis, Kostantinos. 2002. *Abortion in the Ancient World*. London: Duckworth.

King, Helen. 1995. "Self-Help, Self-Knowledge: In Search of the Patient in Hippocratic Gynaecology." In *Women in Antiquity: New Assessments*, edited by Richard Hawley and Barbara Levick, 135–48. London and New York: Routledge.

King, Helen. 1998. *Hippocrates' Woman: Reading the Female Body in Ancient Greece*. London: Routledge.

King, Helen. 2005. "Women's Health and Recovery in the Hippocratic Corpus." In *Health in Antiquity*, edited by Helen King, 150–61. London: Routledge.

King, Helen. 2013. *The One-Sex Body on Trial: The Classical and Early Modern Evidence*. Farnham: Ashgate.

Kotansky, Roy. 1994. *Greek Magical Amulets: The Inscribed Gold, Silver, Copper, and Bronze Lamellae: Text and Commentary*. Opladen: Westdeutcher.

Lanata, Giuliana. 1967. *Medicina magica e religione popolare in Grecia*. Rome: Edizioni dell'Ateneo.

Leitao, David. 2012. *The Pregnant Male as Myth and Metaphor in Classical Greek Literature*. Cambridge and New York: Cambridge University Press.

Lennon, Jack J. 2014. *Pollution and Religion in Ancient Rome*. Cambridge: Cambridge University Press.

LiDonnici, Lynn. 1995. *The Epidaurian Miracle Inscriptions. Text, Translation and Commentary*. Atlanta, GA: Scholars Press.

Marino, Katherine R. 2010. *Setting the Womb in Its Place: Toward a Contextual Archaeology of Graeco-Egyptian Uterine Amulets.* Unpublished Doctoral Thesis, Brown University, Providence, RI.

Michel, Simone. 2004. *Die Magischen Gemmen.* Berlin: Akademie Verlag.

Moyer, Ian, and Dielmann, Jacco. 2003. "Miniaturization and the Opening of the Mouth in a Greek Magical Text (*PGM* XII.270–350)." *JNES* 3: 47–72.

Nagy, Árpad M. 2012. "*Daktylios pharmakites*: Magical Healing Gems and Rings in the Graeco-Roman World." In *Ritual Healing: Magic, Ritual and Medical Therapy from Antiquity until the Early Modern Period*, edited by Ildikó Csepregi and Charles Burnett, 71–106. Florence: Edizioni del Galluzzo.

Nasrallah, Laura S. 2012. "Grief in Corinth: the Roman City and Paul's Corinthian Correspondence." In *Contested Spaces. Houses and Temples in Roman Antiquity and the New Testament*, edited by David L. Balch and Annette Weissenrieder, 109–139. Tübingen: Mohr Siebeck.

Ogden, Daniel. 2009. *Magic, Witchcraft, and Ghosts in the Greek and Roman Worlds.* Oxford and New York: Oxford University Press.

Parker, Holt. 2012. "Women and Medicine." In *A Companion to Women in the Ancient World*, edited by Sharon L. James and Sheila Dillon, 107–24. Oxford: Wiley-Blackwell.

Parker, Robert. 1983. *Miasma. Pollution and Purification in Early Greek Religion.* Oxford: Oxford University Press.

Pepe, Laura. 2014. "Abortion in Ancient Greece." In *Symposion 2013. Vorträge zur griechischen und hellenistischen Rechtsgeschichte*, edited by Michael Gagarin, Adriaan Lanni, 39–63. Wien: VöAW.

Petzl, Georg. 1994. *Die Beichtinschriften Westkleinasiens, Epigraphica Anatolica 22.* Bonn: Habelt.

Petzl, Georg, and Malay, Hasan. 1987. "A New Confession-Inscription from the Katakekaumene." *GRBS* 28: 459–72.

Preisendanz, Karl, and Henrichs, Albert. Eds. 1973–1974². *Papyri Graecae Magicae: Die griechischen Zauberpapyri (PGM).* Stuttgart: Teubner.

Riddle, John M. 1992. *Contraception and Abortion from the Ancient World to the Renaissance.* Cambridge, MA: Harvard University Press.

Salvo, Irene. 2012. "Sweet Revenge: Emotional Factors in the 'Prayers of Justice.'" *Unveiling Emotions: Sources and Methods for the Study of Emotions in the Greek World*, edited by Angelos Chaniotis, 235–66. Stuttgart: Franze Steiner Verlag.

Sax, William S. 2004. "Healing Rituals. A critical performative approach." *Anthropology and Medicine* 11: 293–306.

Scurlock, JoAnn. 2002. "Translating Transfers in Ancient Mesopotamia." In *Magic and Ritual in the Ancient World*, edited by Paul Mirecki and Marvin Meyer, 209–23. Leiden: Brill.

Stears, Karen. 1998. "Death Becomes Her: Gender and Athenian Death-Ritual." In *The Sacred and the Feminine in Ancient Greece*, edited by Sue Blundell and Margareth Williamson, 89–100. London and New York: Routledge.

Stroud, Ronald. 2013. *Corinth XVIII.6: The Sanctuary of Demeter and Kore: The Inscriptions.* Princeton: American School of Classical Studies at Athens.

Stroud, Ronald. 2014. "Religion and Magic in Roman Corinth." In *Corinth in Contrast: Studies in Inequality*, edited by Steven J. Friesen, Sarah A. James, and Daniel N. Schowalter, 187–202. Leiden: Brill.

Tambiah, Stanley J. 1985. *Culture, Thought, and Social Action: An Anthropological Perspective.* Cambridge, MA: Harvard University Press.

148 *Irene Salvo*

Totelin, Laurence M.V. 2009. *Hippocratic Recipes: Oral and Written Transmission of Pharmacological Knowledge in Fifth- and Fourth-Century Greece*. Leiden: Brill.

Versnel, Henk S. 1991. "Some Reflections on the Relationship Magic-Religion." *Numen* 38: 177–97.

Versnel, Henk S. 2010. "Prayers for Justice, East and West: New Finds and Publications since 1990." In *Magical Practice in the Latin West: Papers from the International Conference Held at the University of Zaragoza, 30 Sept. – 1st Oct. 2005*, edited by Richard L. Gordon and Francisco Marco Simón, 275–354. Leiden: Brill.

Von Weiher, Egbert. 1998. *Uruk. Spätbabylonische Texte aus dem Planquadrat U 18/5 (SpTU)*, Mainz am Rhein: von Zabern.

Part III

Control and resistance

8 Bitter constraint? Penelope's web and "season due"

Laurie O'Higgins

Introduction[1]

Three times in Homer's *Odyssey* – near the beginning, three-quarters along in the story, and at the end – the tale of Penelope's web is narrated (Hom. *Od.* 2.89–110; 19.136–61; 24.125–48). The suitor Antinoos relates the story to Telemachus as a rebuke for the latter's complaint about the suitors' depredations upon the household. Penelope herself tells the story to the beggar in Book 19. In Book 24, in an Underworld scene, one of the now dead suitors, Amphimedon, relates the story to Agamemnon. Each time the narrator is different, and yet the three tellings are remarkably similar. Penelope tells her suitors that she must finish a shroud for her father-in-law, Laertes, before she marries again. She weaves by day and unweaves by night until a serving maid or maids betray her and she is compelled to finish. Although it purports to be the story of a ruse discovered, the impasse inexplicably remains. Penelope continues to defer marriage until the story segues into the contest of the bow and the final denouement.

Neo-analysis and the text of the *Odyssey*

The story may not always have been this way. There were other versions. I build my argument on the work of Tilman Krischer, a neo-analyst scholar, who maintains that the current version of the *Odyssey* is a reorganization of an older story (Krischer 1993; the reorganization of material into our current *Odyssey* may have taken place under Peisistratos at Athens; see, for example, Seaford 1994). Indeed, the fact that Penelope's web appears only in reminiscences rather than as part of the action itself, together with the strange inconsequentiality of the ruse's discovery, constitutes Krischer's point of departure for a reconstruction of an older version.

The neo-analytic perspective in no way contradicts the fundamental studies of Milman Parry and Alfred Lord on oral composition and their insights into the formulaic nature of Homeric verse at the level of diction and even of scene. But rather than foregrounding the multiplicity of thematic possibilities open to an oral bard, neo-analysts postulate a specific antecedent, with specific, identifiable "motifs," or plot developments: "The original use of these motifs (i.e. the contexts

152   *Laurie O'Higgins*

in which they were originally used) can still be made out because the motifs are not thoroughly assimilated to their new context" (Kullmann 1984, 309). When poets "redesigned" existing narratives, however adroitly, pieces or shadows of the older tradition remained: the text itself shows signs of those struggles and erasures. In brief, my goal is to excavate in the text we have inherited as the *Odyssey*. I am paying attention to illogicalities in the narrative, which may indicate directions and priorities at odds with the text we have inherited, and consider especially the Homeric language itself, both repetitions and anomalies.

I argue that Penelope's weaving and unweaving, like other behaviors she exhibits, comes out of the world of women's ritual authority and competence. I shall offer two different suggestions regarding the web. One is about the business of unweaving, i.e. the process. The other suggestion concerns the product: the finished web. These suggestions, which are neither interlinked nor mutually exclusive, are just that: a possible way of thinking about Penelope as ritual agent. First, the unweaving may be seen not as an "un-doing" or a retracing of steps to a starting point but rather as a positive act with a particular, ritual end in mind: the management of time. Second, the finished web is unique in its magnitude, sheen, and in the absence of design. It is no ordinary object but belongs in a celestial world. Joseph Russo comments on the web that:

> [H]e [that is, the poet] must surely have known a version of the story, probably in oral epic form, in which Penelope's web was central to the action, as opposed to its marginal position in the *Odyssey*; it is a reasonable supposition that in this older treatment the discovery of the deception coincided with the return of Odysseus.
>
> (Russo, Fernandez-Galiano and Heubeck 1992, 325)

Visual representations, epigraphical data, and literature reveal women's considerable contribution to ancient Greek economies, large and small. (A good place to begin on the bibliography for this topic is Foxhall 2013, especially 90–113; see also Ault 2007; Scheidel 1995.) These all present difficulties of interpretation. The literary sources, however, are particularly difficult, in part because of that mistrustfulness of women that runs through most Greek literature. The weavers of mythology are an ill-omened lot, and the *Odyssey*'s presiding goddess, Athena, seems curiously detached from her own skill of weaving and from Penelope's project. In Book 13, Athena tells Odysseus that she will "weave a plot (*metis*)" with him (13.303). Sheila Murnaghan observes (1995, 64), "The plot that Athena metaphorically weaves in concert with Odysseus supersedes Penelope's plot with the shroud, which by the time the *Odyssey*'s narrative begins, has outlived its usefulness and has been exposed" (see Fig. 8.1).

In literature, weaving was a familiar metaphor for deception, and indeed more than a metaphor. In Hesiod's *Works and Days*, Zeus instructs Athena to teach Pandora to weave the *poludaidalon histon* (the elaborate or variegated web) and Hermes to give her a dog's mind and thievish character. When the gods actually assemble Pandora, we hear only that Athena "girt and adorned" her with a

Bitter constraint? Penelope's web 153

Figure 8.1 Penelope Unraveling Her Work at Night. Dora Wheeler (American, 1856–1940), 1886. Silk embroidered with silk thread; 45 × 68 in. (114.3 × 172.7 cm). NY MMA 2002.230.
Source: Art Resource, NY (ART358074). © The Metropolitan Museum of Art.

beguiling costume and "fitted" to her body the golden jewelry and flowers of Peitho and the Graces. Athena is *not* described as imparting to Pandora the skill in textiles that Zeus requisitioned. Instead that competence seems to have been subsumed beneath the "wheedling words and thievish character" that Hermes does indeed insert into the newly formed girl. Talent at weaving seems almost an afterthought or by-product of the sexual treachery of her disposition. Her elaborate clothes are not presented as valuable artifacts or, like cookery and metallurgy, as a symbol of mortals' elevation above a previous primitive state; like her beautiful face, they serve mainly to hide the predator within.

Weaving and the woman's place

In Homer, spinning and weaving represent a domestic realm in which women may operate and in which they should stay. At *Odyssey* 21.350–3, Telemachus utters the second of two rebukes to his mother when she tries to finesse the conflict between the suitors and the mysterious beggar who wants to string the bow (Telemachus' first rebuke to Penelope occurs at *Od.* 1.345–59). If he wins, she

154 Laurie O'Higgins

promises to give the beggar clothes and weapons and send him on his way. Penelope is asserting authority to provide safe conduct to a threatened stranger. Telemachus tells her that it is not her place to do so (this translation draws partly on Nagler 1993, 249, as does the argument):

> So, go to your place and tend your work,
> Loom and shuttle, and order your handmaids to
> Tend to (their) work; bow (work) will be for men.
> All men – but especially me. For I have the power in the house.

Penelope's reaction (*thambesasa*, an ingressive aorist participle) suggests shock (so Stanford *ad loc.*).

As Nagler observes (1993, 249), this is one of four such passages (Hom. *Il.* 6.490–3; *Od.* 1.345–59; 11.348–54; 21.350–3) in which:

> Men remand women to "their place" and take control of important public activities with this decisive pattern of speech and rhetorical structure. . . . Each of the four "women's place" speeches supplies a different thematic term for the male responsibility that the speaker takes back from his addressee, and the case could be made that the four are complementary and, taken together, exhaustive. . . . [They define] male prerogative over a broad range of activities; the terms are *polemos, mythos, pompe* and *toxon*, for which I would offer the translations "war", "discourse" (both performative speaking and the social construction of meaning itself, which ultimately implies nothing less than culture), "safe conduct" (i.e. for *xenoi*) and finally "bow", or violence used to control one's own community.

It is a substantial list, and yet does *not* include ritual, or the relationship with the divine, that sphere where women held considerable authority. This was a responsibility that *formally* could not be wrested from women, and yet I contend that the *Odyssey* has all but done so, surreptitiously. The text hides or diminishes certain things, for its own purposes, ideological and other. One of the most important of those things, I suggest, is ritual. Amid a generally patriarchal culture, the *Odyssey* stands out as particularly heavy-handed in this regard.

In each account of the ruse, Penelope gives an oddly overdetermined explanation for undertaking the project (*Od.* 2, 96–102; see also 19.141–7; 24.131–7):

> Boys, my suitors, since godlike Odysseus is dead,
> hold off urging me to marry, until
> I finish the cloth, lest my spun yarns go to waste —
> A shroud for Laertes, when
> destructive fate of grievous death should seize him,
> lest any of the Achaian women among us be angry
> that he lie without a winding sheet, a man who has won so much.

Penelope fears that her carefully spun threads may be useless or meaningless, she fears hostile criticism from the women's community where she lives most of her

Bitter constraint? Penelope's web 155

life, *and* she wants Laertes to have a shroud ready for when he dies. The speech folds layer upon layer of contingency and obviated outcomes.

Five different terms characterize the web: *histos, pharos, tapheion, speiron,* and *nemata*. This multiplicity suggests a shift in the web's function over time, as the story changed. Of all the terms, only *tapheion* is specifically a burial cloth or shroud. The web was a rectangular piece of cloth that might be put to different uses: *histos* may refer to the upright of the loom, or the entire web, attached or separate from the loom; *pharos* means a sleeveless tunic, cloak, a shroud, bed spread, rag; *speiron* is a wrapping, such as a beggar might wear – and Odysseus does wear – or it may mean a ship's sail; *nemata* are the fibers or yarns used to weave cloth.

These diffuse and multiple connotations do not diminish the web's symbolic power; on the contrary, this lexical and semantic abundance, in the context of the *Odyssey*'s overall attentiveness to garments' symbolic power, draws our attention. In the *Odyssey*, finished garments appear in key moments, transactions, and transitions. They constitute a key element in that amicable reciprocity linking royal households. (Seaford 1994, 14–25 discusses various kinds of gift exchange in Homer, their power, and their limits.) Sometimes they point to hoped-for transitions, like the fabulous robe made and given by Helen to Telemachus at *Od.* 15.104–29. She takes this robe from a chest, the loveliest in its elaborateness, shining like a star, and asks him to bring it to Penelope, who will store it until he marries, whereupon his bride will wear it. One royal woman honors another and wishes her household well. Antinoos woos Penelope with a robe, beautiful and elaborate, at *Od.* 18.292–4. In *Od.* 6.20–95, Nausicaa and her maids wash clothes in tacit preparation for her imminent wedding. Odysseus, now missing for 20 years, had departed for Troy wearing beautiful and distinctive clothes, a description of which at *Od.* 19.225–35, brings his wife to tears.

In the *Iliad*, also, there is a famous robe, beautiful and elaborate, just as there is also a "remand" to a woman's place, spinning and weaving. In *Il.* 6 Hector speaks for the last time with Andromache, a speech that tells of his own honor-driven responsibility to fight, and his anguished prayer that he not live to see the day of her enslavement. It closes with the famous lines (6.490–4):

> Go back to the house, and attend to your own work,
> the loom and spindle. War will be for men
> — All men born in Troy – but especially me.

This is almost certainly the earliest occurrence of this "women's place" speech, as commentators have noted (Russo, Fernandez-Galiano and Heubeck 1992, on *Od.* 21.350–3). The commission to attend to spinning and weaving does not have the harshness of Telemachus' injunction to Penelope, for many reasons. Here is one: Hector has just asked Hekabe to offer the best and loveliest robe in her possession to Athena in an effort to persuade the goddess to take pity on the Trojans and their wives and children. We watch her give the robe to Theano, Athena's priestess, who lays it across the knees of the goddess' statue as the chief noblewomen of Troy pray. As it happens, the prayer is in vain, for the goddess turns

156   *Laurie O'Higgins*

aside her head. I agree with Andromache Karanika, in this volume, that the text is signaling a series of ritual errors. Nonetheless, the act, and the seriousness with which they perform it, makes clear that it is intended to form the ritual counterpart to men's work of war. Neither Hector's best efforts nor those of the women will avert catastrophe, but this does not detract from the intentional seriousness of their parallel acts: his fight to the death, their prayers. Women, Greek and other, slave and free, made objects worthy to reach and persuade the gods in public crises.

Penelope's weaving and the ritual management of time

As is known from archaeological and epigraphic evidence, weaving and artifacts associated with weaving functioned in ritual contexts. From the Bronze Age onwards, people offered cloth or garments to goddesses (Militello 2007, 45, n. 30). In the Archaic and Classical periods one might offer a goddess woven pieces of clothing, marking life transitions she has overseen. Puberty, marriage, or childbirth might require the weaver to begin a new web and offer its unfinished predecessor to a goddess. Indeed in some respects a web was like a child, as scholars have noted, an offspring knit together with material of the woman's own making, with a gestation period in which the two are intimately linked and a separation at birth. A visual link between weaving and childbirth in relation to a London hydria, attributed to the Painter of Munich 2528, has been noted by Bundrick (2008, 320–1): "a nursemaid or companion hands a male infant to his seated mother, passing the boy over a kalathos; the symbolic link between the bearing of children and weaving of fabric is obvious. This connection was also promoted in contemporary ritual practice: to celebrate a successful childbirth, Athenian women could dedicate textiles to Artemis at the Sanctuary of Brauron or its annex on the Athenian Acropolis."

Although the ritual practices that surely surrounded *domestic* weaving are not known, we may perhaps imagine them, partly from analogy with the great public acts of weaving that occurred in connection with major goddesses. Pausanias (5.16) notes that the Eleans follow ancient custom in (among other things) choosing 16 women every four years to weave a robe for Hera and organize the Heraean games; before they begin, the 16 must purify themselves with a piglet sacrifice and with water from the stream Pieria. Similarly, women wove robes for Athena at the Panathenaia (Sourvinou-Inwood 2011, 263–311). As Mansfield (1985) noted, there were probably *two* robes, one woven annually by especially designated girls and the other made by professional (male) weavers for the Greater Panathenaia and displayed as a sail on the Panathenaic ship. This latter offering, a supplement to the older practice, may be dated to the aftermath of the Persian wars, according to Mansfield (see also Barber 1992, 103–17). Some act of purification or dedication may have begun the individual, domestic process, also, and bound the participants to it.

> Certain days were regarded as preferable for setting up a loom, as Hesiod tells us, the twelfth, at or near the full moon, being optimal, as when the spider

spins her web in the fullness of the day, and the prudent ant gathers her store. The eleventh and twelfth days are good for shearing and gathering harvests. The twelfth is best for setting up a loom

(Hes. *Op.* 773–9; see also schol. Hes. 774–9 [Pertusi 1955])

Twelve is a remarkable number, being three beyond the square of three and falling also into two sets of six, like the gods and goddesses of Olympos. The spider spins a set of concentric circles, remaining at the center to allow equal access to all parts of the web, and spins its web at the brightest time of the day and during the brightest part of the month. As we have seen, weaving could mark time in more than one way; a woven cloth corresponds to a child or an entire lifespan, a flowing continuum that comes to an irrevocable end. An incomplete cloth, conversely, speaks to an unforeseen transition or rupture in the weaver's life.

Each time the tale of Penelope's ruse appears, there are elaborate and multiple references to time: "When the fourth year came, and the seasons came around again," occurs in all three versions. I follow Eustathius in interpreting this to mean that four full years were completed: a ritual cycle. The latter versions of the tale also contain the line, "with the months wearing out and many days were accomplished." "Months wearing out or diminishing" refers to the second half of the lunar month, while the moon was waning, and when some ancient writers claimed that women tended to have their menses (Aristotle *de Generatione Animalium* 767a; Ps. Galen *de victus ratione in morbis acutis ex Hippocratis sententia liber* [ed. Kühn], p. 189). "With all the months wearing out" also hints at Penelope's fidelity. Telemachus will be the only child born within the household.

Days, months, seasons, and years occur in cycles, as do religious festivals; we mortals may feel the sense of return to a fixed point. Of course, as days, months, seasons, and years pass we also apprehend the irreversible trajectory of human life, leading to an undetermined but certain end. Penelope's weaving lasts four years, and by the poem's end it seems to form part of the constellation of events that results in Odysseus' return and murder of the suitors. Eusebius (ad *Od.* II.107) argues that Homer means a full four years, and (at *Od.* II.89ff.) he also notes the multiple excuses that Penelope makes for embarking on the web. That is certainly how Amphimedon, looking back after his death, sees it (*Od.* 24.120–90).

Penelope's weaving and unweaving can be understood as ritual *management* of time. A garment or large web on the loom establishes its own time, and that is what happens in the *Odyssey*. Seaford describes these four years as a period of extended liminality in which Penelope hovers between rejecting and accepting a new marriage (Seaford 1994, 56: "What Katz (1991) sees as the 'indeterminacy' of Penelope's situation I prefer to see as the more specific and concrete phenomenon of (extended) liminality"). The *oikos* and the community on Ithaca are in dissolution and chaos. Thalmann in fact argues that the artful representation of Odysseus as "father" of the community on Ithaca is an ideological move, with the household's hierarchy being the model for the community's social structure

158   *Laurie O'Higgins*

(1998, 124–33). Penelope's state within this chaos is indeed liminal in some respects. She is in a kind of mourning, a state that grants her distance from the world, like the trick of the web itself. She eats nothing while the suitors gorge at their extended wedding feast, and she generally neglects to wash or care for her appearance.

Penelope's hesitation between accepting and rejecting marriage is the antithesis of timidity or confusion. It is the baneful casting right and left of a lion backed into the hunter's nets, an embodied metaphor for her desperate and quietly dangerous heart, casting warily but deliberately between two grievous courses of action. This famous simile occurs at *Od.* 4.791–3. (See Levaniouk 2011, 227: "This is the only Homeric lion whose action is described by *mermerizo.* This verb often refers to deciding between two options, and this makes the strategizing lion of Book 4 all the more similar to the wavering Penelope of Book 19.") The verb *mermerizo,* or "I hesitate between two options," applies only to *this* lion, Penelope, of all Homer's lions. It also characterizes the voice of the nightingale darting to and fro, elusive, anguished, bloody, and wordless.

Moreover Penelope's web is not a "speaking" one, in the sense that it contains no narrative, figured scenes or decorations. In this regard it is unusual. It is *not poikilos* (intricate, many-colored) or *daidaleos* (cleverly wrought), or *kallistos poikiloisi* (most lovely in its intricacies), like the robe offered by the Trojan women. Nor are figural details described, as, for example, on Helen's weaving of scenes from the war in *Iliad* 3. Rather it is fine textured and very large (*lepton kai,* a formula used three times of Penelope's web and nowhere else). In the third account of the episode, *after* being woven it is washed and is said to shine like the sun or the moon by Amphimedon, one of the now-dead suitors, speaking from the dark Underworld at *Od.* 24.148. Woven fabrics were not typically washed directly after construction, so this makes it exceptional too. The apparent absence of decoration, code, or message does not, of course, render this web devoid of meaning. Like everything Penelope says or does, it affords a range of interpretation, and its final meaning, at least as far as the suitors are concerned, emerges only after the fact.

White would be an appropriate color for a shroud (Garland 1985, 24), but the text signals this garment's extraordinary luminousness by the expression *helioi enalinkion ee selenei,* "like the sun or moon." Alkinous' palace and that of Menelaos and Helen also are said to have a radiance like that of the sun or moon (see *Od.* 4.45–6, 7.84–5). The *Telemacheia* and *Phaeacia* were later elements of the story, edging out the centrality of the web ruse. The robe offered by Hekabe, Theano, and the Trojan women in *Iliad* 6 shines *like a star*, as does the robe given by Helen to Telemachus for his eventual bride to be. Baby Astyanax (*Il.* 6.401) also is said to shine like a star; similarly, in Alkman's first *Partheneion*, Agido is said to be preeminent in brightness, being like the sun (lines 39–43). The robe offered by Antinoos to Penelope in *Odyssey* 18 is opulent, *poikilon*, with 12 gold fasteners, but it does not emit radiance. The gifts of jewelry do shine, with Eurymachos'

Bitter constraint? Penelope's web 159

necklace gleaming like the sun. Penelope's web is brighter than a star. In its delicacy and its gleaming, which perhaps supersedes any question of ornament, it resembles the delicate and shining webs of Kirke and Kalypso, pure, free from pollution; it has integrity. Robes suitable for the gods often were said to shine like heavenly bodies. A case in point is the *pharos* offered to the goddess Artemis Ortheia in Alkman's famous first *Partheneion*, bright and formidable as the Dog Star, Sirius. Examples of robes being compared with stars and the like include the *Homeric Hymn to Aphrodite* 86–90 and Nonnos' description of Dionysos' chiton as "starry" (*Dionysiaca* 40.577–80). (I am drawing on the interpretation of Priestley 2007, especially 182, who has successfully argued that Sosibios' reading of the word *pharos* as "plough" is a red herring.)

Penelope as ritual agent

If I may follow this thread for a moment, let me suggest that this web may have served as an offering by Penelope to Athena in an older version of the *Odyssey*. The *Odyssey* in its current form depicts a world in which women's ritual activity is quite curtailed. Odysseus is *friends* with Athena, in a way that seems to obviate the need for a ritual relationship. In the *Iliad*, alternatively, he prays to her, as do Diomedes and Achilles. (In the *Odyssey* Penelope prays to all the gods for requital for all that the household has suffered, but she does so at the behest of Telemachus: *Od.* 17.57–60.) The *Odyssey*'s Odysseus prays only once to Athena, in Book 6 (324–9), following shipwreck on a strange and possibly inhospitable island. Later, Athena appears in her true form only to him, and from Book 13 on they work together as a team. Walter Otto described Athena as "Goddess of Nearness" when dealing with her protégés, but clearly Penelope is no protégée in our poem. As Murnaghan has noted (1995, 71), "Athena's management of Penelope, which is both unusually manipulative and unusually at odds with the inclinations of the human character involved, contrasts markedly with the extraordinary partnership she establishes with Odysseus in Book 13."

There are, however, other signs of Penelope's ritual interventions with Athena, now slightly truncated or obscured in a new context. In *Odyssey* 4, Penelope places barley grains in a basket and makes a prayer to Athena under her cult name of Atrytone, for Telemachus' safety. This brief reference to a basket of barley *tout court*, in what is clearly a ritual sequence, is unparalleled in Greek literature. I suggest that here Penelope originally engaged in a longer set of ritual activities, curtailed in the current version of the *Odyssey*. Barley grains would have served a purpose in an outdoor sacrifice, over which Penelope publicly presided. In our *Odyssey*, their vestigial presence seems to measure the degree to which Penelope's role has been curtailed.

The epithet Atrytone, exclusive to Athena, also is striking. This epithet is exclusive to Athena, occurring five times in the *Iliad*, and twice in the *Odyssey*

160   *Laurie O'Higgins*

(*Il.* 2.157, 5.115, 5.714, 10.284, 21.420, *Od.* 4.762, 6.324), and probably relates to *truo*, meaning to wear out or weary (but see Heubeck, West and Hainsworth 1988, 240–1: "the normal sense of *atrutos* is rather 'incessant, continual, unabating', and it is not used of persons until the Hellenistic age."). It means "Unabating", "Unwearied" – a name that bespeaks focus and constancy. In the *Iliad*, Hera uses it when she urgently summons Athena to intervene with her on the battlefield. When Homer's Diomedes and Odysseus summon her with this epithet, they imply a deeply personal or familial relationship. It has a certain intimacy, at odds with the chilly relationship between Athena and Penelope on display in our poem. As Andromache Karanika observes in this volume, Penelope is, without doubt, a skilled ritual agent. From a narratological point of view, however, something else can be seen, something that does not undermine Karanika's reading. In contextualizing Penelope's prayer, the poem's narrator seems to question Penelope's initiative as ritual agent. She is not young, untried, or resourceless. Why does she need to be prompted? She prays at the behest of Eurykleia, and the form of her prayer is oddly oblique. Instead of making a claim on the goddess in her own right, she says (*Od.* 4.762–71):

> If ever Odysseus burned thigh pieces of oxen or sheep in your honor,
> grant me my son's safety and ward off the obstreperous suitors.
> Following these words, Penelope cried the ololyge (*ololukse*), and
>   the goddess listened to her prayer,
> And the suitors raised their outcry in the shadowed hall,
> And one of the proud youths vaunted:
> "The much-sought queen obviously is preparing
> to marry, and knows not at all that her son's murder has been arranged."

The *ololyge* was in essence and origin a ritual cry, particular to women. It was also in essence and origin joyful and musical and a cry of triumph or jubilation (see Deubner 1941, 10–12), and Rudhardt (1958, 178–80) notes that the *ololyge* is a greeting of some sort to the divine. Perhaps it may be intended to deflect a possible threat accompanying a divine presence; he bases this idea on an interpretation of the *Medea* passage that postulates a servant uttering the *ololyge* when she imagined that Kreousa was (perhaps) momentarily possessed by Pan (Eur. *Med.* 1176–7). Eustathius writes of the passage (*Od.* 4, 756):

> It is a display of an effective prayer, the "following these words she cried the ololyge, and the goddess listened to her prayer." It has been made clear that to cry the ritual prayer is a shrill voiced prayer of women. The suitors perceived Penelope to be shouting somewhat loudly, as she was *ololuzouses* upon her prayer, which is traditional for a woman, and they cried out. . . . Thus they think that she is consenting to marriage, and they are deceived in this. Since they heard the queen not lamenting but praying, as was said. And look how

Bitter constraint? Penelope's web 161

the poet now also is able to create Penelope as she appears to the suitors. Nevertheless she does not do this [agree to marriage], on account of the undoing [of the web].

Eustathius acknowledges the striking disconnection between Penelope's ritual utterance and the suitors' reaction in our version of the poem. In fact, the suitors' reaction to the *ololyge* is not a result of their considerable self-absorption and folly but rather an anomaly resulting from changes to the story. Further, Eustathius, in commenting on *Iliad* 6.301, where the women of Troy raise their voices in a ritual cry as they offer the robe to Athena, refers to Euripides *Medea* 1176–7 and interprets Euripides' words, *antimolpon* (differing from what she had just uttered??), *ololyges*, and *kokyton* (wailing?) as suggesting that the *ololyge* is opposed to the lament (the *kokytos* being, in his view, precisely the same as a *threnos*): "The *ololyge* is a call and prayer, with a certain high pitched, tuneful element that is not rough but very smooth, as the onomatopoeia of the term shows."

In the *Iliad*, when Hekabe, Theano, and the Trojan women offer Athena the robe, at the same time they make the ritual *ololyge*. When Princess Kreousa feels the pain of the poisoned dress in Euripides' *Medea* (1176), she utters howls that run counter to an *ololyge* that had attended her public display of the gorgeous wedding garment. In other words, an *ololyge* was a cry or greeting directed at a god and marking a crisis, a transition, or decision. If the suitors heard it, I suggest that what they were hearing was the finishing of the robe – in a version of the story in which Penelope knew that Odysseus had returned and in which she was working with him. One more point needs to be raised: directly before Penelope tells the beggar in Book 19 her version of the woven and unwoven web ruse, she uses an expression unique in Homer and in the entire Classical tradition: *ego de doulous tolupeuo* (19.138), "I wind up my tricks."

The expression *tolupeuo* means, "I wind carded wool into a ball." As scholars have noted, Athena and Odysseus weave their plot together, seeming to displace the original weaver/plotter that was Penelope. But winding fibers into yarn is a discrete and self-contained stage in the process of making cloth. Winding from the distaff into a ball is not just a precursor to weaving, it is the end of disorder and the formation of a versatile cultural artifact, rich in potential: thread or yarn. It is no accident that when Lysistrata describes sorting through the Athenian polis, eliminating troublemakers and bringing together those who work for the city's good, forming a *tolupe* or ball of yarn is the heart of the metaphor. Weaving a cloak is almost an afterthought, the last two words in a 12-line speech (Ar. *Lys.* 585–6).

The verb *tolupeuo* extended its semantic range, metaphorically, as early as Homer to refer to "winding up" characteristically masculine enterprises, notably war. The formula *polemon tolupeuse* (-a) "I" or "he" "finished up the war" occurs four times in the *Odyssey*, three times of Odysseus. As Chantraine notes (2009, 1085), "The metaphorical development of the verb, sprung from a woman's technique, is remarkable in epic."

162 *Laurie O'Higgins*

Conclusion

In conclusion, Penelope's drawing back the thread from the web was a symbolic and powerful act. Some scholars have interpreted it as symbolizing a women's poetics, an emblem of the process of oral composition itself, retelling a tale from the constituent formulaic elements of the bardic tradition. This is an interesting and fruitful reading, although it focuses on the weaving, which in some ways is less noteworthy than the unweaving, which brings the web back to a ball of yarn. As Orpheus noted, the goddess Athena is the foremost of all at teaching people to weave a web and at spinning wool, in this order (Orph. F 135). Proclus says that the weaving of Athena passes into the life-giving *seira*, the chain, or cord or series of Kore or Persephone. (Kore is a triune goddess, comprising three divine monads, Artemis, Persephone, and Athena.) She conducts life through the spiritual realm but also reverts to her source.

Others have seen deferral and the establishment of autonomous time as the critical aspect of her ruse. Penelope has carved out a special time and space "where women belong to themselves," as Cavarero put it (1995, 17). This also is a valuable insight. Like Achilles, she creates an inalienable place and rank for herself by postponing engagement with the world. Unlike Achilles, she does it backwards and in high heels. Repeatedly, she moves back from stepping over the irrevocable threshold of widowhood and remarriage. Penelope's temporizing, presented by our poem as a trick already exposed, is not just a trick or delay tactic, however, that erases progress so as to come back to one's starting place. That is how Plato expressed it in the *Phaedo* (84a), where he used the image of Penelope's web in a discussion of the futility of freeing one's soul through philosophy and then voluntarily resubmitting oneself to the exigencies of pleasure and pain. I suggest that it is ritual time, which is all about repetition.

Hers is not the to and fro of progress in a web under construction, or the plough in the field. I am also reluctant to see the unweaving as simply affording the opportunity to create a different pattern in a new telling of an ancient tale, although I think this is an interesting and powerful reading. As noted earlier, Homer's thrice-repeated description of the web argues for there being no pattern in it at all, however, only shimmering brightness. Instead, Penelope accomplishes the magical, temporary reversal of the world's order. In Euripides' *Medea* (410–11), the women of Korinth imply that for tales or stories to "turn" (*strepho*) women's lives to having good *kleos*, rivers need to flow uphill, and justice or the world's order has to turn or twist back on itself (*palin strephetai*). These *adunata* explicitly point to a change in direction, a change in status, so that women, formerly critiqued by men, will become the speakers of a new tradition where they do the critiquing. Penelope is not granted a truly independent voice in the *Odyssey*, and, as she is portrayed, she disavows independent ambitions and a speaking part in public discourse. Nonetheless, her actions, albeit somewhat occluded by the producers of the current version of the *Odyssey*, suggest ritual agency that interrupts and reverses the passage of time.

Bitter constraint? Penelope's web   163

Note

1 I dedicate this piece in loving memory of my mother, Dolores Fetherston O'Higgins, September 15, 1934 – June 12, 2015.

Works consulted

Ault, Bradley A. 2007. "Oikos and Oikonomia: Greek Houses, Households and the Domestic Economy." *Annual of the British School at Athens* 15: 259–65.

Barber, Elizabeth J. Wayland. 1992. "The Peplos of Athena." In *Goddess and Polis: The Panathenaic Festival in Ancient Athens*, edited by J. Neils, 103–17. Princeton: Princeton University.

Bundrick, Sheramy D. 2008. "The Fabric of the City: Imaging Textile Production in Classical Athens." *Hesperia* 77: 283–334.

Cavarero, Adriano. 1995. *In Spite of Plato: A Feminist Rewriting of Ancient Philosophy.* New York: Routledge.

Chantraine, Pierre. 2009. *Dictionnaire étymologique de la langue grecque* (2nd edn). Paris: Klincksieck.

Deubner, Ludwig. 1941. *Ololyge und Verwandtes.* Berlin: de Gruyter.

Foxhall, Lin. 2013. *Studying Gender in Classical Antiquity.* Cambridge: Cambridge University Press.

Garland, Richard. 1985. *The Greek Way of Death.* Ithaca, NY: Cornell University Press.

Heubeck, Alfred, West, Stephanie, and Hainsworth, John Bryan (Eds.). 1988. *A Commentary on Homer's Odyssey: Volume I: Introduction and Books I–VIII.* Oxford: Oxford University Press.

Katz, Marilyn A. 1991. *Penelope's Renown: Meaning and Indeterminacy in the Odyssey.* Princeton: Princeton University Press.

Krischer, Tilman. 1993. "Die Webelist der Penelope." *Hermes* 121: 3–11.

Kullmann, Wolfgang. 1984. "Oral Poetry and Neo-Analysis in Homeric Research." *Greek, Roman and Byzantine Studies* 25: 307–23.

Levaniouk, Olga. 2011. *Eve of the Festival: Making Myth in Odyssey 19.* Cambridge, MA: Harvard University Press.

Mansfield, John M. 1985. *The Robe of Athena and the Panathenaic "Peplos."* PhD Diss., Univ. of Berkeley, Berkeley, CA.

Militello, Pietro. 2007. "Textile Industry and Minoan Palaces." In *Ancient Textiles: Production, Crafts, and Society*, edited by Carole Gillis and Marie-Louise Nosch, 36–45. Oakville: Oxbow.

Murnaghan, Sheila. 1995. "The Plan of Athena." In *The Distaff Side: Representing the Female in Homer's Odyssey*, edited by Beth Cohen, 61–80. Oxford: Oxford University Press.

Nagler, Michael. 1993. "'Penelope's Male Hand': Gender and Violence in the *Odyssey*." *Colby Quarterly* 29: 241–57.

Pertusi, Agostino. 1955. *Scholia Vetera in Hesiodi Opera et Dies.* Milan: Università Cattolica del S. Cuore.

Priestley, Jessica M. 2007. "The φαρος of Alcman's 'Partheneion' 1." *Mnemosyne* 60: 175–95.

Rudhardt, Jean. 1958. *Notions fondamentales de la pensée religieuse et actes constitutifs du culte dans la Grèce classique: étude préliminaire pour aider à la compréhension de la piété athénienne au IVme siècle.* Geneva: E. Droz.

Russo, Joseph, Fernandez-Galiano, Manuel and Heubeck, Alfred. 1992. *A Commentary on Homer's Odyssey.* Volume III. Oxford: Clarendon Press.

164 *Laurie O'Higgins*

Scheidel, Walter. 1995. "The Most Silent Women of Greece and Rome: Rural Labour and Women's Life in the Ancient World (I)." *Greece and Rome* 42: 202–17.

Seaford, Richard. 1994. *Reciprocity and Ritual: Homer and Tragedy in the Developing City-State*. Oxford: Clarendon.

Sourvinou-Inwood, Christiane. 2011. *Athenian Myths & Festivals: Aglauros, Erechtheus, Plynteria, Panathenaia, Dionysia.* Oxford: Oxford University Press.

Thalmann, William G. 1998. *The Swineherd and the Bow: Representations of Class in the "Odyssey."* Ithaca: Cornell University Press.

9 Women's ritual competence and domestic dough

Celebrating the Thesmophoria, Haloa, and Dionysian rites in ancient Attica

Matthew Dillon

Introduction: "Women's business"

Males who ventured into the domain of women-only rites in ancient Greece and intruded into the secret and arcane religious world of women did so at their own risk. Amongst the indigenous Koori people of Australia – known to Europeans as "Aborigines" – the situation was a similar one. Contemporary Koori women refer to their secret women-only ceremonies as "women's business," rituals of which the men of the tribe are not to have knowledge under any circumstances. As with many tribal women in Australia, those of the Ngaan-yat-jarra, Pit-jant-jat-jara, Yan-kun-yt-jat-jara and other "tribes" (more correctly, "nations," in the Latin sense of *natio*) celebrate rites that are "women's business." One such rite in central Australia is the ritual called Awelye: it is "women's business," and cannot be performed with men of the nation present (Barwick *et al.* 2013, 197). In much the same way, women in ancient Greece had numerous women-only festivals, focused largely on agrarian rites honoring the goddess Demeter (such as the Thesmophoria and Haloa), as well as secret viticultural rites for Dionysos. But whereas rituals for Dionysos were intended to ensure the production of wine, the Demeter rites were involved with agriculture, the product of which – grain – was one of the intimate concerns of women and one of their main domestic duties: the production of loaves, bread, bread cakes, and porridge from barley and wheat. From Demeter's gift of grain, women produced flour through the laborious process of grinding (Hom. *Od.* 20.105–21), transforming it into dough, and then in her honor manipulating the product of their domestic skills into bread. Two particular festivals were involved with this aspect of women's business: the major festival of the Athenian Thesmophoria celebrated in the city and in the demes, and the less significant Haloa festival, celebrated parochially at nearby Eleusis. Women, through their ritual competence in women-only rites, became cultic citizens and inverted many features of male political organization. (On the Thesmophoria: Parke 1977, 82–8; Simon 1983, 18–22; Detienne 1989; Winkler 1990, 193–9; Versnel 1992; Lowe 1998; Dillon 2002, 110–20; Goff 2004, 125–38; Parker 2005, 270–83; Chlup 2007; Foxhall 2013, 145–6; all with references to older scholarship, of which note esp. Deubner 1932, 50–60.)

166 *Matthew Dillon*

Men's ritual incompetence

An exclusion of men, such as that from the rituals of the Awelye, was also practised a few millennia ago in Archaic and Classical Greece with several mythological narratives concerning the dangers of male intrusion on women-only rites. A well-known didactic anecdote recorded in a fragment of Aelian has as its leading protagonist King Battos (which one is not specified) of Kyrene, whose curiosity about women's secret rituals was such that he insisted on attending the Thesmophoria festival, against the wishes of the priestesses. At a given signal at the celebration, just as the women were slaughtering piglets as offerings to the goddesses Demeter and Persephone (Kore), the women celebrants, faces splattered with sacrificial blood, rose up with their sacrificial knives and castrated him. These knife wielders are specifically referred to as *sphaktriai* ("women who are slaughters"). Now he was a woman, just as they were (Ael. *Fr*. 47). Such a detail concerning sacrificial knives has credibility, for the women at Thesmophoria festivals and other rites throughout the Greek world were ritually competent to sacrifice (Osborne 1993; Dillon 2002, 245–6; 2015, 242–4; contra Detienne 1989, 129–47). Aristophanes' *Thesmophoriazousai* has a mock sacrifice and even refers to the sphagia (the catching of the victim's blood), but in this case, the victim is a wine-skin: there was an altar at the Pynx (the meeting place of the male ekklesia) where they held the festival (752–3) and where this sacrifice presumably took place. Pausanias, too, has an instructive tale of the women at Aigala in Messenia, who were captured when they were celebrating the Thesmophoria by the Messenian hero-leader Aristomenes: they attacked him with their sacrificial knives (Paus. 4.17.1). Herodotos also links the fatal gangrene of the Athenian general Miltiades with his impious profanation of women's space when he approached the temple of Demeter Thesmophoros on the island of Paros with the intent to enter it (Hdt. 6.134.1–135.3, cf. 2.171).

Males in Greek myth suffered for their impious curiosity about women's rites: their willingness to ignore the ritual fact that the performance of ritual competency in these rites was dependent on women was punishable as an impious act. Moreover, the women worshippers did not wait upon the goddess to inflict the penalty but did so themselves (unlike in the Athenian male world, where charges of impiety, whether *asebeia, atheos*, or *anosia*, were matters for public prosecution in the courts). In Aristophanes' *Thesmophoriazousai*, when the women begin to search for the male intruder they have been reliably informed is present at their secret Thesmophoria rite, they refer to such a man as committing impiety (*anosia*) and indicate that he will be punished. Through the collective punishment by the women, a man will then become an example (*paradeigma*) of what happens to men who are guilty of hubris, wickedness, and godlessness (*atheos*) (Ar. *Thes*. 667–85). Such "punishment" stories also delineated that in women-only rituals, men were not welcome; as the Suda *s.v. Thesmophoros* comments: "no man should view forbidden things" (Versnel 1992, 42; Høibye 1995, 43–5; violence of Thesmophoriac women: Detienne 1989; Greek men's interest in women's secret cults: Stehle 2007).

Domestic dough 167

But the social status of these individual men needs to be more fully considered. One was a king (Battos), another a hero-leader of his state (Aristomenes), and the third a general (Miltiades) who saved his country from the Persians in 490 BCE: though at the apex of the political-military pyramid, none of these three were exempt from the gendered exclusivity of the women's celebrations of the Thesmophoria. These men are specifically named (unlike the anonymous women, except for the priestess Timo in the case of Miltiades) because they were powerful: stories about punishment for male intrusion on women's rites, and the necessity of male exclusion, would thus circulate as part of the oral lore of these men's conspicuous and famous careers. Moreover, Thesmophoric women, lacking political power, and in that sense at the other end of the political spectrum from these empowered men, nevertheless successfully imposed their ritual will on the political masters of their day: men were agents of politics, women agents of ritual. In these three cases, men had attempted to impose, through their use of masculine authority and power, their dominance over the religious activities of women, spying on them and therefore threatening their status as ritual agents. In these reports powerful leaders were shown as held to account by the politically disempowered but ritually powerful women.

This inversion was achieved by stunning and successful displays of brutal, bloody violence in which women wielded female instruments of sacrificial power against empowered males (king, hero-leader, general). In the case of the Thesmophoria, women became politicised, informally organising themselves into a dynamic group: making a decision and acting on it as a body. Their religious assembly was transformed into a political assembly taking specific male-like action, and they became politicised through threats to their religious authority. Such violence from women is of course unusual for their gender, as Thucydides notes of the women of Coryca in 427 BCE, who threw roof tiles at the enemy, as he puts it, "in a manner unnatural to their sex" (3.74.1). Moreover, the implements of cultic ritual activity that they are competent to use – and sanctioned to use by the world of men – are used against men with violence. A number of societal and religious inversions in these cases stresses that ritual competency was gender specific.

Such violence similarly permeates the mythology surrounding Pentheus, the young king of Thebes, and his encounter with the maenads: Theban women adherents of the god Dionysos. Rejecting the god, Pentheus was tricked by him into spying on the women in their Bacchic rites. Discovering him observing them, the women, imbued with mania, reacted aggressively, capturing Pentheus and ripping him apart limb from limb, because as a man he was spying on their secret Dionysiac rituals in the hills. His punishment is all the more grotesque because his own mother Agaue and his aunts played the largest role in his dismemberment (*sparagmos*): when Agaue comes to her senses, she is holding her son's decapitated head in her hands (Eur. *Bacch.* 1202–1301). Here, no cultic implements were involved; Agaue herself stresses that she shredded her victim with her bare hands, which took the place of and served as ritual knives.

168   *Matthew Dillon*

Thebes' women, by contrast, are not armed with steel but with their stalks of fennel thyrsoi. With these Agaue calls upon the women to pursue and fight the cowherds and shepherds who have attempted to capture them; she employs a word, *hoplismenai* (women with weapons), which evokes the world of the hoplite citizen and military training (731–3). Citizen men of Thebes, in defending themselves against the women who come into the polis pursuing men, take up metal arms, but to no avail: neither bronze nor iron weapons harmed the women; by contrast, the Bacchants' vegetative thyrsoi draw blood (748–64, cf. 1209–10). Thyrsoi-bearing women from the liminal chora (country-side) have in this way invaded the civilised polis and defeated citizen hoplites. In the face of the ritual authority of the women (lacking citizenship and hence political power), the political and martial authority of men, as represented by their ability to bear arms successfully for the defence of the polis (which entitled them to citizenship), has collapsed. Masculine political authority and the order of the polis have been subverted.

Yet another inversion of roles and implements, one that is far less violent, occurs in the Haloa and the Thesmophoria, when male officials were required to undertake roles with which they were not familiar; this in addition created a role inversion for the women, from their normal state of preparing food for others to a banquet for them. When the Lucianic scholiast (for which, see later) writes that the (male) archons provided the Haloa feast, he is possibly referring to the deme officials of Eleusis. A speaker in a legal case of Isaios (3.80), early in the fourth century BCE, indicates that the feast for the women at the Thesmophoria was a state-imposed liturgy (*leitourgia*): those wealthy citizens with more than three talents in wealth had to pay for it. Liturgies were performed by wealthy citizens paying for expensive services for the state, such as equipping a trireme for the Athenian navy or staging a comedy or tragedy on the stage; basically, liturgies were expensive duties undertaken for the state. The three-talent threshold for paying the expenses of the Thesmophoriac dinners indicates that these were not inexpensive affairs but quite the opposite. Expenses will have been considerable, for a great deal of wine was provided and tables were covered with all the foods of the land and ocean, except those forbidden in the rites, including pomegranates and red-mullet (schol. Luc. *Het*. 2.17.4; Dillon 1997, 163–4).

All of this was an inversion of normal domesticity for the women, whose main role was to prepare food and have it ready for when their men-folk arrived home. The men paid for and set out an elaborate meal for the women rather than having it prepared for them and consuming it themselves. Here is a ritual collective temporality for the women, a time when they all shared in a cultic activity, celebrating the rite and sharing a feast, but it is not a wholly communal one, for men were excluded (cf. Ferrer in this volume).

There were of course male-only cults, as Cole correctly emphasises (1992, 2004, 92–113). Nonetheless, there were far more women-only cults, and thus it is somewhat surprising that there were so few cult regulations (as have survived) that specifically prohibited women's participation. With regard to their own cults, the women embodied particular biological (natural) and domestic (societal) qualities which were crucial for the worship of goddesses such as Demeter, Persephone

Domestic dough   169

(Kore), and Artemis, and hence women were necessary participants in more rituals than men were: yet this need not in itself explain why these rituals had to be kept secret. Perhaps the explanation for this lies in the realm of the potency of the ritual acts in these cults. Conversely, the exclusion of men and the inversion of men and women's roles in women-only rituals suggests male ritual incompetence.

Women's cultic citizenship

When Euripides' kinsman (called Mnesilochos by the scholiast) disguised as a female celebrant plans to infiltrate the women's celebration on the second day of the Thesmophoria, he notes that the dikasteria and the boule do not meet on that day (and hence the assembly of male citizens could not meet either, as the boule acted as the convening political executive: Ar. *Thes.* 78–80). Faraone in fact suggests that on the second day of the Thesmophoria, the Athenian women constituted their own law-court (while the male ones were suspended), hence their "prosecution" of Euripides as a slanderer of women (Faraone 2011, 40–2). Euripides follows this up by noting that on that day women are holding an assembly (ekklesia) and on the agenda was his "destruction," just as the male citizen assembly had a fixed agenda decided upon prior to their ekklesia. The days on which women practised their Thesmophoric (and Haloan, as will be seen later) ritual competence curtailed the religious and political prerogative of the male citizens, and Aristophanes is contrasting the lack of women's political rights with the religio-political competence of the women on this day; they are neo-politicised ritual agents. He creates, as in his *Ekklesiazousai* (mentioned later in this chapter), a cultic, ritual polity of women. (For Athenian citizenship in Aristophanes' plays, see Zumbrunnen 2012.)

Not only did the boule not meet on the second day of the Thesmophoria, but the women at the festival, according to Aristophanes, have their own boule, which they require if they are to hold a meeting of a women's ekklesia, for the male boule had a probouleutic role in organising the male ekklesia. So the women's boule acts like the male equivalent, with Aristophanes parodying the official language of bouleutic decrees: "It was resolved by the women's boule, Timokleia being the epistates (official of the boule acting as its executive on one particular day), Lysilla being grammateus (secretary), Sostrate proposed: an ekklesia will be convened at dawn on the middle day of the Thesmophoria": in precisely the manner as the male boule decreed that an ekklesia would meet. The language is male: resolved (*edoxe*) is of course the official terminology employed in state decrees, with the male officials required – namely, the epistates, grammateus, and a mover of a decree, who proposed it (*eipe*). As in the male ekklesia, there is an announcement for the first speaker to address the motion (which is how to punish Euripides for slandering the women). Myrrhine in fact later instructs her husband Kinesias to vote for peace (*psephiei*, using the verb from a decree of the ekklesia, *psephisma*: 951).

Kritylla instructs the women to pray for the Athenian demos and for the women's demos (305–11, 335–6), echoing the prayers recited before a male ekklesia

170   *Matthew Dillon*

(Habash 1997, 25). Another woman, Mika, comes forward and is given the speaker's wreath to put on her head; she clears her throat, like the *rhetores* in the male ekklesia (372–84). She, as a *rhetor*, begins with a protestation that she is not speaking for her own individual good (*philotimia*) but for the women as a whole; after her speech, the chorus of women sing that she's even better than (the tragic poet) Xenokles at speaking (440–3; Xenokles won first prize at the Dionysia in 415 for a trilogy and satyr play). When Euripides' Kinsman reveals more about women's sexual propensities than even Euripides in his tragedies, and the women protest, Kinsman asserts his right to free speech: for all the women are citizen women (*astai*) and entitled to say what they think (as in the Athenian ekklesia; 541–2). When Kleisthenes (who, he says, always has the women's interests at heart) appears, they listen to him because he is their proxenos (576, 602); Athens had proxenoi in foreign cities to look after the interests of the Athenian demos. Kleisthenes' coming to the women as a proxenos to their ekklesia reflected political norms. Stress is laid on the similarity of the political ekklesia of the males with the religious ekklesia of the women (Bowie 1993, 205–12). For the women's Thesmophoria was celebrated in the Pynx, the venue for the Athenian ekklesia. This was the only open area large enough to accommodate the women and the tents they slept in at night during the festival: the women, in an inversion of the political norm, "ousted" the men and took over their political space. This cultic polity of women might simply be a comic parody of the male citizen assembly, but it serves to delineate that the Thesmophoria entailed the conduct of serious women's business, along the same lines as the business of the Athenian ekklesia, and that these women are ritual agents and, by virtue of their citizenship of Athens, they are cultic citizens.

The same held true at the level of the deme, of which there were 140 throughout Attica and functioning not only as local government but celebrating religious rites. Just as women citizens are referred to as *Athenaiai* in religious contexts, demeswomen, the wives of the Athenian citizen demesmen (*demotoi*) are also found: the speaker of Isaios 8 (19–20), *On the Estate of Kiron*, in fact informs the jurors that he and his siblings must be Athenian citizens, amongst other grounds, because the citizen demes-women, the *demotai*, chose their mother and one other woman to preside over the deme celebration of the Thesmophoria, using the word *archein*, to be an archon (the same verb is used at *IG* II^2 1184 of a deme Thesmophoria). These women were religious officials chosen (presumably elected) by the women of the demes in a deme assembly (such as the men had). (Cf. Men. *Epit*. 749–50: a man contributes financially to the celebration of the Thesmophoria, and the Skira celebrated two days beforehand.) In Aristophanes *Ekklesiazousai*, the women attain their ends, not by convening their own ekklesia separate from the male citizens, but by actually disguising themselves as men and voting as men in the male citizen ekklesia on the Pynx (just as for the Thesmophoria, the women take over the male space). Yet, unlike the parody of Athenian democracy presented in the *Thesmophoriazousai*, the women in the *Ekklesiazousai* have little knowledge of *ekklesia* procedure (Høibye 1995, 49–50) as a means of indicating their ignorance of the world of men.

Domestic dough 171

Domesticity in women's ritual: Incorporation and denial

While women's celebration of the Thesmophoria contains elements of political inversion, so too does this celebration and the Haloa involve inversions of domestic activities, the most important of which were making dough to bake and weaving. Dough was the especial province of the Greek woman. Ischomachos, in a famous passage in Xenophon's *Oikonomikos* in which he advises his new 15-year old wife on her duties within the *oikos*, instructs her that she is to help the slave women to knead the dough. He advises his wife: "It is good exercise to mix and knead . . . with this exercise she would eat better and be healthier, and have a better natural colouring" (Xen. *Oec.* 10.11). Kneading dough therefore in ancient Athens was not a type of work determined by socioeconomic positions – it was a domestic task all citizen women could be expected to undertake. Dough of course was therefore a suitable medium for the women in their cult activities, reflecting one of their main domestic tasks.

In a similar way, weaving was a task the mistress of the *oikos* and her slaves would also perform, as Ischomachos's advice also indicates. In fact, this was the only learned skill that she brought into his *oikos*. Such activity is seen on the famous New York black-figure lekythos attributed to the Amasis Painter, on which the women of the household, mistress and slaves, are depicted as working together (about 550–30 BCE, NY MMA 31.11.10; *ABV* 154.57). This domestic competency of women was reflected in the rituals they practised, most of which were a reflection and indeed counterpoise to their domestic activity. Weaving for the family or for sale was a woman's role, with the weavers (*ergastinai*) each year weaving a new robe for the ancient wooden statue (*xoanon*) of Athena on the acropolis (Goff 2004, 188–9; Sourvinou-Inwood 2011, 67–70; but note Mansfield 1985). Just as women wove for the family or to make an income, weaving this new *peplos* transcended domestic necessity; their service to the goddess enabled them to use their domestic skill for a ritual purpose.

Such points seem both worth making and stressing. For not only were women competent to perform their rituals by virtue of their skills as kneaders of dough and as spinners and weavers, but many of their rituals directly concerned either the physiology of their bodies or the tasks they learned as girls and young women and perfected as wives and mothers. In many ways, to fashion the dough genitalia for the Haloa (see the next section in this chapter) and perhaps to cook them, knowing that they did not serve the utilitarian purpose of feeding one's family but rather were destined for a religious ceremony, must have been, in a very real sense, quite fun and a change from routine. To play and muck about with the dough genitalia must have been a contrast to the otherwise "good exercise" of serious kneading. To produce a foodstuff, dough, and (perhaps) cook it, but certainly not intending it for consumption by their families, is typical of the ritual inversion of so many women's festivals. Moreover, the necessity of kneading and cooking within the *oikos* is here replaced by a foodstuff for entertainment that was in fact part of a ritual! It was no longer a domestic chore and daily duty – even if the pleasurable one of feeding one's family – but a recreational matter of a religious requirement

172   *Matthew Dillon*

for the goddesses. Work became ritual play: feeding the family and placing cooked dough on the family table was replaced by fondling the dough placed humorously on the festal table and being light-hearted with other women. The kitchen of the *oikos*, family duties, and domestic concerns were not only left far behind but were transformed through the ritual performance of the Haloa.

Moreover, women's ritual activities that replace their domestic ones are apparent in the festival of Dionysos in Boiotia, held every two years, when the Theban women literally "took to the hills" for several days to celebrate the festival of this god. This was quite different to Athens, where vases show women worshipping Dionysos in interior rites. Athenian women's Dionysian *enthousiasmos* was restricted to an interior space around a cult image of the god – and while the vases of course cannot show more than a few women, these vases, and the literary tradition at Athens, seem to indicate that only small numbers of women were involved. At Thebes, Euripides' *Bacchae* presents a picture of women *en masse* abandoning their domestic lifestyle. Such spending time away from the *oikos* and the polis, in the chora (territory) of the city, facilitated a physical separation from their routine domesticity, underpinning their liminality. Unfortunately, how women celebrated Dionysiac festivals in other cities is largely unknown (but see Henrichs 1978). There are, however, pertinent Athenian vase scenes – one in which women bring a tray of food before a mask of the god (Athenian red-figure oinochoe, Eretria Painter (?), 450–400 BCE, Athens NM VS318, *ARV*² 1249.13), and others in which women draw wine before a cult image of Dionysos (e.g. an Athenian red-figure stamnos, Villa Guilia Painter, 460 BCE, Boston MFA 90.155a-b, *ARV*² 621). This last typology of depiction can be further subdivided in two subcategories – one in which the women are staid and sedate, and one in which many of them are engaged in maenadic behavior, tossing their heads.

Baking cakes for Dionysiac rituals

Women's ritual involvement could be very food oriented. Two categories of ritual at Athens in particular required the basic foodstuff of dough as produced by women: those of Demeter, and perhaps surprisingly, those of Dionysos. Surprising, for women played no role in viticulture: they did not pick the grapes, press them, or place the liquid into jars to ferment. These were masculine roles, shown on vases being performed by Dionysos' satyrs. But women had a subsequent role as the maenadic devotees of Dionysos. Scenes on Athenian vases show some women drawing wine from jars, while others dance ecstatically, playing music, their hair tossed back. In front of or to the side of the women drawing wine are mask images of Dionysos attached to a wooden pillar. In the various scenes on Athenian pottery that show women worshipping Dionysos, there is a prominent visual domination of foodstuffs belonging to the women's sphere. Whereas the scholarly focus is on women drinking wine in these rites (but in the *Bacchae* they curiously are said not to be drunk) there is a gastronomic dimension to these scenes (but they are not secret for they can be presented on vases). In these scenes, ivy branches stuck into the effigic head of

Dionysos are pierced by round, flattish cakes with numerous dots on them, pricked in them probably at the time of baking.

On the red-figure stamnos by the Villa Giulia Painter of about 460 BCE, mentioned earlier, for example, the flat cakes are actually the shoulders of the god (Boston MFA 90.155a–b, ARV^2 621: Fig. 9.1). Beneath, on the table, lies a large rounded pile of concave cakes, apparently of a different type than the ones the artist has depicted on the god's shoulders. On either side, a woman brings a jar to the god and makes a gesture of adoration with her right hand, while to the right of the god's effigy a woman draws wine from a stamnos into the same kind of vase. There is a similar scene by the same painter, again on a stamnos: flat cakes are shown on the god's shoulder with, once more, a pile of cakes beneath, carefully stacked (Athenian red-figure stamnos, Villa Guilia Painter [as earlier], Rome Villa Giulia 983; ARV^2 621.33). Clearly the artist is depicting a set ritual. Other vases show women drawing wine, with a Dionysos mask adorned with flat cakes, but none on the table beneath (Naples Museo Nazionale Archeologico 2419, ARV^2 1151–2; Berlin F2290, ARV^2 462.48; and Berlin F2290, ARV^2 462.48). In these

Figure 9.1 Woman tending to dough phalloi. Athenian red-figure small pelike, *The Hasselmann Painter*, about 440 BC (BM E819).

Courtesy of the Trustees of the British Museum.

174 *Matthew Dillon*

scenes, women are to be imagined baking the cakes for Dionysos at home, carefully packing them, probably in a ritual basket or tray, and then when arriving at the scene of the ceremony carefully sticking them onto the branches of ivy and possibly later consuming them together.

This theme of women and food is found in a different form on another Athenian vase on which a woman (right) is shown holding a tray of fruit including grapes and round fruit (apples or perhaps pomegranates) for Dionysos; another woman (left) has a kantharos (presumably full of wine); they are presenting these to the mask of Dionysos resting in a liknon (basket) (Athenian red-figure oinochoe, Eretria Painter (?), 450–400 BCE, Athens NM VS318, *ARV*^{2} 1249.13). In most of these depictions, the women adore Dionysos with the gift of wine, produced by men, and add their own particular specialty: baked goods. They bring to the worship of the god the basic elements of the Greek diet: wine and bread. Such presentation of food to Dionysos is also known for a Dionysiac rite in Apulia: an Apulian volute krater depicts a woman approaching a table next to which stands an image of Dionysos. She is bringing a tray, which has a pyramid cake upon it, and what appear to be three cakes with knobs, with a small round item, also probably culinary in nature, by itself on the far right (Naples, Museo Nazionale Archeologico inv. 82922 [H 2411] RVAp 2/8).

Aischrologia **and dough cakes at the Haloa**

The silence imposed by women about their "women's business" has been more effective at the Haloa than for most women's rites. Sufficiently important to attract the interest of a polemical Clement of Alexandria and a later scholiast, details are in shorter supply than usual; yet these methodological cruxes need to be addressed. (On the Haloa: Parke 1977, 98–100; Simon 1983, 35–7; Lowe 1998; Dillon 2002, 120–4; Goff 2004, 144–6; Parker 2005, 119–21.) The main ancient source on the celebration of the Haloa and also of the Thesmophoria is the well-known scholiast to Lucian's *Dialogue of the Hetairai* (7.4). This has often been regarded as an inaccurate source in respects, and Lowe's 1998 examination and critique of this source will long remain a standard point of reference. But it is possible to overcriticize and deconstruct this text, despite its various difficulties. The scholiast's description of the Haloa is divided into two sections – an aetiological one describing the origin of the Haloa festival and then various details about the Haloa itself. Deconstructing the scholiast's account in this way and seeing it as two unsuccessfully linked components (an aetiology to be disconnected from the rite and separated from the actual details of what happened, according to his account) enables a useful reappraisal of this source. This is important, because it then allows greater confidence to be placed in his account of the Thesmophoria as well. What can be identified are some broad details, partly corroborated by other sources. While Lowe seriously challenged the reliability of the scholiast, nevertheless at the core of its account there are clearly sources that he has read, if perhaps a little shallowly and hastily, and it is possible that he has confused some details.

Domestic dough   175

The most glaring error is that the Lucian scholiast on the Haloa has mistakenly connected the festival rite with Dionysos. The Haloa, according to him, was a celebration of this god as well as Demeter and Persephone in the following ways. The scholiast records that Dionysos gave wine to Ikarios, who then gave it to some shepherds; the scene is frequently depicted, as, for example, on an Athenian black-figured amphora, *c.* 540–20 BCE (Affecter Painter (?), BM B153, *ABV* 243.45). Other shepherds, seeing that some of these were asleep and others were maddened (*bakcheuousai*), then killed Ikarios, as they believed he had given them a potent *pharmakon* – a drug to put them in this soporific or enthused state. Dionysos punished them: he took on the appearance of a beautiful, comely youth and so made the shepherds overly sexually stimulated. Having sexually provoked the shepherds, he disappeared, leaving them in a state of heightened arousal but without release. They had become permanently ithyphallic, much as satyrs as are shown on Athenian vases. In response to an oracle, pleading for release from their ithyphallicism, the shepherds fashioned clay phalloi and dedicated these to Dionysos. Having done so, they were released from permanent erections, unlike the uncivilised satyrs.

Other ancient sources indicate that Ikarios' daughter, Erigone, finding him murdered by the shepherds, hung herself; another oracle indicated that a festival of swinging, the Aiora, was to be established, to propitiate Erigone, who had swung from the rope at her own hands. What the scholiast has done is to identify correctly the origin of a religious rite – but the wrong one (the swinging rite is shown on an Athenian red-figure hydria, Washing Painter, 450–400 BCE, Berlin F2394, *ARV²* 1131.172). In this rite, parthenoi swung in order to propitiate Erigone and atone for her suicide. This "swinging" rite has become enmeshed in the scholiast's account because of its relation to the Ikarios myth, but this connection of Dionysos with the Demetriac Haloa is, however, unsustainable. (For the Aiora: Deubner 1932, 118–20; Goff 2004, 39; Parker 2005, 301.)

The scholiast also explains the joking at the Haloa: "Many jokes and frivolities are uttered. . . . And the women may say what they wish; and indeed they do then [when they are alone] say the most disgusting things to one another, and the priestesses approach the women secretly and into their ear urge them to commit adultery, as though it were some sacred secret. All the women shout disgusting, blasphemous things at one another, handling the while indecent images of the body, male and female alike." Jokes and ribaldry are not unfamiliar elements of Greek religious rites; this was *aischrologia*. One well-known example occurred toward the end of the procession from Athens to Eleusis every year as part of the Eleusinian Mysteries, when the mystai (initiates) crossed the Rheitoi streams on the way to the telesterion. It is, in fact, a particularly but not peculiarly Eleusinian trait; in the *Homeric Hymn to Demeter* (195–204), Iambe said things so outrageous to Demeter they made even the bitterly depressed goddess, contemplating the abduction and rape of her daughter, smile, and these jokes lifted her spirits. It is probable that the priestesses were impersonating Iambe, whispering salacious innuendos into the women's ears, as Iambe had to Demeter. Through the manipulation of male and female genitalia, and sexual obscenities to arouse the women's sexual desires, the

176 Matthew Dillon

priestesses invoked women's sensuality and an unbridled sexuality, free from the restraints of marriage and *oikos*. Through suggestions promoting sexual abandon and adultery, the women recognised amongst themselves that sexual activity is exciting, fun, and outrageous. These suggestions of adultery and licentiousness naturally challenged all of Athens' social customs and laws, being a direct affront to the male construction of the necessity of curbing and repressing women's sexual behavior, desires, and needs.

Priestesses at the Haloa represented the formal religious authority of the Athenian state, as did priestesses in other rites and cults. While the actual method of their selection and appointment is unclear, they were either appointed by the city or held their position by virtue of the city's acceptance of hereditary religious positions, such as at Eleusis, where the clan of the Eumolpidai took primacy in all religious matters. The ribaldries repeated by the priestesses subverted the marriage laws of the polis, as well as numerous safeguards concerning the legitimacy of the children of the *oikos*. Adulterous suggestions, even whispered as they were, represented a direct challenge to the numerous provisions made by the state to recognise the legitimacy of its new male citizens, such as the introduction of new male citizens at 18 years old by their fathers into one of the 140 Athenian demes that were a microcosm of the state. It is to be recognised, however, that one of the most important factors in women-only festivals was the chance for women to bond in a milieu that released them from normal social and family roles – escapism, shared jokes, release of tension and repression – accompanied by the ability to do and say things that were strictly forbidden and inappropriate in normal life.

The scholiast also reveals that at the rite the women held a feast where "private parts" were on the table. He writes of aidoia – "shameful things," genitalia – of both sexes. But these are made of "cake"; they are plakountes, not terracotta, as he describes those atoning for the murder of Ikarios. The scholiast has confounded the terracotta phalloi of the shepherds with those made of dough, the scope of women. He has confused the outside, exterior male world of terracotta manufacture with the province of women's interior, domestic dough production. Dough was a natural constituent of Demeter festivals, for dough of course is made from grain, the produce of the fields, and it is as a food item that the dough was manipulated by women into bread and cakes – cakes that were fit even for the gods. Whether these dough parts were cooked or not is unclear. It is possible that the women brought the dough with them and fashioned the models at the festival, or perhaps even made the dough together as one of the ritual activities; they could also have brought the model sexual parts ready made along with them. Once cooked – or even allowed to harden – they would have been easier to handle and, if the respective male and female parts were played with together, would have made the sexual "obscenity" even more stimulating and amusing for the women. Most probably the women prepared the genitalia while and where they were celebrating the Haloa; this would mean that molding the dough will have been a collective experience: as the women worked they will have begun the process of ribald, sexually oriented joking, laughing about adultery and sex while they made and then fondled the genitalia.

Domestic dough   177

Iconographic expression of the Haloa is disappointingly in short supply. Whereas there are numerous scenes of women involved in the worship of Dionysos on Athenian black and then red-figure vases, there is no scene of women feasting and handling dough genitalia. But male phalloi do appear famously on an Athenian red-figure pelike dating to around 430 BCE (BM E819, *ARV*² 1137.25; first discussed by Deubner 1932, p. 3.3; Tiverios 2008, 127; see Fig. 9.1). A smiling woman, who is well-dressed and hence presumably a citizen, stands before four model ithyphalloi, as high as her knees, embedded in the ground. With her left hand she carries a largish bowl, and her outstretched right hand is held palm down over the ithyphalloi; the artist has drawn thin lines between these and her right-hand fingers. She is clearly sprinkling something over the phalloi; usually this is interpreted as water, but it could also be flour.

Around the bases of the phalloi, leaves and tendrils of vegetation have been drawn impressionistically: the phalloi are growing and are shown as similar to the stalks of plants. They have rampant, luscious green growth, presumably because the woman has been tending her garden of phalloi, and they are responding to her nurturing care. The fertility of the phalloi is emphasised by their plant-like nature – the leaves and tendrils show that these are healthy, growing plants, and their luxuriant vegetation shows that they are flourishing. What ritual is involved here has long been a matter of surmise, as is the purpose of this sprinkling. This "Woman watering phalloi" vase has been a well-known iconographical item ever since Deubner first paid it serious attention in his *Attische Feste* (1932). He posited that this scene had something to do with the Haloa, but the iconographic details of the vase do not correlate with the literary ones for the festival. Only phalloi, not women's genitalia, are depicted in the scene, and the woman is an independent worshipper: it is her solitary religious experience. Such an activity could well take place within the *oikos* space of the woman, and possibly this vase records a private domestic rite, but not a secret one, for it can be shown to the viewer of the vase, who acts as a discrete, passive observer of the ceremony who presumably recognized its ritual significance and the competence of the woman to perform this rite. Haloa women did not in fact "grow" their phalloi in the ground but rather fashioned them from grain they had painstakingly ground, kneaded, and shaped.

Thesmophoria

Ancient sources reveal more about the Thesmophoria than the Haloa, for the former was a widespread festival celebrated by women throughout the Greek world – for three days at Athens but an extraordinary 10 days at Syracuse (Diod. 5.4.7). But the festival was nevertheless a secret one. Despite Aristophanes' play *Thesmophoriazousai,* actual details about what the women did there are not known. He could not of course present on the Athenian stage a commentary on a secret festival which only women knew about and whose efficacy was guaranteed by the withholding of details from men about what occurred, lest the ritual potency of the women's worship acts were compromised. Similarly, this must of course also

178   *Matthew Dillon*

apply to a second play that he wrote with the same name (*PCG* 3.2 F331–58), though, according to the scholiast on the first (earlier) play (schol. Thes. 298: *PCG* 3.2 F331), two of the characters were called Kalligeneia and Kourotrophia (F332), the names of two days of the festival (the other being the Nesteia, the day of fasting). Thesmophoric themes must obviously have been one of interest to the Athenians at large if Aristophanes produced two plays on this subject.

The Lucian scholiast, followed closely by Clement (as noted by Lowe 1998: 169), is the main source for the Thesmophoria. Pigs and dough items (phalloi and snakes) were thrown into pits (megara) and allowed to rot and decompose. Clement (*Prot.* 17.1) explains the pigs: a herd of pigs had been nearby when Persephone was abducted by Hades, and when the earth opened up so that he could take her to Hades, it swallowed them into the ground. While this in itself is neatly aetiological from the point of view of Greek mythology, it is more likely that the fecundity of pigs will have something to do with their appearance at this point in the mythical narrative, for of all the domestic animals suitable for sacrifice, it is the sow which produces large numbers of offspring. So piglets were the offering of choice to not only Eleusinian Demeter but also Demeter of the Thesmophoria. Piglets, too, were a sacrifice that women could make easily (both financially and practically). Women known as antletriai ("dredgers") descended into the megara after the pigs and dough had decomposed and brought up the resulting "compost." Because of real snakes in the megara feasting on the dough and sacrificed pigs, "eating up the greater part of the material thrown in" (schol. Luc. *Het.* 2.1), the antletriai made a noise in order to frighten the snakes to away. In the belief that this would lead to a bountiful harvest, the remains were then spread on the fields (schol. Luc. *Het.* 2.1). The order of events is not made clear by the scholiast, but the basic strand of his narrative is that women, piglets, and dough were all part and parcel of the Thesmophoria in honor of Demeter. The antletriai remained ritually pure for three days. In addition, he states that this festival was also known as the "secret things," which is correct as it was a secret ceremony. The capitalisation of his term here, arretophoria, is a modern error (as by Lowe 1998, 165): the scholiast is not referring to the Arrephoria rite of the acropolis but is stating that the Thesmophoria was also a secret rite, in the same way as he provides an etymology for Thesmophoria: Demeter is also known as Thesmophoros, for she laid down customs, such as this festival in her own honor. These rotting pigs have attracted a great deal of interest on semantic and ritual grounds (e.g. Chlup 2007, 76–9, developing Versnel 1992, 1994 while critiquing Robertson 1995, esp. 94–5). But the piglets' primary purpose was, initially, as sacrifices to Demeter by women at the Thesmophoria, and then later they served an "extra" purpose, to fertilise the fields.

Conclusion

Food was crucial to religious rites in antiquity, and when Clement of Alexandria (*Protrep.* 2.19) in the second century CE wanted to mock "pagan" religion, he did so by attacking the sexually oriented nature of food at the Eleusinian Mysteries. His account, however, records commensality that could not possibly relate to the

Eleusinian Mysteries. For he claims that the sacred chests (kistai), which travelled from Eleusis each year to Athens and back again as part of the Eleusinian procession, held numerous types of cakes of various shapes and sizes. It is to be imagined that Clement knew of a ceremony associated with Demeter at Eleusis at which special cakes were displayed or offered: the logical context for these is in fact the Haloa. For the kistai's contents, while still remaining a mystery to modern scholars, will have included material items almost certainly of some antiquity, connected with agriculture or Demeter's stay at Eleusis.

At the Thesmophoria, women handled snakes and genitalia that they themselves made out of dough, throwing these into pits along with piglets they had sacrificed, to be dredged up months later, rotting and putrid. At the Thesmophoria, the cooked was replaced with the raw, what was normally baked and eaten was replaced by the uneaten and the inedible, with the main constituent of women's domesticity – the fire – being absent, as dough and piglets were hurled into a darkened pit. The whole inedible and rotten mess was then at a later date strewn on the fields, making women part of the sowing and the agricultural labor of preparing the fields, another inversion for them.

At the Haloa, dough was manipulated in a similar fashion, coupled once again with the fertility of fields and women. Women's domesticity and skills formed the heart of their ritual competence and experience at the Thesmophoria and the Haloa, but in a much more meaningful way than, for example, their role in pouring libations to their departing warrior hoplite husbands. That libatory act did not transcend their role in the *oikos* but merely transposed it to a ritual plane. In the Thesmophoria and the Haloa, women did not simply transfer one role directly from the *oikos* into a private religious act. Rather, their role as dough makers and preparers of food was translated to a sacred place and polis rite. Their daily grinding of grain and making of dough as the essential precursor to the staple food items of bread and cakes no longer involved the nourishment of their husbands and those they had procreated, their children. Women and the dough genitalia they created and handled need to be seen as an expression not of fertility as such but of women's sexual needs and as an articulation of their gender as sexually aware and active beings who as a communal group at the Haloa expressed their desires and their own gendered construction of their sexuality. The product of sexual activity, childbirth, was a secondary consideration. The women rejected male custom and law that citizen women be largely "asexual," except with respect to childbirth, and without sexual desire. Moreover, their ritual competence was reflected in a cultic citizenship in which they mirrored the usages of the Athenian male ekklesia and that entailed the subversion of male authority (mythically represented by a king, military hero, and a general).

Works consulted

Barwick, Linda, Mary Laughren and Myfany Turpin. 2013. "Sustaining Women's Yawulyu/Awelye: Some Practitioners' and Learners' Perspectives." *Musicology Australia* 35.2: 191–220.

180　*Matthew Dillon*

Bowie, Angus M. 1993. *Aristophanes: Myth, Ritual and Comedy*. Cambridge: Cambridge University Press.

Chlup, Radek. 2007. "The Semantics of Fertility: Levels of Meaning in the Thesmophoria." *Kernos* 20: 69–95.

Cole, Susan G. 1992. "*Gynaikai ou themis*: Gender Difference in the Greek *Leges Sacrae*." *Helios* 19: 104–22.

———. 2004. *Landscapes, Gender, and Ritual Space*. Berkeley: University of California Press.

Detienne, Marcel. 1989. "The Violence of Well-Born Ladies: Women in the Thesmophoria." In *The Cuisine of Sacrifice Among the Greeks*, edited by Marcel Detienne and Jean-Pierre Vernant, trans. P. Wissing, 129–47. Chicago: University of Chicago Press.

Deubner, Ludwig. 1932. *Attische Feste*. Berlin: H. Keller.

Dillon, Matthew. 1997. *Pilgrims and Pilgrimage in Ancient Greece*. London: Routledge.

———. 2002. *Girls and Women in Classical Greek Religion*. London and New York: Routledge.

———. 2015. "Households, Families, and Women." In *The Oxford Handbook of Ancient Greek Religion*, edited by Esther Eidinow and Julia Kindt, 241–55. Oxford: Oxford University Press.

Faraone, Christopher A. 2011. "Curses, Crime Detection and Conflict Resolution at the Festival of Demeter Thesmophoros." *Journal of Hellenic Studies* 131: 25–44.

Foxhall, Lin. 2013. *Studying Gender in Classical Antiquity*. Cambridge: Cambridge University Press.

Goff, Barbara. 2004. *Citizen Bacchae: Women's Ritual Practice in Ancient Greece*. Berkeley: University of California Press.

Habash, Martha. 1997. "The Odd Thesmophoria of Aristophanes' *Thesmophoriazusae*." *GRBS* 38: 19–40.

Henrichs, Albert. 1978. "Greek Maenadism from Olympias to Messalina." *HSCP* 82: 121–60.

Høibye, Anne-Britt. 1995. "A Joke with the Inevitable: Men as Women and Women as Men in Aristophanes' *Thesmophoriazousai* and *Ekklesiazousai*." *Papers from the Norwegian Institute at Athens*: 43–54.

Lowe, Nick. 1998. "Thesmophoria and Haloa. Myth, Physics and Mysteries." In *The Sacred and the Feminine in Ancient Greece*, edited by S. Blundell, 149–73. London: Routledge.

Mansfield, John, M. 1985. *The Robe of Athena and the Panathenaic "Peplos."* Unpublished PhD thesis. Berkeley: University of California.

Osborne, Robin. 1993. "Women and Sacrifice in Classical Greece." *CQ* 43: 392–405.

Parke, Herbert W. 1977. *Festivals of the Athenians*. London: Thames and Hudson.

Parker, Robert. 2005. *Polytheism and Society at Athens*. Oxford: Oxford University Press.

Robertson, Noel. 1995. "The Magic Properties of Female Age-Groups in Greek Ritual." *AncW* 26: 193–203.

Simon, E. 1983. *Festivals of Attica: An Archaeological Commentary*. Madison: Wisconsin University Press.

Sourvinou-Inwood, Christiane. 2011. *Athenian Myths and Festivals. Aglauros, Erechtheus, Plynteria, Panathenaia, Dionysia*. Oxford: Oxford University Press.

Stehle, E. 2007. "Thesmophoria and Eleusinian Mysteries: The Fascination of Women's Secret Ritual." In *Finding Persephone: Women's Rituals in the Ancient Mediterranean*, edited by Maryline Parca and Angeliki Tzanetou, 165–85. Bloomington: Indiana University Press.

Tiverios, Michalis. 2008. "Women of Athens in the Worship of Demeter: Iconographic Evidence from Archaic to Classical Times." In *Worshipping Women. Ritual and Reality in Classical Athens*, edited by Nikolaos Kaltsas and Alan Shapiro, 124–61. Athens: National Archaeological Museum of Athens.

Versnel, Hendrik S. 1992. "The Festival for Bona Dea and the Thesmophoria." *Greece and Rome* 39: 31–55.

———. 1994. *Inconsistencies in Greek and Roman Religion II: Transition and Reversal in Myth and Ritual*. Leiden: Brill.

Winkler, John J. 1990. *The Constraints of Desire: The Anthropology of Sex and Gender in Ancient Greece*. New York: Routledge.

Zumbrunnen, John. 2012. *Aristophanic Comedy and the Challenge of Democratic Citizenship*. Rochester: University of Rochester Press.

10 Inhabiting/subverting the norms

Women's ritual agency in the Greek West

Bonnie MacLachlan

Introduction

During the Classical and Hellenistic periods in South Italy and Sicily, women performed rituals that involved transgressive behavior. Their actions fell outside the gender norms that operated in their nonritual contexts. While conducting festivals for water nymphs, for example, or for Persephone and Demeter (although more commonly Persephone alone), the women often engaged in activity that fell under the category identified by ritual theorists as "rituals of inversion." Some of these analysts have proposed that religious performances of this sort can confer on the participants a type of agency that has the potential to carry over into nonritual contexts. This theoretical position differs substantially from that taken by functionalists, who see these transgressive cult-related activities providing a pressure valve by temporarily releasing tensions that accumulate in the lives of disadvantaged members of the population, such as women living under patriarchal control. On this reading a temporary relaxing of the rules would lessen the risk of destabilizing the normal social order.[1]

This chapter makes the claim that certain festivals of the Greek West empowered women in other social contexts, enabling them to compose erotic songs, for example, or to enjoy the parody of comic theatre and even playfully to denounce wrongdoers in public venues. Examples of this will follow, but I begin with a look at the theoretical insights that have informed my reading of the evidence. This theoretical material will draw upon work in performance theory, anthropology, ritual theory, and social and gender theory that argues for particular rites being sites for contestation of the norms operating in the participants' broader social context. This work challenges not only functionalist approaches to ritual but also other widely accepted interpretations of rituals of inversion.

Theoretical framework

Ritual activities are a type of performance, and recent developments in the field of performance studies have greatly enhanced our understanding of cult activities. One of the areas studied by both performance theorists and anthropologists involves an analysis of religious performances that constitute inversions of normal behavior.

Inhabiting/subverting the norms 183

Eva Stehle argues that transgressive activity by participants in cult-events such as those associated with Demeter can result in a type of personal displacement that has the potential to free up space for dialogue with the circumstances of the performers' day-to-day reality (Stehle 2007, 166 with n. 7; with Leitao 2003, 110). To support her claim Stehle turned to work in comparative anthropology, specifically that of Victor Turner. Turner observed certain features in the experiences of participants during what Van Gennep had referred to as the "liminal" stage of rites of initiation/transition (Van Gennep 1960, 20, *passim*). In his work with the Ndembu tribe in Zambia, Turner identified a type of structural dismantling of individual selfhood that took place in rites of transition. In this liminal phase Turner's initiands were sometimes treated as invisible, as neither male nor female, without normal identification markers, and would undergo, as he observed (1967, 106) a "promiscuous intermingling of the categories of event, experience and knowledge" that left them open for processes of growth and transformation, for the reformulation of old elements in new patterns. Turner saw this as the moment for revelation, for speculation and reflection among ritual participants – an experience for which he coined his now famous phrase *communitas*. Working with Richard Schechner, a professor of performance studies at New York University, Turner also turned to the work of cognitive scientists to argue that the ritual experience of *communitas*, which could be heightened by sonic, visual, and/or rhythmic activity such as singing and dancing, stimulated both hemispheres of the cerebral cortex, producing in the participants a feeling of the fusion of categories normally kept distinct by the binary operation of the left hemisphere (Turner 1986, 15). This he likened to the Christian mystics' description of *unio mystica*, a sense of the unity of all things.

While I am not proposing that in the West Greek rituals in question the Greek women were initiands or necessarily entered a "liminal" space (at least in a narrow sense of the word), there are clear indications that performances taking place during their chthonic rituals would have been at odds with their day-to-day behavior. Like Turner's initiands, the women experienced a *coincidentia oppositorum*, a confrontation of opposites. First documented in Herakleitos and taken up by Mircea Eliade when describing a common mythical pattern in comparative religion, in his description the phrase refers to "one of the most primitive ways of expressing the paradox of divine reality" (1958, 419). If ritual participants such as the women in South Italy experienced the dissolution of the binaries that framed the logical structuring of their lives and experienced life in the subjunctive, not the indicative, mood (Turner 1986, 17, 26), did such experiences suggest new possibilities for arrangements when the women returned to the indicative part of their lives? Barbara Kowalzig, citing Marshall Sahlins and other anthropologists who view ritual as a generative and dynamic force for reconstructing society, argues that ritual is not "a forum in which a static unity of society is celebrated, but one in which a society constantly disassembles and reassembles itself in a social drama that enacts the extremes between normality and crisis" (2007, 36). But the case has also been made for limiting ritual's powers. Bakhtin read performances of reversal tied to

184 *Bonnie MacLachlan*

feast days during the Middle Ages and Renaissance as offering only a short reprieve from oppressive situations and "only a temporary transfer to the utopian world" (Bakhtin 1968, 276). Versnel saw in festivals like the Kronia an inversion of power that allowed itself to be contested ritually in order to consolidate itself more effectively afterward (Versnel 1990, 112, with n. 91).

At the center of widespread rituals of inversion in Europe and elsewhere from the ancient to the early modern period is *paradox*, commonly experienced as the confrontation or fusion of opposites. Turner compared participants in rites of transition to individuals in a meditative state, aware of opposites both as antinomies and as a unified whole; they were aware of this as a paradox and rejoiced in it (Turner 1986, 167). William James spoke of the experience as parallel to that of mystics like St John of the Cross who undergo a "vertigo of self-contradiction" (1985, 246). In his work on paradox, Matthew Bagger argued that its self-refuting nature is nonetheless compelling, and he refers to the work of Roy Rappaport, who made claims for the inherently venerable nature of paradox in religious contexts. Bagger claimed that for mystics paradox does not mark the limits of human consciousness but rather opens up a "plane of exceptional cognition" (Bagger 2007, 2, 5, 9). Babcock took the next step, referring to Bergson and Freud in arguing that this expanded form of cognition, together with the laughter it provoked, had the potential to present a challenge to the social order. For Babcock the laughter-inducing "topsyturvydom" of inversion and comedy can produce an attack on control and on closed systems (1978,17; for more on the place of laughter in religion see Gilhus 1997). Laughter in ancient rituals has been associated with rebirth (examples are given in Richardson's commentary on the *Homeric Hymn to Demeter* 1974 *ad* v. 195). Some specific examples of laughter provoked by ritual follow.

Catherine Bell has discussed the relationship between ritual and the social order, pointing out that the physical body of ritual participants is an important site for the contestation of social norms. Tracing the evolution of the idea of a "ritualized body" and following the shift from scholarship that accepted a dualism between mind and body to the work of those who argued for an "embodied mind," Bell argues that ritual, too, has come to be recognized as embedded – no longer a phenomenon apart from its social matrix (Bell 1990). She cites as a parallel evolution the work on gender undertaken since the last half-century, culminating in discussions of "the erotics of interpretive practice" (2009, 94–5). Relevant to this is the erotic component of West Greek rituals discussed later. Bell refers to Mary Douglas and others who have worked on the relationship between the physical bodies of ritual performers and the social body to which they belong, finding similarities with the work of literary theorists like Hélène Cixous, Julia Kristeva and the "gynocriticism" of Elaine Showalter, where the focus is on the woman's body as the central locus of her lived experience (2009, 96). Bell argues that the ritualized body, both shaped by and shaping in turn the social body, consolidates and contests nonritualized situations through negotiating power relations. And when power is seen as having divine origins, this facilitates a vision of community order that is personally empowering (2009, 107, 116).[2]

Inhabiting/subverting the norms 185

In order to expand the discussion on how ritual performers can exert agency, Bell looks at various models proposed to explain how power operates in the social order. She incorporates the work of Pierre Bourdieu, for whom the established order, invariably arbitrary, "naturalizes" its arbitrariness to create what he calls *doxa*. This order is imprinted on the body of its citizens, producing behavior that he calls *habitus*, "practices." Bourdieu distinguishes these practices from blind obedience to rules, however, and allows for the possibility that the prevailing *doxa* could be challenged, its arbitrariness exposed (see Bourdieu 1977, 164–71 (*doxa*), 72–87 (*habitus*), and 168–9 (challenge to the *doxa*)). Bell also turns to Foucault, whose model of power is a relational one, where it is not imposed directly on the dominated classes but exercised indirectly. For Foucault the dominating class directs the activity of its subjects to produce an organized, hierarchical cluster of relations but leaves open the possibility for movements upward from the bottom (Foucault 1980, 199–200). From her examination of these various models for describing power relationships that operate in the social/ritual order, Bell identifies in each some space for agency on the part of participants.

For Gramsci, who also enters Bell's discussion, dominated classes rarely internalize the values of the hegemonic order in a simple way but find techniques for consenting to a negotiated version of these (2009, 190). Michel de Certeau in *The Practice of Everyday Life* looked at methods used by subjects living within systems of domination who manage to subvert power relations without provoking retaliation or dismantling the system. Likening their actions to Greek *metis* ("cunning"), de Certeau refers to the behavior as a type of "bricolage" (action providing an ad hoc solution), resembling the inventiveness of artisans and enabling them to employ *tactics* with which they can exert agency within an overall *strategy* of domination (de Certeau 1984, xix–xxiv, *passim*). This is consistent with Bell's claim that the ritual experience provides participants with agency outside the ritualized context. This agency enables what she calls "redemptive hegemony," whereby individuals appropriate elements of the hegemonic order and construct a version of it that promises them some personal redemption and an ability to engage with it (2009, *passim*, and in particular 207–9).[3] The source of this agency may be the strength that ritual participants gain from their sense of a connection with the divine order. Here Bell quotes Durkheim: "The believer who has communicated with his god is not merely a man who sees new truths of which the unbeliever is ignorant: he is a man who is *stronger*. He feels within him more force, either to endure the trials of existence, or to conquer them" (Bell 2009, 217–18).

A modern correlate that may be cited here is described by Saba Mahmood, who has studied the current "piety movement" among Islamic women in Egypt. These women, not resisting directly their subordinate position within a conservative Islamic context, accept the moral imperative of modesty for women derived from the *Quran*. The women's bodies function as a sign of this consent by being veiled to various degrees. Women participating in this movement meet together regularly in mosques, receiving instruction from other women trained in the sacred text. Mahmood objects to a charge that would be leveled by Western feminists against these women, whom they would see as displaying and intensifying their

186 *Bonnie MacLachlan*

subordination. Instead she endorses the ways the women "inhabit the norms" of their social context but within these norms exert some agency. Mahmood rejects the absolutism underpinning Western secular feminism, where freedom is an abiding first principle and agency can only be identified in accordance with the binary model of subordination and subversion. Instead, she sees that relations of subordination can actually enable a type of agency, citing as a parallel the discipline that is required to learn a skill (Mahmood 2005, 10–17).

There is always a risk in interpreting signs from our own standpoint. Considering the ritual posture of kneeling, Bell argued that while the act produces a subordinated kneeler, it can also set up a "bifurcation between the external show of subordination and an internal act of resistance" (2009, 100). Another parallel that could be cited here would be the actions of women in the early Christian church, who adopted sexual restraint and celibacy along with the gender subordination that was in keeping with the ideals established by the Church Fathers but, having given their consent, gained the right to travel independently, to found monasteries etc., women like Egeria or Melania the Younger. (For an account of these women, see Salisbury 1991.) Hildegard of Bingen could be cited as another ritual agent who accepted the constraints of the twelfth-century Christian tradition but challenged abbots and other men with ecclesiastical power who attempted to limit hers. Hildegard bypassed their claims to authority by self-identifying as "a feather on the breath of God."

Rituals are performed and, inasmuch as they enact a world distinct from the nonritual environment, they are performatives. Through bodily signs, actions, and words they construct an alternative reality, a construction that has the power to expose the social order to which they belong as an arbitrary one. Hélène Cixous and Elaine Showalter have offered another type of performance that can be seen as parallel to preliterate ritual: writing. They argue that, like Greek women engaged in the erotics of performance in the Thesmophoria or the Haloa, when one's body experiences this, it has the potential to interrogate the social order. For Cixous when a woman's sexuality is embodied in writing it becomes a precursor for transformation, not only of herself but of the social and cultural structures around her (1976, 880). And, like Demeter's response to Iambe, this can produce laughter that has the power to break through paralysis. Cixous uses the figure of Medusa: "You only have to look at the Medusa straight on to see her. And she's not deadly. She's beautiful and she's laughing" (1976, 885). Showalter, in a historical look at women's writing for which she coined the term "gynocritics," regarded writing one's sexuality as having the power to violate taboos and subvert ideologies (1979, 28, 37). We might liken this to *performing* one's sexuality in ritual.

In considering what might have been the effect of women's religious performances in the Greek West that included travesty – and the effects of this on both the performers and their larger context – we can turn to some parallel work by Judith Butler on *gender*. Butler points out that drag performances, by parodying gendered behavior and the sexual binary of the dominant culture, expose the contingent nature of these categories (Butler 1990, 138). This is consistent with the claims made by Bourdieu, de Certeau, Bell and others that the contingency of

Inhabiting/subverting the norms 187

social norms can be exposed during rituals of inversion, through parody. But by pressing the idea of parody I think there is more here that is directly relevant to the ritual context of South Italy and Sicily. In Butler's words, "parodic laughter depends on a context and reception in which subversive confusions can be fostered" (1990,139). We cannot of course obtain direct information about the degree to which parodic ritual actions performed by women led them to indulge in thoughts of subversion or to consider alternative modes of power distribution in their nonritual contexts. But what can be argued, I contend, is that their rituals, publicly acknowledged and supported by their communities, offered them the occasion to see and dialogue about such ideas – with each other and perhaps also with men. Parody and comic inversion invite *laughter*, and laughter entails an opening up of the body. It is homologous with the opening of other bodily orifices such as occurred with sexual activity (see Gilhus 1997, 3). Demeter laughed at the obscene gesture of Iambe, and in her cults the participants opened their mouths with *aischrologia*. The laughter associated with the actions of Iambe or Baubo cannot be explained by the narrative alone: we would have to ask why Iambe or Baubo was in the story in the first place.

The iterative nature of ritual leaves open the possibility that different implications may follow from each ritual occasion. Where parody is involved, an implicit critique of the nonritual context (whether conscious or unconscious among the participants) could address different issues on each occasion. Making specific claims about the various effects of these performances would be unwarranted (however, see Stallsmith 2009, 42). What we can claim, however, is that the power of decontextualization that drives parody always has the potential to be subversive and to expose the contingent nature of what claims to be "natural." And there is an immediacy to this power when sexuality is the principal component of the parody and when the focus on bodily exposure prompts laughter.

These theoretical considerations open up the possibility that Greek women participating in ritual activities had an opportunity to find space for dialogue about the circumstances of their everyday reality and possibly negotiate power relationships that were governed by the binary of the dominating and the dominated. In the experience of performing as individuals who shed their usual personal markers and decontextualized these markers to play with them, the women would be operating in an environment conducive to reflection and transformation, much like the effect of women's writing about their bodies described by Kristeva, Cixous and Showalter. When the ritual experience was visceral, when the focus was on the body as eroticized and the site of parody, laughter boosted the potential for an expanded awareness. We have no evidence, it is true, for the formation of female revolutionaries in Greek sanctuaries, but these rites of inversion may well have left open the possibility that part of the women's ritual agency consisted in the development of a negotiated version of the power relations to which they were subject after the ritual was finished. Confident that they had connected with divine power, a power also endorsed by others in their social context who were not participants in the ritual, the women could conduct these negotiations from a position of – at the very least – nuanced consent.

188 *Bonnie MacLachlan*

From the region where these cults were conducted we have material and textual evidence for cult activity that embraced not only physicality but a playfulness associated with the eroticized body. Keeping in mind the theoretical work already mentioned, this permits us to allow the possibility that the women exercised agency more broadly.

Material and textual evidence

In Epizephyrian Lokri, a *polis* in Southern Italy, ancient sources identify a famous temple of Persephone, indicating that she was a central goddess there (Diod. Sic. 27.4.1–8, Cic. *Nat D.* 3.83, Dion. Hal. *Ant. Rom.* 20.9, Livy 29.18–19, Val. Max. 1.1 ext. 3). The temple was inside the city, but outside the walls on the slope of a hill was another shrine devoted to Persephone where Paolo Orsi found the famous *pinakes* along with other votives attesting to the fact that this was the site of pre-nuptial rites for young Lokrian women during the second half of the fifth century BCE (Orsi 1909). The scenes in relief on the tablets provide a narrative sequence of Kore's marriage to Hades that is markedly different from that found in the *Homeric Hymn to Demeter*. Here the accent clearly was not on Demeter's distress at her daughter's abduction but on Persephone's satisfaction with her marriage and the honors she received as Queen of the Underworld. The iconography of the *pinakes* indicates that the marriage was infused with eroticism through the presence of the chthonic couple Aphrodite and Hermes.

The overall tone of the scenes on the tablets is serious, with a notable exception. On one *pinax* (Prückner 1968, Typ 2) a nuptial couple is offering libations to Aphrodite and Hermes outside a temple. The sobriety and piety of the scene contrasts sharply with the relief on the altar, however, where a satyr is having sex with a deer. No texts survive to describe the ritual that took place at this sanctuary, but assuming the young women participants did not just bring their votive tablets and depart to arrange their wedding, we can only ask ourselves what narrative and ritual actions were performed to inspire this votive object with such a *coincidentia oppositorum*, and in turn what thoughts did this bestiality inspire in the young women? Sourvinou-Inwood (1991, 178) saw this image as manifesting the cosmic principle in ways that "society may classify as perverse." While I agree with the overall interpretation of Sourvinou-Inwood, I see this particular image as reflecting a cultic experience of paradox, with all the potential conveyed by the *coincidentia oppositorum.*

Not far from this site and also outside the walls of Lokri was another location for prenuptial ritual performances of young Lokrian women, at a cave of the Nymphs known as the Grotta Caruso. (For the excavation report see Arias 1946, and for a more complete study see Costabile 1991. For a discussion of the comic material see MacLachlan 2009.) The cave collapsed shortly after being excavated. Although some votive material dates back to the sixth century BCE, most of it indicates that the flowering of the cult was in the fourth century, when stairs led down to a spring-filled basin containing a submerged rock, presumably the seat for ritual bathing, perhaps for a type of baptism. Rising above the water in the basin

Inhabiting/subverting the norms   189

was an altar. In the walls were niches for votives that included figurines of naked seated women, triple heads of nymphs and busts of Persephone but also figures belonging to the comic theatre. Among the votive finds were models of the cave itself with curtains, representing a performance space.

The introduction of material from the comic stage is significant. Somehow the women connected their prenuptial baptism with playfulness and laughter. Perhaps the work of Turner is apposite here for making the connection: with their immersion in the spring-fed basin, the young women symbolically shed their normal personality markers, leaving them open to new possibilities, and this ritual of transformation was an experience in the subjunctive mood. In indicative terms, the women expressed their enthusiasm for comic parody, a cultural genre enjoyed by the Western Greeks even more than their compatriots in Athens (and earlier, according to surviving accounts; see below, p. 190), where the target audience was primarily men.

Crossing the Strait of Messina to Sicily, we find women celebrating Kore/Persephone as a bearer of fertility. According to Diodoros Sikulos (5.4.6), women joined men in a community harvest celebration for the goddess that honored the seasonal return of the Underworld Queen in a ritual known as the *Katagoge Kores* (the "bringing back/restoration of Kore"). This, according to Diodoros Sikulos, was a festival conducted with both *hagneia* and *speuse* ("piety and enthusiasm"). While excavating near Syracuse in 1964 Luigi Bernabò-Brea unearthed an artifact that he identified with this festival for the Underworld bride that celebrated her chthonic wedding (Bernabò-Brea 1973) and, if he is correct, it belongs to the "enthusiastic" side of the ritual. The terracotta figurine dates from the second half of the fifth century and consists of a male–female couple intertwined. The male (the better preserved of the two) is an old man with wrinkles and sagging skin, an enormous stomach, a prominent phallus, and thin arms and legs. He has huge floppy ears, a snub nose and large lips. His left arm is draped around the female figure, who also has large lips and a snub nose. Both figures are nude and wear the *polos*-cap of divinity. The divine couple, these powerful Underworld sovereigns, is depicted as a ridiculous and affectionate pair. This is parody, so undisguised that even we are tempted to smile when contemplating its incongruity. There has been no further analysis of the figure since Bernabò-Brea's first publication, and we can do no more than speculate about its inspiration or the ritual acts to which it belonged, but it is consistent with a related festival that honored Demeter in Sicily during the season of planting the grain. Diodoros Sikulos (5.4.7) refers to the license that took place during these celebrations, a 10-day lavish celebration during which the participants, men as well as women, engaged in *aischrologia*. The historian explains this with reference to the mythical narrative in which stimulating laughter in the goddess was essential to the restoration of Demeter's gifts to humankind.[4] But his gloss on the ritual was likely Eleusinian-inspired[5] and does not give a complete explanation for the activities in Sicily, where the emphasis was not so much on the mother's grief as on the daughter's marriage (Bell 1981, 99; on the nature and extent of Demeter/Kore rituals in Sicily and Magna Graecia see Hinz 1998). For the participants in the Sicilian festivals, a parody of this marriage would be a

190   *Bonnie MacLachlan*

different experience from hearing about Iambe's gesture (whatever it was). It is more in keeping with the report of Athenaios (14.647a, citing as his source a Sicilian writer Herakleides) that during the festival sesame-honey cakes in the shape of female genitalia, *mylloi*, were carried throughout Sicily. Were these representations of Persephone's *pudenda*?

The performance of obscene banter and the handling of pastries in the shape of female genitals are activities reminiscent of those performed by Athenian women during the Thesmophoria, although there the cakes were models of phalluses rather than female genitalia (*Schol. ad* Lucian, *Dial. Meret.* II.1 = Rabe 275–6).[6] Ritual jesting and comic parody such as is reflected in the Syracusan figurine have in common the παρὰ προσδοκίαν, the unexpected, the unconventional, which lies at the heart of parody and performance reversals in certain cult activities. This phrase, denoting language, events or actions that are "contrary to expectation," was coined by rhetoricians of the first century BCE and later, such as Demetrius (*de Elocutione* III.152).[7]

The connection between rituals of inversion and comic drama is reflected, for instance, in the fact that the Athenian Thesmophoria inspired Aristophanes to compose a play that took its name from the female participants. Sicily, where there were many ritual sites honoring Demeter and Kore/Persephone, enjoyed a reputation for producing the first Greek comic poet and earned a reputation for comic parody in other genres as well. Aristotle credited Epicharmus with launching the genre by being the first to develop a plot line in comic performances (*Poet.* 1449b 5–7). Epicharmus was followed by other comic writers, including Sophron, the composer of mimes. Elsewhere (see MacLachlan 2012, 2016) I have argued for the debt of West Greek comic genres to the *para prosdokian* found in chthonic rituals celebrating these goddesses.

Rituals and comic theatre share in a mode of conduct, *performance.* In both formal dramatic performances and in the physical enactment of ritual narratives, as Eva Stehle noted (Stehle 2007, 166), participants had the opportunity to become someone other than themselves. In festivals for Demeter and Kore such as the Athenian Thesmophoria the *mimesis* of the mother-daughter story may have involved role-playing Demeter's grief rather than her joy at the reunion with her daughter, but it also allowed the women, like the Sicilians, to engage with the bodily component of sexuality by playing with pastries shaped like genitalia. Keeping in mind the theoretical discussions of the ritualized and eroticized body, can we suppose that the Western Greek women's ritual actions suggested to them a means of engaging with systems of dominance that they experienced in other contexts? Did it afford them the means to come up with tactics to "inhabit the norms" with authenticity? I now present an example suggesting that perhaps they did.

In 1755 in Bruttium, near Epizephyrian Lokri, a remarkable bronze tablet was discovered, which has been dated to no later than the third century BCE. It is inscribed with words that in part resemble those found on curse tablets, but the text is longer than these usually are, and it is broader in scope. On the tablet a woman, naming herself as "Kollyra," accuses a man and a woman of stealing from her and

Inhabiting/subverting the norms 191

requests that they "not breathe freely" until restoration is made (MacLachlan 2004–5). The script is in the Lokrian dialect and perforated at the top, indicating that it was intended to be hung in a public place rather than buried, as was customary for curse tablets. With her text Kollyra refers to "the goddess" (*tas theo, tai theoi*), phrases identical to those used for Persephone on a dedication at the Manella sanctuary and elsewhere in Lokri, and the tablet may have been hung in the famous Lokrian temple. Kollyra dedicates her stolen objects to the attendants of the goddess, in effect making the thieves temple robbers. She specifies the penalties she requests, indicating that they are consistent with "what the city requires," and they are extreme. The person who stole Kollyra's cloak should dedicate to the goddess 12 times its worth, together with an enormous amount of incense – as should the woman named "Melita" who stole three gold coins from her. If the tablet was hung in the temple, visitors who read it would presumably be prepared to look for the missing cloak, and Melita would have difficulty evading scrutiny for her theft. Kollyra has indeed exerted agency and operates within the valence of the cult(s) of Lokrian Persephone. Kollyra's reference to the city's standard penalties for theft suggests that she does not feel disenfranchised. The agency that women may have gained from cult experiences seems to have been reinforced by the practice of matrilineal descent in Lokri, which enabled them to confer social status on their children (see Redfield 2003, ch. 7).

The bronze tablet bears a resemblance to 13 other tablets found in the nineteenth century in Knidos by C. T. Newman (2011, original publication 1863; for a recent discussion of the inscriptions on the tablets see Blümel 1992). These tablets, made of lead, have been dated to the second or first centuries BCE and were found in a sanctuary of Demeter and other chthonic gods. They were also perforated, hence intended to be hung, and were also a type of curse tablet that registered offences and demanded compensation. Some contain allegations of theft; others refer to unscrupulous business practices, and four contain accusations against women who had lured away the husbands of the dedicatees. On one of the first type the thief is required to return stolen garments to Demeter herself, and the tablet is referred to as a "dedication" to the goddess and Kore. This, like Kollyra's claim, transfers ownership of the stolen property to the divinities, and presumably with this came the expectation that retribution would have divine force behind it. While these tablets do not belong to a Western Greek cult context, they suggest a similar link as in Kollyra's tablet between women's ritual performances for Demeter/Kore and an assumption of competence that carried into the public/social sphere.

Conclusion

The Hellenistic female poet Nossis (*c.* 300 BCE) came from Epizephyrian Lokri, and her epigrams were composed in a strong female voice. We have 12 extant poems, and several refer to female goddesses – Aphrodite, Hera, and Artemis. Aphrodite, who was represented on the Lokrian *pinakes*, figures in several, and clearly inspired an epigram in which Nossis makes the categorical statement that Eros is the sweetest of life's delights (*AP* 5.170). In the second couplet of this epigram Nossis claims that

192   Bonnie MacLachlan

Aphrodite ("Cypris") confers the blossoms of her roses on those she blesses, and Jane Snyder (1989, 78) suggests that the reference to roses (*roda*) is a play on words and could refer, as elsewhere in Greek poetry, to a woman's genitals. A direct connection with cult cannot be claimed for Nossis and her epigram, of course, but it is worth recalling here the *mylloi* carried by Sicilian women and men in festivals for Demeter. In another epigram (*AP* 7.718) Nossis claims that she was inspired by the songs of Sappho. "Theano" was another Lokrian female composer of love-songs that were likened to the Lesbian poet. Theano was a lyre-player whom the *Suda* (*s.v. Theano*) describes as having composed *aismata*, a kind of popular song with erotic content.[8] In one of these *aismata*, preserved by Athenaios (15.697b–c), an adulterous woman is driving her lover out of bed before her husband can return.

We have no idea of the context for the performances of these songs, no details about the audiences who listened to Nossis' epigrams or Theano's *aismata*, but it seems safe to assume that they were performed in public. A direct link to women's performances in Lokrian cults cannot be claimed for them, but the evidence collected in this chapter for Lokrian women claiming the right to seek justice or to enjoy erotic pleasure on a par with men may not be coincidental. It comes from a region where women's competence in performing a variety of rituals had the potential to confer on them a public voice in their West Greek communities, and it was not infrequently playful.

Notes

1   The functional explanation of ritual, first articulated by the sociologist Durkheim (1915), continues to be echoed by a number of theorists who argue for the importance of ritual in channeling conflict (Bell 2009, 171), including, for example, Gluckman (1963, 109), who refers to "rites of rebellion" as a safety valve that diffuses tensions, and Burkert in his seminal work on sacrifice in Greek ritual, who argues that sacrificial ritual functioned within communities to divert violent tendencies that would otherwise result in internecine conflict (Burkert 1983, 1985, 1996).

2   Stehle 2007,166–7, 170, 173 refers to ritual participants connecting and identifying with divinity by reaching a state of *communitas*. In, for example, the Thesmophoria they aroused their female bodies through mocking and obscene speech (*aischrologia*), "producing an alternative valuation of their embodied selves, authorized by the goddess" (174) and by making one another laugh they generated pleasure from within themselves (177).

3   Bell identifies two "dimensions" of the process of a ritual construction of power: in the first the ritualized agents reproduce the structuring schemes within which they live without necessarily being aware of the arbitrariness of these; at the same time, however, they act with resistance and "negotiated appropriation" (2009, 207). In Bell's words, "(a) participant, as a ritualized agent and social body, naturally brings to such activities a self-constituting history that is a patchwork of compliance, resistance, misunderstanding, and a redemptive personal appropriation of the hegemonic order." Resistance might take the form of outward compliance but inner disregard (208). She cites as a parallel example in the American context today the situation of Catholics who consent overall to papal power but modify their compliance by using birth control. In de Certeau's terms these would be tactics that operate with impunity within an overall strategy imposed by the Vatican.

Inhabiting/subverting the norms 193

4 Grain-bearing Sicily had reason to highlight the cults of Demeter and Kore, and the Sicilian tyrants Hieron and Gelon as Deinomenids held the ancestral rights to priesthoods in cults of the two goddesses (Hdt. 7.153).

5 Diodoros' Sicilian record was heavily indebted to that of the fourth/third century BCE historian Timaeus, a Sicilian who spent most of his career in Athens. This could explain why Diodoros accounts for the unbridled behavior at Sicilian festivals for Demeter and Kore with reference to the narrative found in the *Homeric Hymn to Demeter*.

6 Models of male genitalia were also used during the Athenian Haloa, a wine-festival honoring Demeter, Kore and Dionysos, and at Eleusis the women "lifted up" models of both male and female genitalia (*schol. ad* Lucian, *Dial. Meret.* VII.4 = Rabe 279–80). For recent discussions of the scholia and the Athenian Thesmophoria generally see Stehle 2007 and Stallsmith 2009, and Dillon in this volume.

7 On the importance of paradox in religion, see, *inter alia*, Leach 1961,135–6; Babcock 1978; and Bagger 2007, who claim in various ways that paradox is an essential, universal and compelling aspect of religion that triggers cognitive buttons and provides an open plane for cognition. Turner 1986:167 speaks of paradox as activating two modes of the autonomic nervous system, the "ergotropic" (responsible for functioning) and the "trophotropic" (less focused, diffuse, nourishing and endorsing play); equilibrium is maintained by the interrelationship of the two. Logical paradoxes that appear in myth as polar opposites can become unified wholes during the ritual experience.

8 *Suda, s.v.* Θεανώ: Λοκρὶς λυρικὴ αἴσματα Λοκρικὰ καὶ μέλη. Klearchos compares *aismata* to the love-songs of Sappho and Anacreon (fr. 33 Wehrli).

Works consulted

Arias, Paolo Enrico. 1946. *Notizie degli scavi di antichità* 7, ser. 7: 136–61.

Babcock, Barbara A. (ed.). 1978. *The Reversible World: Symbolic Inversion in Art and Society*. Ithaca/London: Cornell University Press.

Bagger, Matthew. 2007. *The Uses of Paradox: Religion, Self-Transformation, and the Absurd*. New York/Chichester/West Sussex: Columbia University Press.

Bakhtin, Mikhail. 1968. *Rabelais and His World*. Translated by Helene Iswolsky. Cambridge, MA: Harvard University Press.

Bell, Catherine. 1990. "The Ritualized Body and the Dynamics of Ritual Power." *Journal of Ritual Studies* 4.2: 299–313.

———. 2009. *Ritual Theory, Ritual Practice*. Oxford and New York: Oxford University Press.

Bell, Malcolm. 1976. "Le terrecotte votive del culto di Persefone a Morgantina," in *Il Tempio Greco in Sicilia. Architettura e Culti.* 140–7 and Plates 40, 41. Catania: Istituto di Archeologia.

———. 1981. *The Terracottas. Morgantina Studies* vol. 1. Princeton: Princeton University Press.

Bernabò-Brea, Luigi. 1973. "Coroplastica ispirata alle Koreia siracusane," *Parola del Passato* 152: 376–84.

——— and Madeliene Cavalier. 2002. *Terracotte teatrali e buffonesche della Sicilia orientale e centrale.* Palermo: Mario Crispo.

Blümel, Wolfgang. (ed.). 1992. "Fluchtafeln aus dem heilige Bezirk der Damater und Kora." In *Die Inschriften von Knidos*, 85–103. Bonn: R. Habelt.

Blundell, Sue and Margaret Williamson. (eds.). 1998. *The Sacred and the Feminine in Ancient Greece*. London/New York: Routledge.

194   *Bonnie MacLachlan*

Bourdieu, Pierre. 1977. *Outline of a Theory of Practice.* Translated by R. Nice from the French edition of 1972. Cambridge: Cambridge University Press.

Burkert, Walter. 1983. *Homo Necans: The Anthropology of Ancient Greek Sacrificial Ritual and Myth.* Translated by P. Bing from the German edition of 1972. Berkeley: University of California Press.

―――. 1985. *Greek Religion.* Translated by J. Raffan from the German edition of 1977. Cambridge, MA: Harvard University Press.

―――. 1996. *Creation of the Sacred: Tracks of Biology in Early Religions.* Cambridge, MA: Harvard University Press.

Butler, Judith. 1990. *Gender Trouble: Feminism and the Subversion of Identity.* New York/London: Routledge.

Cixous, Helene. 1976. "The Laugh of the Medusa." *Signs* 1.4: 875–93.

Costabile, Felice. 1991. *I ninfei di Locri Epizefiri.* Soveria Mannelli, Catanzaro: Rubbettino.

de Certeau, Michelle. 1984. *The Practice of Everyday Life,* vol. 1. Translated by S.F. Rendall. Berkeley/Los Angeles/London: University of California Press.

Dillon, Matthew P. 2002. *Girls and Women in Classical Greek Religion.* London/New York: Routledge.

Douglas, Mary. 1966. *Purity and Danger: An Analysis of Concepts of Pollution and Taboo.* New York: Praeger Publishers.

―――. 1968. "The Social Control of Cognition: Some Factors in Joke Perception." *Man,* n.s. 3: 361–76.

Dowden, Kenneth. 1989. *Death and the Maiden: Girls' Initiation Rites in Greek Mythology.* New York: Routledge.

Dunbabin, Thomas James. 1948. *The Western Greeks: The History of Sicily and South Italy from the Foundation of the Greek Colonies to 480* B.C. Oxford: Clarendon Press.

Duncan, Anne. 2006. *Performance and Identity in the Classical World.* Cambridge/New York: Cambridge University Press.

Durkheim, Emile. 1915. *The Elementary Forms of the Religious Life.* Translated by J.W. Swain. London: Allen and Unwin.

Eliade, Marcel. 1958. *Patterns in Comparative Religion.* Translated by Rosemary Sheed. New York: Sheed and Ward.

Foucault, Michel. 1980. *Power/Knowledge: Selected Interviews and Other Writings 1972–77.* Translated by C. Gordon. New York: Pantheon.

Gilhus, Ingvild Saelid. 1997. *Laughing Gods: Weeping Virgins: Laughter in the History of Religion.* London/New York: Routledge.

Gluckman, Max. 1963. *Order and Rebellion in Tribal Africa.* London: Cohen and West.

Halliwell, Stephen. 2008. *Greek Laughter: A Study of Cultural Psychology from Homer to Early Christianity.* Cambridge: Cambridge University Press.

Hinz, Valentina. 1998. *Der Kult von Demeter und Kore auf Sizilien und in der Magna Graecia.* Wiesbaden: Dr. Ludwig Reichert.

Huizinga, Johan. 1950. *Homo Ludens.* Boston: Beacon Press.

James, William. 1985 (1902). *The Varieties of Religious Experience.* Cambridge, MA: Harvard University Press.

Kowalzig, Barbara. 2007. *Singing for the Gods. Performances of Myth and Ritual in Archaic and Classical Greece.* Oxford/New York: Oxford University Press.

Leach, Edmund Ronald. 1961. "Two Essays Concerning the Symbolic Representation of Time." In *Rethinking Anthropology,* 124–36. London/Toronto: The Athlone Press.

Leitao, David. 2003. "Adolescent Hair-Growing and Hair-Cutting Rituals." In *Initiation in Ancient Greek Rituals and Narratives: New Critical Perspectives*, edited by David B. Dodd and Christopher A. Faraone, 109–29. London/New York: Routledge.

MacLachlan, Bonnie. 2004/5. "Kollyra's Curse." *Minima epigraphica et papyrologica* 7–8: 249–56.

———. 2009. "Women and Nymphs at the Grotta Caruso." In *Mystic Cults in Magna Graecia*, edited by Giovanni Casadio and Patricia A. Johnston, 204–16. Austin, TX: University of Texas Press.

———. 2012. "The Grave's a Fine and Funny Place: Chthonic Rituals and the Comic Theater in the Greek West." In *Theater Outside Athens*, edited by Kathryn Bosher, 343–64. Cambridge: Cambridge University Press.

———. 2016. "Ritual Katábasis and the Comic." *Cahiers des études anciennes* XIII: 83–111.

Mahmood, Saba. 2005. *Politics of Piety: The Islamic Revival and the Feminist Subject*. Princeton: Princeton University Press.

Newman, Charles Thomas. 2011 (1863). *A History of Discoveries at Halicarnassus, Cnidus, and Branchidae* I. Cambridge: Cambridge University Press.

Orsi, Paolo. 1909. "Locri Epizefiri: resoconto sulla terza campagna di scavi Locresi." *Bollettino d'Arte* 3: 1–12.

Padilla, Mark. (ed.). 1999. *Rites of Passage in Ancient Greece: Literature, Religion, Society*. Lewisburg: Bucknell University Press; London/Toronto: Associated University Presses.

Prückner, Helmut. 1968. *Die Lokrischen Tonreliefs*. Mainz: Philipp von Zabern.

Rappaport, Richard. 1999. *Ritual and Religion in the Making of Humanity*. Cambridge/New York: Cambridge University Press.

Redfield, James. 2003. *The Locrian Maidens: Love and Death in Greek Italy*. Princeton: Princeton University Press.

Richardson, Nicholas James. (ed.). 1974. *The Homeric Hymn to Demeter*. Oxford: Clarendon Press.

Salisbury, Joyce E. 1991. *Church Fathers, Independent Virgins*. London/New York: Verso.

Schechner, Richard. 1985. *Between Theater and Anthropology*. Philadelphia: University of Pennsylvania Press.

Showalter, E. 1979. "Toward a Feminist Poetics." In *Women Writing and Writing about Women*, edited by. Mary Jacobus, 22–41. London: Croom Helm Ltd.

Snyder, Jane. 1989. *The Woman and the Lyre: Women Writers in Classical Greece and Rome*. Carbondale/Edwardsville: Southern Illinois University Press.

Sourvinou-Inwood, Christiane. 1991. "Persephone and Aphrodite at Locri: A Model for Personality Definitions in Greek Religion." In *'Reading' Greek Culture: Texts and Images, Rituals and Myths*. Oxford: Clarendon Press, 147–88. (Reprinted from *JHS* 98 [1978] 101–21).

Stallsmith, Allaire B. 2009. "Interpreting the Athenian Thesmophoria." *Classical Bulletin* 84.1: 28–45.

Stallybrass, Peter and Allon White. (eds.). 1986. *The Politics and Poetics of Transgression*. Ithaca: Cornell University Press.

Stehle, Eva. 1997. *Performance and Gender in Ancient Greece: Nondramatic Poetry in Its Setting*. Princeton: Princeton University Press.

———. 2007. "Thesmophoria and Eleusinian Mysteries: The Fascination of Women's Secret Ritual." In *Finding Persephone*, edited by Maryline Parca and Angeliki Tzanetou, 165–85. Bloomington: Indiana University Press.

196   *Bonnie MacLachlan*

Turner, Victor. 1967. *The Forest of Symbols: Aspects of Ndembu Ritual.* Ithaca: Cornell University Press.

———. 1977 (1969). *The Ritual Process.* Ithaca: Cornell University Press.

———. 1982. *From Ritual to Theatre: The Human Seriousness of Play.* New York: PAJ Publications.

———. 1986. *The Anthropology of Performance.* New York: PAJ Publications.

Van Gennep, Arnold. 1960 (1908). *The Rites of Passage.* Translated by M.B. Vizedom and G. L. Caffee. Chicago: University of Chicago Press.

Versnel, Hank S. 1990. *Inconsistencies in Greek and Roman Religion.* II *Transition and Renewal in Myth and Ritual.* Leiden/New York: Brill.

Part IV
Denial and contestation

11 Women's ritual competence and a self-inscribing prophet at Rome

J. Bert Lott[1]

Introduction

The years immediately following 4 CE were difficult ones at Rome. In 5 CE a serious famine began (Garnsey 1988, 219–22). In 6 CE shortages worsened, and several extraordinary measures had to be taken to feed the city (Cass. Dio 55.26.1, Suet. *Aug.* 42.3). At the same time, the Illyrians and Pannonians, who had been mobilized to support a final push into Germany, instead themselves revolted from Rome, causing great alarm due to the surprise, nearness, and strength of the rebels (Wilkes 1969, 69–77). The pattern continued in 7 CE, with revolt spreading to Sardinia and Africa and worsening famine and shortages in the capital. On top of it all, there was a devastating fire in the city, and the implementation of new taxes to deal with the problems caused widespread dissatisfaction (Cass. Dio 55.27.1–3). Augustus conscripted and dispatched to the war new military units drawn from the urban *plebs,* including freedmen and slaves freed for this purpose, a measure that was unwelcome to all involved. Anonymous bills denouncing the *princeps* began to be posted around the city at night. Revolution was in the air (see Swan 2004, 183–4). Pliny the Elder characterizes the period with a long series of misfortunes, including "lack of funds for military pay, rebellion in Illyria, enlistment of slaves, shortage of manpower, disease at Rome, and famine in Italy" (*HN* 7.149).

In his account of growing unrest and panic in the city, Dio includes the story of a certain prophesying woman who attracted so much attention by her actions that Augustus himself intervened:

> κατά τε τῆς πανηγύρεως τῆς μεγάλης ηὔξατο, ὅτι γυνή τις ἐς τὸν βραχίονα γράμματα ἄττα ἐντεμοῦσα ἐθείασέ τινα. ἤσθετο μὲν γαρ ὅτι οὐκ ἐκ θεοῦ κατέσχητο ἀλλ᾽ ἐκ παρασκευῆς αὐτὸ ἐπεποιήκει· ἐπειδὴ δὲ τὸ πλῆθος ἄλλως τε καὶ διὰ τοὺς πολέμους τόν τε λιμόν, ὃς καὶ τότε αὖθις συνέβη, δεινῶς ἐτραπάττετο, πιστεύειν τε καὶ αὐτὸς τοῖς λεχθεῖσιν ἐπλάττετο, καὶ πάνθ᾽ ὅσα παραμυθήσεσθαι τὸν ὅμιλον ἤμελλεν ὡς καὶ ἀναγκαῖα ἔπραττε.

> He (Augustus) vowed *ludi magni* because some woman carved some sort of letters into her arm and prophesied certain things. He understood that she had not been divinely possessed but had done it of her own accord; nevertheless, since the populace was already extremely upset over the war and the

200   *J. Bert Lott*

famine, which had returned, he pretended that he too believed the things she said and judged it necessary to do whatever might calm the crowd.

(55.31.2–3; trans. by the author)

Dio's otherwise unattested story raises several interesting questions. Independent or unofficial prophets or diviners at Rome appear only rarely in our sources for the Republic and early Empire and female ones even more so. Nevertheless, as T. P. Wiseman has shown, such private religious figures were probably numerous at Rome, speaking both to elite and non-elite populations. Wiseman discusses the evidence for independent diviners at Rome (1994, 58) in part as a rebuttal to the work of John North (1989, 578; 1990, 67), who is skeptical about the existence of such private religious actors at Rome. Following Wiseman, it seems likely that professional fortunetellers were an integral part of everyday life at Rome, just as various sorts of seers and diviners were in Greek culture.

When such unofficial prophets do appear in our historical sources, it is normally because they have crossed from the realm of private affairs onto the public stage, as is the case with Dio's prophet, who disturbed the general populace of the city at a difficult time to such an extent that she attracted the attention of the emperor himself. Writing at Rome in the time of Augustus, Livy provides several examples of this pattern (see, for example, Livy 4.30 and 25.1.6–12). Such prophets are mostly characterized as acting in opposition to public religion sanctioned by the ruling elites, offering during moments of crisis competing, even apocalyptic, narratives of the future or courses of religious action (cf. Dion. Hal. *Ant. Rom.* 7.68.1). They are usually discredited but sometimes co-opted by the elites. Livy's accounts emphasize the foreign nature of the nonsanctioned prophecy, the disingenuousness of charlatan prophets who mislead the people, and the corrective actions of the state to suppress incorrect rites and prophecies. This was undoubtedly a view from the top. Richard Gordon points out that popular religious innovation, outside the sanction of the ruling elite, was one of the basic, negative meanings of *superstitio* (2008, 81). Nevertheless, stories of religious con artists swindling people in times of crisis (or perceived crisis) are common. One best example is the false prophet Alexander, who was pilloried by Lucian (*Alex.* 30) for prophesying a coming plague and then selling a line of verse to protect people from disease. The *SHA* (*M. Ant.* 13.6) contains another humorous episode: in order to make a profit during the Antonine plague, a man climbed a fig tree on the Campus Martius and prophesied that if he fell out of the tree and turned into a stork the world would end in fire. Eventually he fell out of the tree and released a stork from under his robe. The emperor pardoned him after he confessed his deception. And, away from fictional narratives, the problem was enough of an issue that in the second century Marcus Aurelius issued a rescript that "anyone who acted in such a way as to frighten the weak minds of men with superstition" should be relegated to an island (*Dig.* 48.19.30).

This is not to say that the Republican state did not adopt and adapt foreign religious practices, especially at times of crisis – it did, as E. Orlin has recently discussed in detail (2010). However, a set of controlling structures normally ensured

A self-inscribing prophet at Rome   201

the primacy of the elite in matters of public prophecy and religion; some scholars (e.g. Ripat 2006) have drawn attention to the dominance of technical modes of divination and expiation – augury, haruspicy, and the interpretation of the Sibylline Books – over inspired, nonexpert divination, such as dreams or possession, to show how state-sponsored experts were normally kept in charge.

The senatorial elite supplied new temples, cults, *ludi*, and other rites, guided by the expert opinions of augurs, *haruspices*, or *decemviri*. On behalf of the state, they sought, accepted, interpreted (with expert help), and responded to all manner of divine manifestations, including omens, prodigies, oracles, divination, and prophecy. The advent of the Empire – Dio's story falls within the reign of the first emperor – led to even stricter controls on the seeking of foreknowledge of public affairs and events, especially in Rome itself. Augustus carefully calibrated his personal involvement in public religion to reinforce his personal divine authority and to emphasize his role as the sole savior of the state and guarantor of public welfare.

Claims to divine favor had played a powerful propagandistic role in justifying the ascendancy of one member of the aristocracy over his peers in the late Republic. Augustus and his successors employed the same strategy on a grander scale (see Potter 1994, 146–82). Conversely, they recognized the dangers posed by uncontrolled claims to divine favor or foreknowledge of public affairs. The official examination and expiation of public prodigies ceased or was greatly curtailed under Augustus (Livy 43.13.1–2, Plin. *HN* 7.36, 10.20; see Galinsky 1996, 293). Moreover, Augustus collected and destroyed more than 2,000 books of prophecies, excepting only the Sibylline Books, which he edited and deposited in his own Palatine temple of Apollo (Suet. *Aug.* 31.1). Repeated bans on astrologers and legal limits on the proper topics for divination show the imperial power trying to protect its authority by maintaining a monopoly on foreknowledge in the political sphere. R. Macmullen collects such instances and includes individuals predicting or seeking to gain foreknowledge about the state and the imperial family in his definition of enemies of the state (1966, 128–62). It must be said that the use of many forms of prognostication by the general public about all sorts of matters that fell short of grand political significance is evidenced nearly everywhere across the Empire. Ripat rightly cautions us that it was likely the distraction and the associated unrest in the city, rather than the mere act of astrological divination, that turned the imperial powers against astrologers (2011). She points out that it was the public pronouncements of astrologers rather than the skill of astrology that was problematic. I would add emphasis to the idea that it was the uncontrolled (that is unregulated and unfiltered by the elite) aspect of public astrologers that created the problem.

Thus, Dio's story, although brief, contributes to our understanding of the creation and maintenance of imperial power at the beginning of the Empire. It allows us to appraise the state's response – really Augustus' response – to the appearance in the city of a disturbing prophet, working outside accepted avenues for state divination at a time when the normal avenues for state action and response were being severely limited and circumscribed by the *princeps*. Under these circumstances,

202   *J. Bert Lott*

we might have expected from the state a punitive and disbelieving response that rejected her claim to divine authority. Indeed, Dio hints at this expected response when he says that Augustus did not himself believe that she was truly inspired. Although it is not addressed in detail in this chapter, Augustus' response, while more accepting of the prophet's validity, did reclaim for the *princeps* the unique competence to act religiously to preserve the state at times of crisis. He vowed *ludi magni,* which were a traditional and well-controlled state response to existential crisis managed by the *pontifex maximus*, an office Augustus himself had held since 12 BCE. The unusual and particular nature of vowing *ludi magni*, along with the unusual actions of the woman, does indicate that Dio is reporting a historical event rather than just retrospectively adding (or repeating the addition of) an omen or prophecy at a moment of crisis.

This chapter focuses not on the state's response but on the prophet herself and her actions. Dio's story provides a few seldom-reported details about a particular sort of prophetic practice outside official means of divination. The prophetic routine of self-inscription is particularly intriguing since it does not correspond exactly to any other such routine or ritual. Moreover, the acceptance of the woman's inspiration and prophecies as valid by the *plebs* and then the *princeps* (Dio's claim of Augustus' skepticism notwithstanding) begs several questions related to religious authority and ritual competence. Should we understand her actions in terms of religious ritual? What ritual system – religion? – did her unusual prophetic routine belong to or grow out of? Why was her authority accepted and prophecy believed at Rome? To examine these questions in the context of ritual competence, I turn to the work of E. Thomas Lawson and Robert McCauley, who have proposed an understanding of religious ritual, ritual form, and ritual competence based in cognitive science. After this discussion, the chapter returns to the details of Dio's prophet in the context of Lawson and McCauley's work. The aim is to use the case of our prophet to examine applicability and usefulness of this theoretical scheme to ancient evidence while, at the same time, providing an analysis of the particular event in question.

Ritual form and ritual competence

In 1990 Lawson and McCauley proposed a cognitive approach to understanding ritual; they developed their theory further, especially with regard to ritual competence, in 2002 (Lawson and McCauley 1990; McCauley and Lawson 2002). Other scholars have also developed their work, with some focus on the ancient world (Barrett and Lawson 2001; Barrett 2002; Barrett 2004; Cragg 2004; Martin 2004; McCauley and Lawson 2007; Engler and Gardiner 2009). Lawson and McCauley argue that religious rituals across cultures demonstrate a structural regularity, and thus religious ritual actions must depend on an underlying universal conceptual scheme, a common ritual form that was independent of cultural context. They identify this common conceptual scheme as an "action-representation system" and suggest that ritual actions (rituals) should be understood as a subtype of general action that can be readily recognized by observers without

A self-inscribing prophet at Rome   203

using any special cognitive machinery distinct from that used to understand other sorts of actions. Lawson and McCauley point to research that the cognitive ability to parse actions is present in all humans from the earliest ages (McCauley and Lawson 2002, 10–11). They argue that ritual actions (rituals) all conform to a standard action-representation system in which someone (an agent) does something to something (an object or patient). They suggest that religious rituals (as a subtype of actions) differ from generic actions in only two ways: first, they involve at some level the intervention or involvement of a superhuman or supernatural being – a god; and, second, they involve outcomes that are not the natural or obvious results of the action taken. Thus, for example, the action of a chorus of youths singing a hymn so that Apollo and Diana will bring Rome prosperity would be understood by observers in the same way as they would understand a group of children singing a song to please their teacher. The identification of the former case as a religious ritual depends on the accepted involvement of superhuman beings (Apollo and Diana) and the nonobvious or observable result (prosperity for Rome).

This leads Lawson and McCauley to a definition of religious ritual that Justin Barrett summarizes as follows: a religious ritual is an action in which (1) someone does (2) something (3) often to someone or something (4) in order to bring about some nonnatural consequence (5) by virtue of the involvement of some superhuman power (Barrett 2004, 266; see McCauley and Lawson 2002, 13). The general conclusion of Lawson and McCauley's theory is that, since the consequence of a ritual is nonobvious and usually nonobservable, ritual observers rely on an intuitive understanding of the correct formation of ritual in order to judge its efficacy rather than any empirical observation of the outcome. Correct formation always conforms to the action-representation system, and ritual competence depends first and foremost on the slots in the action representation scheme being legitimately filled. Thus, observers can make judgments about a ritual's legitimacy and efficacy with only minimal knowledge of the specific ritual being performed.

In determining whether Lawson and McCauley's work can improve our understanding of Dio's prophet, the first question must be, does the prophet in Dio's story meet their relatively narrow definition of religious ritual as a particular kind of action? Although Dio's account is far from detailed, we can see how the various slots in McCauley and Lawson's action-representation formula (numbered earlier) might be filled in the case of our prophet. There is superhuman involvement, the god who possesses the prophet (5). The agent is the woman possessed by a god or the god acting through the woman (1). The action is the self-inscription (2) onto the woman's arms (3) leading to the nonobvious, nonnatural consequence of her speaking prophecies (4). Given that our instance can be described in terms of Lawson and McCauley's definition, a second, more specific question is can their definition contribute to our understanding of a ritual act like that of the prophet, which intuitively seems ritualistic to us but does not conform to any ritual practice we know and lacks the rich cultural context and empirical evidence available to those studying contemporary religion? This is particularly important since Lawson and McCauley designed their theory to be amenable to empirical testing, which

204 *J. Bert Lott*

we cannot do (see Barrett 2002 for examples of such empirical testing). Can we gain any historical insight into the prophet's actions by considering them within the context of Lawson and McCauley's work? The answer is again, yes, but it relies on two particular special conclusions or predictions that Lawson and McCauley argue result from their general understanding of ritual. The first of these stands on its own, the second leads into a detailed discussion of the actions and identity of the female prophet.

First, while the supernatural entity whose involvement is necessary to make an action a religious ritual can be implicated in any of the slots in the action representation system, McCauley and Lawson postulate a division of religious rituals into two categories depending on the role the god plays (McCauley and Lawson 2002, 30–1, 89–123, esp. 120–3; see also the summations of Barrett 2004, 270–4; Cragg 2004, 81–2). Rituals where the god fills or is implicated in the role of the agent – that is the god performs or assists in the performance of the action in the ritual – are called "special agent" rituals; rituals where the god fills the role of object or patient are called "special patient" rituals. Special agent rituals are relatively infrequent, perhaps even unique, and they involve high pageantry and highly emotional content relative to other rituals within the belief system. The high emotional content and sensory pageantry of special agent rituals serves to convince observers that something profound and divine was happening, that a god was acting directly in their presence. They tend to happen at moments of special importance or consequence. Special patient rituals are more quotidian, often repeated, less permanent, and involve less pageantry and emotion (for example, the repeated practice of sacrifices or vows directed at a god in order to gain the god's favor in everyday activities). Special agent rituals, when judged to be legitimate, intuitively carry more weight than special patient rituals. Lawson and McCauley suggest that religious belief systems will seek a balance between the two types of ritual, and that, in particular, belief systems with no or very few special agent rituals tend to develop them over time. Douglas Cragg points out that a striking feature of traditional Roman religion is the near absence of special agent rituals (2004, 82–3). He suggests that this may help us understand the desire of some Romans to be initiated into mystery cults, whose initiatory rites could be special agent rituals where a god acted to change the status of an initiate. Finally, Lawson and McCauley argue that special agent rituals arise in belief systems that lack them not in opposition to traditional beliefs but as an intensification of them and that such new rituals and their observers are usually reabsorbed into the traditional religion, which receives a boost in intensity and emotion (McCauley and Lawson 2002, 192–201).

Dio's prophet provides another example of a special agent ritual: the god acts through the prophet. The reality of the god's presence is demonstrated through the pageantry and emotional power of self-cutting – it was the shocking act of self-harm that interested Dio in the story, at least in part. The ritual happened at a moment of consequence and stress and evidently promised significant rather than mundane change, although we do not know the precise content of the prophecies.

A self-inscribing prophet at Rome   205

Thus if we accept Lawson and McCauley's predictions, the uniqueness of the event (at least in our sources) is not unusual; nor is the powerful and emotional response the prophet evidently triggered; nor should the appearance and acceptance of a special agent ritual at Rome surprise us. Moreover, the acceptance of Dio's prophet by some of the *plebs* can be understood not in terms of political opposition or the failure of traditional religion but rather as an intensification of their religious experience, without rejection of the political religious power of the *princeps*. The cooption of the prophecy back into mainstream religion (which is a point of confusion in this case) is not only allowed but predicted and served in this case to reinvigorate the old Roman ritual of vowing *ludi magni* in times of national danger.

The second specific conclusion that Lawson and McCauley draw from their understanding of ritual is that any particular belief system populates the slots in the action-representation system in specific ways, which taken together they call a religious conceptual scheme (McCauley and Lawson 2002, 16–18). The religious conceptual scheme comprises, at a basic level, a list of those gods, actors, agents, instruments, and objects from which a valid ritual can be constructed along with a set of formation rules that describe how they can be slotted into the action-representation system. Members of a ritual belief system can intuitively identify violations of the religious conceptual scheme without intellectually interrogating the specifics of the ritual process. Ritual competence in any specific instance thus depends on intuitive judgments about a ritual's adherence to the religious conceptual scheme and formation rules. In the case of our prophet, we can begin to answer the question of her legitimacy by looking for how the individual elements of her ritual fit a coherent religious conceptual scheme.

However, not all aspects of a ritual are equally significant in determining ritual competence. Lawson and McCauley argue that, because identifying an agent is the key component to identifying an action, properly filling the role of the agent is of prime importance in determining ritual competence (McCauley and Lawson 2002, 29–30; see Barrett 2004, 268–9). That is, in judging whether a ritual is legitimate and successful, having a proper agent performing the action in a ritual is the most important criterion – a conclusion that has interesting implications generally for our understanding Roman religion as focused on correct performance. Thus in investigating the question of ritual competence in our example, we should emphasize the question of how Dio's inspired prophet may have been understood as a legitimate agent in a ritual that involved cutting and prophecy.

The cutting prophet

With this understanding of ritual competence in mind, we can return to examine the specific case of Dio's prophet. We can begin by reading Dio's passage closely. Dio is vague about the identity of the prophetic woman. She is simply "some woman." His mode of reference (*gune tis*) is dismissive. Dio is equally vague and dismissive about the content of the prophecy. She "prophesied some things" (*etheiase tina*). It was not the woman or her prophecies that interested him. He was interested in her prophetic routine: prior to speaking her prophecies, she cut or

206   *J. Bert Lott*

inscribed letters of some sort into her arm (*es ton brachiona grammata atta ente-mousa*). It was this act of cutting that convinced people that she was truly possessed by a god (*ek theou katescheto; katecho or katochos + ek is* frequently used to signal divine possession or inspiration; see LSJ sv. *katecho* II.10) and thus that the things she said (*tois lechtheisin*) were valid prophecies.

Dio's use of *entemousa* suggests both writing and sacrifice. The verb *entemno* is used both for inscription on stone and for spilling the blood of animal sacrifices. Dio's only other use of the word involves religious arm cutting and sacrifice, but not writing: it is the verb he uses to describe Seneca, as he commits suicide, slicing open his wrist to offer his own blood to Zeus Eleutherios (62.26.4). Heliodoros uses it when a witch cuts her own arms in order to obtain blood for a spell (*Aeth.* 6.14.4). We might conclude that *entemno* was part of a technical phrase for ritual arm cutting. The Romans closely associated the worship of two goddesses, the Great Mother (Magna Mater) and the Syrian Goddess (Dea Syria), with inspired prophecy and self-wounding, especially the self-castration of their eunuch priests (*galli*), but also arm cutting. (For the Magna Mater at Rome, see Roller 1999, 287–327; Borgeaud 2004, 72–90. There is no comprehensive treatment of the Dea Syria/Atargatis at Rome: the best place to start is Lightfoot 2003, 1–85 for an overview of the goddess, but see also Drijvers 1980, 77–121; Hörig 1984; Bilde 1990; for the Greek world, Morin 1960; Baslez 1999; for the Latin and Greek sources, Berg 1972.)

The most complete evidence of arm cutting comes from two works ascribed to the second-century rhetorician Lucian (*De Dea Syria* and *Lucius*) and from Apuleius' *Metamorphoses*. In *De Dea Syria*, Lucian describes an annual spring festival in which people from all over Syria and the eastern Mediterranean come to Hierapolis (the cult center of the goddess) for a giant holocaust sacrifice and festival. Jane Lightfoot (2003) makes a convincing argument for the authenticity of the *De Dea Syria* as a work of Lucian, who was from nearby Samosata and was well versed in Syrian culture, language, and religion; she takes this work as an ethnographic treatment in the vein of Herodotos. As Lucian describes it, during the festival the followers of the Syrian Goddess, both her *galli* and "maddened, deranged women" (*Syr. D.* 43) "perform the rites, cutting their own arms" (*Syr. D.* 50). The other two sources (the *Lucius* and the *Metamorphoses*) tell the story of the unlucky Lucius transformed into an ass. In both accounts, one of the tribulations that Lucius faces in ass form is to be sold to a band of mendicant devotees of the Syrian Goddess (*Met.* 8). The band needs Lucius to carry a statue of the goddess as they travel from town to town begging. When they reach a town or villa they put on a wild show, dressing up, dancing and singing and throwing their heads around to the sound of pipes and cymbals. According to the *Lucius,* "they would cut their forearms with their swords and each would stick his tongue out from his teeth and cut it, so that everything seemed covered in effeminate blood" (*Lucius* 37). In Apuleius the story goes similarly: "Occasionally they would sink their teeth into their own flesh, and as a finale, they each slashed their arms with the two-edged swords which they brandished" (*Met.* 8.27). In the *Lucius,* Lucian uses the same verb as Dio,

A self-inscribing prophet at Rome 207

entemno, for the sacred cutting. In Latin, Apuleius uses *disseco*. In both versions the cutters offer prophecies or oracles after their wounding. These sources are admittedly later than the setting of Dio's story (although Dio would have known them), but arm cutting was already widely enough recognized in the reign of Augustus as an aspect of Eastern ecstatic worship that it could be used as a figure in poetry. When Propertius is asked why he falls in love, he answers, "Why does a man slash and cut his own arms with sacred knifes to mad Phrygian rhythms?" (2.22.15). Not much later, Martial insults the work of a barber by claiming, "White arms are cut with less savage knives when the frenzied throng rages at the Phrygian music" (11.84.3–4).

Dio provides more information about the cutting the woman performed. He says she marked herself not with random slashes but with "letters of some sort" (*grammata atta*) before she prophesied. Importantly, the letters are not the prophecies but part of the enabling routine, the ritual, that preceded the utterance of the prophecies themselves. This is to say that the woman did not write oracles on her skin. Her actions should not be confused with the case of the "skin" of the philosopher Epimenides, which, according to later tradition, the Spartans discovered long after his death to have been marked "with letters" (*grammasi*) that he had kept hidden. "Epimenides' skin" thus became an expression for hidden or secret knowledge (Diogenian 8.28, *Suda* s.v. *Epimenides*, Apostol. *Paroem.* 7.73; cf. Bremmer 1993, 235). As Nicola Reggiani points out, this "skin" has long been thought to be a collection of oracles probably on animal skin, not Epimenides' actual flayed skin (2014, 111–16, with earlier discussion of the topic collected at 113 n. 54–5). In any event, our prophet made her marks publicly in order to validate her prophecies.

Dio either did not know or did not care what the letters were or what they meant. We can look to another kind of sacred writing on the body, sacred marking, branding, or tattooing to find evidence for marking letters on the arm. Christopher Jones has studied such marks in detail (1987, 2000). Decorative tattooing was associated in antiquity only with Thracians (Jones 1987, 145–6; 2000, 2–6). Greeks and Romans used tattoos and branding primarily as a punishment for criminals or, importantly, as a way to conspicuously mark slaves, especially runaways, with the names of their owners (Jones 1987, 147–50; 2000, 7–13).

However, the Romans did know of another sort of body marking: religious marks or tattoos were associated with Syrian cults and especially the Syrian Goddess. Turning to Lucian again, he says of the followers of the Syrian Goddess, "all are marked (tattooed?), some on the wrist, others on the neck" (*Syr. D.* 59). A papyrus from the second century BCE offers corroboration. It describes a runaway female slave from Hierapolis, the cult center of the Dea Syria, as having two "barbarian letters" marked or tattooed on her arm (P. Par. 10=*UPZ* 121). Ulrich Wilken thought the two letters should be the first letters of the names of Atargatis and her consort Hadad in Aramaic (1927, 7–8; see Jones 1987, 144). Jane Lightfoot questions the identification of the marks as religious tattoos, suggesting they might simply be punitive tattoos forced on a runaway slave (2003, 530); but such slave tattoos were normally placed on the forehead or face. That this practice was old

208   *J. Bert Lott*

and broadly applied in Syria is suggested by the law in Leviticus that commanded early Israelites "to not mark writing" on themselves (Leviticus 19.28; see Jones 1987, 144; Lightfoot 2003, 530, n. 10). Later, Isaiah provides some further information, saying that in the end everyone would accept such marks, writing on their wrists "I am the Lord's" (44.5, 49.16; see Jones 1987, 144). Even closer to the time of Dio's prophet, in Revelation, both the faithful and the unfaithful are marked with signs on the hand (7.3, 13.16). In all these cases, the marks seem to be marks of devotion to a god.

We can compare such marks to Herodotos' well-known report that in his day there was a temple of a certain Herakles at a mouth of the Nile where slaves who entered and applied sacred marks to their skin became the property of the god and could not be seized by their former masters (2.113.2). Thus religious marking may have served specifically to identify a person as a "slave" to a god just as marks were used to identify actual runaway slaves. In the case of the cult in Egypt cited by Herodotos, such divine slavery had the ironic result of guaranteeing freedom from a human master. Importantly, the Syrian Goddess served as the divine guarantor of manumission in several Greek cities through the ritual sale of slaves to the goddess, although there is no evidence that her newly acquired "slaves" were marked with her name. For example, at Physiton in Aetolia a body of inscriptions reveal that the goddess (often called "Syrian Aphrodite") served there as witness and guarantor for the manumission of slaves from the third century BCE to the first century CE (*IG* IX, I^2 95–110; see Morin 1960, 44–51; Hörig 1984, 1565–6). The process of manumission, which took place in the temple of the Dea Syria, involved the fictional sale of the slave to the Dea Syria for a nominal price. The slave being freed thus became, notionally, the property and responsibility of the goddess. This process is strikingly similar to that described in Herodotos, although he implies that the temple in Egypt served as an asylum for runaways rather than a functionary in the process of manumission.

To summarize, cutting and self-marking and prophesy were aspects of the worship of the Syrian goddess known at Rome. The association is strengthened by the location of the self-marking on the arms. The parallelism is, of course, far from perfect, and I do not mean that there was a unified, homogeneous cult of the Dea Syria across the Empire to which Dio's prophet belonged. Rather, her actions fell within a known and recognizable ritual conceptual scheme that would have allowed Romans to accept them as legitimate, even if they were not familiar with the details of the cult. Indeed Lawson and McCauley's argument for primacy of agency means that the particular formation of her ritual actions did not need to be precise or well-known to observers so long as the inspired prophet herself was viewed as a legitimate agent. This leads us to a final question: was there a tradition of female prophets associated with the Syrian Goddess that would suggest that Dio's prophet would be judged to be legitimate by a Roman audience when she offered dire prophecies in an ecstatic state?

Romans, of course, knew of the cult of the Dea Syria by at least the second century BCE; and there was a literary tradition at least of inspired female prophets appearing in the city at calamitous moments. For example, the story was

A self-inscribing prophet at Rome 209

told that following the exile of Coriolanus the city was violently disturbed by "women possessed with divine frenzy" foretelling dreadful misfortunes (Dion. Hal. *Ant. Rom.* 7.68.1). The marked slave from Hierapolis was female but not a prophet. There is evidence for female prophets associated with the Dea Syria in Syria: for example, a certain Hochmaea from Niha in Lebanon is described in local inscriptions as a prophetess and virgin of Atargatis (*IGLS* 6.2928–9). In a story that was certainly known at Rome, a certain Syrian woman who, possessed by a god (*katochos ek tou theiou*), prophesied in strange ways had saved Alexander from the Conspiracy of the Pages (Arr. *Anab.* 4.13.5–6). Another story, which comes from Rome itself, is more pertinent: when Marius was preparing to lead the Romans against the invading Cimbri and Teutones at the end of the second century BCE, an inspired Syrian woman named Martha arrived at Rome offering prophetic services in a moment of dire crisis (Plut. *Marius* 17.2–5; see Orlin 2010, 198). Following the story in Plutarch, she first approached the senate, promising to predict the outcome of the war, but the senators rebuffed her (Plut. *Marius* 17.2–5). She then approached their wives. Marius' wife, convinced of Martha's abilities (from Martha's ability to predict the outcome of gladiatorial fights) sent her to her husband, who had marched north with his army. There, Marius had her carried around in a litter, sacrificed in accordance with her directions, and told his troops that he was conducting the war in accordance with divine will. Martha attended the rites wearing an extravagant purple robe and carrying a spear that was wrapped with fillets and garlands. The theatrical nature of her performances led many to wonder, Plutarch says, whether Marius, in parading her about, believed in her divine inspiration or was only pretending to do so. To put the story in the context of ritual competence, Martha brought the emotional power of a special agent ritual at a consequential moment, and Marius co-opted her to intensify and reinvigorate belief and morale among his troops. Unlike Marius, Augustus could act on behalf of the state without the senate's acceptance. There is no evidence of a close doctrinal connection between the Syrian Martha and Dio's prophet, but the story of Martha demonstrates that there was a known tradition of inspired Syrian female prophets with strange prophetic routines appearing in times of crisis. Given the situation and the parallel circumstances, it is not hard to believe that Augustus drew on the tradition of Marius' popular prophet as a model for how he treated our prophet and may even have publicized the connection himself.

Conclusion

Reading Dio's story through the lens of Lawson and McCauley's work on ritual competence has permitted several conclusions. First, this unique (at least in our evidence) event can be judged to have been a religious ritual, since it conforms to the action-representation system. Next, we can address the key question of why the prophet in Dio's story was treated differently from other seemingly similar religious actors who appeared outside the control of the state and meddled in state

210   J. Bert Lott

affairs. The type of ritual action she was involved with was potentially attractive to many in a religious environment that lacked special agent rituals, especially in the midst of the high emotion of a serious crisis. Moreover, we can identify the woman as a legitimate type of agent within a recognizable belief system, and we can see how her actions fit within a constellation of religious actions – arm cutting, self-marking, inspiration, prophecy – that were all part of a coherent ritual conceptual scheme associated with Syrian religion, especially the cult of the Dea Syria. The fact that we cannot precisely parallel the ritual routine of the prophet is not problematic, both because we should expect such routines to be heterogeneous across time and geography and because the recognition of precisely correct ritual components is a tertiary consideration in determining ritual competence, after conformation to the action-representation system and the presence of an intuitively acceptable agent. We should not expect observers – even Augustus – to rely on close intellectual interrogation of the details of the ritual acts and instruments to establish the ritual's validity. Finally but not inconsequentially, the historical details of a poorly attested event are made clearer: we can associate Dio's prophet somewhat confidently with the religious traditions of the Dea Syria, and we can suggest she belonged to a pattern of such inspired prophets appearing at consequential moments.

Note

1 This chapter was greatly improved by discussion among conference attendees at Bates College. The organizers, editors, and anonymous readers also offered valuable comments and saved me from several errors. The editors were especially patient with me. Errors that remain are my own.

Works consulted

Barrett, Justin L. 2002. "Smart Gods, Dumb Gods, and the Role of Social Cognition in Structuring Ritual Intuitions." *Journal of Cognition and Culture* 2: 183–93.

———. 2004. "Bringing Data to Mind: Empirical Claims of Lawson and McCauley's Theory of Religious Ritual." In *Religion as a Human Capacity: A Festschrift in Honor of E. Thomas Lawson*, edited by T. Light and B. C. Wilson, 265–88. Leiden: Brill.

Barrett, Justin and E. Thomas Lawson. 2001. "Ritual Intuitions: Cognitive Contributions to Judgments of Ritual Efficacy." *Journal of Cognition and Culture* 1: 184–201.

Baslez, Marie-Françoise. 1999. "Le culte de la Déesse syrienne dans le monde hellénistique." In *Les syncrétismes religieux dans le monde méditerranéen antique*, edited by C. Bonnet and A. Motte, 229–48. Brussels: Institut Historique Belge de Rome.

Berg, P. L. van. 1972. *Corpus Cultus Deae Syriae*. Leiden: Brill.

Bilde, P. 1990. "Atargatis/Dea Syria: Hellenization of Her Cult in the Hellenistic-Roman Period?" In *Religion and Religious Practice in the Seleucid Kingdom*, edited by P. Bilde, 151–87. Aarhus: Aarhus University Press.

Borgeaud, P. 2004. *Mother of the Gods: From Cybele to the Virgin Mary*. Translated by L. Hochroth. Baltimore: Johns Hopkins University Press.

Bremmer, Jan. 1993. "The Skins of Pherekydes and Epimenides." *Mnemosyne* 46: 234–6.

A self-inscribing prophet at Rome   211

Cragg, Douglas L. 2004. "Old and New in Roman Religion: A Cognitive Account." In *Theorizing Religions Past*, edited by H. Whitehouse and L. H. Martin, 69–86. New York: Altamira Press.

Drijvers, H. J. W. 1980. *Cults and Beliefs at Edessa.* Leiden: Brill.

Engler, Steven and Mark Q. Gardiner. 2009. "Religion as Superhuman Agency: On E. Thomas Lawson and Robert N. McCauley, *Rethinking Religion* (1990)." In *Contemporary Theories of Religion*, edited by M. Strausberg, 22–38. New York: Routledge.

Galinsky, Karl. 1996. *Augustan Culture: An Interpretive Introduction.* Princeton: Princeton.

Garnsey, Peter. 1988. *Famine and Food Supply in the Graeco-Roman World: Responses to Risk and Crisis.* Cambridge and New York: Cambridge University Press.

Gordon, Richard. 2008. "*Superstitio*, Superstition and Religious Repression in the Late Roman Republic and Principate (100 B.C.E.–300 C.E.)." *Past & Present* 199: 79–94.

Hörig, M. 1984. "Dea Syria-Atargatis." *ANRW* 2.17.3: 1536–81.

Jones, Christopher P. 1987. "Stigma: Tattooing and Branding in Graeco-Roman Antiquity." *Journal of Roman Studies* 77: 139–55.

———. 2000. "Stigma and Tattoo." In *Written on the Body: The Tattoo in European and American History*, edited by J. Caplan, 1–16. Princeton: Princeton University Press.

Lawson, E. Thomas and Robert N. McCauley. 1990. *Rethinking Religion: Connecting Cognition and Culture*. Cambridge and New York: Cambridge University Press.

Lightfoot, J. (Ed.). 2003. *Lucian, On the Syrian Goddess.* New York and Oxford: Oxford University Press.

MacMullen, Ramsay. 1966. *Enemies of the Roman Order: Treason, Unrest, and Alienation in the Empire*. Cambridge, MA: Harvard University Press.

Martin, Luther H. 2004. "Ritual Competence and Mithraic Ritual." In *Religion as a Human Capacity: A Festschrift in Honor of E. Thomas Lawson*, edited by T. Light and B. C. Wilson, 245–63. Leiden: Brill.

McCauley, Robert N. and E. Thomas Lawson. 2002. *Bringing Ritual to Mind: Psychological Foundations of Cultural Forms*. Cambridge and New York: Cambridge University Press.

———. 2007. "Cognition, Religious Ritual, and Archaeology." In *The Archaeology of Ritual*, edited by E. Kyriakidis, 209–54. Los Angeles: UCLA.

Morin, J. P. 1960. *The Cult of the Dea Syria in the Greek World.* Dissertation. Ohio State University.

North, John A. 1989. "Religion in Republican Rome." In *Cambridge Ancient History* VII.2². edited by F. W. Walbank, A. E. Astin, M. W. Frederiksen, and R. M. Ogilvie. Cambridge: Cambridge University Press, 573–624.

———. 1990. "Diviners and Divination at Rome." In *Pagan Priests: Religion and Power in the Ancient World*, edited by M. Beard and J. A. North, 51–71. London: Duckworth.

Orlin, Eric M. 2010. *Foreign Cults in Rome: Creating a Roman Empire.* Oxford and New York: Oxford University Press.

Potter, David S. 1994. *Prophets and Emperors: Human and Divine Authority from Augustus to Theodosius*. Cambridge, MA: Harvard University Press.

Reggiani, Nicola. 2014. "La pelle di Epimenide:un corpus di scritture mantiche nell'antica Grecia?" *Ormos – Ricerche di Storia Antica*, n.s. 6: 105–28.

Ripat, Pauline. 2006. "Roman Omens, Roman Audiences, and Roman History." *Greece and Rome* 53: 155–74.

———. 2011. "Expelling Misconceptions: Astrologers at Rome." *CPhil.* 106: 115–54.

212   *J. Bert Lott*

Roller, L. 1999. *In Search of God the Mother: The Cult of Anatolian Cybele.* Los Angeles and Berkeley: California University Press.

Swan, Peter Michael. 2004. *The Augustan Succession: An Historical Commentary on Cassius Dio's Roman History, Books 55–56 (9 B.C.–A.D.).* Oxford and New York: Oxford University Press.

Wilken, U. 1927. "Zu den 'Syrischen Göttern'." In *Studien zur Chronik des Malalas*, edited by W. Weber, 1–19. Tübingen: Siehbeck.

Wilkes, J. J. 1969. *Dalmatia.* Cambridge, MA: Harvard.

Wiseman, T. P. 1994. "Lucretius, Catiline and the Survival of Prophecy." In *Historiography and Imagination: Eight Essays on Roman Culture*, 49–67. Exeter: Exeter University Press.

12 "A devotee and a champion"

Reinterpreting the female "victims" of magic in early Christian texts[1]

Esther Eidinow

Introduction

Scholarship on the practice of ancient magic has increasingly come to recognize the role and activities of women, attempting to locate the female ritual specialists that may be traced within different written sources: for example, the possible writers of particular binding spells, the female figures that may be identified in the *PGM* (see Faraone 1999; Dickie 2000, 2001; Pollard 2001; Eidinow 2013). This approach has generated an intriguing debate. On the one hand, it has revealed evidence of women's agency, difficult to trace in ancient culture. On the other hand, it has been argued that this work has exacerbated an ancient stereotype associating women with "magic" (see discussion Stratton 2014). In turn, new approaches have suggested that it is modern preoccupations with gender and stereotypes – "the scholarly temptation to subject ancient traditions to a glaringly modern gaze" (Reed 2014, 111) – that have reinforced this idea, creating its apparent prevalence. However, despite the welcome exploration of such questions, it remains the case that scholarly discourse on magic primarily focuses on debating the presence, role, and activities of female *practitioners*.

Aside from the magnetic pull of a stereotype, this focus is perhaps also not surprising if we consider the broader context of scholarship on ancient magic, which tends, more generally, to center on practitioners. This has proved an increasingly popular field, with much fascinating work done to establish the ways in which individual practitioners seem to have constructed their claims to magical power. In this respect, a number of different dimensions have been explored, encompassing, for example, the use of particular types of language in magical ritual or the claims made by and about individuals that they belonged to specific social networks (for example, Frankfurter 2002; Flower 2014). This work has helped to nuance the powerful image of the isolated, dissembling magician (as Mauss and Hubert 1902–3, 18–19), and there is now acknowledgement of, and research into, the different social types who may have been involved in or professed to practice "magic" and their activities (for example, Dickie 2001). Nevertheless, that the framework for research remains largely focused on this figure, if not on its stereotypical representation, and the ways in which it constructed its claims to power, still presents limitations.

214   *Esther Eidinow*

As an approach to evoking the environment in which magical activity may have taken place and the ways in which the perceived power of magic was constructed, it offers only one side of what is, I suggest in this chapter, a more multidimensional story. The construction of such claims to power would have occurred within a cultural context and within relationships shaped by that context. As Sherry Ortner (2006, 151) has observed, "individuals or persons or subjects are always embedded in webs of relations, whether of affection and solidarity, or of power and rivalry"; the acquisition and exercise of agency is interactive and dynamic. In trying to understand better how ancient magic "worked" and the ways in which claims to ritual competence and magical power were constructed as effective, a broader focus is required. In that context, this chapter argues that it is fruitful to reflect on the activities and/or agency of the so-called victims of supernatural assault. In this chapter, I will focus on female victims and use the categories of Sherry Ortner to discuss agency (2006, 129–54, as discussed in the introduction to this volume): agencies of power on the one hand and agency of projects on the other. This builds on work on the agency of victimhood in ancient magic (see Eidinow 2017, which uses a cognitive approach to ritual to explore how conceptions of magical power were co-created by spell-makers *and* their so-called victims).

In general, scholarly exploration of the agency of the victim of magic in antiquity has been sparing. Some discussions have examined possible psychological reasons for the acceptance by "victims" of this role (e.g. centering on feelings of fear and guilt; see a compelling account by Tomlin 1988) or interpreted them as exhibiting socially unacceptable behaviors (Bremmer 2003, 57). But most scholarship has, in effect, echoed the ancient sources by describing the process of inference that can be imagined, or we are told was experienced by, the "victim" of a spell and/or demonic assault. With regard specifically to female victims, this approach has resulted in scholarly descriptions of them as passive: their representation conforming to perceived gender stereotypes, their presence merely a medium through which to convey the struggles playing out in a "male" world of sociopolitical power (see Faraone 1999 and Dickie 2001; challenged by Eidinow 2013, esp. ch. 11, followed by, and with similar conclusions, Frankfurter 2014; in this context, Winkler 1990 provides a nuanced examination of the psychological world of male erotic frustration, but cf. Faraone 1999, 80–95).

In this chapter, I want to build on previous scholarship to suggest a different approach to the question of the depiction of women with regard to their role as targets of magic, focusing on a number of early Christian writings. These will include episodes from Irenaeus' *Against Heresies* (dating to the late second century CE, probably 180–9; Markschies 2006); the *Acts of Andrew* (dated to around 150 CE; see Bremmer 2001, 152), specifically, the fragmentary Coptic *Papyrus Utrecht 1*, which was probably written down in the fourth century CE (see Schneemelcher 1992, 118); and the *Acts of Paul and Thekla* (dated to the late second century CE by Barrier 2009, 23–4). Toward the end of this discussion and in the conclusion, I also introduce some relevant analysis of a relatively well-known episode from a much later text, the *Life of St. Hilarion* by Jerome, which dates to the late fourth century CE.

It has been argued by some scholars that the depictions of women found across these documents were intended to undermine the role of women in the early church (Stratton 2007, 111–14, who summarizes previous scholarship, including D'Angelo 1990; Burrus 1995; Cooper 1996, but cf. Cooper 2013, which takes a different approach, for example, to the story of Thekla, discussed later; and, importantly, Bremmer 1996, 58–9, which notes the independence of Thekla). In this argument, the young women described here are, in effect, cyphers: the stories in which they appear, on the one hand, give insight into the debates among Christian communities (by minimizing the role of women) and, on the other hand, reflect the way in which these early writers regarded the power and violence of Rome, personified in the person of the magician depicted in these stories. Stratton, for example, has argued (2007, 113): "By depicting women as victims not as magicians, this rhetorical strategy would reinscribe women's passivity in opposition to the historical reality of some women's lived experiences" and that such texts (*ibid.*, 111, with specific reference to the *Life of St Hilarion* and Irenaeus' presentation of Marcus, discussed later in this chapter) "justify male ecclesiastical control and diminish the power of individual ascetics." The extent to which these narratives can be taken to provide historical insights about the daily, lived experience of the characters of their subjects is debated. Some scholars have argued that such an approach, with its focus on women as representatives of ideologies, may prevent us seeing what information may be available about women's lives (see, for example, Clark 1998; also cited by Stratton 2007, 110; Kraemer 2011). In contrast, a number of these texts have been used to discuss the ways in which the (male) practitioners of magic must have exercised their skills and achieved their effects (see Faraone 1999, 38 for a justification of this approach: he notes how Apuleius' approach to his own defense in the *Apology* suggests "the ready understanding of his audience that there is a close correspondence in the ancient world between life and letters in the case of magical rites").

The gap between ideology and reality is not the primary focus of this chapter – although it will return to this question. This chapter starts from the assumption that since these are works of literature that have been composed to be read or heard in order to persuade their audience, the characters within them (not only the female characters) will have been created so as to speak to the concerns of their audience. As such, they are likely to draw on common assumptions, if not stereotypes. The current scholarly consensus is that the writers of these texts were most probably male (but see Davies 1980; Gamble 1995, 120 cites Eusebius *HE* 6.23.2, which describes how Ambrose, in early third century CE Alexandria, supplied Origen with resources including women "skilled in fine writing"). But it seems that the gender composition of the audiences of these texts is debated (see Cole 1981; Bowie 1996, along with discussion in Barrier 2009, 13–21). It does seem highly likely that women would have been in the audience of at least some of these works. Jan Bremmer (2001, 160–1) has argued in particular that upper-class Christian women were among the readership of the *Apocryphal Acts of the*

216 *Esther Eidinow*

Apostles (*AAA*) (see also Bremmer 1989; Gamble 1995, 148–9 discusses evidence for fourth-century CE women in possession of Christian writings). It has been suggested that they participated in (and perhaps enjoyed, see Barrier 2009, 15) the social reinforcement of the stereotypes that these texts communicated.

In that context, this chapter will focus on the ways in which the women depicted in these texts have been interpreted as targets of magical action. I want to suggest that these texts can be read, individually and together, as suggesting not the passivity of these women in the face of supernatural attack but rather both the need and the potential for women to become competent in the physical, mental, and spiritual discipline offered by the Christian church. Moreover, these narratives suggest that it is only by taking on these disciplines that these women will be able to do battle with the forces of evil – be these supernatural or mortal – that confront them in their daily lives.

Irenaeus: Realization and understanding

Let us start with the description by Irenaeus in *Against Heresies* of the activities of Marcus, the founder of a gnostic group. Here we find a particular focus on the vulnerability of women: Irenaeus portrays them as "foolish," easily taken in by the wily Marcus. We learn that Marcus himself trains his attacks on women in particular (Ir. *Haer.* 1.13.3.27 Μάλιστα γὰρ περὶ γυναῖκας ἀσχολεῖται; all citations here and elsewhere from Rousseau/Doutreleau 1979). Irenaeus describes the ways in which Marcus goes about his deceptions: in some detail, he depicts the steps that Marcus uses to persuade a woman that she can prophesy (*Haer.* 1.13.3.27–58). However, care is needed in using this information about one woman to generalize about Irenaeus's description of "women." Indeed, if this particular character is taken to be representative of Marcus's victims, then she is an example of the individuals of both genders that Marcus deceives. A restored line (*Haer.* 1.13.1.4; Rousseau/Doutreleau 1979, 189) suggests that Irenaeus stated that there were "many men and not a few women" (ἄνδρας τε πολλοὺς καὶ οὐκ ὀλίγα γύναια ἠπάτησε) whom Marcus has inveigled with his magic. More specifically, it has been argued that the prophetic openness of the woman in this episode reflects in turn a sexual openness (see Burrus 1991, 232; also cited by Stratton 2007, 106) and that this effectively silences the women involved insofar as it portrays them "as foolish victims" who are unable to "guard themselves sexually or to exercise self-mastery" and is meant to suggest that they require "male ecclesiastical control" (Stratton 2007, 106, 111). Again, it is certainly the case that these women are portrayed as victims of Marcus, a predator who exploits their sexual and spiritual weaknesses. However, the broader implications then drawn can be queried: the observations about these feminine frailties, their exposure, and their protection can be read very differently if we set them in context.

To begin with, such a discourse about the nature and vulnerability of women was not unique to Marcus's victims but was widespread in antiquity. Taking into account the gendered identity of sexual actors (both male and female; see, for example, the discussion in Williams 2010, esp. 177–251), we see in both literary

"A devotee and a champion" 217

accounts and legislation of the recent period the widespread cultural acknowledgment that it was necessary for men to exert control over the sexual activities of their women – alongside concern over what occurred in the absence of this control. Examples include the association between uncontrolled female sexuality and chaos familiar from the moralizing rhetoric of Roman Imperial writers (see, for a succinct case study, Joshel 1997, 231); while extensive scholarship has highlighted the underlying implications of Augustus' legislation, focused as it was on relating the new regime to the imposition of order through control of, especially female, sexual behavior (e.g. Edwards 1993, 34–62). It has been argued that it was the expression of this fear of social and moral chaos that was responsible for the depiction in Roman literature of the illicit ritual practitioner/witch, of whom a voracious sexual appetite was a frequent characteristic (see Pollard 2014; Spaeth 2014). In this historical context, to describe a woman as sexually open was to observe that she was succumbing to an inherent susceptibility rather than being particularly remarkable for her foolishness; Irenaeus's description depicted the natural state of a woman when she was unprotected. So, if we return to Ortner's terms for agency, Irenaeus presents this woman as one whose true agency is being deconstructed by Marcus: although she is apparently being taught to exercise a competence that offers a form of cultural power, that is, to prophesy, Irenaeus is anxious to explain how that apparent exercise of power, and the power itself, is inauthentic. In his account, this woman's agency (both of power and of projects) is being eroded: her own intentions and desires have become dominated by the appetites of Marcus.

If this was the end of it, then this could indeed be read as suggesting that women, in general, required the control of male officials within the church. However, Irenaeus's account offers some further insights that seem to undermine this idea. Although the passivity of these women is apparently changed through their contact with the church, that protection appears to emerge from within the woman herself and is acquired through her own understanding. This seems to be the implication of Irenaeus's account of his sources for his description of Marcus's claims to magical power, including the creation of *philtra* ('potions', often 'love-potions'). These sources include women who, Irenaeus reports, have realized their mistake themselves and returned to the church; and, he notes, this happens frequently (*Haer.* 1.13.5.83–4). The return of these women to the church can be said, in Ortner's terms, to have given them back their agency of projects, if not of power. Furthermore, the idea that this text suggests that it is male officials of the church who will provide the necessary protection for these women is further undermined by the specific example that Irenaeus gives of one of these woman who, for a brief period, fell victim to Marcus. He reports that it was her husband (a deacon of the church) who actually received Marcus into his house and thus exposed his wife to him (*Haer.* 1.13.5.88–94). In turn, it is the "brethren" (τῶν ἀδελφῶν) who then converted her, suggesting that this was the work of the community to which she belonged rather than the achievement of particular (male) officers of the church.

218   *Esther Eidinow*

Thus, the depiction of his activities clearly identifies Marcus as a sexual predator, but it does not create a straightforward impression that the women he targets are particularly foolish and weak, nor that male officials of the church will protect them. Quite the contrary: as Irenaeus portrays them, the only weakness of these women is their inherent vulnerability. With the protection provided by the church as a body or institution, they realize what has happened to them, recover their agency, and return to the church.

The *Acts of Andrew*: Devotion and combat

This last observation raises the theme of the vulnerability to magical attack not only of women but also of the domestic sphere itself. As we will see, the theme also occurs in the second episode under discussion here, from the *Acts of Andrew*, where it is part of a complex reflection on the importance of rejecting physical comforts. As Jean-Marc Prieur (1992, 114) has noted, the work communicates "a kind of religious and philosophical climate . . . marked by a need to break free from the body and the world and take flight, through striving after union with the deity; in the practical conduct of life it is accompanied by sexual asceticism, a negative attitude toward procreation, a simple mode of diet and the longing for a plain way of life that is not dominated by the passions."

The particular episode discussed here comprises an odd little story that seems odder, no doubt, because of its now fragmentary nature: this Sahidic Coptic version seems to have been "abstracted from the longer apocryphal acts" (Elliott 1993, 233, who notes that this was in fact not unusual). There are some similarities to Gregory of Tours' *Epitome* 18, although the details that interest us here are not included in that account. Most commentators do not make this omission explicit (see, for example, Schneemelcher 1992, 118, 123; Elliott, 1993, 233; but cf. Prieur 1987, 952): they tend to focus on the similarities and differences regarding one aspect – the account of the exorcism of a soldier – and overlook the specifics of the story that Gregory of Tours excised from his version, the tale of the temptation of the soldier's virgin sister.

Quispel (1956, 139) has argued that this section is preserved from an account of Andrew's adventures in Thessalonica, where he faced persecution by the proconsul Varianus. The papyrus appears to say that following some arrests of certain people "on his account" (Schneemelcher 1992, 123), Andrew has gone out into the street to explain that there is no need for the brethren to dissemble. Among those listening are four soldiers (Quispel 1956, 130, suggests they have been sent to arrest Andrew), one of whom is beset by a demon. In the presence of Andrew, the demon cries out, "O Varianus, what have I done to you that you should send me to this god-fearing man?" and he casts down the young man and makes him foam at the mouth. At this point in the story, the account in Gregory's epitome (c. 14) describes the soldier falling down dead; Andrew then brings him back to life and "The whole populace is converted" (Schneemelcher 1992, 120). In the papyrus, the soldier remains alive, and the other soldiers try to hold him up, and Andrew

"A devotee and a champion" 219

remonstrates with them. It appears to be the demon who then recounts the tale of the soldier's sister (Schneemelcher 1992, 124–8).

As with the discussion of women in Irenaeus, the text can be read as focusing on "women's sexuality . . . as the primary site of female identity and self-worth" (as Stratton 2007, 112). Again, we must set these ideas in context: on the one hand, a woman's expected social function was as a mother and child-bearer and her rejection of these roles would be highly significant; on the other hand, she would be perceived as sexually vulnerable, and her capacity to control her sexual activity would be seen as admirable. But the text also gives us other foci: the demon/soldier is reported as describing how this young woman was a *politeutes*, that is someone of discipline, a devotee of Christ (Lampe 1991[12], *s.v.*, gives as the definition "one who behaves, conducts himself as a devotee of Christ" and "follower of Christian life"; but it also has overtones of military discipline, since it can mean a Decurion). That this is a combative role is suggested by the other term used to describe the young woman, *athletes* (Lampe 1991[12], *s.v.*,: "a combatant" or "champion"; the term is used to describe martyrs and ascetics). Her virginity is a sign of her chosen way of life, and it is viewed as part of a larger disciplined regime; the account reports that she is "near to God because of her purity and her prayers and her love" (Schneemelcher 1992, 124). In terms of Ortner's discussion of agency, the depiction of this young woman grants her an agency in which she is not only pursuing her own desires, but her activities also challenge those culturally defined as appropriate for her gender and status; they enact a claim to the power to reject existing social relations. Indeed, what follows in this episode is all about types of and relationships to power.

As this young woman prays on the roof of her house, a great magician who lives nearby sees her. Then, we are told, Semmath – a demon – enters the magician "to contend against this great athlete" (Schneemelcher 1992, 124). The young magician then says to himself: "If I have spent five and twenty years under the instruction of my master until I was trained in this skill, this (then) is the beginning of my craft; should I not be stronger than this virgin, I shall not be able for any work" (Schneemelcher 1992, 125). Using his magic, he summons demons and sends them after the virgin, and they arrive at her house in the form of her brother, where they knock at the door. Thinking her brother is there, the young woman goes down to the door – and here the papyrus becomes very difficult to read. It appears from the fragments that her prayer saves her, and the demons flee. What then follows in the text is badly damaged: it appears to comprise a conversation between the young girl, who is in tears, and another person, whose name and identity is unclear (Quispel 1956, 132 suggests it may be an appearance of Christ; Schneemelcher 1992, 125 suggests the names Teirousia or Erucia). Whoever it is tells her not to weep over her brother and announces that he/she will send him to the apostle Andrew "Not only so that I will heal him, but I shall bring it about that he shall gird himself for the palace" (Schneemelcher 1992, 125; this turns out to be the "heavenly palace," 127). And Andrew does go on to cast the demon out of the young man – the demon pointing out that he never harmed the young man, "thanks to the holy hands

220　*Esther Eidinow*

of his sister" (Schneemelcher 1992, 127) – and the soldier joins Andrew's followers.

In this strange tale, there appear to be a number of embattled individuals beset by magical attack, not just the explicitly targeted woman. First of all, the story is recounted by the demon who has possessed a young man, apparently the target of an attack by a magician. But the magician himself may also be considered a target of some kind of supernatural attack, since we are told that it is Sammath who enters him and who has "decided to take on his adversary." Bremmer (who also discusses the identification of this demon, 2000, 25–6; 2003, 54) has suggested that this is a *parhedros* and that "magicians were traditionally believed to be accompanied by a demon who helped them perform their magic." However, although supporting evidence does suggest the companionship of such a demonic helpmate, it does not indicate that the demon would enter the magician (and the term *parhedros* itself suggests that the demon "sat nearby" as Czachesz 2007, 299; see also the detailed analysis of Scibilia 2002). It is the demon that the magician then himself summons that seems to conform more closely to this role of the *parhedros*. This demon is sent "in the form of the brother" – perhaps indicating another form of possession, and therefore meaning the brother himself – who appears to be sent to attack the young woman. Whether this is intended to be an incestuous attack by the demon/brother or the demon/brother is meant to drag the young woman to the magician is not clear. I incline to the former, since the magician has expressed no sexual interest in the young woman; it appears to be the demon Sammath who is determined to destroy the young woman's virginity. (Stratton 2007, 104, suggests the latter, arguing that this follows the form of an *agoge* spell, and citing Faraone 1999.) Of all these victims, it is in fact the young woman who comes off best: far from being a tale that undermines a woman's role within the church, she appears both disciplined and competent. The terms used to describe her suggest someone who is playing an informed role in her own spiritual and physical life and who can engage successfully in a battle for spiritual power. She may be a target of magical attack, but her connection to the church and the skills she has therefore learned to develop for herself mean that she is capable of repelling that attack. In contrast, the male characters of this episode are described as having far less self-control or capacity to defend themselves.

This returns us to the point at which this section began: like the first, this story offers some intriguing observations regarding the vulnerability to magical attack not only of women but also of the domestic sphere itself. As noted, this young woman has refrained from following the commonly accepted path of her gender and status to become a wife. At first sight, her chosen role, her exercise of agency, has put her into danger. But the nature of that danger is ambiguous: although in essence it comes from an outsider, it is manipulated so that it appears, at least, to come from within her family – in the person of her brother. This is an important detail: it is a reminder that, as would have been clear to a contemporary audience, everyone, male or female, Christian or not, could be the target of a demonic attack. As we have already seen in the account by Irenaeus of the woman

"A devotee and a champion" 221

exposed to danger by her husband, the domestic space and its familiar relationships in fact offer little security; this story also draws attention to the potential dangers of accepting the usual familial roles at face value.

Acts of Paul and Thekla: Apostle and teacher

These themes – of supernatural attack, disciplined men and women of the church, love, magic, and rejection of familial roles – all coincide in our third example, and in something of a playful mode. However serious its final implications and historical influence, the *Acts of Paul and Thekla* has a clear relationship with the genre of the Greek novel (see Aubin 1998, 278; Barrier 2009, 1–9; and, on the interactions more generally between the *Apocryphal Acts of the Apostles* and the ancient novel, Thomas 1998; Bremmer 2001, 164–5). The work narrates how the virgin Thekla falls into the thrall of Paul; rejects her betrothed, Thamyris; leaves her family, home, and town; and faces ordeals, which, without divine intervention, should have killed her. The sequence of events offers what Barrier (2009, 9) calls "the 'adventure' theme' " of the stock ancient novel.

Alongside and interwoven with these adventures run themes of erotic love and marriage; the ordeals of the lovers intensify the impression of their desire as they delay their final unification. But, as many commentators have observed, these recognizable and socially acceptable aspects are radically refashioned for their roles in this narrative. Barrier (2009, 8) notes how "the text clearly seeks to set Paul and Thekla in the leading roles of the young lovers, but with a twist." As Schroeder (2006, 48) observes: "Instead of advocating marriage, the *Apocryphal Acts* use the relationship between apostle and convert to champion sexual abstinence." This message of unremitting chastity – one that did not recognize the importance of sex in marriage – would have posed a dramatic challenge to prevalent social values. In that context, these narratives subvert familiar themes to produce texts whose messages are (Perkins 1995, 26) "rigorously anti-social, unremittingly opting for the dissolution of social categories and relationships."

From the perspective of re-examining the role of the targets of magic, we find yet another twist in this tale. Just as the account adopts and adapts themes of erotic love and marriage from the ancient novel, the description of Thekla's apparent love for Paul is described in terms that, in a number of ways, evoke erotic magic, as Jackson-McCabe (2010) has observed. *Agoge* spells were concerned with making their target focus on the spell-caster and forget all other attachments. This happens to Thekla, and her behavior certainly produces a marked antisocial effect: the whole family becomes distressed at the way in which Thekla is behaving and its significance (*AP* 3.10 trans. here and throughout, Barrier 2009): "And those in the house were weeping bitterly, Thamyris, for the loss of a wife; Theokleia (for the loss) of a child, but the female slaves (for the loss) of a mistress. Therefore a great confusion of mourning was in the house." And, indeed, the language used to describe Thekla's response to Paul evokes the terminology of binding spells: Thekla's mother explains how Thekla stays by the window (3.9) "held (*dedemene*) to

222   *Esther Eidinow*

a new desire and a frightful passion" (see also Bremmer 1996, 42, who gives relevant examples of binding spells; the terminology is repeated later in the story; see later in the chapter). But there are also some significant differences between Paul's effects on Thekla and those imagined/described as the usual effects of an erotic magical spell. These differences evoke the theme of female spiritual discipline that we have already seen in the previous episode.

An *agoge* spell was understood to provoke not just attachment in its target but also violent and frenzied behavior. Examples of spells can be cited (as Jackson-McCabe 2010, 269) that describe the extreme agitation that should afflict a spell's victim: for example (*SM* 45.44–50, Betz), "Seize Euphemia and fetch her for me, Theon, to love me with mad love, and bind her with indissoluble, strong adamantine fetters to love me, Theon; and do not let her eat, or drink, or find sleep, or have fun, or laugh; but make her run away from every place and from every house, and leave father, mother, brothers, sisters, until she comes to me. . . . But if she has another one at her bosom, move her to push him away and forget him and hate him"; similarly, *PGM* IV.2756–62 (Betz), "In frenzy may she (NN) come fast to my doors | Forgetting children and her life with her parents | and loathing all the race of men | and women except me, but may she hold me alone | and come subdued in heart by love's great force." As well as these spell recipes, we also have a vivid picture of the perceived physical and mental effects of such a spell in the tale told by Jerome in the *Life of St. Hilarion* (*Migne PL* 23). In this account we hear of a young woman in Gaza who is attacked by a youth who is desperately in love with her. It is clear that she gives him no encouragement: she is one of God's virgins, we are told, and the usual social feints – touches, jests, nods, and whispers (*tactu, jocis, nutibus, sibilis*) – have had no effect. The youth resorts to magic: he takes instruction for a year from a priest of Asklepios and then returns to Gaza and places an inscribed brass plate (*aeris Cyprii lamina*) under the threshold of the girl's house. The effects are terrible: the girl appears to go insane (*insanire virgo*), throwing aside her head-covering, tearing her hair, and gnashing her teeth. She calls on the youth loudly by name, she enters a frenzied state of intense desire.

In contrast, Thekla's response to her emotions is remarkably controlled. Although, as we are told, there are many women and virgins who are going to visit Paul, Thekla, despite her longing (*epepothei*), keeps away from him in person (see Barrier 2009, 87). Instead, she stays (*AP* 3.7) "sitting at a nearby window of the house listening night and day to the things concerning purity which were being said by Paul." So, to begin with, Thekla does not appear completely to forget her previous social connections or the expectations of her social role; indeed, the conflict between her desires and knowledge of her social role appear to cause her some discomfort. As her mother notes (*AP* 3.8): "For three days and three nights, Thekla has not risen from the door, neither to eat nor to drink, but she is gazing intently as though enraptured, thus she is closely attached to a foreign man who is teaching deceptive and divisive words, so that I marvel how one of such modesty as of the virgin is being burdened (so painfully)." Moreover, when she does leave

"A devotee and a champion" 223

the house – to visit Paul, who is now imprisoned – there is no sense in the text of her being under the control or guidance of some supernatural force (*AP* 3.18). Rather, the text describes her as pursuing her own, nonsexual desires and finding her own way toward her goal. She resolves the obstacles in her path using her own resources, bribing the gatekeeper with her bracelets and the jailer with a silver mirror.

Similarly, when she is found in the prison, terminology that evokes the magical practice of binding spells is again used – and the expectations that it raises are again subverted. Thekla is described as συνδεδεμένην τῇ στοργῇ "united by means of love" (3.19). The participle used here still retains a sense of control or restraint, but instead of being "bound down," it rather evokes Thekla's more equal relationship with Paul: they are "bound together." Indeed, in a physical sense, it is Paul who is actually bound. Barrier (2009, 116–17) observes that the phrase need not suggest sexual union, but sounds erotic undertones: the story is, as he notes (117), "speaking of chastity in the language of the romance." And this ambiguous erotic motif of the relationship between Paul and Thekla is more overtly evoked elsewhere in the text: for example, *AP* 3.18, where Thekla kisses the bonds of the imprisoned Paul. Finally, in terms of magical motifs, even the accusations made against Paul that he is a *magos* (*AP* 3.15) are subverted: when Thamyris, Thekla's betrothed, criticizes Paul to others, he does not argue that he is attempting to corrupt virgins. Instead, Paul is a "man of deception" . . . "deceiving the souls of young ones and defrauding virgins, in order that they might not become married but that they should remain as they are" (*AP* 3.11). The usual theme of trickery and seduction (part of the accusation made against Marcus by Irenaeus, mentioned earlier) is itself redirected to this new context: this is a *magos* who does not seek to seduce these young women, but to maintain their virginity.

While building links to familiar genres – of romance and erotic magic – this text destabilizes expectations. The portrayal of Thekla's spiritual journey offers further surprises, including its depiction of the character of Paul and the balance of spiritual understanding between the two figures. Over the course of events, Thekla develops into the main protagonist, overtaking Paul in her appreciation of her role in service to God. When Paul and Thekla meet again, after Thekla's miraculous salvation from death, she states her desire to become an apostle of Paul's and then requests baptism (*AP* 3.25). Paul appears to refuse, although Thekla clearly has received God's approval: the final outcome of the story – in which she returns to Ikonion as a teacher (*AP* 4.17–18) – will reveal Paul's error. Barrier (2009, 136) points out the ways in which, at this point, Paul is painted as inferior to Thekla. He observes that "it is almost as if the author of the text is presenting a Paul, who, formerly being ignorant concerning the role of women in the church is now beginning to understand what Paul once thought shameless."

Although Thekla leaves behind traditional female roles, it is too simple to describe her as being gradually constructed as masculine (as Kraemer 2011, 139). Perhaps surprisingly, it is the erotic elements of the story, including the intimations of erotic magic, which problematize such an analysis. These details not only

224   *Esther Eidinow*

entertain the reader, they also help to sustain the femininity of Thekla – even as they subvert the usual motifs of the genre of the ancient novel. The final result is a complex character, perhaps one that would provoke a strong response among contemporary readers (as Kate Cooper 2013, 92, 94–8). For the purposes of this chapter, the story of Thekla, in all its complexity, depicts how a woman's connection to the church could provide her with a new agency, sometimes simply to pursue her own intentions or desires but, more frequently, to engage with cultural and/or supernatural forms of power.

Conclusion

This chapter has suggested some ways in which we might re-examine the presentation of female so-called "victims" of magical attack in some early Christian texts. It posits that characters in these texts were not limited simply to "victims" vs. "magicians," passive vs. active, but were more nuanced in their presentation. In their depictions of these female figures, these texts do not evoke submissive recipients of the power of others – be those others demons or officers of the church. Instead, in each case, a more complex account of their role is apparent, in which these female characters develop, using the language of Sherry Ortner's approach to agency, not only an agency of projects but even an agency of power. Thekla, the anonymous young woman of the *Acts of Andrew*, even those women whom Irenaeus describes simply as returning to the church, are portrayed as developing a new level of spiritual competence, knowledge, and understanding that enables them to confront and repel both mortal and supernatural assailants.

This interpretation of these texts has a number of implications for different areas of scholarship. Most obviously, it raises questions about our understanding of the rhetoric of these documents within the early church and the portrayal of women in that context. Granted, this material presents its characters so as to represent or further particular ideologies, but this reading suggests the possibility that, regarding women, these ideologies were more nuanced than simply the undermining of female competence and agency. This, in turn, may then support other arguments made about the attractions that Christianity held for women and the opportunities it offered for their intellectual and social expression. With regard to Thekla's story, it has been argued (Cooper 2013, 77–8, quotation 78) that, however the text came to be written, whatever its connection to historical reality, it shows that "ancient readers were hungry for detail about the lives of Paul's women." Others have argued (e.g. Kraemer 2011, esp. 146–52) that there may be some historical and social verisimilitude in this story; indeed, Jan Bremmer (1989, 42), considering other aspects of early Christianity, notes that: "Membership of the Christian community . . . seems to have enabled rich women to be heard and to participate in meaningful intellectual discussions."

In terms of approaches to the topic of ancient magic, this chapter has suggested that closer examination of the presentation of the "victim" can aid our understanding of the contemporary construction of claims to power and the

"A devotee and a champion" 225

ways in which these were developed in different contexts. As a final illustration of this aspect, I return to the tale recounted by Jerome in the *Life of St. Hilarion* (see earlier in the chapter for the first part of this story, in which a young woman shows all the symptoms of erotic demonic possession). When the family brings the young woman to the monastery to visit Hilarion, the demon that has possessed her makes himself known: he argues that he is there against his will (he prefers to beguile the men of Memphis in their dreams), bound under the threshold. In the ensuing debate with Hilarion, he argues that he is trying to preserve the virginity of the girl – and had not entered the body of the youth who had summoned him, since that young man was already in alliance with the demon of love (*amoris daemonen*). What follows is puzzling: we are told that Hilarion insisted that the virgin undergo a process of purgation before the young man or the charm be sought out. This was in case it was perceived that the demon had been released by incantations or that Hilarion had been taken in by the demon's explanations. Hilarion then offers the lesson that demons are deceitful and well able to dissemble; he rebukes the virgin for offering the demon the chance to enter.

Again, it has been argued that we should see this as an account that emphasizes male power (e.g. Stratton 2007, 89–90). But a second, closer look at the story, along with a reflection on the wider context of the text, may prompt a different interpretation. First, the story itself: the virgin is not rebuked for being simply open to demonic possession; rather, we find that it is her activities that have made her vulnerable. In the attempt to understand what those could be (she is after all still a virgin, so it seems unlikely that this includes leading a dissolute life), the other miracles reported in the *Life* may offer a helpful comparison. The virgin is not the only one who is scolded in the course of being healed: most of the individuals that are afflicted by demons and then cured by Hilarion are given strict instruction about their past, present, or future behavior, whether they are male or female. Moreover, the nature of Hilarion's reproofs in these cases is significant: they all relate to the ways in which normative activities of everyday life are inadequate when compared to the advantages of taking on the training and discipline of the Christian life.

Hilarion instructs both men and women in this way: for example, we learn of a woman from Facidia who is told she should not have wasted money on physicians to cure her blindness but given those funds to the poor and trusted in Jesus (15); a charioteer from Gaza is told that he cannot be cured of his physical stiffness unless he first believes in Christ and forsakes his former occupation (16). In these examples, and in the tale of the rebuked virgin, we see again a theme already noted: the dangers – or perhaps better put, the lack of security – offered by the familiar, everyday roles of family life and the domestic space. Once the story of the virgin's demonic possession is viewed in this light, then she is no longer simply the passive instrument of supernatural struggle. Instead, she becomes one of many, male and female, whose interactions with Hilarion have offered them a glimpse of a very different future, one that includes the possibility of a new role – with the potential for a new and powerful agency.

226 *Esther Eidinow*

Note

1 With thanks to the original conference participants for their comments, and also to Lisa Maurizio and Jan Bremmer for their thoughtful advice.

Works consulted

Aubin, M. 1998. "Reversing Romance? The Acts of Thecla and the Ancient Novel." In *Ancient Fiction* in *Early Christian Narrative*, edited by R. F. Hock, J. Bradley Chance, and J. Perkins. Atlanta: Society of Biblical Literature, 257–72.

Barrier, Jeremy W. 2009. *The Acts of Paul and Thecla: A Critical Introduction and Commentary*. Tübingen: Mohr Siebeck.

Betz, Hans, Dieter. ed. 1992. *The Greek Magical Papyri in Translation.* 2nd ed. Chicago: University of Chicago Press.

Bowie, Ewen. 1996. "The Ancient Readers of the Greek Novels." In *The Novel in the Ancient World*, edited by Gareth Schmeling, 87–106. Leiden: Brill.

Bremmer, Jan. 1989. "Why Did Early Christianity Attract Upper-Class Women?" In *Fructus centesimus: Mélanges offerts à Gerard J. M. Bartelink à l'occasion de son soixante-cinquième anniversaire*, edited by Anton Bastiaensen, Antonius Hilhorst, and Corneille Kneepkens, 37–47. Steenbrugge and Dordrecht: S. Pietersabdij and Kluwer.

Bremmer, Jan. 1996. "Magic, Martyrdom and Women's Liberation in the Acts of Paul and Thecla." In *The Apocryphal Acts of Paul and Thecla*, edited by Jan Bremmer, 36–59. Kampen: Kok Pharos.

Bremmer, Jan. 2000. "Man, Magic, and Martyrdom in the *Acts of Andrew*." In *The Apocryphal Acts of Andrew*, Studies on the Apocryphal Acts of the Apostles 5, edited by Jan Bremmer, 15–34. Leuven: Peeters.

Bremmer, Jan. 2001. "The *Apocryphal Acts*: Authors, Place, Time and Readership." In *The Apocryphal Acts of Thomas*, Studies on the Apocryphal Acts of the Apostles 6, edited by Jan Bremmer, 149–70. Leuven: Peeters.

Bremmer, Jan. 2003. "Magic in the *Apocryphal Acts of the Apostles*." In *The Metamorphosis of Magic from Late Antiquity to the Early Modern Period*, edited by Jan Bremmer and Jan Veenstra, Leuven: Peeters, 51–70.

Burrus, Virginia. 1991. "The Heretical Woman as Symbol in Alexander, Athanasius, Epiphanius and Jerome." *Harvard Theological Review* 84: 229–48.

Burrus, Virginia. 1995. *The Making of a Heretic: Gender, Authority, and the Priscillianist Controversy*, Transformation of the Classical Heritage, 24. Berkeley: University of California Press.

Clark, Elizabeth A. 1998. "The Lady Vanishes: Dilemmas of a Feminist Historian after the 'Linguistic Turn.'" *Church History* 67: 1–31.

Cole, Susan. 1981. "Could Greek Women Read and Write?" In *Reflections of Women in Antiquity*, edited by Helene P. Foley, 219–45. New York: Gordon and Breach.

Cooper, Kate. 1996. *The Virgin and the Bride: Idealized Womanhood in Late Antiquity.* Cambridge, MA and London: Harvard University Press.

Cooper, Kate. 2013. *Band of Angels: The Forgotten World of Early Christian Women.* London: Atlantic Books and New York: Overlook Press.

Czachesz, Istvan. 2007. "Magic and Mind: Toward a New Cognitive Theory of Magic, With Special Attention to the Canonical and Apocryphal Acts of the Apostles." In *Neues Testament und Magie: Verhältnisbestimmungen*, edited by Tobias Nicklas and Thomas J. Kraus, special issue of *Annali di Storia dell'Esegesi* 24, 295–321.

"A devotee and a champion" 227

D'Angelo, Mary Rose. 1990. "Women in Luke-Acts: A Redactional View." *Journal of Biblical Literature* 109: 441–61.

Davies, Stevan L. 1980. *The Revolt of the Widows: The Social World of the Apocryphal Acts.* Carbondale: Southern Illinois University Press.

Dickie, Matthew. 2000. "Who Practised Love-Magic in Classical Antiquity and in the Late Roman World?" *Classical Quarterly*, n.s. 50(2): 563–83.

Dickie, Matthew. 2001. *Magic and Magicians in the Greco-Roman World.* London: Routledge.

Edwards, C. 1993. *Politics of Immorality in Ancient Rome.* Cambridge: Cambridge University Press.

Eidinow, Esther. 2013. [2007]. *Oracles, Curses, and Risk among the Ancient Greeks.* Oxford: Oxford University Press.

Eidinow, Esther. forthcoming 2017. "Ancient Magic and the Agency of Victimhood." *Numen* 64(4).

Elliott, James Keith. 1993. *The Apocryphal New Testament: A Collection of Apocryphal Christian Literature in an English Translation by M. R. James.* Oxford: Oxford University Press.

Faraone, Christopher. 1999. *Ancient Greek Love Magic.* Cambridge, MA: Harvard University Press.

Flower, Michael. 2008. *The Seer in Ancient Greece.* Berkeley: University of California Press.

Frankfurter, David. 2002. "Dynamics of Ritual Expertise in Antiquity and Beyond: Towards a New Taxonomy of 'Magicians'." In *Magic and Ritual in the Ancient World*, edited by Paul Mirecki and Marvin Meyer, 159–78. Leiden: Brill.

Frankfurter, David. 2014. *The Social Context of Women's Erotic Magic in Antiquity.* In *Daughters of Hecate: Women and Magic in the Ancient World*, edited by Kimberley B. Stratton and Dayna Kalleres, 319–39. Oxford: Oxford University Press.

Gamble, Harry. 1995. *Books and Readers in the Early Church: A History of Early Christian Texts.* New Haven and London: Yale University Press.

Jackson-McCabe, Matthew. 2010. "Women and Eros in Greek Magic and the Acts of Paul and Thecla." In *Women and Gender in Ancient Religions: Interdisciplinary Approaches*, edited by Stephen P. Ahearne-Kroll, Paul A. Holloway, and James A. Kelhoffer, 267–78. Tübingen: Mohr Siebeck.

Joshel, Sandra. 1997. "Female Desire and the Discourse of Empire: Tacitus's Messalina." In *Roman Sexualities*, edited by Judith P. Hallett and Marilyn. B. Skinner, 221–54. Princeton: Princeton University Press.

Kraemer, Ross Shephard. 2011. *Unreliable Witnesses: Religion, Gender, and History in the Greco-Roman Mediterranean.* Oxford: Oxford University Press.

Lampe, G.W.H. ed. 1991. *A Patristic* Greek *Lexicon.* 12th edition. Oxford: Clarendon Press.

Markschies, Christoph. 2006 (First appeared online). "Eirenaeus, Irenaeus." In *Brill's New Pauly.* Antiquity volumes edited by Hubert Cancik and Helmuth Schneider. Brill Online, 2015. Accessed: UFB Erfurt/Gotha. 15 October 2015 http://referenceworks.brillonline.com/entries/brill-s-new-pauly/eirenaeus-irenaeus-e327520

Mauss, Marcel and H. Hubert. 1902–3. "Esquisse d'une théorie générale de la magie." *Année Sociologique* 7: 1–146.

Ortner, Sherry. 2006. *Anthropology and Social Theory: Culture, Power, and the Acting Subject.* Durham, NC: Duke University Press Books.

Perkins, Judith. 1995. *The Suffering Self: Pain and Narrative Representation in the Early Christian Era.* London and New York: Routledge.

Pollard, Elizabeth Ann. 2014. "Magic Accusations Against Women in Tacitus's *Annals*." In *Daughters of Hecate: Women and Magic in the Ancient World*, edited by Kimberley B. Stratton and Dayna Kalleres, 183–218. Oxford: Oxford University Press.

228   *Esther Eidinow*

Pollard, Elizabeth Jane. 2001. *Magic Accusations Against Women in the Greco-Roman World from the First Through the Fifth Centuries*. PhD Diss. Philadelphia: University of Pennsylvania.

Prieur, Jean-Marc. 1987. *Écrits apocryphes chrétiens I*. Paris: Editions Gallimard.

Prieur, Jean-Marc. 1992. "The Acts of Andrew: Introduction." In *New Testament Apocrypha II: Writings Relating to the Apostles; Apocalypses and Related Subjects*, edited by Wilhelm Schneemelcher; translated and edited by Robert McLachlan Wilson. Rev. ed., 101–18. Cambridge: James Clarke and Co. Ltd.

Quispel, Gilles. 1956. "An Unknown Fragment of the Acts of Andrew (Pap. Copt. Utrecht N.1)." *Vigiliae Christianae* 10: 129–48.

Reed, Annette Yoshiko. 2014. "Gendering Heavenly Secrets? Women, Angels, and the Problem of Misogyny and Magic." In *Daughters of Hecate: Women and Magic in the Ancient World*, edited by Kimberley B. Stratton and Dayna Kalleres, 108–51. Oxford: Oxford University Press.

Rousseau, Adelin and Louis Doutreleau. 1979. *Irénée de Lyon, Contre les Hérésies II*. Paris: Éditions du Cerf.

Schneemelcher, Wilhelm. 1992. "The Acts of Andrew: Texts." In *New Testament Apocrypha II: Writings Relating to the Apostles; Apocalypses and Related Subjects*, edited by Wilhelm Schneemelcher; translated and edited by Robert McLachlan Wilson. Rev. ed., 118–51. Cambridge: James Clarke and Co. Ltd.

Schroeder, Caroline. 2006. "The Erotic Asceticism of the Passion of Andrew: The Apocryphal Acts of Andrew, the Greek Novel and Platonic Philosophy." In. *A Feminist Companion to the New Testament Apocrypha*, edited by Amy-Jill Levine and Maria Mayo Robbins, 47–59. London: T&T Clark.

Scibilia, Anna. 2002. "Supernatural Assistance in the Greek Magical Papyri: The Figure of the Parhedros." In *The Metamorphosis of Magic from Late Antiquity to the Early Modern Period*, edited by Jan Bremmer and Jan Veenstra, 71–86. Leiden: Brill.

Spaeth, Barbette Stanley. 2014. "From Goddess to Hag: The Greek and the Roman Witch in Classical Literature." In *Daughters of Hecate: Women and Magic in the Ancient World*, edited by Kimberley B. Stratton and Dayna Kalleres, 41–70. Oxford: Oxford University Press.

Stratton, Kimberley. 2007. "The Rhetoric of 'Magic' in Early Christian Discourse: Gender, Power and the Construction of 'Heresy.'" In *Mapping Gender in Ancient Religious Discourses*, edited by Todd Penner and Caroline Vander Stichele, 89–114. Leiden: Brill.

Stratton, Kimberley. 2014. "Interrogating the Magic-Gender Connection." In *Daughters of Hecate: Women and Magic in the Ancient World*, edited by Kimberley B. Stratton and Dayna Kalleres, 1–37. Oxford: Oxford University Press.

Thomas, Christine. 1998. "Stories without Texts and without Authors: The Problem of Fluidity in Ancient Novelistic Texts and Early Christian Literature'." In *Ancient Fiction and Early Christian Literature*, edited by Ronald Hock, J. Bradley Chance, and Judith Perkins, 273–91. Atlanta: Scholars Press.

Tomlin, Roger S. O. 1988. "The Curse Tablets." In *The Temple of Sulis Minerva at Bath, vol. 2: The Finds from the Sacred Spring*, edited by Barry Cunliffe, 59–277. Oxford: Oxford University Press.

Williams, Craig. A. 2010. *Roman Homosexuality: Ideologies of Masculinity in Classical Antiquity*. 2nd ed. New York: Oxford University Press.

Winkler, John. 1990. *The Constraints of Desire: The Anthropology of Sex and Gender in Ancient Greece*. London and New York: Routledge.

13 "What the women know"

Plutarch and Pausanias on female ritual competence

Deborah Lyons

Introduction

This chapter addresses the problem of access to sacred knowledge and how it affects ancient understandings of ancient Greek women's rituals.[1] I propose to consider the problem from several angles: the difficulty, already in antiquity, of understanding rituals that may have fallen into disuse or changed over time; the difficulty of understanding rituals marked as mysteries or bounded by ritual prohibitions; and finally strategies for dealing with these difficulties on the part of the ancient writers on whom we depend for our scant knowledge of obscure practices. I will focus on Plutarch and Pausanias, two authors whose relationship to the customs they discuss is made both interesting and problematic by ritual prohibitions and the passage of time (see Preston 2001, 109–10 on Plutarch's problematic relation to the present), thus putting them in a less dire version of the same predicament in which we modern scholars of ancient religion find ourselves. The example of these two authors shows that, in stark contrast to others about whom I have written elsewhere (Lyons 2007), ritually enforced male ignorance does not necessarily lead to suspicion and contempt but may at times serve to enhance the prestige of the rituals and to foster recognition of and respect for women's ritual.

This chapter will not attempt to wring hidden details from recalcitrant texts but rather to show that awareness of women's mysteries, together with ignorance of their details, could sometimes go hand in hand with a recognition and appreciation of the ritual competence of these often undervalued practitioners. Particularly in the works of these two near-contemporaries, we find respectful treatment of female-only rituals of which they knew little and revealed less.

The difficulty of obtaining reliable knowledge about ancient Greek women's religious observances is well known. As with other ancient rituals attended by both men and women, the details of women's ritual observances are rarely recorded with any precision. Like other cultural information handed down from generation to generation, no one felt the need to record them.

Vague formulas like "the accustomed [rites or practices]" (*ta nenomismena, e.g.* Plut. *Quaest. Rom.* 20, 268e; see Parker 2005, 27) routinely appear in inscriptions and literary texts, where they are applied to rituals performed by men and women alike.

230 *Deborah Lyons*

The lack of information is much more acute in the case of *mysteria*, which were kept secret from non-initiates under pain of severe penalties. These prohibitions were so completely respected that surviving information is scant. The little we do know is somewhat suspect, in many cases filtered through the hostile attitudes of Christian writers, such as Clement of Alexandria and Hippolytus, who had no reason to respect the prohibitions and strong motivations for distorting whatever they had heard. Hippolytus presumably had no first-hand knowledge of the mysteries, so his statements in the *Refutation of All Heresies* (*Elenchus*; 5.8.39) are especially problematic. Clement, author of the *Exhortation to the Greeks* (*Protreptikos*), was a convert to Christianity and may well have been initiated, in which case he would have had actual knowledge of the proceedings (which he discusses at 2.21.22). Even so, one must be cautious about taking his account of the ritual at face value, since conversion is usually accompanied by a complete revaluation of one's previous religious beliefs and practices. Indeed, both these writers take pains to make the mysteries sound absurd, obscene, or both.

In addition, many women's festivals and sacrifices were off-limits to men, and therefore, even if not technically secret, only entered the public record obliquely – and even then frequently in a dismissive fashion. Ritual exclusions, not always gender-based, were common in Greek religion, and I will have more to say about them later.

Two antiquarians

I focus my analysis on Plutarch (*c.* 45–120 CE) and Pausanias (*c.* 120–180 CE), who share an interest in Greek antiquities and religious customs and are rich sources of information about ancient ritual. Each alludes frequently to the religious practices of women in their writings. Despite their desire to preserve every crumb of the vanishing lore of Archaic and Classical Greece, they avoid divulging or even inquiring about *mysteria*, secret rites that must not be revealed. Among the rituals they avoid discussing are many enacted by women only. It is hard to know whether they intentionally preserve a pious silence about what they know or are unable to break their silence because they lack knowledge about the rites. Perhaps the rhetoric of respect for women's mysteries results from a combination of both. Certainly we can observe in these passages a tension between curiosity – not to say voyeurism – and piety.

Plutarch took a lively and not entirely academic interest in religious practices. He served as a priest at Delphi and had an active role in the revival of the sanctuary there. His *Greek and Roman Questions* offer a unique opportunity to observe an ancient scholar of religion coming to grips with the sometimes obscure rituals still remembered, if not always still practiced, in his own day. It is from these two treatises that I will draw my Plutarchan examples. I refer to these texts by their traditional English titles, as *questions*, although Plutarch seems to have called them *aitia*, causes. To call them questions is not a mere nod to tradition. It also addresses two facts about them: their form and the tradition of *problemata*, or problem literature, from which they clearly emerge. (On similarities and differences between

"What the women know" 231

these texts and the *Problemata*, see Preston 2001, 95–9.) The pseudo-Aristotelian *Problemata*, like many of the *Greek and Roman Questions*, introduce their questions with the formula *dia ti* ("why?"). As Blair (2000, 173) comments, they ask "about the cause of a fact that is presumed so well known that it is not even stated before it is explained."

In these texts we see the antiquarian and religious practitioner attempting to elucidate traditions that are, to varying degrees, separated from his own experience by time, space, and cultural difference. A Greek subject of Rome, Plutarch embodies the paradox of Greek cultural prestige in the face of Roman imperial power, a topic that has attracted considerable attention in recent years (Alcock *et al.* 2001; Goldhill 2001). While he lived for many years in Rome and had many Roman friends, they may not have been the primary audience for these works, which aim not only to preserve a record of local Greek customs, but also to explain, if not justify, Rome's ways to Greece. This may explain his tendency to prefer explanations of Roman customs that ascribe a moral purpose. A third set of *aitia*, the *aitia barbarica*, unfortunately do not survive to help break down the dichotomy between Greece and Rome. Artificial as it may be, it was nevertheless a dichotomy in which Plutarch himself was heavily invested, as the enterprise of the *Parallel Lives* bears witness.

In his attempts to elucidate Greek and Roman rituals, Plutarch is both ancient and modern. To us, he is an "ancient," but vis-à-vis many of the traditions he discusses, his position is similar to that of the modern scholar confronting customs whose meaning has been obscured by time and whose information about those customs is not always reliable. While our own situation is far more dire, nonetheless Plutarch's predicament at times resembles our own. It is in fact not always easy to know when he is speaking of contemporary practices and when he is using the so-called "ethnographic present," as some contemporary anthropologists still do, when citing customs observed by ethnographers more than 50 years ago (Parker 1996, 271; this much-criticized phenomenon has recently come in for reconsideration and even rehabilitation; see, for example, de Pina-Cabral 2000).

Analysis of Plutarch's explanatory strategies shows that many of them – principally etymologizing, mythologizing, and "common sense" – allow him to fall back on his own Greek cultural and linguistic assumptions. Preston (2001, 105 n. 98) finds 27 answers that appeal to what is "natural," "proper," or "reasonable." In the following passage (*Quaest. Rom.* 87, 285b-d), we can see several of these strategies applied to a Roman custom (all translations from Plutarch are by Frank Cole Babbitt, in some places with minor revisions):

Why do they part the hair of brides with the point of a spear? Does this symbolize the marriage of the first Roman wives by violence with attendant war, or do the wives thus learn, now that they are mated to brave and warlike men, to welcome an unaffected, unfeminine, and simple mode of beautification? Even as Lykourgos, by giving orders to make the doors and roofs of house with the saw and the axe only, and to use absolutely no other tool, banished all over-refinement and extravagance.

232 *Deborah Lyons*

Or does this procedure hint at the manner of their separation, that with steel alone can their marriage be dissolved?

Or is it that most of the marriage customs were connected with Juno? Now, the spear is commonly held to be sacred to Juno, and most of her statues represent her leaning on a spear, and the goddess herself is surnamed *Quiritis*; for the men of old used to call the spear *curis*.

In the *Greek Questions*, Plutarch is dealing with a tradition that is culturally familiar, even if some of the customs have changed or fallen into disuse, while the still-living Roman rituals are more obscure in their origins both to him as a non-Roman and – because of a paucity of written sources – apparently to the Romans themselves. His hellenocentrism is reflected stylistically and methodologically in the two treatises, most of all in the relative confidence with which he approaches the Greek material and his habit of using Greek customs to elucidate Roman ones, as earlier in the far-fetched reference to Lykourgos. Although Plutarch is clearly well read in Roman authors, they were not part of his educational formation, as were the Greek authors to whom he frequently refers. When Plutarch asks Greek questions, he generally knows the answers. The Greek questions elicit answers, usually no more than one per question, while the Roman questions usually lead into a series of further questions. Preston contrasts the definitive Greek answers to the open-ended Roman ones, with their suggestion that Roman culture is "the subject of considerable uncertainty" (2001, 97).

I have already quoted a rather typical Roman question. A typical Greek question (*Quaest. Graec.* 31; 298b-c) is the following:

Why is it that at the Thesmophoria the Eretrian women cook their meat, not by fire, but by the rays of the sun; and why do they not call upon Kalligeneia?

Is it because it happened that the captive women whom Agamemnon was bringing home from Troy were celebrating the Thesmophoria at this place, but when the conditions for sailing suddenly appeared favorable, they put out to sea leaving behind the sacrifice uncompleted?

Kalligeneia was the name of the third and final day of the festival as it was celebrated at Athens and may also have been a title of Demeter. According to Plutarch, circumstances did not allow the women to complete their celebrations (or their cooking), and therefore they did not arrive at the part of the rites traditionally dedicated to Kalligeneia. By this means, he explains the difference in the festival as celebrated at Athens and at Eretria. Interestingly, in this passage Plutarch seems to anticipate the modern habit of seeing Athens and its customs as normative – so normative, in fact, that he does not even feel it necessary to explain why one might expect the women to call on Kalligeneia or to name the city where the women do invoke Demeter by this name. The rest of his answer depends on another source of cultural currency, the Trojan War. We are used to appeals to Homer in nearly all

"What the women know" 233

successive Greek literature, but in this case, Plutarch refers to an episode after the fall of Troy and outside the scope of the *Iliad*.

I have observed that most Greek questions receive a single answer. It is notable that among the few exceptions to the single answer rule for Greek questions are several that address women's religious practice, which are also – like the Roman ones – answered by multiple questions. Here is one example (*Quaest. Graec.* 36, 299a–b):

> Why is it that the women of the Eleans, when they sing hymns to Dionysos, call upon him to come to them "with the foot of a bull"?
>
> Is it because some address the god as "kine-born" or as "bull"? Or by "ox-foot" do they mean "with a mighty foot" even as the poet used "ox-eyes" to signify "large-eyed," and "bully" for "loud-mouthed"?
>
> Or is it rather because the foot of the bull is harmless, but the part that bears horns is harmful, and thus they call upon the god to come in a gentle and painless manner?
>
> Or is it because many believe that the god was the pioneer in both ploughing and sowing?

For Plutarch, then, one might argue that women's ritual culture is as foreign as Roman culture and that his attempts to answer the questions it poses result only in more questions.

Pausanias was no less inclined than Plutarch to take women and their religious observations seriously. In his description of the temple of Eileithyia in Athens, he credits them with various kinds of information (all translations from Pausanias are by W.H.S. Jones, although I have revised them in some cases): "The women [presumably local women attached to the temple] told me that the two [wooden figures in the temple] are Cretan, being offerings of Phaedra, and that the third, which is the oldest, Erysichthon brought from Delos" (1.18.5). He likewise confesses that he never understood a certain verse in the *Odyssey* (9.581) until enlightened by women:

> The former passage in which Homer speaks of the beautiful dancing floors of Panopeus, I could not understand until I was taught (*prin ē edidachthēn*) by the women whom the Athenians call Thyiads. The Thyiads are Attic women, who with the Delphian women go to Parnassus every year and celebrate orgies in honor of Dionysos. It is the custom for these Thyiads to hold dances at places, including Panopeus, along the road from Athens. The epithet [*kallichoros*] Homer applies to Panopeus is thought to refer to the dances of the Thyiads.
>
> (10.4.3a–b)

Enlightenment, however, was not always forthcoming. What these authors may at times have most wanted to know they could not ask, nor could the women tell them. Pausanias (2.35.3–8) recounts details of the worship of Demeter Chthonia

234 *Deborah Lyons*

at Hermione, consisting of those rituals open to all, those performed by women but known to men, and finally mysteries known only to women (Johnston 2012, 216). Pirenne-Delforge postulates that Pausanias was actually present at the celebration of this festival. All the same, much of his knowledge must be second-hand, and there are limits even to that (Pirenne-Delforge 2008, 202–5). After describing the unusual sacrifice performed by women, he alludes to the mysteries in the following terms: "But the thing itself that they worship more than all else, I never saw, nor yet has any other man, whether stranger or Hermionian." He ends his account with what sounds almost like a ritual formula, apotropaically forswearing any desire to learn what is forbidden: "Of what sort of thing it is, only the old women know" (*monoi de hopoion ti estin hai graes istōsan* [my translation])." That there might be consequences for physically invading women's rites he was surely aware: at 4.17.1, he tells the story of Aristomenes, who barely escaped with his life after infiltrating the Thesmophoria.

As Elsner notes, Pausanias in this passage is repeating a pattern that can be found throughout the work (1992, 21–5). In several instances, most notably at Eleusis (1.38.7), he tells us that a dream has indicated the limits of the permissible: "My dream forbade the description of things within the walls of the sanctuary, and the uninitiated are of course not permitted to learn that which they are prevented from seeing." In his discussion of the sacrifice to Zeus Lykaios on Mount Lykaion (8.38.7), it is presumably scruples of a different sort that lead him to remark that, "it was not a pleasant idea for me to ask any more questions about the sacrifice. Let it be as it is and as it was from the beginning." Once again, he closes his demurral with what sounds like a ritual formula.

Neither of these men was hostile to women or resistant to learning from them, as can be seen by the number of times they mention information gleaned from local female sources. Plutarch, moreover, was a close friend of the Delphic priestess Klea, to whom he dedicated two works (one of which was *On the Bravery of Women*), and was also the author of a treatise on the sayings of Spartan women. In his *Lives*, he complains more than once about the difficulty of learning the names of the mothers of the famous men of whom he writes, a problem caused by the taboo against naming respectable women in public in ancient Athens; for example at *Alcibiades* 1.2, he complains that the name of his subject's nurse is known but not that of his mother (Schaps 1977; Bremmer 1981). In his efforts to uncover the names of women, as well as his interest in women's ritual, we see his historian's desire for knowledge trumping whatever culturally determined tendency he might have had to regard women as extraneous to history.

Ritual prohibitions and exclusions

Plutarch, in his *Greek Questions*, demonstrates a keen interest in ritual prohibitions, asking questions like the following: "Why is it that among the Rhodians a herald does not enter the shrine of the hero Ocridion?" (*Quaest. Graec.* 27, 297c–d); "Why is it that among the inhabitants of Tenedos, a flute-player may not enter the shrine of Tenes, nor may anyone mention Achilles' name within the shrine?"

"What the women know" 235

(28); "Who was the hero Eumostos in Tanagra, and why may no women enter his grove?" (40). Pausanias, in his *Periegesis*, also records ritual prohibitions: at a temple of Eileithyia in Elis in western Greece, in the inner part where the god Sosipolis is worshipped, no one may enter except the old woman who tends the god, and she must wrap her head and face in a white veil (6.20.3).

Such prohibitions were commonplace in ancient Greek and Roman rituals and frequently resulted in the exclusion of women from religious rites, as Susan Cole (1992, 2004) has shown in her study of ritual exclusions in Greek *leges sacrae* (inscriptions laying out the proper cultic observances). Ritual prohibitions may regulate the kinds of offerings or practices due a particular deity in a particular sanctuary – no meat sacrifices, no fire, no "take-out" (*ou phora*), to give only a few examples. In addition to the laws regulating ritual behaviors, others specifically address the classes of people who may have access to the shrine and those who may participate in or observe the rites. Although it would be impossible to arrive at an accurate reckoning, it appears that ritual exclusion of women was more common than that of men, flute-players, mentioners of Achilles, or any other category of being.

And yet, because they were male, it is the exclusion of men that really attracts the attention of ancient writers on Greek religious practices. Pausanias tells us (7.27.10) that at the temple of Demeter Musaion near Pellene in Achaia, they hold a seven-day long festival for Demeter: "On the third day of the festival the men withdraw, and the women are left to perform on that night the ritual that custom demands. Not only are men excluded, but even male dogs. On the following day, the men come to the sanctuary, and the men and women laugh and jeer at one another in turn." This is the practice known as *aischrologia*, better known from descriptions of the rites leading up to the mysteries at Eleusis (Brumfield 1992; O'Higgins 2001, 2003).

Plutarch, in a Roman rather than a Greek example, tells us (*Quaest. Rom.* 20, 268e7–8) that during the festival of the Bona Dea, the women "not only exclude their husbands, but they drive everything male out of the house whenever they conduct the customary ceremonies in honor of the goddess" (Lyons 2007, esp. 43–4). The language of these passages is similar: "the ritual that custom demands" (*hoposa nomos estin autais*) or "the customary ceremonies" (*ta nenomismena*). This is no doubt the obvious way to refer to these ritual practices, but it has the added advantage of being both vague and respectful.

Although apparently less common, judging from the survey carried out by Cole (2004), the exclusion of men – the main recorders of culture in this period – has consequently a far larger presence in ancient writings on religion than the more common exclusion of women. And Cole's survey discusses not only ritual exclusions of women in the context of gender-segregated rituals (92–104) but also (104–13) those exclusions resulting from polluting conditions such as childbirth (see also Cole 1992). What is more, the activities of women, which are often off limits to men, are thereby made more mysterious to them and are apt to be given the label of "mysteries," whether that is indeed an appropriate description of their nature or not. Certainly they are mysteries in the modern sense of the word, and,

236 *Deborah Lyons*

in more than a few cases, it is clear from the cautious language used by these two writers that the rituals involved certain esoteric practices that nonparticipants were forbidden to know. In more than one context, Pausanias recounts the dire consequences of violating ritual prohibitions. For example, he twice mentions Aigyptos, who broke the prohibition against entering the sanctuary of Poseidon Hippios near Mantineia, and was punished with blindness and death (8.5.5; 8.10.3; see Elsner 1992, 24).

Plutarch shows a similar delicacy in describing a festival called Heroïs (Heroine) that took place at Delphi (*Quaest. Graec.* 93, 293d): "The greater part of the Heroïs has a secret import (*mystikon logon*) which the Thyiads know; but *from the portions of the rites that are performed in public* [my emphasis], one might conjecture that it represents the leading up (*anagogē*) of Semele" (Trans. Babbitt, slightly revised). He wants to know as much as possible, but at the same time takes pains to indicate that his conjectures are based entirely on information that it is lawful for him to have.

Whether caused by ritual prohibition, gender segregation, protection of mystic knowledge, or simply the passage of time, the effect of the recurring silences at the heart of these texts is paradoxically to highlight the ritual knowledge and competence of women and the respect in which these were held by both Plutarch and Pausanias. In this way, these two writers provide a valuable corrective to the censorious and disdainful attitudes both of tragic characters like Euripides' Pentheus and of early Christian writers like Clement of Alexandria. In so doing, they remind us how much ancient Greek men relied on their female counterparts to carry out the essential ritual work that was theirs alone. As much recent scholarship has shown, it is in the area of religious practice that women in ancient Greece most clearly exercised agency in public life. If much of it seems private to our antiquarians or to us today, that is an artifact of the gendered division of labor, which allotted to women the performance of certain indispensable rituals on which the favor of the gods depended but to men the recording of that which the culture considered worth writing down. In the case of women's secret rituals, this dichotomy is exploded by the realization that some of what is most important cannot be revealed, much less recorded.

The (female, ritual) past is a foreign country

I assume throughout this chapter that by the time of our two authors, some if not many of the traditional rituals of Archaic and Classical Greece were no longer practiced, but this is by no means an uncontroversial assumption. Robert Parker (1996, 256) has addressed this problem in the form "[w]hen should a history of Athenian religion come to an end?" He notes that many well-known festivals disappear from the historical record after 300 BCE. But he also observes that new ritual practices come into being, many of them tied to the importation of foreign cults, emperor worship, and the commemoration of recent events (Parker 1996, 272–4). Although his question – which is admittedly somewhat artificial – is really about the end of Classical Greek religion, he does marshal evidence that the

"What the women know" 237

traditional observances of the sort that interested our antiquarians were losing importance and disappearing – if not from daily life, then at least from the historical record. Burkert (1985, 6), on the other hand, stresses continuity from the Bronze Age to the period under discussion here. His comment that "many of the rituals which Plutarch and Pausanias observed must be of high antiquity" assumes that these rituals were still being practiced at least into the first half of the second century BCE. The assumption of continuity and consistency over time has been discussed with careful nuance by Pirenne-Delforge, who stresses the centrality of ritual in Pausanias' construction of a "recomposed" Greek identity (2008, 349). In her words, *Les rituels sont conçus comme le lieu privilegié de la continuité, même si le mémoire des traditions anciennes a pu faillir parfois.* ("The rituals are conceived as a privileged site of continuity, even if the memory of ancient traditions has sometimes faded.")

In his guidebook to the ancient monuments of mainland Greece, Pausanias is so intent on recreating the pre-Roman Greek past that (with few exceptions) he does not even mention the Roman monuments he encounters in his travels (as noted by Habicht 1985). As Elsner puts it (1992, 15 n. 45), Pausanias' project of constructing a new kind of Greek identity rests on the creation of a "nostalgic ideology of sacred and ancient Greece." Preston (2001, 111) speaks in similar terms of Plutarch's "highly selective version of the present [that] elides the contemporary realities of Roman rule." Pausanias goes to great lengths to foreground the Greek monuments and to uncover the truth about them, consulting local archives, religious practitioners, or anyone else who can provide him with an account, even one that he may go on to reject. The greatest obstacle to his project is the work of time, which destroys ancient objects or obscures their meaning. In one poignant example, when he makes the arduous journey to the cave of Demeter Melaine on Mt. Elaios, he is sorely disappointed: not only is the famous horse-headed cult image long gone (8.42.4–5) but even the bronze image meant to replace it is nowhere to be seen and has vanished from local memory (8.42.12; see Elsner 1992, 8).

But time is not the only obstacle to the recreation of a coherent Greek past. Like Plutarch, Pausanias must also reckon with certain ritual exclusions that make the knowledge he desires off-limits to men. Here several conflicting tendencies collide: his eagerness for esoteric knowledge bumps up against his piety and respect for religious prohibitions, while his willingness to learn from women conflicts with his perhaps frustrated awareness that certain kinds of knowledge are their prerogative alone.

At times it is tempting to relate the frustrated desire to know more of women's ritual practices to the nostalgia for an authentic and unchanging Greek culture that permeates the texts of both these antiquarians. In the couple of generations that separate them, the desired object has continued to recede. Plutarch displays a degree of cultural confidence that allows him to keep his ethnocentrism intact, and he can barely write about Rome without writing about Greece. Pausanias, on the other hand, can only write his *Description of Greece* by deliberately ignoring the many Roman monuments that have cropped up among the Greek ones. He, especially, appears reluctant to admit that many of the customs he describes may have

238   *Deborah Lyons*

fallen into disuse or changed beyond recognition, although the occasional word gives the game away. He tells us (3.20.3) that at Brysiai in Lakonia, "there *still* (my emphasis) remains here a temple of Dionysos with an image in the open. But the image in the temple, women only may see, for women perform the sacrificial rites by themselves in secret." Similarly, as Parker has remarked, Plutarch frequently uses the phrases *kai nun* and *eti nun*. While noting the use of these phrases, for example in the *Life of Theseus*, he is unwilling to say whether their absence in other passages describing ancient rituals constitutes positive evidence for the disappearance of those rituals (1996, 270). On the other hand, it must be admitted that Plutarch, at least, does not hesitate to discuss changes and lapses in ritual customs, as is shown by his two essays on the Delphic Oracle, known in English as "The Oracles at Delphi No Longer Given in Verse" (especially 402b–409d) and "On the Obsolescence of Oracles" (throughout).

Perhaps the rituals of women, because they were never well known to men, help – even more than those that are accessible to all – to preserve the illusion that nothing has changed. This may help to explain the reluctance to question whether these female rituals as witnessed by or described to our authors represent an unbroken transmission from Archaic times. The exclusion of men from these practices serves as a kind of alibi for our nostalgic antiquarians. In both these authors, women – often unnamed – seem to exist outside of history. The notion of women's existence in some timeless zone outside of a history created by men is prominent in ancient Greek and Roman thinking (Lyons 2007). This idea is, however, not unique to these societies but can be found across many cultures (Weiner 1979, esp. 20). It is in part attributable to a division of labor that allocates to women the maintenance of relations with certain divine forces but to men the recording of human deeds. When women are exiled from recorded history, their culturally important practices tend to be devalued, even as men recognize that they must be performed. If those practices exclude men, this provides an opportunity for knowledge to be replaced by fantasy, often of sexual license.

I have explored this tension before (Lyons 2007), where I concentrated on the negative reception of women's rituals. What sets apart Pausanias and Plutarch is that they are capable of respecting women's rituals and the secrecy they require without using them as a screen on which to project their own lurid imaginings. That is not to say that no projection is taking place. The phrase, "the women say . . ." introduces many of these reported scraps of information, and perhaps it is reassuring for these champions of Hellenic culture, in the face of so much change, to imagine these nameless women, never very firmly rooted in history – which was after all a masculine product – continuing forever to carry out their unseen rites.

I end with an image from Pausanias (2.11.6) that can stand for the situation in which our antiquarians find themselves:

> One cannot learn of what wood or metal the image is, nor do they know the name of the maker, though one or two attribute it to Alexanor himself. Of the image can be seen only the face, hands, and feet, for it has about it a tunic of white wool and a cloak. There is a similar image of Health; this too one cannot

"What the women know" 239

easily see because it is so surrounded with the locks of women, who cut them off and offer them to the goddess, and with strips of Babylonian raiment.

In the face of the tremendous loss of cultural integrity that deeply concerned both of these men, that which is obscured by the timeless and eternal rituals of women is somehow more comforting than that which has been simply worn away by time.

Note

1 Thanks are due to the editors of this volume for their helpful suggestions. They are not to blame if I have insufficiently heeded them.

Works consulted

Alcock, Susan E., John F. Cherry, and Jaś Elsner, eds. 2001. *Pausanias: Travel and Memory in Roman Greece*. Oxford: Oxford University Press.

Babbett, Frank Cole. 1936. *Plutarch's Moralia*. Vol. 4. Cambridge, MA: Harvard University Press.

Blair, Ann. 2000. "The *Problemata* as a Natural Philosophical Genre." In *Natural Particulars: Nature and the Disciplines in Renaissance Europe*, edited by Anthony Grafton and Nancy Siraisi, 171–204. Cambridge, MA: MIT Press.

Bremmer, Jan. 1981. "Plutarch and the Naming of Greek Women." *AJP* 102: 425–6.

Brumfield, Allaire. 1992. "Aporreta: Verbal and Ritual Obscenity in the Cults of Ancient Women." In *The Role of Religion in the Early Greek Polis*, edited by Robin Hägg, 67–76. Stockholm: Paul Åströms Forlag.

Burkert, Walter. 1985. *Greek Religion*. Trans. John Raffan. Cambridge, MA: Harvard University Press [Stuttgart 1977].

Cole, Susan G. 1992. "Gunaiki ou themis: Sexual Difference in the *Leges Sacrae*." *Helios* 19: 104–22.

———. 2004. *Landscapes, Gender, and Ritual Space: The Ancient Greek Experience*. Berkeley: University of California Press.

de Pina-Cabral, João. 2000. "The Ethnographic Present Revisited." *Social Anthropology* 8: 341–8.

Dillon, Matthew. 2002. *Girls and Women in Classical Greek Religion*. London: Routledge.

Elsner, John. 1992. "Pausanias: A Greek Pilgrim in the Roman World." *Past & Present* 135: 3–29.

Goldhill, Simon, ed. 2001. *Being Greek Under Rome: Cultural Identity, the Second Sophistic and the Development of Empire*. Cambridge: Cambridge University Press.

Habicht, Christian. 1985. *Pausanias' Guide to Ancient Greece*. Berkeley: University of California Press.

Johnston, Sarah Iles. 2012. "Demeter in Hermione: Sacrifice and Ritual Polyvalence." *Arethusa* 45: 211–41.

Jones, W.H.S., ed. and trans. 1918–35. *Pausanias: Description of Greece. Loeb Classical Library*. 5 Vols. Cambridge, MA: Harvard University Press.

Lyons, Deborah. 2007. "The Scandal of Women's Ritual." In *Finding Persephone: Women's Rituals in the Ancient Mediterranean*, edited by Angeliki Tzanetou and Maryline Parca, 29–51. Bloomington: Indiana University Press.

240 *Deborah Lyons*

O'Higgins, Laurie. 2001. "Women's Cultic Joking and Mockery: Some Perspectives." In *Making Silence Speak: Womens' Voices in Greek Literature and Society*, edited by Laura McClure and André Lardinois, 138–60. Princeton: Princeton University Press.

———. 2003. *Women and Humor in Classical Greece*. Cambridge: Cambridge University Press.

Parker, Robert. 1996. *Athenian Religion: A History*. Oxford: Clarendon Press.

———. 2005. *Polytheism and Society at Athens*. Oxford: Oxford University Press.

Pirenne-Delforge, Vinciane. 2006. "Ritual Dynamics in Pausanias: The Laphria." In *Ritual and Communication in the Graeco-Roman World*, edited by Eftychia Stavrianopoulou, 111–29. Liège: Presses Universitaires de Liège.

———. 2008. *Retour à la source: Pausanias et la religion grecque* (*Kernos* Supplement 20). Liège: Centre International d'Etude de la Religion Grecque Antique.

Preston, Rebecca. 2001. "Roman Questions, Greek Answers: Plutarch and the Construction of Identity." In *Being Greek Under Rome: Cultural Identity, the Second Sophistic and the Development of Empire*, edited by Simon Goldhill, 86–120. Cambridge: Cambridge University Press.

Schaps, David. 1977. "The Woman Least Mentioned: Etiquette and Women's Names." *Classical Quarterly* 27: 323–30.

Stehle, Eva. 2007. "Thesmophoria and Eleusininian Mysteries: The Fascination of Women's Secret Ritual." In *Finding Persephone*: *Women's Rituals in the Ancient Mediterranean*, edited by Angeliki Tzanetou and Maryline Parca, 165–85. Bloomington: Indiana University Press.

Weiner, Annette. 1979. *Men of Value, Women of Renown*. Austin: University of Texas Press.

Index

acropolis: *peplos* in act of offering 41–2; statues of *arrhephoroi* 41; *see also* Sicilian acropoleis

Acts of Andrew 214, 218–21, 224

Acts of Paul and Thekla 214, 221–4

Against Heresies (Irenaeus) 214, 216

Agamemnon 106, 124, 232; lament 107; prayer 38

Agaue 166–7

agency 6, 32–3; acquisition and exercise of 214; external and internal conceptions of 46, 58; female 17, 144, 191; gender 11; Iphigeneia's 116; passive/active 12, 24, 85, 177, 214, 224; practice theory 5; primacy of 208; redemptive hegemony 185; ritual 5–6, 162, 182, 185–8; women's 12–13, 213, 217–20, 224, 236

agency of power 5, 214, 224

agency of projects 5, 214, 217, 224

agent, ritual 1, 144, 203–5, 208–10; dimensions of process 192*n*3; Hildegard of Bingen 186; objects 40, 43; Penelope as 152, 159–61; women 46, 167, 169–70

Ahrens, Heinrich Ludolf 100

aischrologia ('dirty talk') 174, 175, 189, 235

Alexiou, Margaret 99

amulet(s) 131, 132, 137–8, 141–3

Andromache (Euripides) 99; Hektor's speech to 155; lament for Hektor 108, 110, 111*n*2

animal: consumption of meat 17–19; representation of 18

Antinous (suitor of Penelope) 151, 155, 158

Apocryphal Acts of the Apostles (*AAA*) 215–16, 221

archaeology, Sicilian records and women 11–13

Aristomenes, infiltrating the Thesmophoria 166–7

arm-cutting ritual 204, 205–8, 210

Artal-Isbrand, Paula 87*n*1

Artemis Brauronia *see* Brauron

Athena at Argos 57; and cult of Artemis 115–16, 122, 127; Penelope's prayer to 35–6, 38; *peplos* at Athens 40–1, 52, 156, 171; prayer of 34, 37, 38; unsuccessfully supplicated by Trojan women 38–9, 47, 49, 155–6, 161; weaver 152–3, 162; wooden image 121; *see* festivals, Plynteria

Augustus, and the self-inscribing prophetess 199–202, 207, 209

Aurelius, Marcus 200

authority: divine 201–2; Hildegard of Bingen 186; masculine 167, 168, 179; religious 106, 115–21, 125–6, 167, 176; ritual of priestess 124, 125, 127; women 6, 152, 154, 168

Babbia, Karpime 133–5, 137, 139, 143

Babbitt, Frank Cole 231, 236

Bagger, Matthew 184, 193*n*7

Barbarossa Hypogaeum 74

Barrett, Justin 203

Battos 105; infiltrating the Thesmophoria 166–7

Bell, Catherine 3, 4, 184–6, 192*n*1, 192*n*3

binding spells *see* curse tablets; magic

blame, women's laments 108–9

body: and agency 58; and amulets 141; and behavior 1; as constraint 218; dead 75, 78, 82, 102, 103, 107, 127; eroticized 187, 188, 190; female 68, 132, 184; of a god 50, 152; language 44; marking 207–8, 210; movement 33; and nature 136; opening up 187; in Orphic treatise 140; possessed 225; ritualized 184, 190

Bonucci, Carlo 73

242 *Index*

Bourdieu, Pierre 5, 185, 186
Boyer, Pascal 105
Brauron: cult statues in sanctuary 54–7;
    temple inventory 47–8, 54
bricolage 185
Briseis: lament 103
Bronze Age 81, 156, 237

Canosa, Italy: Daunian civilization 73–5;
    funerary "drama" 81–2; funerary
    tradition insights 86–7; map of Daunia
    66; statues and their context 73–5;
    statues bridging two worlds 78–81;
    terracotta statues in 65; terracotta
    statues of maidens from 69, 70, 71, 72;
    underground tombs 73–5; women and
    funerary rites in 75–8
castration, as ritual empowerment 166
ceramics hierarchy 12
Cerberus Hypogaeum 76, 78
Christian: definition 219–20; role of
    women 186, 214–16; texts/writings 5, 6,
    214–16, 224–5; unity of all things 183;
    writers 230, 236
chthonic gods: Aphrodite and Hermes 188;
    invocation to 80–1, 87, 88n3; rituals
    183, 189, 190, 191
citizenship, cultic 54, 117, 165, 169–70,
    179; cultic polity of women 169–70;
    women 54, 117, 165, 169–70, 179
Cixous, Hélène 184, 186–7
Clement of Alexandria 174, 178–9, 230, 236
Cole, Susan 2, 121, 128, 168, 235
collective commensality 15
comic theatre/drama 170, 182, 187–91
communal ritual spaces, Sicilian
    acropoleis 13, 15
community rituals: centrality of women in
    Sicilian 20, 22–4; consuming alcohol and
    meat on acropoleis 17–19; drinking and
    eating 15–17; Sicilian acropoleis 13, 15
competence: materiality and ritual, in
    Odyssey 34–8; ritual 4, 32; *see also*
    ritual competence
confession inscription 139–40
cookware, *pignatte* and communal
    ceremonies in Sicily 20, 22–4
Cozzi, Salvatore 74
Cragg, Douglas 204
curse 34, 39, 43, 98
curse tablets/binding spells 131–7, 139, 143,
    144, 190–1, 213, 221–3; *see also* magic
cutting ritual 204, 205–8, 210

dance 233
dancers 84, 172
dancing floors 233
Daunian civilization: Canosa, Italy 73–5;
    Romanization of 87; *see also* terracotta
    statues
deception 200, 216, 223; Iphigeneia's 116,
    119; ritual 124–5; weaving as metaphor
    for 152
de Certeau, Michel 5, 185–6, 192n3
Delphic oracle: oracular "I" 104–8; verse
    oracles 100–1; women's laments 98–9
Demeter 36, 47, 48, 50, 53, 80, 98, 120, 132,
    136, 144, 182, 183, 184, 193, 237; curse
    tablet 190–1; goddess of Thesmophoria
    165, 166, 168, 172, 175, 176, 178–9,
    189–90, 232; laughter 186–7, 189;
    women only cults 166–7, 233, 235
Dignas, Beate 118–19
Diomedes 159, 160; Trojan women pray
    for his destruction 34, 39
Dionysos: baking cakes for 172–4; rituals
    for 165, 167, 170, 175, 177, 193n6,
    233, 238
discipline 186, 216, 219–22, 225
discourse 154; lamenter's 34, 109; public
    162; ritual 32, 117, 213; women's 6,
    12, 216
domestic duties: baking cakes for
    Dionysiac rituals 172–4; dough cakes
    at the Haloa 174–7; food and religious
    rites 165, 178–9; sacred temple duties
    resembling 119–20; Thesmophoria
    177–8; weaving and woman's place
    153–6; women and grain 165; women's
    ritual 171–2
Douglas, Mary 184
Douny, Laurence 61
drinking 15–19, 23–4, 115, 172, 222
Durkheim, Emile 185, 192n1

eating 15–19, 23, 178, 222
ekphora, terracotta statues on platform
    82, 83
elegies, funerary laments 101–4
Eliade, Mircea 183
empowerment/disempowerment: men 167;
    women 43, 182, 184
Euripides 4, 6, 115, 169–70, 172, 236;
    see also Andromache (Euripides);
    Iphigeneia in Tauris (Euripides)
Eurykleia: instructs Penelope in ritual 35,
    37, 43, 160

Index   243

experience: collective 176; of disease 131,
140; domestic duties 177, 179; fertility
and reproduction 134, 136, 144; magic
214–15; multisensual 33; religious 177,
205, 231; ritual 1–3, 6, 15, 117, 183;
rituals of inversion 184–91

feminism/feminists 11, 185–6
Fernandez-Delgado, J. A. 101
festivals 69, 86, 102, 117, 118, 157, 172,
182–3, 230, 236; Anthesteria 56; Bona
Dea 235; Choes 115; of Demeter 189,
192, 233–4, 235; Demeter and Kore
190; Dionysiac 172; Haloa 166, 174–7;
Heroïs 236; of Kore/Persephone 189;
Kronia 184; Lenaia 56; Panathenaia
40–1, 57, 156; Plynteria 119, 126, 159;
Syrian goddess 206; Thesmophoria 134,
144, 166, 170, 174, 177–9, 233
Fick, August 100
Flower, Michael 101
Freedberg, David 59
funerary rites: drama of 81–2; procession
81–2, 83; terracotta statues as attendants
84–6; terracotta statues bridging two
worlds 78–81; women in South Italy
75–8; women's laments 100, 101–4,
109–10

Galli 206
Garcia, John 105–6
Gehrke, Hans Joachim 110
Gell, Alfred 5, 46, 57–8
gender: ritual and 1–2; segregation 43,
235–6; sexuality 137, 176, 179, 186–7,
190, 217, 219
gestures: domestics 173; funerary rites
75–6, 78–81, 85, 87; gynecological
problems 144; Iambe's 187, 190;
material 43; prayer 33–4, 38; terracotta
statues 70–2
Giddens, Anthony 5
Goff, Barbara 5, 117
Golden Bough (Frazer) 1
Gordon, Richard 58, 200
grammar of ritual 4
Greek Magical Papyri see PGM
Grimes, Richard L. 4

Haloa: dough cakes at 174–7, 179;
honoring goddess Demeter 165; role
inversion 168, 171; women's ritual
competence 169, 171–2, 186, 193n6

Harris, Susanna 61
healing rituals, reproduction 131–2
Hekabe 103, 104; and Hektor's request to
supplicate Athena 38–9, 42, 155–6
Hektor 108; requesting Trojan women
to supplicate Athena 38–9, 42, 155–6;
speech to Andromache 155; women's
lament for 101, 103, 107, 108
Helen 39, 155, 158; as diviner 97–9
Hera: temple-key 120; textiles dedicated to
47, 53, 55–6, 156, 191
Heraion, inventory of 55, 56
Hermes 152, 153, 188; in *PGM* 133–4;
women dedicate clothes to 55
Herzfeld, Michael 98
hexameter: elegy genre 101–4; verse
oracles 100–1
hierarchies: class 185; gender and
ecclesiastical 61; household 157; power
26; relationships 13; social 23–4, 26, 131
Homer: *Iliad* 38–42, 46–7; *Odyssey*
34–8; prayers in poetry 32–4; ritual
competence in poems 42–4
humor 172, 200
hypomnesis, reminding cue 35

iconography: funerary terracotta statues
72–3, 76; maidens from Canosa 69–72;
mourning women in art 86; *pinakes* 188;
ritual use of textiles 56; of terracotta
statues 66–73; Underworld deities 80, 82
identity: asserting 107; collective 110, 123;
communicating 60; community 16, 87;
cultural 144; of female prophet 204–5;
Greek 237; group 15; sexual 216, 219;
social 132, 134
ideology: community's 15; of cult 40–1;
gap between reality and 215; of *oikos*
53–4, 81, 157; of *polis* 117; of prayer
33; sacred and ancient Greece 237
ignorance, ritual 124, 127, 170, 185,
223, 229
Iliad (Homer) 99, 103; elegiac funerary
laments 103–4, 111n2; materiality and
ritual incompetence in 38–42; textiles
for temple 46–7; women's laments in
107–8, 109–10
impiety 166; *see also* "piety movement"
incompetence: materiality and ritual, in
Iliad 38–42; ritual 4, 166–9
inscriptions 6, 131, 144, 229, 235;
'confession inscriptions' 140, 143;
specific inscriptions: *ID* 1417A 55, 56;

244 *Index*

1428 56; 1442B 55; 1444A 56; 1450A 56; *IG* II² 1034 40; 1184 170; 1365 138; 1366 138; 1514–30 47, 54; *IG* II/III² 3564 57; 3634 41; 3644 57; 4771 57; 4772 57; 4818 57; *IG* VII.2421 48; *IG* IX, I² 95–110 208; *IG* IX, 2 1107b 57; *IG* XI, 2 154A 56; 2 161B 55; 2 203 55; 2 204 55; 287A2 56; *IG* XII, suppl. 571 57; *IGLS* 6.2928–9 209; *SEG* 44.463 102; 45.1163 55; 47.1314 55; *see also* amulet(s); curse tablets
inversion: domestic 167–9, 171, 179; political 170, 171; rituals of 182, 184, 186–7, 190; social 167, 171, 182
Iphigeneia in Tauris (Euripides) 4, 115–28; cult statue 120–2; keys to temple 119–20; new polis for Taurian Artemis 117–18; priestess of Taurian Artemis 117–18; purity 122–3; ritual competency 118–19; ritual deception 124–5; sacrifice 122–3; use/abuse of ritual 125–7; women, religion and the polis 117
Italy *see* Canosa, Italy

James, William 184
Jeammet, Violaine 68, 74–5, 81, 88*n*2
Jones, Christopher 207
Jones, W.H.S. 233

Kalligeneia, third day of the Thesmophoria 178, 232
Karpime Babbia, curse against 133–5, 137, 139, 143
knowledge: access to sacred 229; ancient Greek women's 229–30, 234, 238–9; hidden/secret 207; reproduction rituals 143–4; ritual competence 32, 43–4; ritual procedure 6, 125–6, 144, 203, 236–7; textile dedication 46–7, 61; women's 222, 224
Kowalzig, Barbara 183
Krischer, Tilman 151
Kristeva, Julia 184, 187
Kron, Uta 120

Lagrasta I Hypogaeum 74
Lagrasta II Hypogaeum 73
language, ritual of prayer 32–4
laughter 5, 184, 187, 189
Lawson, E. Thomas 4, 33, 202–5, 208
Life of St. Hilarion (Jerome) 215, 222, 225
Lightfoot, Jane 206, 207
liminality 60, 68, 78, 87, 157–8, 168, 172, 183

Livy 200–1
logic of persuasion 32, 37
Lord, Alfred 151
Lysistrata (Aristophanes) 117, 128

MacLeod, Wallace E. 100, 101
Macmullen, Ramsay 201
maenad(s) 56, 84, 167
magic: *Acts of Andrew* and 218–21; *Acts of Paul and Thekla* and 221–4; aggressive 132–7, 190; binding spells/curse tablets 131–7, 139, 143, 144, 190–1, 213, 221–3; reproduction and 132–7; victims of attack 191, 214–15, 221–5; women's agency 213; *see* amulet(s); curse tablets; *PGM*
Mahmood, Saba 185–6
maidens, terracotta statues of Canosan 69, 70, 71, 72
manipulation: birthing process 144; community identity 15–16; dough 165, 171–2, 176–7; female complicity 125; male and female genitalia 175–6; reproduction 137–41; ritual procedures 127; time 152, 156–9
marking, body 207–8, 210
Martha, Marius' prophetess 209
Martin, Richard P. 97
masculinization 102, 110
McCauley, Robert N. 4, 33, 202–5, 208
memory 35, 37; collective 19, 44; communal 108–9; episodic 34, 42; implicit 34; objects having 40; ritual 40, 237; of trauma 118
Mentor, Athena disguised as 37–8
methodology 1–2, 15, 131, 174, 232
Miltiades, infiltrating the Thesmophoria 166–7
Montagnola di Marineo 14, 24, 25
Monte Maranfusa: *pignatte* from domestic contexts of 20, 21; western Sicily 12, 14
Monte Polizzo: acropolis of 12–13, 18, 20, 21; deer hunting at 15; map of Sicily 14; meat consumption 18; *pignatte* from 20–2; planimetry of 19
movement, ritual 81
Murnaghan, Sheila 152, 159
Myrrhine 128, 169

Nagy, Gregory 102–3
Nausicaa 155
negotiated appropriation 192*n*3
Newman, C. T. 191
Nieto Ibánez, J. M. 101

North, John 200
Ny Carlsberg Glyptotek 70, 79, 80

Odysseus 124, 125, 161; Athena and
  157, 159; as beggar 152, 154–55, 161;
  Penelope praying for 35–6, 160; woman
  praying for 42–3
Odyssey (Homer) 99, 103, 151–62;
  materiality of prayer 34–8; neo-analysis
  and text of 151–3; Penelope as ritual
  agent 159–61; Penelope's weaving 156–9;
  ritual management of time 156–9;
  weaving and woman's place 153–6
Orestes 115–16, 121–5, 127
Orlin, E. 200
Orphica *Lithica* 140
Ortner, Sherry 5, 214, 217, 219, 224
Osborne, Robin 47–8

Page, Denys 101–2, 111*n*2
Parker, Robert 236, 238
Parry, Milman 151
participation: active 11, 16, 20, 23–4, 26;
  choral performance 123; in cults 168;
  exclusion of men 166, 167, 169, 238;
  funerary rites 81, 85; political 117; ritual
  exclusions 230, 234–6, 237
passivity 215–16, 217
patriarchal culture 154, 182
Pausanias 6, 104, 121, 156, 166, 229–30,
  233–9
Peisistratos (Homeric), and prayer 38
Peisistratos (tyrant of Athens), and
  redaction of Homeric texts 151
Penelope 4, 120; lament of 34–5; prayer of
  35–7; as ritual agent 159–61; weaving
  of 151–62
peplos: dedication and ritual use 52;
  women and textile production 52–4;
  women and weaving 39–42
performance, ritual 3, 104, 106–7, 124,
  143, 172, 182–8, 191; comic theatre
  170, 182, 187–91
performative futures 97, 99, 104
PGM (*Greek Magical Papyri*): causing
  menstruation (in oneself or a pregnant
  enemy) 132, 136, 137, 138–9, 141;
  erotic 222; specific spells: III.164 137;
  IV.675–676 141; IV.1081 141; IV.2756–62
  222; VII.260–71 132; VII.359–361 141;
  VII.973 136; VII.2439 136; XII.234
  137; XII.96.313 141; XXXVI.235–236
  141; LXII.76–106 138; women in 213
"piety movement" 185

pignatte: communal ceremonies in Sicily
  20, 22–4; from Monte Maranfusa
  20, 21; from Monte Polizzo 20–2;
  morphology of 20
pinakes: goddesses depictions 188, 191;
  Greek sanctuaries 50–1
pithos, Boiotian relief 48, 49
Plutarch 6, 120–1, 209, 229–39
polis religion 117, 118, 124, 127–8
politicisation of women 167, 169–70
pollution 159; fear of 125–7; matricide
  115, 123, 125; ritual 78, 99
power, agency of 5
praise, women's laments 108–9
Praxiergidai, textile rituals 52, 57, 119
prayer: defining 34; female 42–4; *Iliad*
  (Homer) 38–42; materiality of, in
  Odyssey 34–8; ritual 32–4, 42–4; ritual
  competence, in *Odyssey* 34–8; ritual
  discourse 32–4; ritual incompetence, in
  Iliad 38–42
prayers: for justice 134; ululation 36, 38–9
Priam 34; lament for Hektor 103
prohibitions, ritual 229–30, 234–7
prophesying woman: ritual form and
  competence of 202–5; Rome 199–202;
  self-cutting 205–9
Proverbs (Zenobios) 52
Prückner, Helmut 50
purification, rituals 80, 82, 85, 87, 116–19,
  121–3, 125–7, 156
purity, sacrifice and 122–3
Pythia 4, 6, 98–101, 104–9

Rappaport, Roy 184
rebellion 192*n*1, 199
rebuke/rebuking 151, 153, 225
redemptive hegemony 185
reproduction: amuletic gems in birthing
  chamber 141–3; confession inscription
  139–40; cursing the womb 132–7;
  magic for controlling fertility 131–2;
  manipulating by magic 137–41; rituals
  143–4
ritual acts: baking 3, 171, 172–4, 179;
  body marking 207–8, 210; cleaning 15,
  119, 120; cooking 12–13, 18, 20, 22–4,
  26, 107, 171–2, 175, 179, 232; cutting
  204, 205–8, 210; dressing 46, 54–9, 61,
  81, 120, 206; drinking 15–19, 23–4,
  115, 172, 222; eating 15–19, 23, 178,
  222; offerings 2, 33–5, 37–44, 46–51,
  53–4, 56, 61, 65, 84–5, 125, 156, 159,
  166, 178, 233, 235; praying 65, 78, 80,

246   *Index*

84, 87, 160; singing 97, 101–2, 183, 203, 206; washing 41, 57–8, 61, 124; weaving 3, 37, 40–2, 53, 152–9, 161–2, 171; *see also* sacrifice
ritual agent *see* agent, ritual
ritual attendants, terracotta statues as 84–6
ritual autonomy: activities 6; of women 116, 117, 125–6, 128, 143–4
ritual competence: definition 4, 32; doctrinal 34–7, 43; efficacy 32; Homeric poems highlighting 42–4; imagistic 34, 37–8, 42, 44; Iphigeneia's 118–19; ritual form and 202–5; theory 32, 34
ritual grammar *see* grammar of ritual
ritual incompetence: men's 166–9; women's 38–42
ritual movement *see* movement, ritual
ritual offerings 35, 37, 40, 43, 84
ritual performer 40, 46, 97, 101, 183, 185, 186
ritualization 3, 13, 14
ritualized body 184, 190
rituals: cognitive approach to 202–5; consuming alcohol and meat on acropoleis 17–19; domesticity in women's 171–2; dressing cult images 54–7; drinking and eating 15–17; funerary drama of Canosan statues 81–2; members of *Praxiergidai* 52, 57, 119; potency of 97, 169, 177; prayer 32–4, 42–4; prohibitions and exclusions 234–6; religious 3–4, 170, 175, 178, 202–5, 209, 235; research into 1–2; role of 2; special agent 204–5, 209–10; textiles dressing cult statues 54–7; theoretical approaches 3–4; use and abuse of 125–7; women and funerary rites in South Italy 75–8; women and weaving of *peplos* 39–42
Rossi, L. E. 101
Royal Museum of Naples 74
Russo, Joseph 152

Sabetai, Victoria 54
sacrifice 2–3, 18, 35–9, 41–2, 49, 61, 80–1, 115, 117–20, 122–3, 125–7, 156, 166–7, 178, 192*n*1, 204, 206, 209, 230, 234–5
Sahlins, Marshall 5, 183
sanctuary of Artemis Brauronia *see* Brauron
Sant' Aloia Hypogaeum 76, 77, 78
Schechner, Richard 183
Scheid, Joseph 41
Scocchera B Hypogaeum 74–5

Scott, James 5
Seaford, Richard 117, 157
secrecy 43, 61, 238
secret rite/ritual 119, 166, 178, 230, 236
self-marking 207–8, 210
senses: hearing/sound 36, 161, 206; sight 58, 106, 121, 125–7; smell 60, 81, 107; taste 26, 36; touch 60–1, 120–2
sensual religion 60–1
Seremetakis, Nadia 97–8
sexuality 137, 176, 179, 186–7, 190, 217, 219
Showalter, Elaine 184, 186–7
Sicilian acropoleis: communal ritual spaces in 13, 15; community ceremonies and women 20–4; consuming alcohol and meat on 17–19; drinking and eating on 15–17; *pignatta* cookware 20–4; porridges on 20–4; women and communal ceremonies 25–6
Sicily: communal ritual spaces in 13, 15; map of 14
Snyder, Jane 192
Socrates 136
Sourvinou-Inwood, Christiane 117
space: ceremonial 24, 25; ritual 6, 12, 13, 23, 115; sacred 118, 119, 125–8; time and 11, 32, 43, 143, 162; women's 2, 11, 166
special agent rituals 204–5, 209–10
special patient rituals 204
speech: direct 34, 103–4; Homeric 33; lament-like 34–6, 38; performer 97–9; ritual 4, 105–6; women's 43, 75, 110
statues *see* terracotta statues
status: alcohol 17; biological 78; funerary 98, 107; liminal 87; marital 220; men's 11, 54; priestess 118, 120–1, 127; social 48, 53, 78, 167, 191, 219; socioeconomic 65; women's 37, 49, 54, 68, 78, 162
Stehle, Eva 183, 190, 192*n*2
stereotypes 124, 213–16
subversion 179, 186–7; behavior as type of bricolage 185; ideologies 186–7; rituals and comic theatre 170, 182, 187–91
Svenbro, Jesper 41
symbolism/symbolic 5, 12, 16, 32, 43, 58–9, 116, 142, 155–6, 162, 189

Tambiah, Stanley J. 32
Tanagra: marble *stele* from 48, 55; temple inventory 47–8, 55; terracotta statue from 78

Taurian Artemis, priestess of 117–18
Telemachus 35, 36, 97, 151, 158, 159; rebuke of Penelope 153–4, 155
temple: sacred duties of priestess 119–20; textiles 47–9, 54–6, 58
terracotta statues 65; arm positions of 79–80; bridging two worlds 78–81; context of 73–5; depicting burial 83; *ekphora* 82, 83; funerary 72–3; funerary "drama" 81–2; iconography of 66–73, 81–2, 84–6; insights into funerary traditions 86–7; maiden from Canosa 69, 70, 71, 72; reconstruction drawing of 83; as ritual attendants 84–6; technique of 66–73
textiles: anthropology of touch 57–60; dedicating in Greek sanctuaries 46–54; dressing the gods 54–7; functions in rituals 59–60; *peplophoria* for transport of 51–2; *pinakes* (plaques/tablets) 50–1; temple inventories 47–9, 54–6, 58; women in production of 52–4
Theano 41, 192; dedication of *peplos* and prayers to Athena 39, 44, 47, 49, 155, 158, 161
Thebes, temple inventory 47–8
Theseus 41, 238
Thesmophoria: exclusion of men 166–9, 234; rituals for goddess Demeter 134, 165; women's celebration of 171, 174, 177–8, 179, 186, 190, 192*n*2, 193*n*6, 232; women's cultic citizenship 169–70
Thoas, cult of *Iphigeneia in Tauris* 116, 121, 122, 125, 126, 127
time: management of 152, 156–9; space and 11, 32, 43, 143, 162
Timo, priestess of Demeter 167
tombs: Daunian civilization 73–5; women and funerary rights 75–8
touch: anthropology of 57–60; power of 60–1; *see also* senses
Turner, Victor 183–4, 189, 193*n*7

ululation *see* prayers
unacceptable ritual 4

Underworld: funerary rites 78, 80–1; Hermes to 133; *Odyssey* (Homer) 151, 158; Persephone 188–9; wall painting of journey to 77

values, Homeric 40, 109–10
van der Wielen-van Ommeren, Frederike 68, 88*n*2
voices: prophetic 105; ritual 108–9, 136, 144, 161, 192; women's 109, 160, 191–2
vulnerability 216, 218–20, 225

weaving: Penelope's 156–9; woman's place and 153–6; women and *peplos* 39–42
West, M. L. 101
Whitehouse, Harvey 34
Whitehouse, Ruth 11
Wiseman, T. P. 200
women: clothing cult images 54–7; cultic citizenship 54, 117, 165, 169–70, 179; dedicating textiles in Greek religion 46–54; funerary rites in South Italy 75–8; knowledge about ancient Greek 229–30, 234, 238–9; members of *Praxiergidai* 52, 57, 119; porridges on acropoleis 20–4; religion and the polis 117; restricting participation of, during funerals 85–6; terracotta statues as ritual attendants 84–6; terracotta statues of maiden 69, 70, 71, 72; textile production 52–4; textiles and anthropology of touch 57–60; textile transport 51–2; as "victims" of magic 213–14, 216–25
women's business 165, 170, 174
women's laments: Delphic oracles 98–9; elegiac funerary 101–4; legal restrictions 99–100; praise and blame 108–9
"Women's Ritual Competence in the Ancient Mediterranean" conference 3
Worcester Art Museum 71, 76, 79, 80, 87*n*1, 88*n*2

Zeus 36, 39, 99, 104, 107, 120, 152, 153, 206, 234; sending omen to woman 42

Printed in the United States
By Bookmasters